Lecture Notes in Artificial Inte

Edited by J. G. Carbonell and J. Siekmann

Subseries of Lecture Notes in Computer Science

Springer
Berlin
Heidelberg
New York
Hong Kong
London
Milan
Paris
Tokyo

Series Editors

Jaime G. Carbonell, Carnegie Mellon University, Pittsburgh, PA, USA
Jörg Siekmann, University of Saarland, Saarbrücken, Germany

Volume Editors

Toru Ishida
Kyoto University
Department of Social Informatics
Yoshida-Honmachi, Kyoto, 606-8501, Japan
E-mail: ishida@i.kyoto-u.ac.jp

Les Gasser
University of Illinois at Urbana-Champaign
Graduate School of Library and Information Science
501 East Daniel St., Champaign, IL 61820, USA
E-mail: gasser@uiuc.edu

Hideyuki Nakashima
Future University - Hakodate
116-2 Kameda-Nakanocho, Hakodate, Hokkaido, 041-8655, Japan
E-mail: h.nakashima@fun.ac.jp

Library of Congress Control Number: 2005927899

CR Subject Classification (1998): I.2.11, I.2, C.2.4, H.4, H.5.3

ISSN   0302-9743
ISBN-10   3-540-26974-6 Springer Berlin Heidelberg New York
ISBN-13   978-3-540-26974-8 Springer Berlin Heidelberg New York

Springer is a part of Springer Science+Business Media

springeronline.com

© Springer-Verlag Berlin Heidelberg 2005
Printed in Germany

Typesetting: Camera-ready by author, data conversion by Scientific Publishing Services, Chennai, India
Printed on acid-free paper   SPIN: 11512073   06/3142   5 4 3 2 1 0

Preface

We are now in the era of ubiquitous computing and networking: millions of electronic devices with computing facilities in the public space are connected with each other in ad hoc ways, but are required to behave coherently. Massively multiagent systems (MMAS) can be a major design paradigm or an implementation method for ubiquitous computing and ambient intelligence. As the infrastructure of massively multiagent systems, technologies such as grid computing together with semantic annotation can be combined with agent technologies. A new system design approach, society-centered design, may be realized by embedding participatory technologies in human society. Applications include large-scale navigation, scientific or social simulations, e-home, e-offices, e-cities, and e-science.

The First International Workshop on Massively Multiagent Systems (MMAS-04), was held from December 10 to 11 in Kyoto, Japan. The workshop consisted of 12 invited talks, 3 chair talks, 20 oral and poster presentations, and excursions to world heritage sites in Kyoto. Participation in the workshop was by invitation only, and was limited to around 50 professionals who have made significant contributions to the topics of the meeting. Attendees were from many countries including Algeria, Australia, China, France, Korea, Luxembourg, the US, and Japan. This volume includes 25 of the papers presented at the workshop. The papers cover the area of massively multiagent technology, teams and organization, ubiquitous computing and ambient intelligence; all are related to massively multiagent systems in the public space.

At the end of the workshop, we had discussions on why MMAS should be the focus of attention rather than just MAS. Massively multiagent systems create applications for society as a whole; this raises the possibility of having a new structure in our social life via mass-support rather than individual-support. "Massive" means "beyond resource limitation:" the number of agents exceeds local computer resources, or the situations are too complex to design/program given human cognitive resource limits. The discussion will be continued at the next workshop, which will be held in 2006.

March 2005

Toru Ishida
Les Gasser
Hideyuki Nakashima

Organization

Workshop Chairs

General Chair
Koiti Hasida   Information Technology Research Institute, AIST, Japan

Program Co-chairs
Toru Ishida   Department of Social Informatics, Kyoto University, Japan
Les Gasser   University of Illinois at Urbana-Champaign, USA
Hideyuki Nakashima   Future University — Hakodate, Japan

Organization Co-chairs
Hideyuki Nakanishi   Department of Social Informatics, Kyoto University, Japan
Itsuki Noda   Information Technology Research Institute, AIST, Japan

Program Committee

Robert Axtell   The Brookings Institution
Francois Bousquet   IRRI, CIRAD
Dan Corkill   University of Massachusetts
Alexis Drogoul   Laboratoire d'Informatique de Paris 6
Satoru Fujita   Internet System Research Laboratories, NEC Corporation
Nick Gibbins   University of Southampton
Hiroshi Ishiguro   Osaka University
Nadeem Jamali   University of Saskatchewan
WooYoung Kim   Univ. of Illinois at Urbana-Champaign
David Kinny   Agentis Software
Yasuhiko Kitamura   Kwansei Gakuin University
Satoshi Kurihara   NTT Network Innovation Labs.
Koichi Kurumatani   Information Technology Research Institute, AIST
Kazuhiro Kuwabara   ATR Intelligent Robotics and Communication Laboratories
Victor Lesser   University of Massachusetts
Jiming Liu   Hong Kong Baptist University
Ryusuke Masuoka   Fujitsu Laboratories of America, Inc.
Azuma Ohuchi   Hokkaido University
Ei-ichi Osawa   Future University – Hakodate
Akihiko Ohsuga   Toshiba Corporation
Van Parunak   ALTARUM
Jeffrey S. Rosenschein Hebrew University
Larry Rudolph   MIT Laboratory for Computer Science
Norman M. Sadeh   School of Computer Science, Carnegie Mellon University
Ichiro Satoh   National Institute of Informatics
Paul Scerri   Robotics Institute, Carnegie Mellon University

Toshiharu Sugawara	NTT Communication Science Laboratory
Satoshi Tadokoro	Kobe University
Millind Tambe	University of Southern California
Walt Truszkowski	NASA Goddard Space Flight Center
Gaku Yamamoto	IBM Research, Tokyo Research Lab.
Makoto Yokoo	Kyushu University

Sponsored by

National Institute of Advanced Industrial Science and Technology (AIST)
Center of Excellence on Knowledge Society, Kyoto University
Future University — Hakodate

Supported by

Japan Science and Technology Agency (JST)
IEICE Special Interest Group for Artificial Intelligence and Knowledge Processing (SIG-AI)
IPSJ Special Interest Group for Ubiquitous Computing Systems
JSSST Special Interest Group for Multi-agent and Cooperative Computation
Support Center for Advanced Telecommunications Technology Research
The Obayashi Foundation
Microsoft Corporation
IBM Japan, Ltd.

Table of Contents

Massively Multi-agent Technology

Team and Organization

Ubiquitous Computing and Ambient Intelligence

Massively Multi-agent Systems in Public Space

Agent Server Technology for Managing Millions of Agents

Gaku Yamamoto

IBM Research, Tokyo Research Laboratory,
1623-14, Shimo-tsuruma, Yamato-shi,
Kanagawa-ken 242, Japan
+81-462-73-4639
yamamoto@jp.ibm.com

Abstract. In this paper, we describe technologies for an agent server capable of hosting millions of agents. The agent server needs a thread management mechanism, a memory management mechanism, and a recovery management mechanism. We have developed a framework and agent execution environment named Caribbean. First, we describe the programming model of Caribbean. Following the description, we explain technologies for managing millions of agents. Some application scenarios of real commercial systems using the technology are also introduced. We describe what we learned from the development of the real applications.

1 Introduction

We used a multiagent programming model for a real commercial system in 1998. The application is a service that provides information on airline tickets to consumers through the Internet. In this service, consumers have their own computer agents. Consumers input their query conditions on flights. In the system, travel agencies also have their own computer agents providing airline ticket information. A travel agency's agent has the agency's own sales policies. When a consumer inputs his or her query conditions, the consumer's computer agent sends a query condition message to the travel agency's computer agents. A travel agency's agent replies with a message containing airline ticket recommendations in accordance with its sales policies. The consumer's agent shows the airline ticket recommendations from the travel agency's agents using a Web browser. The agent also retains the input query conditions and the airline ticket information, and can show the information anytime when the consumer uses the agent again. The lifetime of a consumer agent is one week.

Through the development of the system, we found that the multiagent programming model is flexible, and it is easy to design and develop a system. However, we had to solve the serious problem that there was no multiagent platform that managed a very large number of agents. Since each consumer has an agent in the system and each agent lives in the system for a week in the commercial system, the number of consumer agents may be in the tens of thousands. Therefore, we developed our first multiagent platform that manages tens of thousands of agents on top of the

T. Ishida, L. Gasser, and H. Nakashima (Eds.): MMAS 2004, LNAI 3446, pp. 1–12, 2005.

Aglets framework, a mobile agent framework [1]. In 2000, we redesigned the platform and developed a new multiagent platform named Caribbean, which can manage hundreds of thousands of agents on a single platform [2-9]. In 2003, we added a server clustering function to Caribbean so that millions of agents can be managed in one system.

In this paper, we describe the technologies for a multiagent platform capable of hosting millions of agents. We call the multiagent platform that manages many agents the "agent server" in this paper. In Section 2, we describe the programming model of Caribbean. Section 3 describes the runtime structure of a Caribbean agent server. A server clustering mechanism of Caribbean is introduced in this section. Several application scenarios will be introduced in Section 4. The lessons learned from developing real applications will be described in Section 5. Conclusion is written in Section 6.

2 Caribbean Programming Model and Framework

2.1 Programming Model

In the Caribbean programming model, an agent is responsible for given roles and performs its tasks to meet its design objectives. In the typical application scenario shown in a later section, an agent is a proxy of a user. All agents are created in a server and stay in the server for a long time. Agents in Caribbean are reactive agents that execute jobs by receiving messages or events. This means that the agent does not own a thread. Occasionally, an agent requires a special service like a timer service. Such a service is provided by a "Service Object." A service object can own threads. An agent communicates with other agents by using asynchronous peer-to-peer messaging. Messages sent by an agent are put into the message queue of the destination agent. A Caribbean agent server creates a message queue for each agent. An agent server delivers a message stored in a queue to the destination agent at an appropriate time. When a message is delivered to an agent, a callback method of the agent's methods will be invoked. In that method, the agent performs its job and may send messages to other agents.

An agent server provides agents with fundamental functions such as agent creation, agent removal, and messaging. An agent server must host a large number of agents. If each agent owns a thread, the agent server will be overloaded. If too many agents are in memory, an agent server will also fail because of the resulting memory shortage. Therefore, an agent server must manage the activities of agents to control thread assignment and memory usage.

An agent server does not provide intelligent agent capabilities. If an application requires intelligent agent capabilities, the capabilities can be added as agent logic.

2.2 Framework

Figure 1 shows an overview of the Caribbean framework.

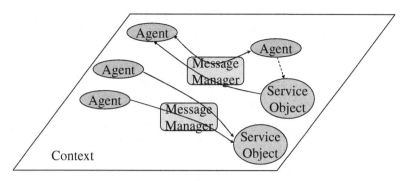

Fig. 1. Caribbean Framework

ObjectBase. The base class of agents is the "ObjectBase" class. An agent is an instance of a class extended from this class. An agent is identified by a unique identifier whose class is "OID." An agent can belong to an agent group. An application can define an agent group in a system configuration file. In the configuration file, properties for an agent group can be defined. An agent can obtain the properties from "Context." An agent must not deliver to other agents an object reference to itself. Instead, it delivers its own identifier. Instead of method calls, an agent sends other agents messages, which are instances of either the "Message" class or a class extended from the "Message" class. An agent program is based on a message-driven programming model. When an agent receives a message, a callback method "handleMessage" of the agent will be calledbacked. The delivered message is handled as an argument of the method. The agent executes the task corresponding to the message within a short period. An agent excepting an instance of the ServiceObject class described later must not own any threads. Because of memory limitations, an agent might be moved into storage by an agent server and loaded from storage back into memory. The methods that an agent must implement are as follows;

```
public void onCreation(Object arg)
```

   arg: an argument of Context#create()

```
public void onDisposing()
```

   This method is called by an agent server just before this agent is disposed.

```
public void onActivation()
```

   This method is called by an agent server just after this agent is loaded into memory.

```
public void onDeactivating()
```

   This method is called by an agent server just before this agent is stored into storage.

```
public boolean handleMessage(OID sender, Message msg,
MessageManager msgman)
```

   sender: an agent identifier of a sender agent
   msg: a message

msgman: an object reference to the message manager which the sender agent used to send the message.
This method is called to handle the message.

The following methods are provided by the "ObjectBase" class.

```
public Context getContext()
```

Get an object reference to a context.

```
public String getGroup()
```

Get the name of the group to which this agent belongs.

```
public OID getOID()
```

Get an agent identifier.

```
public Properties getProperties(OID oid)
```

oid: an agent identifier
Get properties of a group to which the agent specified by an agent identifier belongs

Context. Agents invoke use the agent server's functions provided through the "Context" interface. The interface provides methods for creating agents, disposing of agents, getting lists of agents in an agent server, etc. "Context" provides the following methods:

```
public OID create(String classname, Object arg)
```

classname: a class name of a created agent
arg: an argument passed to the onCreation method of ObjectBase.
Create an agent. Return the identifier of the created agent.

```
public OID create(String classname, String agentgroup,
Object arg)
```

classname: a class name of a created agent
agentgroup: an agent group name
arg: an argument passed to the onCreation method of ObjectBase.
Create an agent. The created agent belongs to the agent group. Return the identifier of the created agent.

```
public void dispose(OID oid)
```

oid: An agent identifier
Dispose of an agent.

```
public OID[] getAllOIDs()
```

Get an array of the identifiers of all agents in this agent server.

```
public OID[] getAllOIDs(String agentgroup)
```

group: an agent group

Get an array of the identifiers of all agents belong to the agent group. Return an array of agent identifiers.

```
public String getGroup(OID oid)
```

oid: an agent identifier
Get the name of the agent group to which an agent belongs

```
public MessageManager getMessageManager(String name)
```

name: the name of the messaging manager
Get an object reference of a messaging manager.

```
public SimpleMessageManager getSimpleMessageManager()
```

Get an object reference to the default messaging manager.

```
public ServiceObjectBase lookupService(String name)
```

name: a name of a service object
Get an object reference to the service object.

MessageManager. A MessageManager is an object that provides messaging functions to agents. It provides an asynchronous messaging function and a multicast messaging function to agents as fundamental functions. "MessageManager" class is an abstract class. The Caribbean package provides "SimpleMessageManager" class as a default message manager. An application can define an application-dependent MessageManager and can plug it into an agent server. For example, an application may need an anonymous messaging function that distributes a message to an appropriate agent in accordance with a message name. An application-dependent MessageManager is defined in a system configuration file. An agent server registers it into a message manager repository at system startup time. An agent obtains an object reference to a MessageManager from Context, and sends messages using those messaging functions. Context manages multiple MessageManager objects that are identified by names. The methods provided by "SimpleMessageManager" class are as follows;

```
public void post(OID[] oids, Message msg)
```

oids: an array of identifiers of destination agents
msg: a message
Multicast a message to destination agents.

```
public void post(OID oid, Message msg)
```

oid: an identifier of a destination agent
msg: a message
Post a message to a destination agent. This method does not wait until the destination agent handles the message.

ServiceObjectBase. A "Service Object" is the object that provides agents with services. A service object is an instance of a class extended from "ServiceObjectBase" class, a subclass of "ObjectBase" class. A service object has all the functions of agents. It can send messages to other agents. It also can receive messages. Moreover, a service object can own threads. An agent can obtain an object reference to a service object and can call it by using a method call. A service object is associated with a service name and is defined in a system configuration file. An agent server registers the service object into the service registry of an agent server at system startup time. An agent can then obtain an object reference to the service object.

Service objects are also used for extending the Caribbean framework. For example, the Caribbean package provides the RMI gateway service object that a client program sends to an agent, the mail delivery service object that an agent uses to send a mail message to a user, the event transfer service object that an external program can use to send a Caribbean message to agents, etc.

3   Agent Server

The Caribbean agent server runtime is designed in order to manage many agents. Figure 2 shows an internal architecture of Caribbean agent server runtime. A thread management mechanism is needed to improve performance, and a memory management mechanism for limiting the amount of memory occupied by the agents is also needed. In addition, agents should be protected against system failures, and therefore a recovery management mechanism is needed. There are several different types of agents in a single application. For example, the number of user agents, which are created for each user, might be in the hundreds of thousands. On the other hand, an agent server has only one the service object (which provides DBMS access services for the user agents). Obviously, the management policies for user agents are different from those of the service agent. Therefore, Caribbean provides a function for defining management policies for each type of agent.

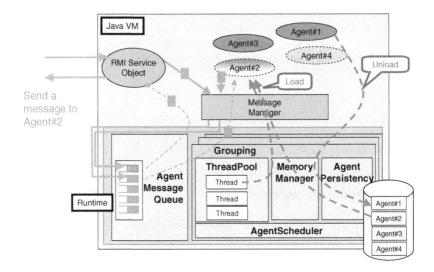

Fig. 2. Internal Architecture of Caribbean

3.1 Memory Management

The Caribbean agent server hosts hundreds of thousands of agents. An agent is a Java object whose size in a typical application may be tens of kilobytes. Even if each agent is not very big, the amount of memory occupied by all of the agents will significant, and may amount to hundreds of megabytes. Therefore the agent server needs a mechanism for minimizing the amount of memory occupied by hundreds of thousands of agents.

Agents should be kept in memory, but physical memory is limited. Therefore, the Caribbean agent server has a mechanism for swapping agents in and out. Some agents can be located in memory and others in secondary storage. If an agent in secondary storage receives messages, then the mechanism reads a memory image of the agent from the storage and activates the agent. This is called "swapping in." At the same time, the mechanism moves another agent into storage. This is called "swapping out." The agent server automatically swaps agents in and out in order to limit the number of agents in memory.

3.2 Thread Management

Since there may be hundreds of thousands of user agents, running agents without an appropriate schedule may cause overloading of the agent server. In the case of applications in which a user agent communicates with many agents accessing a database, a single request from a user may cause many simultaneous database accesses, causing an overload of the database. To avoid system overloads, a mechanism for controlling the threads is needed.

The Caribbean agent server uses thread pools and limits the number of running threads. It also has a thread scheduler in order to improve the performance. To reduce the number of swaps, the scheduler assigns higher priority to the agents in memory over the agents in secondary storage.

3.3 Recovery Management

Agents should be persistent within their lifetimes, even if the agent server fails. This means that an agent should be able to recover after the server is restarted. Agents that do not modify their data can be created afresh, but those that modify their data should be recovered together with the data. Therefore an agent server needs an agent recovery mechanism.

The Caribbean agent server has an agent persistency mechanism that takes a snapshot of an agent whenever it modifies its data. The agent modifies its data through a callback method named "handleMessage" that returns a Boolean value. If the return value is true, the server takes a snapshot of the agent. Later, the server can recover agents from their snapshots stored in the agent log.

3.4 Grouping of Agents

Many types of agents run on the Caribbean agent server. Their behaviors can be categorized according to their roles. For example, the number of user agents created for individual users might be in the hundreds of thousands. On the other hand, the number of service objects is typically less than 100, and none of them modifies its own data. However the objects are invoked frequently, since they are shared by all user agents. Therefore, the agent server should swap user agents in and out and keep the service objects in memory. It should also take snapshots of the user agents, but it does not need to take snapshots of the service objects.

The Caribbean agent server manages agents and service objects on the basis of groups defined by a system administrator. The administrator can set parameters limiting the number of agents in memory and the number of threads, and enable or disable the agent logging mechanism for each group.

3.5 Agent Server Cluster

A single agent server can host millions of agents because the Caribbean agent server uses the memory management mechanism described above. However, the number of agents hosted by a single agent server is actually performance limited. Therefore, clustering of agent servers is needed.

The clustering support provides a single view of a cluster for client programs and agents. A client program can send a message to an agent on any agent server in an agent server cluster. It can also multicast a message to agents on all agent servers in an agent server cluster. As well as a client program, an agent can send a message to an agent on a remote agent server through a "MessageManager" interface.

The cluster support enhances not only the performance but also the reliability of the system. The cluster recovers from a local component failure automatically by merely restarting the failed component. During the time a component is unavailable, the cluster can continue to work as long as the operations do not depend on the unavailable component. For example, creation and posting of messages to agents residing at the available servers continues even if a particular agent server is down. When the agent server recovers, the cluster recognizes it automatically, and resumes normal use of the server from that point.

4 Application Scenarios

We already applied the agent server technology to several real commercial applications. In this section, we introduce three applications. The first application is built on top of a predecessor of Caribbean and the third application is built on top of a successor of Caribbean that is compliant with J2EE. The frameworks of those agent servers are different from the framework described in this paper, but the concepts of the programming models are the same as in the programming model described in this paper.

4.1 A Commercial Service Site Providing Airline Tickets Information

TabiCan (1998-2000) was a commercial service site providing airline tickets and package tours including plane flights and hotel stays. Users accessed this server via their Web browsers and searched for airline tickets and package tours. They could obtain information from several travel agencies in a single search.

Travel agencies and users were represented as shop agents and consumer agents, respectively. The agents interacted to exchange information on airline tickets and package tours. A user instantiated his own agent on the TabiCan server and input search conditions. For example, "New York" for the destination, "Narita" for the point of departure, May 10 for the departure date, "Japan Airlines" for the airline, and "$1,000" for the maximum price. He then clicked on the "Start search" button, and his agent questioned all of the shop agents that could provide the requested airline tickets. Each shop agent queried a database several times to obtain exactly matching items and recommended items, and returned these results to the consumer agent. Recommended items were items that did not exactly match the consumer's search conditions but that the shop hoped to sell. For example, a shop agent can offer a ticket on "United Airlines" whose price is only $700. Each shop has its own selling policies. After the consumer agent has received airline tickets from all of the shop agents, the agent notifies the user of the results.

Shop agents live during the server runs. Consumer agents live for two days and are removed by the system when their lifetime is over. A user can access his consumer agent many times while it is alive. Even if he switches off his computer, his agent will still be alive, so he can access it again when he switches the computer back on.

4.2 A Notification Service for Profits and Losses for Foreign Currency Assets

The notification service is provided through a Web browser. A user registers information on foreign currency assets at the Web site. The user chooses foreign currencies and registers for the amounts in each foreign currency and sets notification thresholds for profit (loss) for each asset. Since the currency rates are updated daily, the profit (loss) of the assets changes daily. If the profit (loss) crosses the threshold set by the user, an email notification of the value is sent. For example, a user buys US$ of 1,000,000 yen at 110 yen, and also sets profit and loss thresholds of 50,000 yen. When the US dollar rate changes to 120 yen, the profit is +90,909 yen. Since this is over 50,000 yen, the value is sent by email. After the notification, the registered threshold is disabled until the user resets it. The threshold of US dollars is displayed with a mark indicating a notification threshold.

In this service, an agent is created for each user. An agent has information on its owner's foreign currency assets and a threshold. A service object manages information on currency rates. An agent can obtain the latest currency rates from the service object by invoking a method of the service object. When rates of currencies are updated, the service object gets an update event and retrieves the latest currency rates from a database. Then, the service object multicasts an event to all agents. When an agent receives the event, it obtains the latest rates of the currencies that its owner has registered and calculates profits (losses). If profit (loss) exceeds the threshold which the owner has registered, then the agent sends a notification mail to its owner.

4.3 Location-Aware Personalized Information Notification Service

Goopas is a location-aware personalized information notification service provided by Omron. It is coupled with automated ticket gates in railway stations, and when a user of the service passes the gate, it can send e-mail messages to the user's mobile phone.

The users input their properties such as age, job, and personal preferences when they register in the system, so the e-mail includes information that is not only associated with the station's neighborhood, but is also personalized. In this system, an agent is created for each user. The agent has its owner's properties. When a user passes through an automated ticket gate in a train station, an event indicating that the user has passed through the gate is sent to the user's agent. The agent sends mail containing relevant information about the station where the user is. The mail is sent from the system within a couple of seconds after passing through the automated ticket gate. Since the system load to create the mail for each user is significant, it is difficult to send the email quickly. Therefore, the mail content is prepared during the night or at times when new information is added to the system. An agent keeps the generated email content and sends it when the user passes through an automated ticket gate.

5 Discussion

We have applied the agent server technology to applications that handle events using personalized information. Through these projects we learned that the agent programming model described in this paper is easy for application developers to understand.

5.1 Reactive Agent Model

In the applications we developed, when a system receives an event, it executes processes for individual users. An executed process is isolated for an individual user. This means that a process for one user does not access information on other users. The process is started when a system receives an event. The model of reactive agents is suitable for these applications. The agent programming model in the agent server is based on these reactive agents [10]. However, the agent programming model adds restrictions on a thread-based model of reactive agents. A reactive agent can continue to work after it receives a message. This means that the agent can hold a thread. However, in the agent programming model, the threads are resources pooled in an agent server runtime module. An agent server gives a thread to an agent when the agent handles a message. When the agent finishes handling a message, the thread has to be returned to the thread pool and the agent server runtime module gives the thread to another agent. From the point of view of the model of reactive agents, this seems to be a strong restriction. However, the restriction was not problematic for the applications we developed.

5.2 Simple Programming Model

Since the agent programming model is simple, even non-technical people can understand the model. They can think of an agent's activities as similar to a person's activities. In the application we developed, even the non-technical people who were in charge of business processes could determine the roles of agents and define the agents appearing in the applications. Of course, the definitions were very rough and an actual application designer had to modify the definitions in the design phase, but the definitions were roughly correct. Another interesting point is that the non-technical people who were in charge of business processes and the IT architects could talk with each other by referring to the agent model of the target application. This point is important because it can reduce problems caused by miscommunications.

5.3 Concurrent Development

The programming model also makes designing and developing an application easy. During typical design activities using the model, a designer first identifies roles appearing in the target application. Second, he or she decides on the agents to be used in the application. Third, the designer designs the messages that will be exchanged among the agents or external programs. An initial rough design is completed at this point. Then he or she starts designing each agent and each service object. This can be done separately for each type of agent because each agent is isolated in the agent programming model. There are three benefits of this approach. First is that a designer can do the implementation design in a natural way based on the initial rough design. At this stage, the designer can delegate the design of each agent to the sub-designers. Second is that the developer can understand the roles of each agent intuitively and clearly. Third is that multiple developers can work concurrently with few dependencies among agents, since each developer can develop each agent separately.

In the applications we developed, agents occasionally need to use common resources. In the notification service of the profits and losses for foreign currency assets, each agent has to convert a foreign currency code to a foreign currency name to show it on the user's Web browser. The converter component is a resource used by the agents. In the agent programming model, such components are implemented as service objects. Service objects are very useful for developing real systems. It also provides high extendability.

5.4 Development Duration

These characteristics give significant benefits for developing an application quickly. In each of the projects for the applications described above, the duration of design and development was a few months. When the time for design and development is short, the writing of code is often started before the detailed application specifications are fixed. In the agent programming model, designers and developers can have a clear view of the application structure. For example, designers and developers can quickly have a clear grasp of the area for modification caused by updating an application specification. In most cases, the modification is limited to a particular agent or a particular service object.

6 Conclusion

We introduced the Caribbean agent programming model and the framework of the model in this paper. The agent programming model is based on the "reactive agent" model. In the typical applications using the framework, each user has an agent in a server. The number of agents is very large, perhaps hundreds of thousands or more. The runtime module for the framework needs powerful capabilities to support such large numbers of agents. The Caribbean runtime provides a memory management mechanism and a thread management mechanism. The system also needs to ensure that agents remain alive even if a system hosting the agents fails. The runtime has a recovery management mechanism. A single server might not be sufficient to host millions of agents in a system. Caribbean supports a server clustering function.

We applied the agent programming model and the framework to several commercial systems that handle events using personalized information. Through the development of these systems, we proved that the designers, developers, and even non-technical people could easily understand the agent programming model. This characteristic provides significant benefits in developing an application quickly. The applications we applied the agent programming model to are applications that handle events using personalized information. We expect that the model can offer benefits to other types of applications, such as multiagent simulations.

References

[1]   Aglets System Development Kit, http://www.trl.ibm.com/aglets.
[2]   G. Yamamoto and Y. Nakamura: Architecture and Performance Evaluation of a Massive Multi-agent System, Autonomous Agents '99.
[3]   Y. Nakamura and G. Yamamoto: Aglets-Based e-Marketplace: Concept, Architecture, and Applications, IBM Research, Tokyo Research Laboratory, Research Report, RT0253 (1998).
[4]   Y. Nakamura and G. Yamamoto: An XML Schema for Agent Interaction Protocols, IBM Research, Tokyo Research Laboratory, Research Report, RT0271 (1998).
[5]   G. Yamamoto and H. Tai: Architecture of an Agent Server Capable of Hosting Tens of Thousands of Agents, Research Report RT0330, IBM Research, 1999 (a shorter version of this paper was published in Proceedings of Autonomous Agents 2000, ACM Press, 2000)
[6]   G. Yamamoto and H. Tai: Performance Evaluation of An Agent Server Capable of Hosting Large Numbers of Agents, Proceedings of Autonomous Agents 2001, ACM Press, 2001
[7]   H. Tai and G. Yamamoto: An Agent Server for the Next Generation of Web Applications, The 11th International Workshop on Database and Expert Systems Applications (DEXA-2000), IEEE Computer Society Press, 2000
[8]   G. Yamamoto and H. Tai: Event Distribution Patterns on an Agent Server Capable of Hosting a Large Number of Agents, Research Report RT0382, IBM Research, 1999
[9]   G. Yamamoto and H. Tai: Agent Server Technology for Next Generation of Web Applications, 4th International Conference on Computational Intelligence and Multimedia Applications, IEEE Computer Society Press, 2001
[10] J. M. Bradshaw, ed., Software Agents, The MIT Press, 1997
[11] K. P. Sycara, Multiagent Systems, pp. 79 - 92, AI Magazine, Summer 1998.
[12] P. A. Bernstein, and E. Newcomer, Principles of Transaction Processing, Morgan Kaufmann Publishers, Inc. 1997

Exploring Flows in the Intelligent Agent Grid Environment[1]

Hai Zhuge

China Knowledge Grid Research Group,
Institute of Computing Technology, Chinese Academy of Sciences, Beijing, China
zhuge@ict.ac.cn

Abstract. The Intelligent Agent Grid Environment is a scalable, live, sustainable and intelligent networking environment where humans, agents, machines and nature can harmoniously co-exist, work and evolve. It automatically collects useful information from nature and society according to requirements, transforms it into resources in the environment, and then after intelligent processing, affects nature and society through machines. According to the regulations and principles of the environment, people, agents and resources can intelligently cooperate with each other to accomplish tasks, generate knowledge and solve problems by actively participating in versatile flow cycles in the environment through roles and machines. The Environment is the unity of the natural material world, virtual world and cognitive world. Various types of attraction in the environment drive the flows. The rules of flows guide the development and management of the environment.

1   Introduction

Our modern society requires the future interconnection environment to go beyond the scope of the traditional automatic machine intelligence, because the computing environment has evolved from personal computers to network, to human-computer environments, and to large-scale human-computer environments, where dynamics, evolution, cooperation, fusion, sustainability, and society issues of computing resources become the major concerns.

The Intelligent Agent Grid Environment is an ideal interconnection environment that involves in the objective natural world, the virtual electronic world and the subjective cognitive world. Flows in real world such as water flow, goods flow and electronic flow are processes of material or energy transmission, which follow the natural laws and economical principles. The balanced flows ensure the harmonious development of the natural environment [11]. The virtual electronic world holds information flow, knowledge flow [9] and service flow. The cognitive world holds the information flow and knowledge flow in other forms. Various flows cooperate with each other to ensure the effectiveness of the environment. Just as goods transportation in supply chain management, the material flows in the environment obeys the laws of

---

[1] Supported by National Basic Research Program (973 project No. 2003CB317001) and National Science Foundation (Grant No. 60273020 and 70271007) of China.

T. Ishida, L. Gasser, and H. Nakashima (Eds.): MMAS 2004, LNAI 3446, pp. 13–24, 2005.

physics and economics and cooperates with the information, knowledge and service flows.

Information flows through the Internet to support applications via TCP/IP protocols. The Grid is to provide advanced computing services by effectively organizing and sharing distributed computing resources [5]. Workflow technologies are to support effective teamwork.

The Semantic Web intends to improve the current Web by establishing machine-understandable semantics for Web applications [4]. Semantics is the basis for knowledge sharing.

Peer-to-Peer (P2P) networks widely exist in one form or another in society such as the epidemic spread network. The idea has been successfully used to share files and computing resources in large-scale dynamic networks especially on the Internet [2]. Its major advantages are autonomy and scalability. But it is hard to support high-level complex applications that require understanding, coordination and scheduling among computing resources. P2P also supports resource sharing among massive agents.

Combining Grid and P2P technology could obtain the advantages of both. Bringing characteristics such as semantics and trust into P2P would bridge the gap between P2P/Grid and high-level complex applications. By establishing some standard mechanisms and using autonomous computing objects, the Intelligent Agent Grid Environment could be a self-managed network that adapts to change and supports high-level intelligent applications.

It should absorb the theories and technologies of the Web, the Semantic Web, the Grid and the Peer-to-Peer computing, and go beyond their scopes. Our research method is to carry out cross-disciplinary research, to draw models and discover rules from making analogies between disciplines such as ecology, physics, and society, to verify the models through simulation, and improve them in real applications.

The Intelligent Agent Grid Environment has *time* and *scale* [11]. Flows in different scale obey different rules, just as the physical law in macrocosm is different from that in microcosm.

2   From Link to Flow

Various links are ties within and between the real world, the virtual world and the spiritual world.

Hyperlinks reflect the relationship between Web pages and form the scale-free structure of the Web [1, 3, 7]. The growth of the Web forms the difference between nodes' status. The high rank nodes have higher attraction to new pages than the low rank nodes do. This phenomenon leads to "the rich gets richer" phenomenon. The hyperlink network implies some information structure. The human browse behavior on the Web implies certain interest communities. However, hyperlinks are rather static and semantically poor.

The semantic link extends hyperlinks by attaching semantics to links. By defining various types of semantics such as the spatial, classification and logical semantics, semantic link networks support intelligent Web applications. Simple semantic link can be defined by attaching a word with commonsense or daily-life semantics to describe the relationship between two resources. Complex semantics can be defined as a semantic link network or a link pointing to semantic description. To describe the semantic relationship that cannot be described in simple semantic links, we extend our previous semantic link representation A—α→B to A—α(link)→B, where α(link) describes a well-defined interconnection semantics.

Different from the static links, flow is dynamic and has the following elements:

1. Starting node and ending node. Nodes are resources in the environment, can process machine-understandable semantics, and can receive and emit flows. Doing this needs a new resource model. In contrast, Web pages' semantics are passive and not machine-understandable.
2. Flow's content. A flow's content will keep stable during the period from leaving a node to arriving a node, but it may change when it goes through a node. In contrast, links do not contain rich content flow.
3. Driving force. The content of a node reflects its energy. A flow directs from high energy to low energy points. In contrast, the high rank node in the hyperlink network can be regarded as having more attraction to new links.

A flow can be formally represented as $c(\Delta t)$: $e(n) \rightarrow e(n')$, which means that content c tends to flow from node n with energy $e(n)$ to node n' with energy $e(n')$ during Δt. Different types of flows need different ways to measure the energy.

An effective flow requires that its receiver needs the content. The receiver needs if it does not have the content. The distribution of flows does not follow the power-law, because the newly added nodes would receive more flows than old nodes.

3   Information Flow and Its Self-organization Phenomenon

The Internet uses TCP/IP and HTTP to realize file transmission, which causes information flows.

Email flow is a typical information flow. Texts go through mailboxes to form the email flow network. The nodes can play different roles at different times. The hub nodes receive and emit many information flows. The characteristic is that the node is static, but the node' rank and the flow frequently change with time. The node's rank is relevant to the owner's role in a period of time. For example, a conference mailbox' rank is high before conference, but it goes down quickly after conference.

Information flow network can be described as follows:

InformationFlowNetwork=(*Nodes, Flows, Ranks, time, Owners*).
Rank(*node*)=*Rank*(*owner*(*node*)).

Emails carry information flows to form self-organization communities because the sender and receiver of an email share some common interest. Various email self-organize diverse virtual interest groups within a team that could be different from real organization. This also shows that the information flows influence the effectiveness of teamwork. We can assess the performance of a team by analyzing its email flows.

To observe the phenomenon of information flow self-organization, we record the emails of a research team with 27 team members in the period of seven months. Fig. 1 shows a map of this experiment, where the nodes are team members and the lines are information flows. The lighter and thinner lines represent smaller flows, and the heavier and thicker lines represent larger flows.

Fig. 1. Map of information flow self-organization in a real research team

Compared with the organization of research groups within the laboratory, we find that the information flows' self-organization function makes the groups' boundaries vague, but the contact between the leaders (the thick and dark lines) and the contact between the leader and the members (the dark lines) can still be clearly seen.

The experiment also tells us the following characteristics.

Characteristic 1. The formation of task-relevant information flow networks is not sensitive to the geographical distances between members.

Characteristic 2. Geographically dispersed members have more task-irrelevant flows than geographically centered members.

The information flow network evolves with the evolution of the knowledge of team members. The evolution of knowledge changes team members' interest and behavior. The recruitment of team members changes the team's knowledge structure so influences the information flow network. So the evolution of knowledge flow network influences the information flow network.

The information flow network also shapes and evolves with cultural and economical factors.

The genetic information flows between generations to control the evolution of species in the future interconnection environment [11]. Resources in the future interconnection environment are living, active and intelligent. New resources are generated by inheriting from existing resources. The basic principle of this kind of information flow is to keep the variety of species in the environment. So, inheritance rules are needed to guide the fusion of information flows.

4   From Information Flow to Knowledge Flow

A team is organized for tasks, but information flows involve various personal interests, some are relevant and helpful, some are irrelevant to the team task. So it is hard
to find the correspondence between the team organization and the self-organized
information flow network. The correspondence can be seen when we extract the task
relevant information flow network out of the information flow network. Removing
knowledge irrelevant information flow like the announcement of meetings, the task
relevant information flows carrying knowledge can be clearly seen. The relationship
among organization, information flows and knowledge flows is shown in Fig.2.

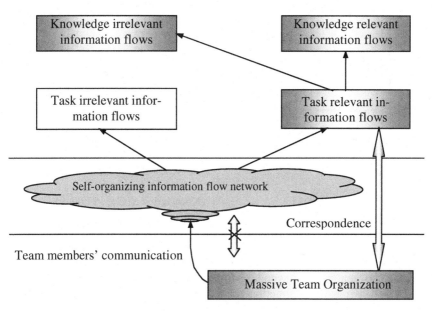

Fig. 2. The relationship among organization, information flows and knowledge flows

Information flows inspire, enrich and verify knowledge flows during being used.
Knowledge flows in turn stimulate new task-relevant information flows. Knowledge
flows within team to accomplish team task and influence cooperation and productivity.

Knowledge flows within the knowledge nodes (human and other knowledge processing mechanism) are internal knowledge flows. The output flow of a node depends
on the input flows, the processing mechanism, and the flowing internal knowledge.
The formation and understanding of knowledge flow concern epistemology and ontology [10].

5   Fusion of Knowledge Flows

A knowledge node in knowledge flow network is composed of a knowledge processing mechanism and a multi-dimensional knowledge space. Knowledge areas and

knowledge levels are two dimensions of the space. Fig. 3 shows two bi-dimensional knowledge spaces, each has three knowledge areas and four knowledge levels that systematic knowledge usually has: *concepts, axioms, rules* and *methods*. The axioms are the relationships between concepts, which need not to be proved. Rules refer to the derived relationships between concepts, between axioms, between rules, and even between methods. Rules can be used for reasoning, and new rules can be proved by axioms and existing rules. The methods include the processes or solutions to problems as well as experience and skill in form of <*Situation, Action, SuccessRate*>.

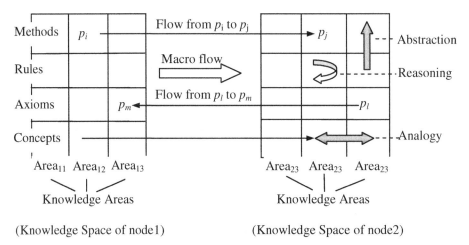

(Knowledge Space of node1)   (Knowledge Space of node2)

Fig. 3. Knowledge fusion between and within knowledge nodes

Every point in the space represents a subspace of definite area and level. Knowledge flows between knowledge nodes and fuses within nodes through merging within points as well as making abstraction between levels and analogy across areas. Abstraction can also carry out within each point. A node emitting knowledge flow can also receive flow from the receiver or other nodes at the same time.

The *knowledge energy* measures the knowledge of a node in a network [10]. The energy difference between points can be but not the must condition of knowledge fusing between points. In macrocosm, knowledge generally flows from high to low energy nodes just as water flows from high to low energy places. For example, knowledge generally flows from teacher to student though teacher may also learn from student simultaneously.

Multiple types of knowledge flowing between the points of the same pair of nodes imply different *attractions* between nodes. Such an attraction drives the behavior of emitting and accepting knowledge. A knowledge flow from p_i to p_j concerns attractions from two directions.

For point p_i, attraction from point p_j, $A_{i \leftarrow j}$ can be measured by considering the amount of knowledge in p_j that p_i does not have (i.e., $|C(p_j) - C(p_i)|$) and the amount of knowledge in p_i (i.e., $|C(p_i)|$) as follows:

$A_{i \leftarrow j} = h(|C(p_j) - C(p_i)| / |C(p_i)|)$ such that $A_{i \leftarrow j} = 0$ if $C(p_i) = C(p_j) \neq 0$ and $A_{i \leftarrow j} = 1$ if $C(p_i) = 0$ and $|C(p_j)| > 0$.

The inspiration function h will amplify the attraction if the flowing knowledge activates thinking and generates some benefit, e.g., triggers analogy, abstraction and reasoning, as well as generates new knowledge and promotes mutual-trust, interest and happy.

Further, if we consider the social factor, e.g., different nodes has different impacts in the same area, the attraction can be improved as follows:

$A_{i \leftarrow j} = h(|C(p_j) - C(p_i)| / |C(p_i)|) \times (1 + |\alpha_j - \alpha_i|)$, where α_j and $\alpha_i \in [0, 1]$ are impact factors of p_j and p_i respectively in the knowledge flow network, and $|\alpha_j - \alpha_i| = 0$ if $\alpha_j \leq \alpha_i$.

Further more, attraction changes with the change of knowledge in nodes in a period of time $\Delta t = end\text{-}time - start\text{-}time$. Taking this into account, we have:

$$A_{i \leftarrow j}(\Delta t) = h(|C(p_j, \Delta t) - C(p_i, \Delta t)| / |C(p_i, \Delta t)|) \times (1 + |\alpha_j(\Delta t) - \alpha_i(\Delta t)|).$$

A strong attraction between nodes is a precondition of an effective knowledge flow. A knowledge flow network is dynamic in nature because the internal knowledge flows keep growing and updating, and the external knowledge flows adapt to the change of the attraction between nodes. Due to the knowledge fusion, we have the following principle.

Principle. Attraction between knowledge nodes always tends to decrease in a knowledge flow network.

This principle drives the team members to obtain new knowledge to keep or improve their status in team.

A knowledge point can accept knowledge flow from multiple points of the same node and from multiple nodes. These incoming flows are integrated according to the knowledge representation in these points. One representation should be transformed to the other if they use different representations. If they are sets, then set union is the way of fusing. Consistency checking and maintaining should be carried out within the point. Knowledge flow fusing carries out by integration, abstraction, analogy, reasoning, conflict resolving, and verifying during the use of knowledge.

A node can broadcast requirements for special knowledge when solving problems. Such requirements form attraction to appropriate knowledge in other nodes. In nature, knowledge should pursue the requirement to gain the maximum profit of teamwork.

A market mechanism can be also established to reward knowledge providers. In this case, the attraction depends on reward, and thus the inspiration function h can be deemed as the function of multiple factors: $h(a_1, \ldots, a_n)$.

The experience of peer-to-peer communication helps a node effectively communicate with another. For example, a node can emit different flows to different nodes according to their interest, bias, and the expertise knowledge areas and levels.

6 Routing Knowledge Flows in Peer-to-Peer Network

It is more important for a knowledge team to effectively share knowledge than to own knowledge [8]. On the other hand, the Intelligent Agent Grid Environment needs the support from a large-scale and scalable network environment. The knowledge flow network can be regarded as a special peer-to-peer network: a node attracts nodes with different intensities. To avoid unnecessary knowledge delivery is a way to raise the efficiency of teamwork. Then, how to route knowledge flow to obtain high efficiency?

Our strategy is to map the equal network onto the probability world. The most attractive node has the largest probability to provide with appropriate knowledge. Therefore, a node will select the most attractive node to ask questions (question-answering is a major means to make knowledge flow).

The usefulness of the knowledge gained from knowledge flows influences the attraction between nodes. It can be measured by the total times of query and the number of satisfied answers:

$\beta_{i \leftarrow j}(t+1) = \beta_{i \leftarrow j}(t)(1 + satisfied\text{-}answer_{i \leftarrow j}(t) / query\text{-}times_{i \leftarrow j}(t))$, where $\beta_{i \leftarrow j}(0) = 1$ and $satisfied\text{-}answer_{i \leftarrow j}(0)/query\text{-}times_{i \leftarrow j}(0) = 0$.

Considering the usefulness, the attraction can be further measured by the following formula:

$$A_{i \leftarrow j}(\Delta t) = \beta_{i \leftarrow j}(\Delta t) \times h(|C(p_j, \Delta t) - C(p_i, \Delta t)| / |C(p_i, \Delta t)|) \times (1 + |\alpha_j(\Delta t) - \alpha_i(\Delta t)|).$$

Fig. 4 shows the result of experiment for comparing the efficiency of knowledge flows in the equal and unequal peer-to-peer networks.

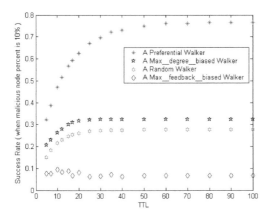

Fig. 4. Experiment of knowledge flow routing strategy

The result shows that the approach adopting the attraction (called the preferential walker) is better than other approaches (the Random Walk: a peer forwards queries to a randomly chosen neighbor, the Max-Degree-biased Walk: a peer forwards queries to the highest-degree neighbor, and the Max-Feedback-biased Walk: a peer forwards queries to the highest-feedback neighbor at each hop).

7   Service Flow

A service flow is a process of the execution of a set of inter-dependent services, represented as SFN=(*Services, ProcessDefinition, InteractionDefinition, Constraint*).

Service flow networks are dynamic service logistic processes during which information and knowledge flows are triggered to serve the service flow. The process definition includes the following logical relationships among service flows.

Sequential routing is a segment of a process instance where services are executed in a logical sequence, which satisfies:

1. The start order: the predecessor starts before the successor.
2. The termination order: the predecessor terminates before the successor.
3. The input-output relationship: the output of the predecessor is the input of the successor.
4. The mark passing rule: the start mark will be delivered to the successor from the predecessor when the successor starts, and the termination mark will be delivered to the successor from the predecessor when the predecessor terminates.

And-join connection between services means that two or more logically parallel-executing services converge into a single common thread of control, and satisfies:

1. The start order: the successor starts after the start of all its predecessors.
2. The termination order: the successor terminates after the termination of all its predecessors.
3. The input-output relationship: the outputs of all the predecessors are as the input of the successor.
4. The mark passing: the start marks of all the predecessors will be merged as one start mark, which will be delivered to the successor when the successor starts. The termination marks will be merged as one termination mark, which will be delivered to the successor when all the predecessors have been terminated.

And-split is a single thread of control splits into two or more parallel services, and satisfies:

1. The start order: all the successors start after the starting of their common predecessor.
2. The termination order: all the successors terminate after the termination of their common predecessor.
3. The input-output relationship: the output of the predecessor is as the inputs of all its successors.
4. The mark passing rule: the start mark will be split and delivered to all of its successors respectively when these successors start, and the termination mark will be split and delivered to all of its successors when the predecessor terminates.

Or-join is a connection way that two or more service branches re-converge into a single thread of control without any synchronization, and satisfies:

1. The start order: the successor should start after the start of its active predecessor(s) (because not all of the predecessors are active at the same time).
2. The termination order: the successor terminates after the termination of its active predecessor(s).
3. The input-output relationship: the outputs of the active predecessors are as the input of the successor or are selected by the successor as its input.
4. The mark passing rule: the start mark of an active predecessor will be delivered to the successor when the successor starts, and the termination mark of an active predecessor will be delivered to the successor when the predecessor terminates.

Or-split means a single thread of control makes a decision upon which branch to take when encountered within multiple service branches, and satisfies:

1. The start order: the active successor(s) start(s) after the predecessor starts.
2. The termination order: the active successor(s) terminate(s) after the termination of the predecessor.
3. The input-output relationship: the output of the predecessor is as the input(s) of the active successor(s).
4. The mark passing rule: the start mark will be delivered to the active successor(s) when it (they) start(s), and the termination mark will be delivered to the successor(s) after the predecessor terminates.

8   Cooperation of Flows

A complex application needs the logistic service flows rather than a single service. Effective logistic service flow depends on the effective cooperation of relevant information flow and knowledge flow, and the operation of the service flow can also generate feedback to enrich and update the knowledge and information flows. Fig. 5 shows the scenario of the cooperation among the information flow, knowledge flow and service flow. An example of flow cooperation for arranging an academic visiting is described in Table 1.

Such cooperation brings the following three features:

1. The logistic process of the service flow can obtain the support from the optimized information and knowledge flows.
2. Different functions of a service can obtain information and knowledge separately on demand.
3. The evolution and fusion effect is formed when new knowledge and information generated during the operation of the service flow are fed and fused with the information and knowledge flows. New knowledge also comes from the mining in the information flow.

The semantic gaps prevent machines and human to collaborate with each other. For example, software tools are difficult to collaborate to provide integrated services, and workflows are difficult to collaborate with each other for cooperation. Effort has been down in the Semantic Web area such as domain ontology and semantic annotation, Semantic Web services, and open-source middleware (semantic virtual machine for process model). But semantics are still the technological obstacle to the self-organization of services.

On-demand service provision is an ideal of Web Services, but services could be organized and provided on-demand only in communism. It is almost impossible if the service production and provision have cost. In free market economic systems, services are organized according to market principle. Services should compete each other to gain reputation and trust, and consumers should pay for qualified services. Service providers and consumers form a network via the media of services. The providers gain trust when consumers use services they provided.

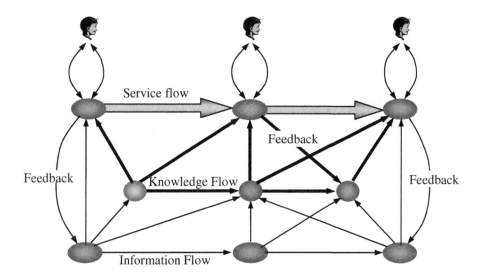

Fig. 5. Cooperation of flows

Table 1. Cooperation of flows to arrange a scholar's visiting process

Steps	Service Flow	Involved flows
1	The user uses search service to find appropriate peers	Information flow
2	The user uses email service to settle visiting	Information flow, Knowledge flows
3	The user uses service to exchange ideas and papers	Information flow
4	The user uses service to apply visa	Information flow
5	The user uses service to book ticket and hotel	Information flow
6	The user uses travel service	Material flow, information flow
7	Visiting activity (talk, discussion, and studying)	Knowledge flow, information flow
8	The user uses travel service	Material flow, information flow

An interesting question is whether the self-organization of information and knowledge flows influences the efficiency of the cooperation of flows. In worldwide region, it is difficult for services to accurately obtain the required knowledge and information, and store new knowledge and information in appropriate places. Knowing the self-organization phenomenon, services could contact the high rank nodes to obtain the efficiency.

9   Conclusion

This paper explores the rules of flows in the future interconnection environment — Intelligent Agent Grid Environment. Information flow, knowledge flow and service flow cooperate to functioning the sustainable development, operation and evolution of the environment according to their own rules.

Intelligence, *Grid* and *Environment* represent humanity's three aspirations for the future working and living environment. The intelligence reflects humanity's pursuit of recognizing themselves and the society. The Grid reflects humanity's pursuit of optimization and systematization. The environment reflects the humanity's pursuit of recognizing nature and its harmony.

Ongoing work is to explore more rules in the environment like the rules for inheritance among the unified resource model soft-devices [12], and to apply the proposed approaches to construct a real environment for the culture protection and exhibition domain.

Acknowledgement

The author thanks all the team members of the China Knowledge Grid Research Group (http://kg.ict.ac.cn) for their cooperation and support, especially X.Chen, L.Ding and Z.Gu for their help in the experiments of this paper.

References

1. Adamic, L.A. and Huberman, B.A. Power-Law Distribution of the World Wide Web. *Science*, 287, 24 (2000) 2115.
2. Balakrishnan, H. et al. Looking Up Data in P2P Systems. *Communications of the ACM*, 46, 2 (2003) 43-48.
3. Barabási, A.L. and Albert, R. Emergence of Scaling in Random Networks. *Science*, 286, (1999) 509-512.
4. Berners-Lee, T., Hendler, J., and Lassila, O. Semantic Web. *Scientific American*, 284, 5 (2001) 34-43.
5. Foster, I. Internet Computing and the Emerging Grid. *Nature*, 408, 6815 (2000) www.nature.com/nature/webmatters/grid/grid.html.
6. Hendler, J. Agents and the Semantic Web. IEEE Intelligent Systems, 16, 2 (2001) 30-37.
7. Kleinberg, J. and Lawrence, S. The Structure of the Web. *Science*, 294, 30 (2001) 1849-1850.
8. O'Leary, D.E. Enterprise Knowledge Management. *Computer*, 31, 3 (1998) 54-61.
9. Zhuge, H. A Knowledge Flow Model for Peer-to-Peer Team Knowledge Sharing and Management. *Expert Systems with Applications*, 23, 1 (2002) 23-30.
10. Zhuge, H. The Knowledge Grid. *World Scientific Publishing Co.* Singapore, 2004.
11. Zhuge, H. Toward the Eco-Grid: A Harmoniously Evolved Interconnection Environment. *Communications of the ACM*, 47, 9 (2004) 79-83.
12. Zhuge, H. Clustering Soft-devices in Semantic Grid. *Computing in Science and Engineering*, 4, 6 (2002) 60-63.

Adaptive Agent Allocation for Massively Multi-agent Applications

Myeong-Wuk Jang and Gul Agha

Department of Computer Science,
University of Illinois at Urbana-Champaign,
Urbana IL 61801, USA
{mjang, agha}@uiuc.edu

Abstract. Although distributed computing is necessary to execute massively multi-agent applications, the distribution of agents is challenging especially when the communication patterns among agents are continuously changing. This paper proposes two adaptive agent allocation mechanisms for massively multi-agent applications: one mechanism aims at minimizing agent communication cost, while the other mechanism attempts to prevent overloaded computer nodes from negatively affecting overall performance. We synthesize these two mechanisms in a multi-agent framework called *Adaptive Actor Architecture (AAA)*. In AAA, each agent platform monitors the workload of its computer node and the communication patterns of agents executing on it. An agent platform periodically reallocates agents according to their communication localities. When an agent platform is overloaded, the platform migrates a set of agents, which have more intra-group communication than inter-group or inter-node communication, to a lightly loaded agent platform. These adaptive agent allocation mechanisms are developed as fully distributed algorithms, and they move the selected agents as a group. In order to evaluate these mechanisms, preliminary experimental results with large-scale micro UAV (Unmanned Aerial Vehicle) simulations are described.

1 Introduction

Large-scale multi-agent simulations have recently been carried out [8, 12]. These large-scale applications may be executed on a cluster of computers to benefit from distributed computing. When agents participating in a large-scale application communicate intensively with each other, the distribution of agents on the cluster may significantly affect the performance of multi-agent systems: overloaded computer nodes may become the bottleneck for concurrent execution, or inter-node communication may considerably delay computation.

Many load balancing and task assignment algorithms have been developed to assign tasks on distributed computer nodes [13]. These algorithms mainly use information about the amount of computation and the inter-process communication cost; a task requires a small amount of computational time to finish, and the communication cost of tasks is known *a priori*. However, in many multi-agent

T. Ishida, L. Gasser, and H. Nakashima (Eds.): MMAS 2004, LNAI 3446, pp. 25–39, 2005.

applications, agents do not cease from execution until their system finishes the entire operation [5]. Furthermore, since the communication patterns among cooperative agents are continuously changing during execution, it may be infeasible to estimate the inter-agent communication cost for a certain time period. Therefore, task-based load balancing algorithms may not be applicable to multi-agent applications.

This paper proposes two agent allocation mechanisms to handle the dynamic change of the communication patterns of agents participating in a massively multi-agent application and to move agents on overloaded computer nodes to lightly loaded computer nodes. *Adaptive Actor Architecture* (*AAA*), the extended multi-agent framework of *Actor Architecture* [9], monitors the status of computer nodes and the communication patterns of agents, and migrates agents to collocate intensively communicating agents on a single computer node. In order to move agents to another computer node, an agent platform on a single node manages agent groups whose member agents have more intra-group communication than inter-group or inter-node communication. In order to evaluate our approach, large-scale micro UAV (Unmanned Aerial Vehicle) simulations including up to 10,000 agents were tested.

This paper is organized as follows. Section 2 introduces the overall architecture of our agent system. Section 3 explains in details two adaptive agent allocation mechanisms used in our agent system. Section 4 shows the preliminary experimental results to evaluate these allocation mechanisms, and Section 5 describes related work. Finally, Section 6 concludes this paper with our future work.

2   Adaptive Actor Architecture

AAA provides a light-weight implementation of agents as active objects or actors [1]; agents in AAA are implemented as threads instead of processes, and they communicate using object messages instead of string messages. Adaptive Actor Architecture consists of two main parts:

- *AAA platforms* which provide the system environment in which agents exist and interact with other agents. In order to execute agents, each computer node must have one AAA platform. AAA platforms provide agent state management, agent communication, agent migration, agent monitoring, and middle agent services.
- *Actor library* which is a set of APIs that facilitate the development of agents on the AAA platforms by providing the user with a high level abstraction of service primitives. At execution time, the actor library works as the interface between agents and their respective AAA platforms.

An AAA platform consists of ten components (see Fig. 1): Message Manager, Transport Manager, Transport Sender, Transport Receiver, Delayed Message Manager, Actor Manager, Actor Migration Manager, Actor Allocation Manager, System Monitor, and ATSpace.

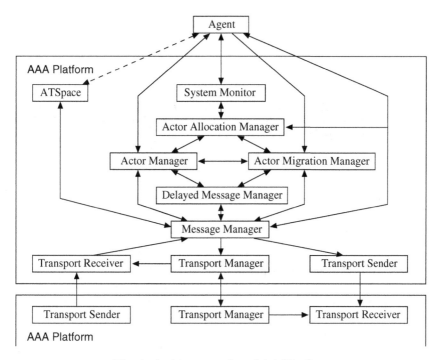

Fig. 1. Architecture of an AAA Platform

The *Message Manager* (MM) handles message passing between agents. Every message passes through at least one Message Manager. If the receiver agent of a message exists on the same AAA platform as the sender agent, the MM of the platform directly delivers the message to the receiver agent. However, if the receiver agent is not on the same AAA platform, this MM delivers the message to the MM of the platform where the receiver currently resides, and finally the MM delivers the message to the receiver. The *Transport Manager* (TM) maintains a public port for message passing between different AAA platforms. When a sender agent sends a message to a receiver agent on a different AAA platform, the *Transport Sender* (TS) residing on the same platform as the sender receives the message from the MM of the sender agent and delivers it to the *Transport Receiver* (TR) on the AAA platform of the receiver. If there is no built-in connection between these two AAA platforms, the TS contacts the TM of the AAA platform of the receiver agent to open a connection so that the TM creates a TR for the new connection. Finally, the TR receives the message and delivers it to the MM on the same platform.

The *Delayed Message Manager* (DMM) temporarily holds messages for mobile agents while they are moving from their AAA platforms to other AAA platforms. The *Actor Manager* (AM) manages states of the agents that are currently executing and the locations of the mobile agents created on the AAA platform. The *Actor Migration Manager* (AMM) supports agent migration.

The *System Monitor* (SM) periodically checks the workload of its computer node, and the *Actor Allocation Manager* (AAM) analyzes the communication patterns of agents. With the collected information, the AAM makes decisions for either agents or agent groups to deliver to other AAA platforms with the help of the Actor Migration Manager. The AAM negotiates with other AAMs to check the feasibility of migrations before starting agent migration.

The *ATSpace* provides middle agent services, such as matchmaking and brokering services. Unlike other system components, the ATSpace is implemented as an agent. Therefore, any agent can create an ATSpace, and hence, an AAA platform may have more than one ATSpaces. The ATSpace created by an AAA platform is called the *default ATSpace* of the platform, and all agents can obtain the agent names of default ATSpaces. Once an agent has the name of an ATSpace, the agent may send the ATSpace messages in order to use its services, and the messages are delivered through the Message Manager.

3   Adaptive Agent Allocation

In order to develop large-scale distributed multi-agent applications, the multi-agent systems must be scalable. This scalability cannot be achieved if the application or the infrastructure includes centralized components which can become a bottleneck. Moreover, the scalability requires relatively balanced workload on computer nodes. Otherwise, the slowest node may become a bottleneck. However, balancing the workload between computer nodes requires significant overhead: the relevant global state information needs to be gathered, and agents have to be transferred sufficiently frequently between computer nodes. Therefore, when the number of computer nodes and/or the number of agents is very large, load balancing is difficult to achieve. AAA uses the *load sharing approach* in which agents on an overloaded agent platform are moved to other lightly loaded agent platforms, but balanced workload among computer nodes is not required.

Another important factor for the scalability of multi-agent systems is the communication overhead. When agents on separate computer nodes communicate intensively with each other, this factor may significantly affect the performance of multi-agent systems. Even though the speed of local networks has increased considerably, the intra-node communication speed for agent message passing is much faster than inter-node communication. Therefore, if we can collocate together agents which communicate intensively with each other, communication time significantly decreases. It is not generally feasible for a user to distribute agents based on their communication patterns, because the communication patterns among agents may change over time in unpredictable ways. Therefore, agents should be reallocated dynamically according to their communication patterns, and this procedure should be managed by a middleware system, such as agent platforms. Each agent platform in AAA monitors the status of its computer node and the communication patterns of agents on it, and the platform dynamically reallocates agents according to the information gathered.

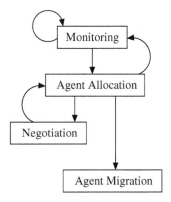

Fig. 2. Four Phases for Basic Adaptive Agent Allocation

3.1   Agent Allocation for Communication Locality

An agent allocation mechanism used in AAA handles the dynamic change of the communication patterns among agents. This mechanism consists of four phases: *monitoring*, *agent allocating*, *negotiation*, and *agent migration* (see Fig 2).

Monitoring Phase. The Actor Allocation Manager monitors the communication patterns of agents with the assistance from the Message Manager. Specifically, the Actor Allocation Manager checks the number of messages between sender agents on its agent platform and agent platforms of receiver agents. This information is maintained with a two dimensional matrix variable M.

Periodically or when requested by a system agent, the Actor Allocation Manager updates the communication patterns between agents and agent platforms with the following equation:

$$C_{ij}(t) = \alpha \left(\frac{M_{ij}(t)}{\sum_k M_{ik}(t)} \right) + (1 - \alpha)C_{ij}(t - 1)$$

where $C_{ij}(t)$ is the communication dependency between agent i and agent platform j at the time step t; $M_{ij}(t)$ is the number of messages sent from agent i to agent platform j during the t-th time step; and α is a coefficient for the relative importance between recent information and old information.

For analyzing the communication patterns of agents, agents in AAA are classified into two types: *stationary* and *movable*. Any agent in AAA can move itself according to its decision, even though it is either stationary or movable. However, the Actor Allocation Manager does not consider stationary agents as candidates for agent allocation; an agent platform can migrate only movable agents. These types of agents are initially decided by agent programmers, and may be changed during execution by the agents, but not by agent platforms.

Agent Allocation Phase. After a certain number of repeated monitoring phases, the Actor Allocation Manager computes the communication dependency ratio of an agent between its current agent platform and another agent platform:

$$R_{ij} = \frac{C_{ij}}{C_{in}}, \quad j \neq n$$

where R_{ij} is the communication dependency ratio of agent i between its current agent platform n and agent platform j.

When the maximum ratio of an agent is larger than a predefined threshold, the Actor Allocation Manager assigns this agent to a *virtual agent group* that represents a remote agent platform:

$$k = \arg\max_{j}(R_{ij}) \ \wedge \ R_{ik} > \theta \ \rightarrow \ a_i \in G_k$$

where θ is the threshold for agent migration, a_i represents agent i, and G_k means agent group k.

When the Actor Allocation Manager has checked all agents and assigned some of them to virtual agent groups, this Manager starts the negotiation phase. After the agent allocation phase, information about the communication dependencies of agents is reset.

Negotiation Phase. Before an agent platform migrates the agents in a virtual agent group to its corresponding agent platform, the Actor Allocation Manager of the sender agent platform communicates with that of the destination agent platform to check its current status. If the destination agent platform has enough space and available computational resources for new agents, its Actor Allocation Manager accepts the request for the agent group migration. Otherwise, the destination agent platform sends the number of agents that it can accept. Therefore, the granularity of this negotiation between agent platforms is an agent.

When the Actor Allocation Manager receives a reply from the destination agent platform, this Manager sends as many agents to the destination agent platform as the number of agents recorded in the reply message. When the number in the reply message is less than the number of agents in the virtual group, the agents to be migrated are selected according to their communication dependency ratios.

Agent Migration Phase. When a destination agent platform can accept new agents, the Actor Allocation Manager of the sender agent platform initiates the migration of entire or part of agents in the selected virtual agent group. After the current operation of a selected agent finishes, the Actor Migration Manager moves the agent to the destination agent platform decided by the Actor Allocation Manager. After the agent is migrated, it carries out its remaining operations.

3.2   Agent Allocation for Load Sharing

With the previous agent allocation mechanism, AAA handles the dynamic change of the communication patterns of agents. However, this mechanism may increase the workload of certain agent platforms and then decrease the overall performance of entire systems. Therefore, the second agent allocation has been developed to mitigate this problem. When an agent platform is overloaded, the System Monitor detects this and activates the agent reallocation procedure to move agents to lightly loaded agent platforms. Since agents had been assigned to their current agent platforms according to their communication patterns, choosing agents randomly to migrate might result in moving them back to their original agent platforms by the Actor Allocation Managers of their new agent platforms. This is because the moved agents may still have a high communication with their previous agent platform. This agent allocation mechanism consists of five phases: *monitoring*, *agent grouping*, *group allocation*, *negotiation*, and *agent migration* (see Fig 3).

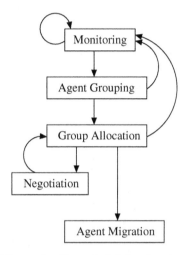

Fig. 3. Five Phases for Extended Adaptive Agent Allocation

Monitoring Phase. In the second agent allocation mechanism, the System Monitor periodically checks the state of its agent platform; this component gathers information about the current processor usage and the memory usage of its computer node. When the System Monitor decides that its agent platform is overloaded, it activates an agent allocation procedure. When the Actor Allocation Manager is notified by the System Monitor, it starts monitoring the local communication patterns among agents to partition them to *local agent groups*.

To check the communication patterns of agents, the Actor Allocation Manager uses information about the sender agent, the agent platform of the receiver agent, and the agent group of the receiver agent of each message. In addition to the number M_{ij} of messages sent from agent i to agent platform j, the number m_{ik} of messages sent from agent i to local agent group k is updated when the receiver agent exists on the same agent platform. The summation of all m variables of an agent is equal to the number of messages sent by the agent to its current agent platform: $\sum_k m_{ik} = M_{in}$ where the index of the current agent platform is n.

After a predetermined time interval, or in response to a request from a system agent, the Actor Allocation Manager updates the communication patterns between agents and agent groups on the same agent platform using the following equation:

$$c_{ij}(t) = \beta \left(\frac{m_{ij}(t)}{M_{in}(t)} \right) + (1 - \beta)c_{ij}(t - 1)$$

where $c_{ij}(t)$ is the communication dependency between agent i and local agent group j at the time step t; $m_{ij}(t)$ is the number of messages sent from agent i to agents in local agent group j during the t-th time step; $M_{in}(t)$ is the number of messages sent from agent i to its current agent platform n during the t-th time step; and β is a coefficient for deciding the relative importance between recent information and old information.

Agent Grouping Phase. After a certain number of repeated monitoring phases, each agent i is assigned to a local agent group whose index is decided by $\arg\max_{j} (c_{ij}(t))$; this group has the maximum value of the communication localities $c_{ij}(t)$ of agent i. Since the initial group assignment of agents may not be optimized, the monitoring and agent grouping phases are repeated several times.

After each agent grouping phase, information about the communication dependency of agents is reset. During the agent grouping phase, the number of agent groups can be changed. When two groups have much smaller populations than others, these two groups may be merged into one group. When one group has a much larger population than others, the agent group may be split into two groups. The minimum number and maximum number of agent groups are predefined.

Group Allocation Phase. After a certain number of repeated monitoring and agent grouping phases, the Actor Allocation Manager makes a decision to move a local agent group to another agent platform. The group selection is based on the communication dependencies between agent groups and agent platforms; the communication dependency D_{ij} between local agent group i and agent platform j is decided by the summation of the communication dependencies between all agents in the agent group and the agent platform:

$$D_{ij} = \sum_{k} C_{kj}(t) \quad where \quad a_k \in A_i$$

where A_i represents local agent group i, and a_k is a member agent of the agent group A_i.

The agent group which has the least dependency to the current agent platform is selected using the following equation:

$$\arg\max_{j} \left(\frac{\sum_{j, j \neq n} D_{ij}}{D_{in}} \right)$$

where n is the index of the current agent platform. The destination agent platform of the selected agent group i is decided by the communication dependency between the agent group and agent platforms using the following equation.

$$\arg\max_{j}(D_{ij}) \quad where \quad j \neq n$$

Negotiation Phase. If one local agent group and its destination agent platform are decided, the Actor Allocation Manager of the sender agent platform communicates with that of the destination agent platform. If the destination agent platform accepts all agents in the group, the Actor Allocation Manager of the sender agent platform starts the agent migration phase. Otherwise, this Actor Allocation Manager communicates with that of the second best destination platform until it finds an available destination agent platform or checks the possibility of all other agent platforms.

This phase of the second agent allocation mechanism is similar to that of the previous agent allocation mechanism, but there are some differences. One important difference between these two negotiation phases is the granularity of negotiation. If the destination agent platform has enough space and available computation power for all agents in the selected agent group, the Actor Allocation Manager of the destination agent platform accepts the request for the agent group migration. Otherwise, the destination agent platform refuses the request. The granularity of this negotiation between agent platforms is an agent group; the destination agent platform cannot accept part of an agent group.

Agent Migration Phase. When the sender agent platform receives the acceptance reply from the destination agent platform, the Actor Allocation Manager of the sender agent platform initiates the migration of agents in the selected local agent group. The procedure for the following steps in the second agent allocation mechanism is the same as that in the previous agent allocation mechanism.

3.3   Characteristics

Transparent Distributed Algorithm. Our adaptive agent allocation mechanisms are developed as fully distributed algorithms; each agent platform independently performs its agent allocation mechanism according to information about its workload and the communication patterns of agents on it. There are no centralized components to manage the overall procedure of agent allocation. These mechanisms are transparent to multi-agent applications. The only requirement for application developers is to declare candidate agents for agent allocation as movable.

Load Balancing vs. Load Sharing. The second agent allocation mechanism is not a load balancing mechanism but a load sharing mechanism; it does not try to balance the workload of computer nodes participating in an application. The goal of our multi-agent system is to reduce the turnaround time of applications with optimized agent allocation. Therefore, only overloaded agent platforms perform the second agent distribution mechanism, and agents are moved from overloaded agent platforms to lightly loaded agent platforms.

Individual Agent-Based Allocation vs. Agent Group-Based Allocation. With the agent group-based allocation mechanism, some communication locality problems may be naturally solved. First, when two agents on the same agent platform communicate intensively with each other but not with other agents on the same platform, these agents may continuously stay on the current agent platform even though they have a large amount of communication with agents on another agent platform. If these two agents can move together to the remote agent platform, the overall performance can be improved. However, an individual agent-based allocation mechanism does not handle this situation. Second, individual agent-based allocation may require much platform-level message passing among agent platforms for the negotiation. For example, in order to send agents to other agent platforms, agent platforms should negotiate with each other to avoid sending too many agents to a certain agent platform, thus overloading the agent platform. However, if an agent platform handles a set of agents at one time, the agent platforms may reduce negotiation messages and negotiation time.

Stop-and-Repartitioning vs. Implicit Agent Allocation. Some object reallocation systems require the global synchronization. This kind approach is called the *stop-and-repartitioning* [2]. Our agent allocation mechanisms are concurrently executed with agent applications. The monitoring and agent allocation phases do not interrupt the execution of application agents.

Size of a Time Step. In the monitoring phase, the size of each time step may be fixed. However, this step size may be adjusted by an agent application. For example, in multi-agent based simulations, this size may be the same as the size of a simulation time step. Thus, the size of time steps may be flexible according to the workload of each simulation step and the processor power. To use dynamic step size, our agent system has a *reflective mechanism*; agents in applications are affected by multi-agent platform services, and the services of the multi-agent platform may be adjusted by agents in applications.

4   Experimental Results

For the purpose of evaluation, we provide experimental results related to micro UAV (Unmanned Aerial Vehicle) simulations. These simulations include from 2,000 to 10,000 agents; half of them are UAVs, and the others are targets. Micro UAVs perform a surveillance mission on a mission area to detect and serve moving targets. During the mission time, these UAVs communicate with their neighboring UAVs to perform the mission together. The size of a simulation time step is one half second, and the total simulation time is around 37 minutes. The

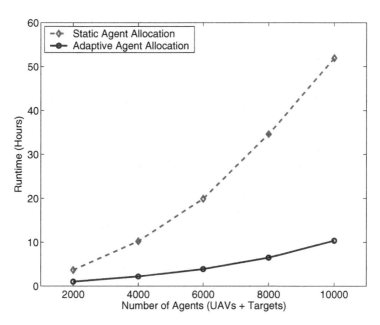

Fig. 4. Runtime for Static and Adaptive Agent Allocation

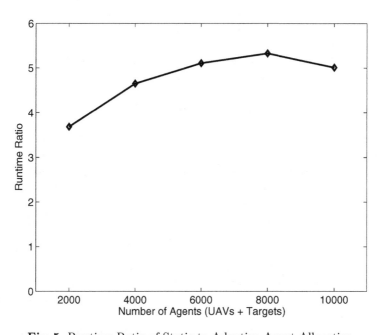

Fig. 5. Runtime Ratio of Static-to-Adaptive Agent Allocation

runtime of each simulation depends on the number of agents and the collaboration policy among agents. For these experiments, we have used four computers (3.4 GHz Intel CPU and 2 GB main memory) with a Giga-bit switch.

For UAV simulations, the *agent-environment interaction* model has been used [3]; all UAVs and targets are implemented as intelligent agents, and the navigation space and radar censors of all UAVs are implemented as environment agents. To remove centralized components in distributed computing, each environment agent on a single computer node takes charge of a certain navigation area. UAVs communicate directly with each other and indirectly with neighboring UAVs and targets through environment agents. Environment agents provide application agent-oriented brokering services with the ATSpace [10]. During simulation, UAVs and targets move from one divided area to another, and UAVs and targets communicate intensively either directly or indirectly.

Fig. 4 depicts the difference of runtime in two cases: adaptive agent allocation and static agent allocation. Fig. 5 shows the ratio of runtime in both cases. These two figures show the potential performance benefit of adaptive agent allocation. In our particular example, as the number of agents is increased, the ratio also generally increases. With 10,000 agents, simulations using the adaptive agent allocation are five times faster than simulations using a static agent allocation.

5   Related Work

The mechanisms used in dynamic load balancing may be compared to those in AAA. *Zoltan* [7], *PREMA/ILB* [2], and *Charm++* [4] support dynamic load balancing with object migration. Zoltan uses a loosely coupled approach between applications and load balancing algorithms using an object-oriented callback function interface [7]. However, this library-based load balancing approach depends on information given by applications, and applications activate object decomposition. Therefore, without developers' thorough analysis about applications, the change of dynamic access patterns of objects may not correctly be detected, and object decomposition may not be performed at the proper time. The ILB of PREMA also interacts with objects using callback routines to collect information to be used for the load balancing decision making, and to pack and unpack objects [2]. Charm++ uses the *Converse* runtime system to maintain message passing among objects, and hence, the runtime system may collect information to analyze communication dependencies among objects [4]. However, this system also requires callback methods for packing and unpacking objects as others do. In AAA, the Actor Allocation Manager does not interact with agents, but it receives necessary information from the Message Manager and the System Monitor to analyze the communication patterns of agents and the workload of its agent platform. Also, developers do not need to define any callback method for load balancing.

J-Orchestra [15], *Addistant* [14], and *JavaParty* [11] are automatic application partitioning systems for Java applications. They transform input Java applications into distributed applications using a bytecode rewriting technique.

They can migrate Java objects to take advantage of locality. However, they differ from AAA in two ways. First, while they move objects to take advantage of data locality, AAA migrates agents to take advantage of communication locality. Second, the access pattern of an object differs from the communication pattern of an agent. For example, although a data object may be moved whenever it is accessed by other objects on different platforms, an agent cannot be migrated whenever it communicates with other agents on different platforms. This is because an object is accessed by another single object, but an agent communicates with other multiple agents at the same time.

The *Comet* algorithm assigns agents to computer nodes according to their credit [5]. The credit of an agent is decided by its computation load, intra-communication load, and inter-communication load. Chow and Kwok have emphasized the importance of the relationship between intra-communication and inter-communication of each agent. However, there are some important differences. The authors' system includes a centralized component to make decisions for agent assignment, and their experiments include a small number of agents, i.e., 120 agents. AAA uses fully distributed algorithm, and experiments include 10,000 agents. Because of the large number of agents, the Actor Allocation Manager do not analyze the communication dependencies among all individual agents, but only those between agents and agent platforms and those between agent groups and agent platforms.

The *IO* of *SALSA* [6] provides various load balancing mechanisms for multi-agent applications. The IO also analyzes the communication patterns among individual agents. Therefore, it may not be applied to massively multi-agent applications because of the large computational overhead.

6 Conclusion and Future Work

This paper has explained two adaptive agent allocation mechanisms for massively multi-agent applications. These agent allocation mechanisms allocate agents according to their communication localities and the workload of computer nodes. The main contribution of this paper is to provide adaptive agent allocation mechanisms to handle a large number of agents which communicate intensively with each other and dynamically change their communication localities. Because of the large number of agents, these agent allocation mechanisms focus on the communication dependencies between agents and agent platforms and the dependencies between agent groups and agent platforms, instead of the communication dependencies among individual agents. Our experimental results show that micro UAV simulations using the adaptive agent allocation are approximately five times faster than those with a static agent allocation.

The proposed mechanisms introduce an additional overhead for monitoring and decision making for adaptive agent allocation. However, our experiments suggest that this overhead are more than compensated if multi-agent applications have the following attributes: first, an application includes a large number of agents so that the performance on a single computer node is not acceptable;

second, some agents communicate more intensively with each other than with other agents, and thus the communication locality of each agent is an important factor in the overall performance of the massively multi-agent application; third, the communication patterns of agents are continuously changing, and hence, static agent allocation mechanisms are not sufficient.

Although we have proposed an agent allocation mechanism to move an over-loaded computer node to a lightly loaded computer node, our experiments suggest that increased load does not necessarily result in a decrease in the performance of massively multi-agent applications. When the number of agent platforms for an application exceeds a certain limit, the inter-node communication cost even becomes larger than the benefit of distributed computing. Therefore, we plan to develop algorithms to determine the appropriate number of agent platforms for a given massively multi-agent application.

Acknowledgements

This research is sponsored by the Defense Advanced Research Projects Agency under contract number F30602-00-2-0586.

References

1. G. Agha. *Actors: A Model of Concurrent Computation in Distributed Systems.* MIT Press, 1986.
2. K. Barker, A. Chernikov, N. Chrisochoides, and K. Pingali. A Load Balancing Framework for Adaptive and Asynchronous Applications. *IEEE Transactions on Parallel and Distributed Systems*, 15(2):183–192, February 2004.
3. M. Bouzid, V. Chevrier, S. Vialle, and F. Charpillet. Parallel Simulation of a Stochastic Agent/Environment Interaction. *Integrated Computer-Aided Engineering*, 8(3):189–203, 2001.
4. R.K. Brunner and L.V. Kalé. Adaptive to Load on Workstation Clusters. In *The Seventh Symposium on the Frontiers of Massively Parallel Computation*, pages 106–112, February 1999.
5. K. Chow and Y. Kwok. On Load Balancing for Distributed Multiagent Computing. *IEEE Transactions on Parallel and Distributed Systems*, 13(8):787–801, August 2002.
6. T. Desell, K. El Maghraoui, and C. Varela. Load Balancing of Autonomous Actors over Dynamic Networks. In *Hawaii International Conference on System Sciences HICSS-37 Software Technology Track*, Hawaii, January 2004.
7. K. Devine, B. Hendrickson, E. Boman, M. St. Jhon, and C. Vaughan. Design of Dynamic Load-Balancing Tools for Parallel Applications. In *Proceedings of the International Conference on Supercomputing*, pages 110–118, Santa Fe, 2000.
8. L. Gasser and K. Kakugawa. MACE3J: Fast Flexible Distributed Simulation of Large, Large-Grain Multi-Agent Systems. In *Proceedings of the First International Conference on Autonomous Agents & Multiagent Systems (AAMAS)*, pages 745–752, Bologna, Italy, July 2002.

9. M. Jang and G. Agha. On Efficient Communication and Service Agent Discovery in Multi-agent Systems. In *Third International Workshop on Software Engineering for Large-Scale Multi-Agent Systems (SELMAS '04)*, pages 27–33, Edinburgh, Scotland, May 24-25 2004.

10. M. Jang, A. Abdel Momen, and G. Agha. ATSpace: A Middle Agent to Support Application-Oriented Matchmaking and Brokering Services. In *IEEE/WIC/ACM IAT(Intelligent Agent Technology)-2004*, pages 393–396, Beijing, China, September 20-24 2004.

11. M. Philippsen and M. Zenger. JavaParty - Transparent Remote Objects in Java. *Concurrency: Practice and Experience*, 9(11):1225–1242, 1997.

12. K. Popov, V. Vlassov, M. Rafea, F. Holmgren, P. Brand, and S. Haridi. Parallel Agent-Based Simulation on a Cluster of Workstations. *Parallel Processing Letters*, 13(4):629–641, 2003.

13. P.K. Sinha. Chapter 7. Resource Management. In *Distributed Operating Systems*, pages 347–380. IEEE Press, 1997.

14. M. Tatsubori, T. Sasaki, S. Chiba, and K. Itano. A Bytecode Translator for Distributed Execution of 'Legacy' Java Software. In *Proceedings of the 15th European Conference on Object-Oriented Programming (ECOOP)*, pages 236–255, Budapest, June 2001.

15. E. Tilevich and Y. Smaragdakis. J-Orchestra: Automatic Java Application Partitioning. In *Proceedings of the 16th European Conference on Object-Oriented Programming (ECOOP)*, Malaga, June 2002. http://j-orchestra.org/.

Hierarchical Resource Usage Coordination for Large-Scale Multi-agent Systems

Nadeem Jamali and Xinghui Zhao

Department of Computer Science, University of Saskatchewan,
176 Thorvaldson Building, 110 Science Place,
Saskatoon, SK, S7N 5C9, Canada
{n.jamali, x.zhao}@usask.ca

Abstract. Scalable coordination is a key challenge in deploying massively multi-agent systems. Resource usage is one part of agent behavior which naturally lends itself to abstraction. CyberOrgs is a model for hierarchical coordination of resource usage by multi-agent applications in a network of peer-owned resources. Programming constructs based on CyberOrgs allow resource trade and control reification while maintaining a separation between functional and resource concerns. An operational semantics of CyberOrgs is presented. Expressive power of programming constructs based on CyberOrgs is illustrated with examples.

Hierarchical control presents challenges in scalability. However, some types of resource coordination are amenable to efficient implementation using CyberOrgs. Hierarchical control of processor time, for instance, can be implemented scalably by efficiently flattening the hierarchical schedule on the fly. Experimental results demonstrate scalability of the technique. Generalizations of this solution for hierarchical control of processor, network and other computational resources in a distributed system are discussed.

1   Introduction

A computation distributed into semi-autonomous subcomputations collectively solving a problem, inevitably suffers from a degree of uncertainty. In the context of multi-agent systems, when an agent's decision about the action to take next depends on actions taken by other agents, *coordination* between the agents is required to achieve optimal results [5]. Not only is coordination recognized as a key concern in distributed computing [4], it has also been argued that computation and coordination are separate and orthogonal dimensions of all useful computing [6], necessitating coordination to be addressed explicitly.

Computations sharing an execution space inevitably compete for the resources in that space. In an *open system* [7], there may be both *logical* and *resource* dependencies [5] between agents, with the resource dependencies sometimes leading to logical dependencies. Unrestricted competition for resources between agents collaborating to achieve a shared goal may hamper progress toward the goal. Coordinating resource access by agents is hence critical to reducing uncertainty and enabling agents to make control decisions for the best global performance [9].

T. Ishida, L. Gasser, and H. Nakashima (Eds.): MMAS 2004, LNAI 3446, pp. 40–54, 2005.

In a bounded resource environment, if a computation can launch other computations as in a multi-agent system, it is difficult to control resource consumption reactively. If an erroneous or malicious agent begins creating other agents with similar characteristics, and if the only mechanism employed for identifying such agents is observation of their own threatening behavior, the rate of growth in the number of agents can be shown to be exponential. Intuitively, this means that irrespective of how conservatively the system tries to purge misbehaving agents, so long as the mechanism relies solely on the observation of suspicious activity, by the time the system reacts, it may be already too late: other agents have potentially been created about whose behavior the system will know nothing until it has observed them individually.

A back of the envelope calculation illustrates the difficulty. Consider a scheduler that schedules agents for fixed time slices in a round robin fashion. If the probability of an agent creating another agent when given an opportunity is p, and the system purges an agent when it observes its behavior to exhibit a creation probability of k, if we begin with n such agents, at the end of the end of the cth cycle of the scheduler, the number agents is $(n(1 - p/k))^c$, which represents an exponential growth.

An effective mechanism for controlling such behavior would require tracking groups of agents. In other words, at the time of purging an agent, if there were a way of identifying other agents whose creation is rooted at the purged agent, all of them could be purged together. However, because of the exponential growth described above, a book-keeping solution of this problem is impractical. Specifically, the cost of maintaining information about which agents are created by which other agents – to be used for purging all agents which were created (directly or indirectly) by an agent being purged – also grows exponentially.

An alternate approach to control is by bounding resource consumption at the outset, and limiting resources available to a computation and all sub-computations originating from it. In this approach, each agent would receive a resource consumption allowance, which it could utilize or give a part of to other agents.

Ether [11] was the first language to address explicit allocation of resource in concurrent systems. Sponsors were assigned to processes to support their computations. This idea was later incorporated in the Actor language *Acore* [13]. *Sponsor actors* accompanied computation requests, and they carried ticks that could be used in processing a request. Using a similar scheme, in *Telescript* [16], processes were awarded funds in terms of *teleclicks* which they were supposed to use to accomplish their results.

The Quantum [14] framework is the most relevant to our work on CyberOrgs. Motivated by the need for managing finite resources shared by multiple computations, Quantum models resources as *energy* which computations require for execution. Computation tasks are contained in *groups* which also serve as *tanks* of energy. Groups are hierarchical, so that a group may create subgroups with its subcomputations. When a group's computations terminate, its energy is absorbed into the energy of its parent group; when it has exhausted its energy, it may receive more energy from its parent. Although the original formulation of Quantum did not support migration over multiple hosts, it has since been extended [15] to handle management of distributed and multi-type resources, which does address migration in a limited manner.

2 CyberOrgs

CyberOrgs [8] is a model for resource sharing in a network of self-interested peers, where application agents may migrate in order to make avail of remotely located peer-owned resources. CyberOrgs organize computational resources as a market, and their control as a hierarchy. Specifically, each cyberorg encapsulates one or more multi-agent computations (to be referred to as computations contained in the cyberorg), and distributed resources available to it (to be referred to as resources owned by the cyberorg) for carrying out its computations or for resale. Cyberorgs act as principals in a market of resources, where they can buy or sell resources among themselves using *eCash* in a shared currency. To avail themselves of acquired resources, cyberorgs migrate in the space of cyberorgs.

CyberOrgs treat computational resources as being defined in time and space. Sale of a resource is represented by a *contract* stipulating availability of resources to the buyer for a cost. Delivery of resources to cyberorgs is determined by a hierarchy of control decisions. In other words, cyberorg a makes control decisions required for delivery of resources purchased from it by cyberorg b; cyberorg b in turn makes control decisions determining how the resources purchased from it by cyberorg c are to be delivered.

Our approach in formalizing CyberOrgs is to separate concerns of computations from those of the resources required to complete them. Because our focus is on the usage of resources, we represent the resource requirements of each computation by the sequence of resources required to complete the computation. To simplify the model, we assume that resource requirements are known in advance. As an instantiation, we assume that the computations are carried out by systems of actors.

2.1 Actors

Actors [1] provide a formal model for building and representing the behavior of concurrent objects and thus serve as a foundation for concurrent object-oriented programming.

Actors are autonomous, interacting computing elements, which encapsulate a behavior (data and procedure) as well as a process. Different actors carry out their actions asynchronously and communicate with each other by sending messages. The basic mechanism for communication is also asynchronous and buffered; however, other forms of message passing can be defined in the context of the model. Finally, actors may be dynamically created and reconfigured, which provides considerable flexibility in organizing concurrent activity.

It is possible to extend any sequential language with actor constructs. For example, the call-by-value λ-calculus is extended in [3].

Agents are naturally modeled by the Actor formalism. In fact, many implementations of agents have typically been implementations of actor systems. An actor is autonomous and persistent. Actors are inherently concurrent and autonomous enabling efficient parallel execution [10] and facilitating mobility [2].

2.2 Instantiating CyberOrgs with Actors

An instantaneous snapshot of a system of cyberorgs is represented by $\langle \Gamma | \mathcal{M} | \mathcal{C} | \Theta | \mathcal{D} \rangle$. Γ represents the set of cyberorgs in the system, $\mathcal{M}$ is a name table which maps cyberorgs and actors to cyberorgs hosting them, C is the set of contracts between client cyberorgs and their host cyberorgs, Θ is the multiset of directed resources in the system, and finally $\mathcal{D}$ is a matrix which keeps track of distances between cyberorgs and actors.

The hosting relationship between two cyberorgs is not represented by syntactic containment. Instead, $\mathcal{M}$ maintains information about which cyberorg each cyberorg is hosted by. However, the containment of actors within cyberorgs is represented as syntactic containment as shown later.

We abstract computational resources as *ticks*, which determine the granularity of availability and consumption of resources. In other words, resources are provided to cyberorgs in terms of numbers of ticks, and computations consume resources in multiples of ticks. Ticks are defined in time and space and are sequentially ordered. If a tick is available in a cyberorg which cannot consume it, or if it is available at a time at which it cannot be consumed, it expires. Because a tick is the basic unit of resource, introduction of ticks into the system defines the system clock. The clock advances as ticks are introduced; consequently, *absolute* rates of availability of ticks to cyberorgs are with respect to the introduction of ticks into the system.

Because the model abstracts over physical machines, distances among cyberorgs, among actors, and between cyberorgs and actors are explicitly represented with $\mathcal{D}$. The distance from a cyberorg is defined only when all actors of the cyberorg are at zero distance from each other. In other words, if a cyberorg is distributed over a distance, it's distance from actors or other cyberorgs is undefined.

Each cyberorg in the system is represented by $[\![\alpha, \mu, \$]\!]_{c_i}^{\xi, \omega}$, where α represents a set of actors whose computation is managed by the cyberorg,; μ is a set of actor messages with local or remote recipients; $\$$ is the amount of eCash in the cyberorg;; ξ and ω are the resources required by the cyberorg for execution, and those offered by it to potential clients, respectively; and c_i is the cyberorg's unique name.

The current state of an actor in the model, at any instant, is represented by a state in the future and the resources required to reach that state. Specifically, actor a's state is written as $[n \circ s]_a$, where s is the state it would reach after receiving n ticks. An actor is said to have reached a state when the count of ticks required has reached zero.

Progress. Progress in a system of cyberorgs is represented by transitions occurring with introduction of ticks into the system. When a tick is inserted into a cyberorg, the cyberorg may pass it on to a client cyberorg, it may use it for progressing on one of its actors. Whether a tick is passed on to a client or used locally depends on the contracts that the cyberorg has with its clients.

Contracts determine the total number of ticks that the clients must receive, and the rates at which they must receive them. Rates of receipt of ticks are as a ratio of the total number of ticks inserted into the system at the root. Contracts also determine the costs which the clients are supposed to be charged for the ticks.

Surplus ticks after a cyberorg's contractual obligations to its clients have been satisfied, may be distributed among the local actors.

When the function T_{c_1} representing the decision process for cyberorg c_1 returns actor a as the recipient of the tick $t(c_1)$ for c_1, given the cyberorg's state $st(c_1)$ and its set of contracts $co(c_1)$, the system progresses by decrementing the number of ticks to a's next state from n to $n - 1$.

$$\langle [\{ [n \circ e]_a, \alpha \}, \mu, \$]_{c_1}^{\xi,\omega}, \Gamma | \mathcal{M} | \mathcal{C} | t(c_1), \Theta | \mathcal{D} \rangle$$
$$\longrightarrow \langle [\{ [(n-1) \circ e]_a, \alpha' \}, \mu', \$]_{c_1}^{\xi',\omega'}, \Gamma | \mathcal{M} | \mathcal{C} | \Theta | \mathcal{D} \rangle$$
$$T_{c_1}(st(c_1), co(c_1)) = a, n > 0$$

As a result of delivery of this tick to actor a, new actors and messages may be created in the cyberorg, changing the set of other actors from α to α', and the multiset of messages from μ to μ'. Similarly, the resource offerings and requirements of the cyberorg may also change.

When an actor's number of ticks required to reach the next state reduces to zero, the state is said to be reached. At this point, the state may be rewritten to reflect the number of ticks required to reach the following state e'. Because this is a rewriting of the current state rather than a change of state, the transition does not require any ticks to carry out.

$$\langle [\{ [0 \circ e]_a, \alpha \}, \mu, \$]_{c_1}^{\xi,\omega}, \Gamma | \mathcal{M} | \mathcal{C} | \Theta | \mathcal{D} \rangle$$
$$\longrightarrow \langle [\{ [n \circ e']_a, \alpha' \}, \mu', \$]_{c_1}^{\xi',\omega'}, \Gamma | \mathcal{M} | \mathcal{C} | \Theta | \mathcal{D} \rangle$$

If there is a cyberorg c_2 being hosted by c_1 and the new tick is to be passed on to c_2, then, the tick is redirected to c_2, and an amount of eCash Δ representing the cost of the tick – determined by the contract $co(c_1, c_2)$ between c_1 and c_2, and $st(c_1)$, the state of c_1 – is transferred from c_2 to c_1.

$$\langle [\alpha_1, \mu_1, \$_1]_{c_1}^{\xi_1,\omega_1}, [\alpha_2, \mu_2, \$_2]_{c_2}^{\xi_2,\omega_2}, \Gamma | \mathcal{M} | \mathcal{C} | \Theta | \mathcal{D} \rangle$$
$$\longrightarrow \langle [\alpha_1, \mu_1, \$_1 + \Delta]_{c_1}^{\xi_1,\omega_1'}, [\alpha_2, \mu_2, \$_2 - \Delta]_{c_2}^{\xi_2,\omega_2}, \Gamma | \mathcal{M} | \mathcal{C} | t(c_2), \Theta | \mathcal{D} \rangle$$
if $<c_1, c_2> \in \mathcal{M}, T_{c_1}(st(c_1), co(c_1)) = c_2$, where $\Delta = cost_t(st(c_1), co(c_1, c2))$

If there are no active actors or cyberorgs to be given a tick, the tick expires:

$$\langle [\alpha, \mu, \$]_{c_1}^{\xi,\omega}, \Gamma | \mathcal{M} | \mathcal{C} | t(c_1), \Theta | \mathcal{D} \rangle \longrightarrow \langle [\alpha, \mu, \$]_{c_1}^{\xi',\omega'}, \Gamma | \mathcal{M} | \mathcal{C} | \Theta | \mathcal{D} \rangle$$
$$T_{c_1}(st(c_1), co(c_1)) = \phi$$

CyberOrgs Primitives. In addition to transitions corresponding to progress in actor computations, there are a number of transitions in the system which correspond to Cy-berOrgs primitives. These transitions happen through invocation of CyberOrgs commands from *helper* actors, which in turn are created by the cyberorg's *facilitator* actor. A facilitator actor monitors the state of the current host as well as the cyberorg's resource requirements, and creates helpers to carry out CyberOrgs primitives. Facilitators and helpers are different from application actors hosted by a cyberorg in that they do not have names, and hence, may not receive messages from other actors. They also do not participate in the computations pursued by the application actors. Finally, because no actors have helpers' names, they safely disappear from the system after carrying out their operations.

Creation and Absorption. As illustrated in Figure 1a, a new cyberorg is created by using the isolate primitive, which collects a set of actors, messages, and electronic cash,

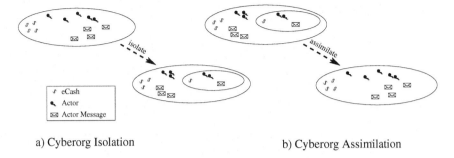

a) Cyberorg Isolation   b) Cyberorg Assimilation

Fig. 1. Creation and Absorption

and creates a new cyberorg hosted locally. The construct `isolate` takes as parameters a subset of the actors in c_1, α_2, a subset of the messages, μ_2, and a part of its cash $\$_2$, as well as representations of what the new cyberorg aught to offer other cyberorgs and require from other cyberorgs (currently c_1 itself), and creates a new cyberorg inside c_1's boundaries with a fresh name c_2. As a result, a new entry is placed in the name table depicting c_2's presence inside c_1, and entries for locations for actors inside c_2 are modified to depict the change.

$$\langle [\!\{ [0 \circ \mathtt{isolate}(\alpha_2, \mu_2, \$_2, \xi_2, \omega_2)]_\phi, \alpha_1 \}, \mu_1, \$_1]\!]^{\xi_1, \omega_1}_{c_1}, \Gamma | \mathcal{M} | \mathcal{C} | \Theta | \mathcal{D} \rangle$$
$$\longrightarrow \langle [\!\alpha_1 - \alpha_2, \mu_1 - \mu_2, \$_1 - \$_2]\!]^{\xi_1, \omega_1}_{c_1}, [\!\alpha_2, \mu_2, \$_2]\!]^{\xi_2, \omega_2}_{c_2}, \Gamma | \mathcal{M}' | \mathcal{C}' | \Theta | \mathcal{D} \rangle$$
$$\alpha_2 \subset \alpha_1, \mu_2 \subset \mu_1, \$_2 \le \$_1, c_2 \text{ fresh}$$

As shown in Figure 1b, a cyberorg disappears by assimilating into its host cyberorg using the `asmlt` primitive, relinquishing control of its contents - actors, messages and eCash - to its host. The assimilating cyberorg disappears, and its host becomes the container for its contents.

$$\langle [\!\alpha_1, \mu_1, \$_1]\!]^{\xi_1, \omega_1}_{c_1}, [\!\{ [0 \circ \mathtt{asmlt}]_\phi, \alpha_2 \}, \mu_2, \$_2]\!]^{\xi_2, \omega_2}_{c_2}, \Gamma | \mathcal{M} | \mathcal{C} | \Theta | \mathcal{D} \rangle$$
$$\longrightarrow \langle [\!\alpha_1 \cup \alpha_2, \mu_1 \cup \mu_2, \$_1 + \$_2]\!]^{\xi_1, \omega_1}_{c_1}, \Gamma | \mathcal{M}' | \mathcal{C}' | \Theta | \mathcal{D} \rangle$$
$$\text{if } < c_1, c_2 > \in \mathcal{M}, \nexists c_3 \text{ such that } < c_2, c_3 > \in \mathcal{M}$$

Assimilation of a client cyberorg into its host can potentially be a dangerous operation to allow. Although the primitive hands the client's eCash to the host to use at its discretion, its computations also join the host's computations and may interact or interfere in undesirable ways. The host is however protected because it alone decides whether the assimilated cyberorg's computations are allowed to advance in their processing. In other words, when a cyberorg decides to assimilate into its host, it relinquishes all control over its contents: its contract with the host dissolves, its eCash is added to the host's eCash, and its computations may or may not receive any ticks from the host without any contractual obligations.

Mobility. A facilitator may realize that its resource requirements exceed what is available by its contract with the host cyberorg. As a result, it creates a helper to search for alternate hosts:

$$\langle [\![\alpha, \mu, \$]\!]_{c_1}^{\xi,\omega}, \Gamma | \mathcal{M} | \mathcal{C} | \Theta | \mathcal{D}\rangle$$
$$\longrightarrow \langle [\![\{[n \circ \texttt{search}(\xi)]_\phi, \alpha\}, \mu, \$]\!]_{c_1}^{\xi,\omega}, \Gamma | \mathcal{M} | \mathcal{C} | \Theta | \mathcal{D}\rangle$$
$$\text{if } \xi > av(co(c_1, c_2)) \text{ where } < c_1, c_2 > \in \mathcal{M}$$

Cyberorgs may migrate from one host (cyberorg) to another. However, this must be preceded by negotiation of the terms under which the client may be hosted. The tasks required for a cyberorg to migrate are as follows:[1]

1. **Search** for a potential host. This makes use of the yellow page services provided by the system to search for cyberorgs which may offer needed ticks for an acceptable price.

$$\langle [\![\{[0 \circ \texttt{search}(\xi_1)]_\phi, \alpha_1\}, \mu_1, \$_1]\!]_{c_1}^{\xi_1,\omega_1}, \Gamma | \mathcal{M} | \mathcal{C} | \Theta | \mathcal{D}\rangle$$
$$\longrightarrow \langle [\![\{[n \circ \texttt{negotiate}(C)]_\phi, \alpha_1\}, \mu_1, \$_1]\!]_{c_1}^{\xi_1,\omega_1}, \Gamma | \mathcal{M} | \mathcal{C} | \Theta | \mathcal{D}\rangle$$
where C is the set of cyberorgs found $\{c_k, c_{k+1}, \cdots, c_l\}$, possibly including c_1

2. **Negotiate** a contract with potential hosts. Negotiation involves interaction with potential hosts for possible access to their ticks. Negotiation may be initiated by a cyberorg wanting to migrate itself or wanting to migrate part of its computation. On successful culmination of a negotiation, a contract is reached with a potential host cyberorg, which would hold between the migrating cyberorg and the host[2].

$$\langle [\![\{[0 \circ \texttt{negotiate}(C)]_\phi, \alpha_1\}, \mu_1, \$_1]\!]_{c_1}^{\xi_1,\omega_1}, [\![\alpha_2, \mu_2, \$_2]\!]_{c_2}^{\xi_2,\omega_2}, \Gamma | \mathcal{M} | \mathcal{C} | \Theta | \mathcal{D}\rangle$$
$$\longrightarrow \langle [\![\{[n \circ \texttt{migrate}(c_2)]_\phi, \alpha_1\}, \mu_1, \$_1]\!]_{c_1}^{\xi_1,\omega_1}, [\![\alpha_2, \mu_2, \$_2]\!]_{c_2}^{\xi_2,\omega_2}, \Gamma | \mathcal{M} | \mathcal{C}' | \Theta | \mathcal{D}\rangle$$
$$\text{if } C \neq \phi, \text{where } c_2 \in C = \{c_k, c_{k+1}, \cdots, c_l\} \text{ such that } \xi_1 < \omega_2, C' \supseteq C$$

If there are no cyberorgs which can serve c_1's resource requirements, no negotiation can happen, and c_1 adapts to its current resource availability:

$$\langle [\![\{[0 \circ \texttt{negotiate}(C)]_\phi, \alpha_1\}, \mu_1, \$_1]\!]_{c_1}^{\xi_1,\omega_1}, \Gamma | \mathcal{M} | \mathcal{C} | \Theta | \mathcal{D}\rangle$$
$$\longrightarrow \langle [\![\alpha_1, \mu_1, \$_1]\!]_{c_1}^{\xi_1',\omega_1}, \Gamma | \mathcal{M} | \mathcal{C} | \Theta | \mathcal{D}\rangle$$
$$\text{if } C = \phi \vee \nexists c_i \in C = \{c_k, c_{k+1}, \cdots, c_l\} \text{ such that } \xi_1 < \omega_i$$

3. **Migrate** to the selected host. If a contract has been successfully negotiated, a client can relocate to the host using the `migrate` primitive as shown in Figure 2.

$$\langle [\![\{[0 \circ \texttt{migrate}(c_2)]_\phi, \alpha_1\}, \mu_1, \$_1]\!]_{c_1}^{\xi_1,\omega_1}, [\![\alpha_2, \mu_2, \$_2]\!]_{c_2}^{\xi_2,\omega_2}, \Gamma | \mathcal{M} | \mathcal{C} | \Theta | \mathcal{D}\rangle$$
$$\longrightarrow \langle [\![\alpha_1, \mu_1, \$_1]\!]_{c_1}^{\xi_1',\omega_1'}, [\![\alpha_2, \mu_2, \$_2]\!]_{c_2}^{\xi_2',\omega_2'}, \Gamma | \mathcal{M}' | \mathcal{C} | \Theta | \mathcal{D}'\rangle$$
$$\text{if } \{co(c_1, c_2)\} \in \mathcal{C}$$
where $\mathcal{M}'$ reflects the change in location of c_1

---

[1] Migration of a part of a cyberorg's computation would require isolation first.
[2] A migrating cyberorg may not exist at the time of negotiation; it may be created following a successful negotiation.

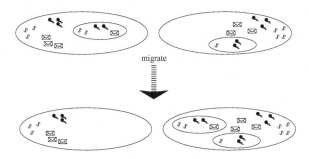

Fig. 2. Cyberorg Migration

where $\mathcal{D}'$ is the revised distance matrix representing any changes in distances that might have occurred as a result of migration.

If a contract was not successfully negotiated, and c_1 adapts to its current resource availability:

$$\langle [\![\{ [0 \circ \texttt{migrate}(c_2)]_\phi, \alpha_1, \mu_1, \$_1]\!]_{c_1}^{\xi_1,\omega_1}, [\![\alpha_2, \mu_2, \$_2]\!]_{c_2}^{\xi_2,\omega_2}, \Gamma | \mathcal{M} | \mathcal{C} | \Theta | \mathcal{D} \rangle$$
$$\longrightarrow \langle [\![\alpha_1, \mu_1, \$_1]\!]_{c_1}^{\xi'_1,\omega'_1}, [\![\alpha_2, \mu_2, \$_2]\!]_{c_2}^{\xi_2,\omega_2}, \Gamma | \mathcal{M} | \mathcal{C} | \Theta | \mathcal{D} \rangle$$
$$\text{if } \{co(c_1, c_2)\} \notin \mathcal{C}$$

Cyberorgs progress as a result of insertion of ticks into the system, one tick at a time. On receiving a tick, a cyberorg determines whether to pass it on to a client cyberorg, one of its computations, or use it to perform one of its system tasks, based on the contracts it is obliged to honor, and needs of its local computations it must complete.

Insertion of ticks one at a time, and their expiration when no computation is ready to use them is a simpler representation of the way processor resource becomes available, than granting of an approximate number of ticks followed by corrective mechanisms. It may also be viewed as a more accurate modeling in an ideal world where resource needs are known *a priori* or may be dictated.

Furthermore, awarding ticks one at a time allows management of rates of use of resource. cyberorgs may offer absolute rates of availability of resources as functions of ticks becoming available to the root cyberorg.

It is acknowledged that for an implementation to manage processor ticks one at a time, would mean incurring prohibitive overheads. Transfers of ticks from server cyberorgs to client cyberorgs - which are stipulated by contracts - may be easily optimized because known contracts rather than needs of clients determine how many ticks to provide. Awarding of ticks by cyberorgs to the computations they manage may be approximated by using a scheme that guesses and then adjusts as necessary.

Distribution of resources a local decision but the decision process is not shown. This can be used for resource-oriented coordination.

If a tick is received by a cyberorg when it does not have a computation or a cyberorg that can use it, the tick expires. This is consistent with the nature of many resources. For example, processor cycles can be used only if there is a task that can use them; they cannot be saved for future use. If there are no tasks ready for execution, the cycles pass unutilized. Similarly for network bandwidth. If communications are not ready to proceed at a time when there is idle bandwidth, it goes to waste; it may not be saved for future use.

3   Prototype

A prototype implementation of CyberOrgs has been built using *Actor Foundry* [12], a library of Java classes supporting Actor functionality. Actor Foundry is meant to be a research tool, and hence is designed with the goals of modularity and extensibility rather than pure efficiency. Actor programs may be written and executed in a run time that supports operational semantics of the Actor model. Specifically, cyberorgs are implemented as a library of Actor Foundry code.

A cyberorg system consists of actors carrying out application tasks (which we will call *application actors*), and cyberorgs managing resource utilization of the actors. The unit of resource is a *tick*. Each method of an actor requires a number of ticks to execute, depending on the parameters passed to it. Ticks are transferred between cyberorgs based on contracts between them. These contracts are negotiated bilaterally between the cyberorgs. Ticks received by a cyberorg are autonomously distributed by the cyberorg among the application actors it manages. Ticks received by an actor may be used by the actor for invoking any of the methods ready for invocation (as a result of received messages). Both cyberorgs and actors use their own tick distribution/utilization strategies.

3.1   Implementing an Application

To implement an application as a system of cyberorgs, a programmer writes classes defining the cyberorgs, and the application actors. A cyberorg class definition identifies events that would trigger cyberorg behaviors, as well as defines these behaviors in terms of basic cyberorg primitives. Application actor classes are similar to actor classes in *Actor Foundry*, except that for each method defined, the class contains another method to compute the resource requirements of executing the method with the passed parameters.

Cyberorgs may pick from a number of available negotiation protocols to use for negotiating contracts. The two negotiating parties would communicate using a basic pre-negotiation protocol to decide which negotiation protocol to use. These protocols may either be provided as part of a library, or they may be written by a programmer especially for a particular application.

A system of cyberorgs is implemented by directly subclassing from Cyberorg and AppActor classes, which are subclasses of the `Actor` class of Actor Foundry. Additionally, a programmer may customize negotiation protocols and strategies to suit the application.

Cyberorgs. A class of cyberorgs can be implemented as a subclass of the `Cyberorg` class. By subclassing from the `Cyberorg` class, the implemented class inherits a cyberorg's behavior, which provides a runtime system, which manages the consumption of *ticks* by application actors, and secures *tick* resource for their execution from other cyberorgs. The class typically contains one method overriding the `checkForTriggers`

```
public void checkForTriggers() {
        if (activeActors.numElements() > 30)
                    chores.enqueue("isolate");
        if (activeActors.numElements() < 3)
                    chores.enqueue("assimilate");
        if (neededTicks > myTickRate)
                    chores.enqueue("migrate");
}
```

Fig. 3. checkForTriggers method

method defined in the CyberOrg class which is invoked periodically to see if a cyberorg primitive needs to be triggered. This method may rely on local information about the cyberorg as well as information about its host cyberorg, which is available from the host cyberorg upon request. Figure 3 shows an example implementation of checkForTriggers. This method checks for three conditions: if the number of actors in the cyberorg exceeds a threshold, the *isolate* primitive is triggered to create a new cyberorg; if the number of actors drops below a threshold, the *assimilate* primitive is triggered to merges the cyberorg's contents into its hosting cyberorg; if the number of ticks required is greater than the rate of availability of ticks as stipulated by the contract with the current host, the *migrate* primitive is triggered. Additionally, a cyberorg class may also override methods for the behaviors to be triggered when a particular primitive operation is to be carried out. For example, a possible implementation of the initiateMigrationSequence method for carrying out the migrate primitive is shown in Figure 4.

```
public void initiateMigrationSequence() {

    // ask YP service to find a potential server

    ActorName server =
        call (myYellowPages, myCurrentRequirements().ticks(),
            myCurrentRequirements().ticksRate());

    // attempt to negotiate with the server

    send (server, "resRequest", self(),
        myCurrentRequirements().ticks(),
        myCurrentRequirements().ticksRate());

    // if the server is interested in negotiation,
    // contract negotiations commence.  If a contract
    // is successfully negotiated, the cyberorg is
    // migrated.
}
```

Fig. 4. initiateMigrateSequence method

In addition to being triggered in response to the state, primitive cyberorg operations may also be explicitly requested by application actors. A cyberorg class may override default methods for servicing such requests.

Finally, a cyberorg class may override the method for distributing ticks among its application actors, which - by default - distributes a fixed identical number of ticks to each active application actor at a time. The class may also override the method containing the default negotiation strategy which accepts any price for selling ticks so long as it does not represent a loss,[3] and any price for buying ticks that the cyberorg has enough *eCash* to pay.

Application Actors. Implementation of a class of application actors subclasses from the `AppActor` class. The class defines methods describing behaviors for the application actors as they are defined in subclasses of the `Actor` class in *Actor Foundry*. However, instead of the usual Actor class primitives of `create` and `send`, the programmer uses `createActor` and `sendMessage` respectively, with otherwise identical syntax as for class `Actor`.

For each behavior method, the programmer also includes a method which returns an integer estimating the number of ticks required for the method's completion given the parameters. By convention, the names of these methods are the behavior method names concatenated with the string "`Cost`".

Negotiators. Cyberorgs may instantiate given classes of client and server negotiators for negotiating on their behalf or define their own negotiator classes subclassed from the given classes, in which they may customize their negotiation strategies. In either case, negotiators agree on a communication protocol prior to commencing negotiation, and the negotiation behavior must conform to the agreed protocol for the negotiation to successfully conclude.

3.2   User Interface

A user can interface with the system using the Actor Foundry shell program called `ashell`. `ashell` makes the user the root cyberorg for the system. The user initiates an application run by creating a cyberorg of the desired Cyberorg class with a desired amount of eCash; and next creating an application actor of the desired AppActor class, which would in turn be managed by the cyberorg. Following these creations, the computation progresses simply as the user provides ticks to the cyberorg by sending it `tick()` messages with an integer parameter specifying the number of ticks being given. Only the user may create eCash or provide ticks.

4   Scheduling Cyberorgs

An important hurdle in efficiently implementing CyberOrgs is the model's hierarchical structure. A naive way to enforce the hierarchical schedule of a cyberorg tree would be

---

[3] Meaning that the price paid for obtaining the ticks is lower than the price at which they are being sold.

by implementing a hierarchy of schedulers. The overhead incurred by such a hierarchical scheduler would be prohibitive even for a single processor.

It turns out that enforcing cyberorgs' hierarchical distribution of cpu time does not require a hierarchical scheduler. Because availability of resources is in terms of what is available to the root cyberorg, and the availability for each cyberorg is in terms of resources its parent possesses (as stipulated by their contract), absolute availability of resources for each cyberorg can be maintained by simply looking at the contract and the parent's resources. By simple induction, the absolute resource availability for each cyberorg can hence be maintained in time proportional to the number of changes. Consequently, a global schedule can be created in which each cyberorg receives the resources it is promised as a function of the resources entering the system.. In other words, instead of launching a new scheduler for each cyberorg, all cyberorgs' internal schedules are composed into a single *flat schedule* of actors which is equivalent to the hierarchical schedule. Maintenance of the *flat schedule* can happen on the fly in response to primitive cyberorg operations, with a constant cost for each type of update.

A number of experiments were carried out on a prototypical Java implementation of the efficient scheduler for cyberorgs, to compare the overhead with the overhead of using a simple fair scheduler, or of letting Java's default scheduler schedule the threads.

4.1   CyberOrgs Scheduler

The scheduler is implemented using two classes. The `Scheduler` class defines a thread scheduler which simply schedules threads (corresponding to actors at the tree's leaves) for amounts of time for which they are to be scheduled. The scheduler uses Java's `suspend` and `resume` primitives to schedule threads. Another class, `ScheduleManager`, defines an update manager which receives requests for updating the cyberorg tree, and carries out the required changes in the flat schedule.

Table 1. Comparison of scheduling choices for cpu intensive computations. Time is in milliseconds. Height is height of cyberorg tree; Cyberorgs is the final number of cyberorgs. Columns min, mean and max show time slices used by a fair scheduler corresponding to the minimum, mean and maximum of time slices awarded by the cyberorg scheduler for the same number of threads

Threads	CyberOrg Scheduler			Fair Scheduler							No
(Actors)	Height	Cyberorgs	Time	Max	Time	Mean	Time	Min	Time		Scheduler
10	2	4	356	14	272	8	280	2	334		319
50	4	17	1040	183	999	33	1087	2	1022		1020
100	3	15	1967	146	1878	17	1969	2	2016		2201
200	4	27	4058	250	3720	15	3750	2	3775		3399
300	5	40	5372	370	5412	19	5908	2	6074		5017
400	5	67	7544	356	6685	21	7202	2	7931		6299
500	5	59	8946	239	7823	13	8313	2	9043		7922
600	5	71	11040	352	10121	11	10507	2	10943		9938
700	5	102	13866	390	11607	11	12736	2	13291		10906
800	5	74	14754	330	14203	11	14359	2	15614		12892
900	6	129	17061	634	15617	16	16177	2	16568		13998
1000	6	140	18736	324	16548	14	17715	2	18087		16781

There are two parameters used by the system for managing the overhead by adjusting the granularity of control. Parameter `smallestSlice` puts a lower limit on how small a request for time slice can be, and parameter. However, requests for smaller time slices are not outrightly rejected. When a time slice lower than `smallestSlice` is requested, the time slices of each thread are scaled up so that the newest thread receives at least `smallestSlice`. The cost of this scale-up is in the total amount of time that one cycle of the scheduler takes, which coarsens the granularity of control. The second parameter, `largestSlice`, puts an upper limit on the size of a slice. This parameter becomes relevant at the time of accommodating a request for a time slice smaller than `smallestSlice`. If the scale-up required to award the new time slice is such that the highest time slices becomes larger than `largestSlice`, then the request is denied.

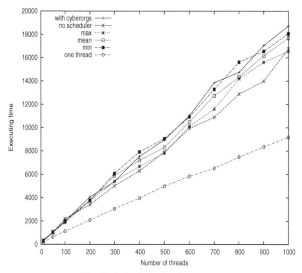

Fig. 5. Scheduler Performance

4.2   Experiments

Experiments were carried out for comparing performance of four broad scheduling choices for cpu intensive computations (Table 1). The first choice was to allow Java's default thread scheduler to schedule the concurrently executing threads carrying out the computations; second was a fair scheduler that awarded uniform time slices to all threads; third was the cyberorg scheduler for scheduling cyberorgs according to the requested time slice allocations. The final choice was to sequentialize all computations carried out concurrently in the previous cases, to be carried out by a single thread.

Because there is a relationship between the sizes of time slices and the scheduling overhead, to keep the comparison fair, the fair scheduler experiments were carried out with three different time slices, corresponding to the smallest, mean and largest time slices for which the cyberorg scheduler scheduled its actor threads.

As illustrated by the graph corresponding to Table 1 in Figure 5, no significant over-head is incurred in enforcing the hierarchical schedule of a tree of cyberorgs. Specifi-cally, the overhead is proportional to the number of threads (actors) in the system irre-spective of the number of cyberorgs and the height of the cyberorg tree.

4.3   Distributed Hierarchical Scheduler

A distributed scheduler would control processor resources on a number of connected machines. However, implementing such a scheduler is complicated by communication delays. Specifically, a fine-grained cpu scheduler must be local to the processes it is scheduling. A distributed scheduler, therefore, must be a network of communicating lo-cal schedulers. Schedules for such a scheduler must explicitly address communication delays. In the context of CyberOrgs, it is possible to create such schedules by examining communication delays which can be estimated once the network resource is controlled. In other words, once an amount of network bandwidth has been secured for a cyberorg, cpu scheduling of its distributed agents may rely on predictable communication de-lays. Work is currently ongoing to implement efficient hierarchical control of network bandwidth and to develop a distributed version of the CyberOrg scheduler.

5   Conclusions

Agents sharing an execution environment invariably compete for available resources, possibly in ways impacting global performance of a multi-agent application. However, resource usage is one aspect of multi-agent behavior which naturally lends itself to abstraction. CyberOrgs offer a model for hierarchical coordination of resource usage by multi-agent applications in a network of peer-owned resources, allowing multi-agent applications to execute in an environment of predictable resource availability. The model achieves a separation of concerns by representing resource requirements of an application separately from its functionality. We have introduced programming constructs for implementing systems of cyberorgs as well as described scheduling tech-niques for efficient distribution of processor resource.

Work is ongoing to generalize the method of flattening a hierarchical schedule to achieve efficient distribution and control of other computational resources. A distributed version of the cyberorg scheduler is under development which relies on predictability of communication delays resulting from effective control of network bandwidth.

Acknowledgements. This research is supported in part by an NSERC Discovery Grant.

References

1. G. Agha. *Actors: A Model of Concurrent Computation in Distributed Systems.* MIT Press, Cambridge, Mass., 1986.
2. G. Agha and N. Jamali. Concurrent programming for distributed artificial intelligence. In G. Weiss, editor, *Multiagent Systems: A Modern Approach to DAI.*, chapter 12. MIT Press, 1999.

3. G. Agha, I. A. Mason, S. F. Smith, and C. L. Talcott. A foundation for actor computation. *Journal of Functional Programming*, 1996. to appear.

4. A. Bond and L. Gasser, editors. *Readings in Distributed Artificial Intelligence.* Morgan Kaufman Publishers, San Mateo, California, 1988.

5. L. Gasser. DAI approaches to coordination. In N. M. Avouris and L. Gasser, editors, *Distributed Artificial Intelligence: Theory and Praxis*, pages 31–51. Kluwer Academic Publishers, 1992.

6. D. Gelernter and N. Carriero. Coordination languages and their significance. *Communications of the ACM*, 35(2):97–107, February 1992.

7. C. Hewitt and P. de Jong. Open systems. In J. Mylopoulos, J. W. Schmidt, and M. L. Brodie, editors, *On Conceptual Modeling*, chapter 6, pages 147–164. Springer Verlag, 1984.

8. N. Jamali. *CyberOrgs: A Model for Resource Bounded Complex Agents.* PhD thesis, University of Illinois at Urbana-Champaign, 2004.

9. N. R. Jennings. Commitments and conventions: The foundation of coordination in multi-agent systems. *The Knowledge Engineering Review*, 8(3):223–250, 1993.

10. W. Kim and G. Agha. Efficient Support of Location Transparency in Concurrent Object-Oriented Programming Languages. In *Proceedings of Supercomputing'95*, 1995.

11. W. A. Kornfeld and C. Hewitt. The scientific community metaphor. *IEEE Transactions on System, Man, and Cybernetics*, 11(1):24–33, January 1981.

12. Open Systems Laboratory. The Actor Foundry: A Java-based actor programming environment. *Available for download at ⟨http://www-osl.cs.uiuc.edu/ foundry⟩.*

13. C. Manning. Introduction to programming actors in acore. In C. Hewitt and G. Agha, editors, *Towards Open Information Systems Science*, chapter 2, pages 33–80. MIT Press, Cambridge Mass, 1990.

14. L. Moreau and C. Queinnec. Design and semantics of quantum: a language to control resource consumption in distributed computing. In *Usenix Conference on Domain-Specific Languages (DSL'97)*, pages 183–197, Santa-Barbara, California, 1997.

15. L. Moreau and C. Queinnec. Distributed and Multi-Type Resource Management. In *ECOOP'02 Workshop on Resource Management for Safe Languages*, Malaga, Spain, June 2002.

16. J. E. White. Telescript Technology: The Foundation for the Electronic Marketplace. Technical report, General Magic Inc., Mountainview, CA, 1994.

Towards Fault-Tolerant Massively Multiagent Systems

Zahia Guessoum[1,2], Jean-Pierre Briot[1], and Nora Faci[2]

[1] LIP6, Université Pierre et Marie Curie (Paris 6),
8 rue du Capitaine Scott, 75015 Paris, France
{Zahia.Guessoum, Jean-Pierre.Briot}@lip6.fr
[2] MODECO-CReSTIC - IUT de Reims, 51687 Reims Cedex 2, France
faci@leri.univ-reims.fr

Abstract. In order to construct and deploy massively multiagent systems, we must address one of the fundamental issues of distributed systems, the possibility of partial failures. In this paper, we discuss the issues and propose an approach for fault-tolerance of massively multiagent systems. The starting idea is the application of replication strategies to agents. As criticality of agents may evolve during the course of computation and problem solving, and as resources are bounded, we need to dynamically and automatically adapt the number of replicas of agents, in order to maximize their reliability and availability. We will describe our approach and related mechanisms for evaluating the criticality of a given agent and how to parameterize it (e.g., number of replicas). We also will report on experiments conducted with our prototype architecture (named DarX).

1 Introduction

The possibility of partial failures is a fundamental characteristic of distributed applications. The fault-tolerance research community has developed solutions (algorithms and architectures), mostly based on the concept of replication, applied for instance to data bases. But, these techniques are almost always applied explicitly and statically, at design time. In such approaches, this is the responsibility of the designer of the application to identify explicitly which critical servers should be made robust and also to decide which strategies (active or passive replication...) and their configurations (how many replicas, their placement...).

New cooperative applications, e.g., air traffic control, cooperative work, and e-commerce, are much more dynamic and massive. It is thus very difficult, or even impossible, to identify in advance the most critical software components of the application. Furthermore, criticality can vary over run time, information that should be used to best allocate the scarce replication resources. Such cooperative applications are now increasingly designed as a set of autonomous and interactive entities, named agents, which interact and coordinate (multiagent system). In

T. Ishida, L. Gasser, and H. Nakashima (Eds.): MMAS 2004, LNAI 3446, pp. 55–69, 2005.

such applications, the roles and relative importance of the agents can greatly vary during the course of computation, of interaction and of cooperation, the agents being able to change roles, strategies. Also, new agents may also join or leave the application (open system).

In addition, such applications may be massive. And the fact that the underlying distributed system is massive makes it unstable by nature, at least in currently deployed technologies. That increases the needs for mechanism for adaptive fiabilisation of the application.

Our approach is in consequence to give the capacity to the multiagent system itself to dynamically identify the most critical agents and to decide which fiabilisation strategies to apply to them. This is analog to "load balancing" but for fiabilisation. We want to **automatically** and **dynamically** apply fiabilisation (mostly through replication mechanisms) **where** (to which agents) and **when** they are most needed. To guide the adaptive fiabilisation, we intend to use various levels of information, system level, like communication load, and application/agent level, like roles or plans.

This paper is organized as follows: Section 2 presents the related work and Section 3 presents fault tolerance concepts and replication principles. Section 4 presents the DarX framework that we developed to replicate agents. This framework introduces novel features for dynamic control of replication. Section 5 describes our approach to compute agent criticality in order to guide replication. Section 6 describes the implementation of this solution and our preliminary experiments.

2   Related Work

Several approaches address the multi-faced problem of fault tolerance in multiagent systems. These approaches can be classified in two main categories. A first category focuses especially on the reliability of an agent within a multiagent system. This approach handles the serious problems of communication, interaction and coordination of agents with the other agents of the system. The second category addresses the difficulties of making reliable mobile agents which are more exposed to security problems [12]. This second category is beyond the scope of this paper.

Within the family of reactive multiagent systems, some systems offer high redundancy. A good example is a system based on the metaphor of ant nests. Unfortunately:

– we cannot design any application in terms of such reactive multiagent systems. Basically we do not have yet a good methodology. Moreover, these systems are more suitable for simulations.
– we cannot apply such simple redundancy scheme onto more cognitive multiagent systems as this would cause inconsistencies between copies of a single agent. We need to control its redundancy.

S. Hagg introduces sentinels to protect the agents from some undesirable states [8]. Sentinels represent the control structure of their multiagent system. They need to build models of each agent and monitor communications in order to react to faults. Each sentinel is associated by the designer to one functionality of the multiagent system. This sentinel handles the different agents which interact to achieve the functionality. The analysis of its beliefs on the other agents enables the sentinel to detect a fault when it occurs. Adding sentinels to multiagent systems seems to be a good approach, however the sentinels themselves represent failure points for the multiagent system. Moreover, the problem solving agents themselves participate in the fault-tolerance process.

A. Fedoruk and R. Deters [2] propose to use proxies to make transparent the use of agent replication, i.e. enabling the replicas of an agent to act as a same entity regarding the other agents. The proxy manages the state of the replicas. All the external and internal communications of the group are redirected to the proxy. However this increases the workload of the proxy which is a quasi central entity. To make it reliable, they propose to build a hierarchy of proxies for each group of replicas. They point out the specific problems of read/write consistency, resource locking also discussed in [13]. This approach lacks flexibility and reusability in particular concerning the replication control. The experiments have been done with FIPA-OS which does not provide any replication mechanism. The replication is therefore realized by the designer before run time.

Kaminka et al. [9] adapt a monitoring approach in order to detect and recover faults. They use models of relations between mental states of agents. They adopt a procedural plan-recognition based approach to identify the inconsistencies. However, the adaptation is only structural, the relation models may change but the contents of plans are static. Their main hypothesis is that any failure comes from incompleteness of beliefs. This monitoring approach relies on agent knowledge. The design of such multiagent systems is very complex. Moreover, the behavior of agent cannot be adaptive and the system cannot be open.

In distributed computing, many toolkits include replication facilities to build reliable application. However, many of products are not enough flexible to implement an adaptive replication. MetaXa [4] implements in Java active and passive replication in a flexible way. Authors extended Java with a reactive metalevel architecture. Like in DarX, the replication is transparent. However, MetaXa relies on a modified Java interpreter. GARF [5] realizes fault-tolerant Smalltalk machines using active replication. Similar to MetaXa, GARF uses a reflexive architecture and provides different replication strategies. But, it does not provide adaptive mechanism to apply these strategies.

The work by Kraus et al [10] proposes a solution for deciding allocation of extra resources (replicas) for agents. They proceed by reformulating the problem in two successive operational research problems (knapsack and then bin packing). Their approach and results are very interesting but it is based on too many restrictive hypothesis to be made adaptive.

3   Requirements and Techniques for Fault-Tolerance

3.1   Principles of Replication

Replication of data and/or computation is an effective way to achieve fault tolerance in distributed systems. A replicated software component is defined as a software component that possesses a representation on two or more hosts [5]. There are two main types of replication protocols:

- active replication, in which all replicas process concurrently all input messages,
- passive replication, in which only one of the replicas processes all input messages and periodically transmits its current state to the other replicas in order to maintain consistency.

Active replication strategies provide short recovery but lead to a high overhead. Passive replication minimizes processor utilization by activating redundant replicas only in case of failures. It requires less CPU resources than the active approach but it needs a checkpoint management which remains expensive in processing time and space.

3.2   Limits of Current Replication Techniques

Many toolkits (e.g., [5] and [14]) include replication facilities to build reliable applications. However, most of them are not quite suitable for implementing adaptive replication mechanisms. For example, although the strategy can be modified in the course of the computation, no indication is given as to which new strategy ought to be applied; moreover, such a change must have been devised by the application developer before runtime. Besides, as each group structure is left to be designed by the user, the task of conceiving a software appears tremendously complex.

Therefore we designed a specific and novel framework for replication, named DarX (see details in Section 5), which allows dynamic replication and dynamic adaptation of the replication policy (e.g., passive to active, changing the number of replicas). Moreover, DarX has been designed to easily integrate various agent architectures, and the mechanisms that ensure dependability are kept as transparent as possible to the application.

4   DarX: A Framework for Dynamic Replication

DarX [1] is a framework to design reliable distributed applications which include a set of distributed communicating entities (agents). Each agent can be replicated an unlimited number of times and with different replication strategies (passive and active). Note that we are working on the integration of other replication strategies in DarX, including quorum-based strategies. However, this

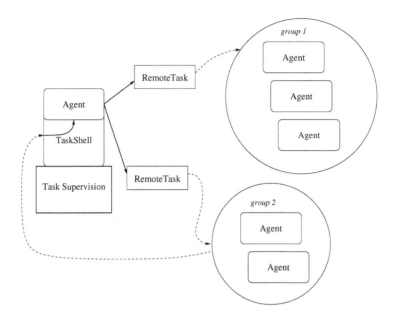

Fig. 1. DarX application architecture

paper does not address the design of particular strategies, but describes the infrastructure that will enable to switch to the most suitable dependability protocol. The number of replicas may be adapted dynamically. Also, and this is a novel feature, the replication strategy is reified such as one may dynamically change the replication strategy.

4.1   DarX Architecture

DarX includes group membership management to dynamically add or remove replicas. It also provides atomic and ordered multi-cast for the replication groups' internal communication. Messages between agents, that are communication external to the group are also logged by each replica, and sequences of messages can be re-emitted for recovery purposes. For portability and compatibility issues, DarX is implemented in Java.

4.2   Agent Replication

A replication group is an opaque entity underlying every application agent. The number of replicas and the internal strategy of a specific agent are totally hidden to the other application agents. Each replication group has exactly one leader which communicates with the other agents. The leader also checks the liveness of each replica and is responsible for reliable broadcasting. In case of failure of a leader, a new one is automatically elected among the set of remaining replicas.

DarX provides global naming. Each agent has a global name which is independent of the current location of its replicas. The underlying system allows to handle the agent's execution and communication. Each agent is itself wrapped into a TaskShell (Figure 1), which acts as a replication group manager and is responsible for delivering received messages to all the members of the replication group, thus preserving the transparency for the supported application. Input messages are intercepted by the TaskShell, enabling message caching. Hence all messages get to be processed in the same order within a replication group.

An agent can communicate with a remote agent, unregarding whether it is a single agent or a replication group, by using a local proxy implemented by the RemoteTask interface. Each RemoteTask references a distinct remote entity considered as its replication group leader. The reliability features are thus brought to agents by an instance of a DarX server (DarxServer) running on every location. Each DarxServer implements the required replication services, backed up by a common global naming/location service.

5   Adaptive Control of Replication

DarX provides the needed adaptive mechanisms to replicate agents and to modify the replication strategy. Meanwhile, we cannot always replicate all the agents of the system because the available resources are usually limited. In the given example (Section 6.1), we can consider more than 100 distributed assistant agents and resources that do not allow to duplicate more than 60 agents. The problem therefore is to determine the most critical agents and then the needed number of replicas of these agents. The resources are thus allocated to critical agents.

We distinguish two cases: 1) the agent's criticality is static and 2) the agent's criticality is dynamic. In the first case, multiagent systems have often static organization structures, static behaviors of agents, and a small number of agents. Critical agents can be therefore identified by the designer and can be replicated by the programmer before run time.

In the second case, multiagent systems may have dynamic organization structures, dynamic behaviors of agents, and a large number of agents. So, the agents criticality cannot be determined before run time. The agent criticality can be therefore based on these dynamic organizational structures. The problem is how to determine dynamically these structures to evaluate the agent criticality?

Thus, we propose a new approach for observing the domain agents and evaluating dynamically their criticality. We will now detail our approach for dynamically evaluating criticality of each agent in order to perform dynamic replication where and when best needed.

5.1   Hypothesis and Principles

We want some automatic mechanism for generality reasons. But in order to be efficient, we also need some prior input from the designer of the application.

This designer can choose among several approaches of replication: static and dynamic.

In the proposed dynamic approach, the agent criticality relies on two kinds of information:

- System-level information. It will be based on standard measurements (communication load, processing time...). We are currently evaluating their significance to measure the activity of an agent.
- Semantic-level information.

Several aspects may be considered (importance of agents, independence of agents, importance of messages...). We decided to use the concept of role [11], because it captures the importance of an agent in an organization, and its dependencies to other agents.

Note that our approach is generic and that it is not related to a specific interaction language or application domain. We just suppose that agents communicate with some agent communication language such as ACL [3].

5.2   Architecture

In order to track the dynamical adoption of roles by agents, we propose a role recognition method. Our approach is based on the observation of the agent execution and their interactions to recognize the roles of each agent and to evaluate its processing activity. This is used to dynamically compute the criticality of an agent.

In most existing multiagent architectures, the observation mechanism is centralized. The acquired information is typically used off-line to explain and to improve the system's behavior. Moreover, the considered application domains typically only involve a small number of agents and *a priori* well-known organizational structures.

These centralized observation architectures are not suited for large-scale and complex systems where the observed information needs to be analyzed in real-time to adapt the multiagent structure to the evolution of its environment.

We thus propose to distribute the observation and monitoring mechanism to improve its efficiency and robustness. This distributed mechanism relies on a reactive-agent organization. These reactive agents have two roles:

- they observe and control the domain agents,
- they build global information and minimize communication.

These two roles are assigned to two kinds of agents: domain agent monitors (named agent-monitors) and host monitors (named host-monitors). An agent-monitor is associated to each domain agent and a host-monitor is associated to each host (see Figure 2).

The monitoring agents (agent-monitors and host-monitors) are hierarchically organized. Each agent-monitor communicates only with one host-monitor. Host-monitors exchange their local information to build global information (global number of messages, global exchanged quantity of information...).

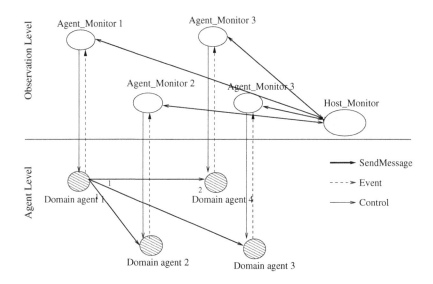

Fig. 2. Multiagent architecture

Distribution and observation mechanisms are provided by the middleware. Our implementation relies on DarX (see Section 4). In this middleware, each machine runs a DarX server and each server provides an observation module. This module collects events (sent and received messages) and data. Each agent-monitor registers to its host-monitor to receive information and events related to the associated domain agent.

After each interval of time Δt, the host-monitor sends the collected events and data to the corresponding agent-monitors. An agent-monitor executes then the following behavior:

– read messages received from the host-monitor,
– activate the role analysis (see section 5.3),
– compute the domain-agent criticality (see sections 5.4 and 5.5),
– determine the number of its replicas (see section 5.6).

When the criticality of the domain agent is significantly modified, the agent-monitor notifies its host-monitor. The latter informs the other host-monitors to update global information. In turn, agent-monitors are informed by their host-monitors when global information changes significantly.

5.3   Role Analysis

We consider two cases. In the first case, each agent displays explicitly its roles or interaction protocols. The roles of each agent are thus easily deduced from its interaction events. In the second case, agents do not display their roles nor their

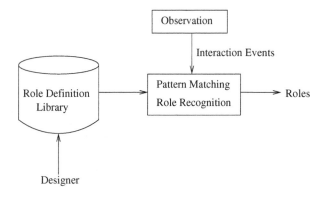

Fig. 3. Roles recognition

interaction protocols. The agent roles are deduced from the interaction events by the role analysis module.

In this analysis, attention is focused on the precise ordering of interaction events. The `role analysis` module captures and represents the set of interaction events resulting from the domain agent interactions (sent and received messages). These events are then used to determine the roles of the agent. Figure 3 illustrates the various steps of this analysis.

To represent the agent interactions, several methods have been proposed such as state machines and Petri nets. For our application, state machines provide a well suitable representation. Each role interaction model is represented by a state machine. A transition represents an interaction event (sending or receiving a message). Figure 4 shows an example of machine state that represents the interaction model of the role Initiator.

Interaction events represent the exchanged messages. We distinguish two kinds of interaction events: ReceiveMessage and SendMessage. The attributes of the SendMessage and ReceiveMessage interaction events are similar to the attributes of ACL messages:

- SendMessage(Communicative act, sender, receiver, content, reply-with, ...).
- ReceiveMessage(Communicative act, sender, receiver, content, reply-with, ...).

In order to be able to filter various messages, we introduce the "wild card" character ?. For example, in the interaction event ReceiveMessage ("CFP", "X", "Y", ?), the content is unconstrained. So, this interaction event can match any other interaction event with the communication act CFP, the sender "X", the receiver "Y" and any content.

In the example of scheduling meetings (see Section 6.1), the assistant agents use the contract net protocol to schedule a meeting. The interaction models of the initiator and the participant are deduced from the contract net protocol. The initiator is described in Figure 4. The description represents the different

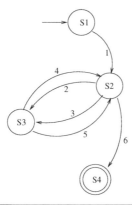

1	(SendMessageEvent("cfp",Agent,?,?,M1)).
2	((ReceiveMessageEvent("propose",?,Agent,?,M2,M1)) |
3	(ReceiveMessageEvent("refuse",?,Agent,?,M2,M1))).
4	((SendMessageEvent("reject",Agent,?,?,M2,M1)) |
5	(SendMessageEvent("accept",Agent,?,?,M2,M1))).
6	(ReceiveMessageEvent("inform",?,Agent,?,M2))

Fig. 4. Machine State for the Initiator

steps (sent and received messages) of the role. The description of the Initiator can be interpreted as follows:

- A call for proposals message is sent to the participants from the initiator following the FIPA Contract Net protocol.
- The participants reply to the initiator with the proposed meeting times. The form of this message is either a proposal or a refusal.
- The initiator sends accept or reject messages to participants.
- The participants which agree to the proposed meeting inform the initiator that they have completed the request to schedule a meeting (confirm).

An agent may simultaneously fulfill more than one role. Each agent-monitor may therefore have one or more active role recognition process.

5.4   Activity Analysis

In multiagent systems, the internal activity of agents cannot be observed, because it is private. The observation is restricted to events. To evaluate the degree of the agent activity, we use system data that are collected at the system level. We are considering two kinds of measures: CPU time and communication load. We are currently evaluating the significance of these measures as indicators of agent activity, to be useful to calculate agent criticality.

For an agent $Agent_i$ and a given time interval Δt, these measures provide:

- The used time of CPU (cp_i),
- The communication load (cl_i).

cp_i and cl_i may be then used to measure the agent degree of activity aw_i as follows:

$$aw_i(t) = (d_1 * cp_i/\Delta t + d_2 * cl_i/CL)/(d_1 + d_2) \qquad (1)$$

where:

- CL is the global communication load,
- d_1 and d_2 are weights introduced by the user.

5.5 Agent Criticality

The analysis of events and measures (system data and interaction events) provides two kinds of information: the roles and the degree of activity of each agent. This information is then processed by the agent's criticality module. The latter relies on a table T that defines the weights of roles. This table is initialized by the application designer.

The criticality of the agent $Agent_i$ which fulfills the roles r_{i1} to r_{im} is computed as follows:

$$w_i(t) = (a_1 * aggregation(T[r_{ij}]_{j=1,m}) + a_2 * aw_i(t))/(a1 + a2) \qquad (2)$$

Where a_1 and a_2 are the weights given to the two kinds of parameters (roles and degree of activity). They are introduced by the designer.

For each Agent A_i, its criticality w_i is used to compute the number of its replicas.

5.6 Replication

An agent is replicated according to:

- w_i: its criticality,
- W: the sum of the domain agents' criticality,
- rm: the minimum number of replicas which is introduced by the designer,
- Rm: the available resources which define the maximum number of possible simultaneous replicas.

The number of replicas nb_i of $Agent_i$ can be determined as follows:

$$nb_i(t) = rounded(rm + w_i(t) * Rm/W) \qquad (3)$$

The number of replicas is then used to update the number of replicas of the domain agent. When this number of replicas increases, the associated monitor-agent sends a call for proposal to all the host-monitors. Each host monitor sends a proposal if it has a non-allocated resource. The agent-monitor then selects the needed resources. The selection process relies mainly on the communication cost between the two hosts. Moreover, when the number of replicas decreases, the agent-monitor selects $nb_i(t + \Delta t)$ - $nb_i(t)$ of its replicas and sends a message to the corresponding host-monitors to cancel the location of the resources.

6   Experiments

To validate the proposed approach, we realized an integration of DarX with the multiagent platform DIMA [6]. This integration provides a generic fault-tolerant multiagent platform. In order to validate this fault-tolerant multiagent platform, we carried out several experiments.

Measures were obtained using a set of 20 Pentium PCs running linux with JDK1.2 and linked by a fast Ethernet (10Mb/s).

6.1   A First and Simple Example

We consider the example of a distributed multiagent system that helps at scheduling meetings. Each user has a personal assistant agent which manages its calendar. This agent interacts with:

– the user to receive its meeting requests and the associated information (a title, a description, possible dates, participants, priority, etc.),
– the other agents of the system to schedule meetings.

If the assistant agent of one important participant (initiator or prime participant) in a meeting fails (e.g., its machine crashes), this may disorganize the whole process. As the application is very dynamic - new meeting negotiations start and complete dynamically and simultaneously - decision for replication should be done automatically and dynamically.

6.2   Performances

Monitoring is a useful mechanism. However, its cost seems important. Thus, our first experiment measures the monitoring cost in the proposed architecture. We consider, a multiagent system with n distributed agents that execute the same scenario, each agent has a fixed scenario. The number of agents (n) is an important factor because our framework was specially designed for massively multiagent systems. For each n (100, 150, ..., 400), we realized two kinds of measures (with and without monitoring). Each machine runs 20 agents. We use thus the 20 machines for the last experiment (n=400) and we repeat each experiment 10 times.

Figure 5 gives the average execution time for each n. It shows that the monitoring cost is almost a constant function. It does not increase with the number of agents. That can be explained by the proposed optimization in the multiagent architecture such as the communication between the agent-monitors and host-monitors. For instance, to build global information (global communication load ...), the host-monitors communicate only if the local information changes.

6.3   Robustness

We considered 100 assistant agents which are distributed on 10 machines. These agents may have two roles: initiator and participant. We define a scenario with 20

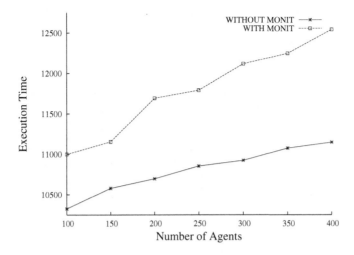

Fig. 5. Monitoring cost

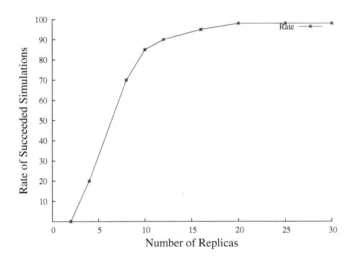

Fig. 6. Rate of succeeded simulations for each number of replicas

initiators. These agents have thus two roles: initiator and participant. Moreover, we consider 80 agents which have one role: participant. These agents are thus less critical.

We run each experiment 10mn and we introduced 100 faults. To simulate the presence of faults, we implemented a failure simulator randomly stopping the thread of an agent (chosen randomly). We repeated several times the experiments with a variable number of extra resources (number of replicas that can be used).

We consider here the following variables:

$$ReplicationRate = \frac{Number of ExtraReplicas}{NumberOf Agents} \tag{4}$$

and the rate of simulations which succeeded (i.e., which did not fail):

$$SuccessRate = \frac{Number of Successful Simulations}{NumberOf Simulations} \tag{5}$$

Figure 6 shows the success rate as a function of the replication rate. From these experiments, we notice that the rate of succeeded simulation becomes interesting (greater than 90%) when the number of extra resource reaches the number of critical agents. Therefore, the number of extra resources should be at least equal to the number of critical agents. Each critical agent should thus have at least one replica.

Although preliminary, we believe these results are encouraging. Note that the results are similar for the two replication strategies.

7   Conclusion

Massively multiagent systems are often distributed and must run without any interruption. To make these systems reliable, we proposed a new approach to evaluate dynamically the criticality of agents [7]. This approach is based on the concepts of roles and degree of activity. The agent criticality is then used to replicate agents in order to maximize their reliability and availability based on available resources.

To validate the proposed approach, we realized a fault-tolerant framework (DarX) and we used a multiagent platform (DIMA [6]) to implement multiagent systems. The integration of DarX with the multiagent platform DIMA provides a generic fault-tolerant multiagent platform. In order to validate this fault-tolerant multiagent platform, two small applications have been developed (meetings scheduling and crisis management system). They are intended at evaluating our model and architecture viability.

In the realized experiments the role definition library (see Section 5.3) and the role criticality are defined by the designer before runtime. It seems interesting to improve the monitor-agent behavior to learn new roles and learn their criticality by observing agent interactions.

Moreover, the obtained results are interesting and promising. However, more experiments with real-life applications are needed to validate the proposed approach.

Acknowledgement

The authors would like to thank the members of *Fault-Tolerant Multi-agent Systems* project for many useful discussions and suggestions.

References

1. M. Bertier, O. Marin, and P. Sens. Implementation and performance evaluation of an adaptable failure detector. In *the International Conference on Dependable Systems and Networks*, Washington, USA, 2002.
2. A. Fedoruk and R. Deters. Improving fault-tolerance by replicating agents. In *AAMAS2002*, pages 373–744, Bologna, Italy, 2002.
3. FIPA. Agent communication language, foundation for intelligent physical agents, Geneva, Switzerland. http://www.cselt.stet.it/ufv/leonardo/fipa/index.htm, 1997.
4. M. Golm. Metaxa and the future of reflection. In *OOPSLA -Workshop on Reflective Programming in C++ and Java*, pages 238–256, 1998.
5. R. Guerraoui, B. Garbinato, and K. Mazouni. Lessons from designing and implementing GARF. In *Object-Based Parallel and Distributed Computation*, number 791 in LNCS, pages 238–256, 1995.
6. Z. Guessoum and J.-P. Briot. From active objects to autonomous agents. *IEEE Concurrency*, 7(3):68–76, 1999.
7. Z. Guessoum, J.-P. Briot, and S. Charpentier. Dynamic and adaptative replication for large-scale reliable multi-agent systems. In *Proceedings of the ICSE'02 First International Workshop on Software Engineering for Large-Scale Multi-Agent Systems (SELMAS'02)*, Orlando FL, U.S.A., may 2002. ACM.
8. S. Hagg. A sentinel approach to fault handling in multi-agent systems. In C. Zhang and D. Lukose, editors, *Multi-Agent Systems, Methodologies and Applications*, number 1286 in LNCS, pages 190–195, 1997.
9. G. A. Kaminka, D. V. Pynadath, and M. Tambe. Monitoring teams by overhearing: A multi-agent plan-recognition approach. *Journal of Intelligence Artificial Research*, 17:83–135, 2002.
10. S. Kraus, V.S. Subrahmanian, and N. Cihan Tacs. Probabilistically survivable MASs. In *IJCAI'03*, pages 789–795, 2003.
11. J. J. Odell, H. V. Dyke Parunak, and B. Bauer. Representing agent interaction protocols in UML. In *Fourth International Conference on Autonomous Agents*, pages 121–140, 2000.
12. F. De Assis Silva and R. Popescu-Zeletin. An approach for providing mobile agent fault tolerance. In S. N. Maheshwari, editor, *Second International Workshop on Mobile Agents*, number 1477 in LNCS, pages 14–25. Springer Verlag, 1998.
13. L. Silva, V. Batista, and J. Silva. Fault-tolerant execution of mobile agents. In *International Conference on Dependable Systems and Networks*, pages 135–143, 2000.
14. R. van Renesse, K. Birman, and S. Maffeis. Horus: A flexible group communication system. *Communications of the ACM*, 39(4):76–83, 1996.

Virtual Space Ontologies for Scripting Agents

Zhiqiang Gao[1], Liqun Ren[1], Yuzhong Qu[1], and Toru Ishida[2]

[1] Department of Computer Science and Engineering, Southeast University,
210096, P. R. China
{zqgao,yzqu}@seu.edu.cn
renliqq@163.com
[2] Department of Social Informatics, Kyoto University, Japan
ishida@i.kyoto-u.ac.jp

Abstract. Interactive multi-agent system improves reusability of agents by separating application design from agent design. However, it remains difficult for application designers (usually non-computer professionals) to script massive multi-agents. This is especially true for scripting hundreds of *NPC*s (Non Player Characters, agents) hosted by hostile, dynamic and complex 3D (three-dimensional) environments in military simulation. Out of perspective of *interaction between agents and environments*, namely virtual spaces, we introduce *virtual space ontologies* to facilitate *interaction between humans and agents*. Three advantages are obtained by using *virtual space ontologies*: 1) A hybrid approach of integrating qualitative and quantitative spatial reasoning is achieved so that application designers can specify arguments of *action*s (scenario primitives) *qualitatively*. 2) Primitive actions of agents are abstracted hierarchically so that application designers can *sketch* scenarios for units of agents. 3) Better intent communication between humans and agents is realized so that application users can control agents easily in real time.

1 Introduction

Massive multi-agent simulations are needed for domains such as military, space operation, disaster recovery and commerce, where there are many inter-related, complex activities to be performed by many agents. In this paper, we build a massive multi-agent system, *COMMANDER*, to train sub-ordinate commanders in anti-terrorist actions. After super-ordinate commanders (trainers) generate an anti-terrorist event, sub-ordinate commanders (trainees) design course of actions, and resolve unexpected situations in real time. Roles of *NPC*s include soldier, terrorist, hostage, and crowd, and their total number exceeds several hundreds. Trainees control soldier agents, which are organized as units of squad, platoon, company and battalion. Soldier agents keep formations and cooperate under different situations. All agents find paths to destinations and plan action sequences. In order to meet training requirements, two major difficulties arise: *How for trainees to control massive multi-agents? How for agents to interpret and execute commands from trainees?* We use *Q* scenarios [14] to express *what trainees require massive multi-agents to do*. We use *virtual space ontologies* to help agents sense environments and decide *how to behave*

T. Ishida, L. Gasser, and H. Nakashima (Eds.): MMAS 2004, LNAI 3446, pp. 70–85, 2005.

under various situations in accordance with scenarios. The benefits of using *virtual space ontologies* include: 1) Trainees can specify location parameters of scenarios in names of objects instead of coordinates. They can also inquire properties of objects to help design scenarios, such as the width of a road, the distance and visibility between two locations. 2) Grid arrays of virtual spaces are created automatically, and agents rely on these arrays or maps to find paths and make decisions. Because ditches, rivers, tunnels, hills, even doors and windows of buildings are annotated, it become easy for agents to select attacking, hiding and sneaking positions. 3) Visual effects of interaction between agents and virtual spaces are improved. After one building is bombed, it is replaced by another destroyed one according to *virtual space ontologies.* The color, size and type of particles showing bombing effects are chosen according to the type of terrain. Therefore, *virtual space ontologies* facilitate scenario generation, help agents make decisions and plan, improve visual effects of interaction between agents and virtual spaces.

Interactive multi-agent system increases reusability of agents by separating application design from agent design [13]. Ishida [14] has emphasized *interaction design between humans and agents* by introducing scenarios to describe a human request to a large number of agents with different roles. The scenarios also establish a bridge between agent designers and application designers [8, 9]. Murakami [16] made it easier to describe scenarios of evacuation simulation by using *IPC* (Interaction Pattern Card). Wang [17] discussed the application of *Q*-based architecture for semantic information interoperability on *Semantic Web.*

However, *interaction between agents and environments* has not been emphasized. One goal of *Semantic Web* is to describe the world in ways that are easy for agents to think about. *Semantic Web* brings structure to the meaningful contents of *Web* resources, and creates an environment where software agents roaming from page to page [2, 4]. Tremendous effort has been made to annotate current *Web* semantically [3, 5, 11, 12]. Nevertheless, little attention has been paid to non-text resources. *SVG* (Scalable Vector Graphics) describes the majority of two-dimensional vector and raster graphical features (http://www.w3.org/TR/SVG12). *MPEG-7* group develops a rich set of standardized tools to enable both humans and machines to generate and understand audiovisual descriptions [15]. *Inverse causality* was introduced whereby objects in the environment told an animated agent how it should interact with them [10]. Doyle [6] introduced the concept of annotated environment in text-based *MUD* (Multi-User Dungeon) world.

The rest of this paper is organized as below. We first propose a framework for designing interactive massive multi-agent system, introduce scenario markup language *SML*, and discuss the difficulties for scripting massive agents. In section 3, we design entities and properties for *virtual space ontologies.* Advantages obtained are analyzed in section 4. In section 5, a massive multi-agent system *COMMANDER* for army commander training is illustrated. Then, we review related works for spatial representation and reasoning in section 6, and close with conclusions in section 7.

2 Backgrounds

In this section, a framework is proposed for different roles of humans to collaborate to design massive multi-agent system. Scenario markup language *SML* is outlined and difficulties for scripting massive multi-agents are discussed.

2.1 Framework for Designing Interactive Massive Multi-agent System

The framework of interactive massive multi-agent system takes into consideration both the *interaction between humans and agents* as well as the *interaction between agents and virtual spaces*. It relates different roles of humans who collaborate to design massive multi-agent system and do social simulations. See Fig.1 for detail. *Model creators* are usually architects and artists, who build virtual spaces and design *virtual space ontologies*. *Agent designers* are computer professionals who implement *cue*s and *action*s of agents. *Application designers* write scenarios for agents, who are often ordinary people such as sales managers, publicity officers, and social psychologists. *Application users* control agents in real time by speech commands, which are mapped to *action*-like format for agents to interpret. *Scenarios* represent what and how humans require agents to do. *Agents* communicate with others, perceive annotated virtual spaces, and act in virtual spaces.

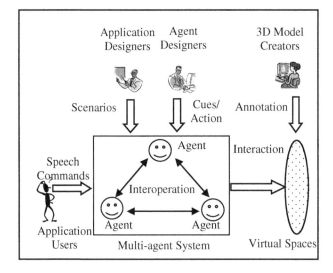

Fig. 1. A framework for designing interactive massive multi-agent system

2.2 A Scenario Markup Language *SML*

Scenario markup language *SML* is based on scenario description language Q [13]. We extend *Scheme* by introducing sensing/acting functions and guarded commands to realize Q, which describes how an agent should behave and interact with its environment. The salient features of Q language are summarized as follows: **1) Cues.**

A sensing function is defined as a *cue*. There is no side effect to sensing. *Cues* request agents to observe their environment. **2) Actions**. An acting function is defined as an *action*, which may change the environment of multi-agent system. Some *action*s allow other *action*s to be executed in parallel. **3) Scenarios**. Guarded commands are introduced for the situation wherein agents need to observe multiple *cues* simultaneously. A guarded command combines *cues* and *actions*. After one of the *cues* becomes true, the corresponding *action* is performed. **4) Agents**. An agent is defined by a scenario, which specifies what the agent should do. Even if a crowd of agents executes the same scenario, the agents exhibit different *action*s as they interact

Table 1. Primitive actions in *COMMANDER*

Type	Name	Arguments
Ready	!stand_ready	:last (float time)
	!kneel_ready	:last (float time)
	!prone_ready	:last (float time)
Aim	!stand_aim	:at (POSITION position)
		:last (float time)
	!kneel_aim	:at (POSITION position)
		:last (float time)
	!prone_aim	:at (POSITION position)
		:last (float time)
Move	!walk	:to (POSITION position)
		:speed (float speed)
	!walk_lo	:to (POSITION position)
		:speed (float speed)
	!walk_back	:to (POSITION position)
		:speed (float speed)
	!walk_back_lo	:to (POSITION position)
		:speed (float speed)
	!run	:to (POSITION position)
		:speed (float speed)
	!jog	:to (POSITION position)
		:speed (float speed)
	!crawl	:to (POSITION position)
		:speed (float speed)
Turn	!turn_left	
	!turn_right	
	!turn_back	
	!turn_angle	:angle (float angle)
Shot	!shot	:at (POSITION position)
	!throw_grenade	:at (POSITION position)
Dead	!dead	
Speak	!speak	:what (STRING sentence)
		:last (float duration)

with their local environment. **5) Avatars**. Avatars controlled by humans do not require any scenario. Thus, *Q* is a language for describing hierarchical *FSA* (Finite State Automata), in which one scene or a guarded command is an automaton. Guarded commands are used to realize state transition and *cue*s are events to be guarded.

Although we can fluently describe the interaction between humans and agents by introducing *cue*s and *actions,* and tools had been created for non-programmers to describe behaviors of agents [16], it is difficult to implement *meta-level* architecture of *Q* [8]. On the other hand, since *XML* has been adopted as a meta-language by *W3C* (http://www.w3.org/XML/), we implement *SML* by using *XML* as its mother language. In order to reduce the complexity of scenario design, recursive scenario is not allowed in *SML*. *Scene* shifting in one scenario is treated as an *action* command, provided the *action* name is replaced with the *scene* name. Two new constructs have been added: **1) Chance**. It is a command permitting agents to choose *scene*s in accidence and causes uncertainty of agents' behavior. Unpredictability of agents' behavior is increased greatly by using this construct. **2) Concurrence**. It associates scenes with others and allows agents to execute *actions* in one scene and monitor other *scenes* simultaneously. When one *cue* in concurrent scene succeeds during the execution of an *action*, agents shift to the corresponding scene immediately. Thus, *SML* extends *Q* language for trainees to require non-deterministic and parallel behaviors of agents. Primitive *cue*s and *action*s in *COMMANDER* are related to military operations. Primitive *cue*s are *?see*, *?hear* and *?sense_body*, and primitive *action*s are listed in Table 1.

2.3 Meta-level Interaction Between Application User and Agents

It is impractical to assign scenarios to agents, and agents execute them until scenarios are finished. Because multi-agent systems are intrinsically dynamic: what an agent assumes to be true may become false as a consequence of the actions of other agents in the system. Thus, a *meta-level* architecture of interaction between application user and agents is proposed to cope with the challenge for scenario control. For simplicity,

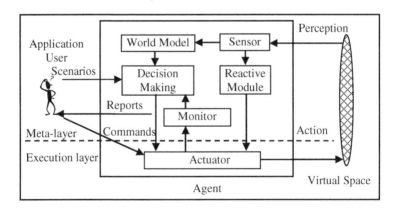

Fig. 2. Meta-level interaction between application user and agents

application designer who designs scenarios and application user who uses scenarios to control agents are assumed the same. In *meta-level* architecture shown in Fig. 2, urgent events are sent directly to *reactive module*, and *actuator* changes virtual spaces. Agents combine *scenario, world model* and *commands* to make decisions. Action results are monitored by *monitor* component, and agents send *Reports* to application user. Application user controls agents by *action*-like sentences obtained from speech commands [8].

2.4 Difficulties for Scripting Massive Multi-agents

Usually, one scenario is generated for one unit of agents. However, in order to discuss the difficulties for scripting agents, a scenario for one agent *John* to ambush *Blue* is illustrated in Fig. 3. The initial position of *John* is P_0 (0, 0, 2), and he follows the path P_1 (4, 0, 6), P_2 (4, 0, 8), P_3 (8, 0, 8), P_4 (12, 0, 8) or P_5 (8, 0, 11) to attack *Blue*. Application designer requires *John* run to position P_1, P_2, P_3, wait for 15 seconds there, and then crawl to position P_4 or P_5 by chance. Meanwhile, if *John* could see *Blue* when moving to P_3, he has to return to P_1. Part of the scenario is shown in Fig. 4.

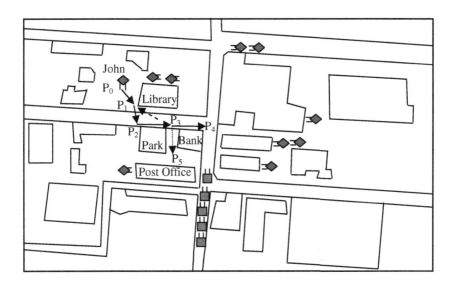

Fig. 3. A route for agent *John* to ambush Blue

The following difficulties for scripting massive multi-agents arise: **1) Application designers (scenario writers) have to specify arguments of *actions* quantitatively.** However, it is difficult and unnecessary for scenario writers to specify coordinates of positions. Scenario writers usually say: Cross the street and wait for a while at the corner of the post office, crawl to the window of the building and shot at the target. **2) It is tedious and error-prone for scenario writers to generate complex scenarios for massive multi-agents.** Scenario writers hope to specify arguments of *action*s

```
<scenario name="John">
  <scene name="ambush"
     <concurrence> run_back </concurrence>
     <guard>
        <cue> TRUE </cue>
          <action> !run :to (4, 0,6) :speed (5) </action>
          <action> !run :to (4, 0,8) :speed (5) </action>
          <action> !run :to (8, 0,8) :speed (5) </action>
          <action> !stand_ready :last (15) </action>
          <action scene="(attack_north) (attack_west)"> chance </action>
     </guard>
  </scene>
  <scene name="run_back">
     <concurrence> </concurrence>
       <guard>
         <cue> ?see :whom (ENEMY)  </cue>
         <action> !run :to (4, 0,6) :speed (7) </action>
         ……
       </guard>
  </scene>
  <scene name="attack_north">
     <concurrence> </concurrence>
     <guard>
        <cue> TRUE </cue>
        <action> !walk_lo :to (12, 0,8) :speed (3) </action>
        <action> !shot :at (ENEMY) </action>
         ……
     </guard>
  </scene>
  <scene name="attack_west">
        ……
       <action> !walk_lo :to (8, 0,11) :speed (3) </action>
       ……
  </scene>
</scenario>
```

Fig. 4. A scenario segment for agent *John* to ambush Blue

qualitatively and use *abstract actions* to reduce the burden for scenario design. Although massive multi-agents are organized as units and one unit uses the same scenario, it is hard for agents to make decisions and coordinate in hostile, complex and dynamic environments.

3 Designing Virtual Space Ontologies

Virtual space ontologies are inspired by the recognition that even human beings rely on information gleaned from the environment to assist them in deciding how to act.

Analogously, agents should operate in annotated virtual spaces that contain representations of the content and semantics [6]. In this section, we discuss entities and properties of *virtual space ontologies*, and answer the questions of how to access *virtual space ontologies*. For managing visual database of 3D models, we adopt *OpenFlight* format (www.multigen.com), which has become the standard for most real time systems.

3.1 Entity and Property of Virtual Space Ontologies

Generally speaking, vocabulary of *virtual space ontologies* is specific to the needs of a particular class of environments. However, commonalities do exist. For example, what entities are scenes composed of? What properties do these entities have? What are the interaction effects among entities? The composition of virtual spaces is shown in Fig. 5. Both *is-a* and *has-part* relationships between classes are shown in solid lines and dashed lines respectively. Topics of *virtual space ontologies* include: **1) Entity**. Building, bridge, road, tree, obstacle, grass, lake, river, door, window, weather, safe point, attack point, pinch point, weapon, vehicle, aircraft, ferry line, railway, etc. **2) Property**. In addition to geometry properties in spatial and geographical ontologies as discussed later in section 6, physical properties of entities are emphasized in *virtual space ontologies*, which are name, visibility, traffic ability, concealing grade, cover grade, etc. They are not shown in the class hierarchy. **3) Interaction**. Sound effects and special effects are generated when agents or entities interact with other entities. For example, when rifle bullets run into walls, smoke effects are generated.

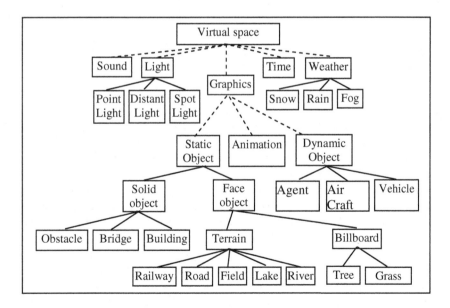

Fig. 5. Composition and class hierarchy of virtual spaces. Solid lines denote *is-a* relationship, and dashed lines denote *has-part* relationship

3.2 Accessing Virtual Space Ontologies

Entities are usually organized hierarchically in geometry databases, such as *VRML* (http://vrml.sgi.com/) and *OpenFlight*. Model creators can attach *virtual space ontologies* in the "Comment" properties of entities, and access ontologies by node hierarchy. A node is the fundamental element for constructing the database hierarchy. Beginning with the database (*DB*) node, a general database structure follows this order. **1)** *DB* **node**. *DB* node contains descriptive information about the entire database itself. Only one *DB* node can be at the top of the structure. **2) Master groups**. A master group node represents the entire model. All component hierarchies are ultimately attached to this common point. **3) Significant groups**. A number of group nodes represent major components of visual database. **4) Objects**. Objects can only contain face nodes (polygons), and are used to mark single objects. **5) Faces**. Face nodes can be attached to groups, objects, or other faces. **6) Vertex**. Vertex attributes are characteristics of face attributes and have no hierarchal significance.

Database hierarchy defines the relationship of nodes to each other. Nodes in the hierarchy are linked together in an inverted tree, which grows from a single database header node at the top, down to object, face, and vertex nodes at the bottom. Thus, *virtual space ontologies could be accessed and reasoned by node hierarchy.*

4   Reasoning About Virtual Space Ontologies

We generate grid arrays from *virtual space ontologies* for quantitative spatial reasoning, including tactical analysis and path finding. Arguments of *action*s are reasoned qualitatively. *Primitive action*s are abstracted to *abstract actions*, and advantages obtained from *virtual space ontologies* are given.

4.1 Automatic Generation of Grid Arrays

As shown in Fig. 4, path finding or planning is one of the major difficulties for scripting agents. There are two different techniques to create world graphs for path planning: grid arrays and *Voronoi* graphs. A grid array maps obstacles in virtual space to an array of numbers. A large value representing infinite cost is placed in each element in the array that an obstacle maps to, and the array can be searched using standard search algorithms, such as A* algorithm. *Voronoi* graphs are often used for path planning, and algorithms exist for generating one [7]. Because a grid array takes into account obstacle dimensions when creating the graph, it can generate safe paths around the obstacles. Furthermore, a grid array can be efficiently and automatically computed from spatial descriptions, such as *virtual space ontologies*. Consequently, we generate grid arrays of traffic ability for tactical analysis and path finding.

Traffic ability is the ability of an agent, vehicle or unit to move across a specified piece of terrain. Model creators annotate traffic ability as one of the properties of terrain. Note, traffic ability of the same piece of terrain is different for agents and for vehicles due to their different size and weight. So, there are different grid arrays for different agents in a virtual space. We divide traffic ability of terrain into 8 grades in

COMMANDER. The larger the value is, the more difficult for agents and vehicles to move. For example, severely restricted means impassable, restricted means one can get through, although perhaps slowly or with damage, and unrestricted means that agent can travel unhindered by that terrain.

Overlaying the virtual space with square grids and retrieving the traffic ability property of the piece of terrain automatically compute grid arrays. The grid array of a town for agents is shown in Fig. 8 (b).

4.2 Qualitative Arguments of Actions

Since simultaneous low-level control of all agents is difficult, directives from the human operator must be at a suitably high level. In the context of our application, most important high-level directives have to do with point-to-point movement through the virtual space. As discussed in Section 2.4, specifying arguments of *action*s is tedious and error-prone. Consequently, *Qualitative* reasoning about arguments of *action*s may facilitate scenario generation, especially for those arguments of position (region) and orientation.

How to identify candidate point set (grid set) for a region name and choose one representative point of that region? Assume agent *John* has an *action !walk :to (A-Hotel)*. Identification of the argument *A-Hotel* is divided into three steps. **1) Identify the entity *A-Hotel* from virtual space ontologies**. *John* queries each entity in the geometry database for the property *HasName*, which is annotated as part of the *virtual space ontologies* discussed in section 4. There exist three situations: If there is no such entity with name *A-Hotel*, then *John* does nothing at all, and the scenario is to be debugged by application user. If there is just one entity with the name *A-Hotel*, then this entity is returned. If more then two entities have the same name *A-Hotel*, then the one nearest to *John* is selected. **2) Identify candidate point set**. Linking the entity with grid array, a candidate point set is generated. **3) Choose one representative point**. If all of these candidate points are impassable, then select one passable point near these points randomly. Else, one passable point from these candidate points is chosen. In this way, we transform the region to a candidate point.

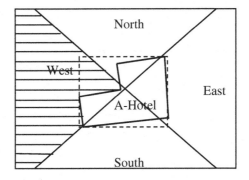

Fig. 6. Reasoning about position (region) and orientation

How to identify candidate point set from orientation? If the action name is *!walk :to (West of A-Hotel)*, we have to reason about orientation. We identify the entity as discussed above, and then calculate the bounding box of the region, as shown in Fig. 6. The center of the bounding box is computed, and four rays starting from the center divide the whole field into 4 parts. The candidate point set is the subtraction of all points in *West* sub-field and the points occupied by entity *A-Hotel*. Shadowed points shows the candidate point set for the orientation of *West of A-Hotel*. In the same way, orientation of southeast, southwest, northeast and northwest could be calculated. However, orientations related to *context*s have not been considered yet, such as *front of the car*, which is related to moving direction of the car, position and viewpoint.

4.3 Tactical Analysis and Path Finding

Agents can choose a target point and find a path to it by reasoning about grid arrays, which are generated automatically from *virtual space ontologies*. Target point selection is divided into two levels, i.e., tactical analysis and path finding. We demonstrate how to choose danger points and safe points in *COMMANDER*. Let V_k denotes the set of points visible from agent k. Danger points V_d is the union of all points nearer and visible to enemy agents, i.e., $V_d=V_1 \cup V_2 \cup \ldots \cup V_n$, 1…n is the number of enemy agents. Then, safe points V_s are the complement of danger points $V_s=V-V_d$. V is all the grid points in the grid array. After target points have been chosen, an agent has to select one according to location parameter specified in scenario. Let V_a denote point set specified by trainees and chosen by agents through spatial reasoning discussed above. Then the candidate target points are $V_t= V_a \cap V_s$. At last, the nearest one to the agent in V_t is chosen as the target point. At the second level, the best path from current agent position to target point is searched by standard *A** algorithm. We use both distances and threats in heuristics function.

4.4 Abstract Actions

With *virtual space ontologies* and grid array, agents can do tactical analysis. This provides the possibility for agents to execute high-level *abstract actions*. *Primitive actions* listed in Table 1 form a hierarchy [1]. The lowest levels are actuators. The set

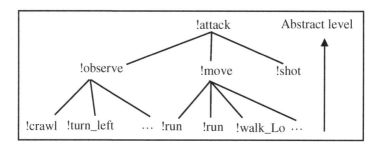

Fig. 7. Abstraction hierarchy of action *!attack*

Table 2. Abstract actions in *COMMANDER*

Name	Arguments
!wait	:last (float time)
!defense	:for (WHERE region_name)
!attack	:at (WHERE region_name)
!move	:to (WHERE region_name)
!shot	
!observe	:last (float duration)
!dead	
!communicate	:content (STRING sentence)

of actuators are *primitive actions* such as move the agent, turn it and firing a weapon. Complex actions are built from these primitive ones. *!Attack action*, for example, may move an agent to a target's location and fire at it, see Fig. 7. As one goes up the hierarchy, *action*s become increasingly abstract and powerful. Application designers use both *primitive actions* and higher-level *action*s to generate scenarios. Comparing Table 1 with Table 2, it is found that the number of *action*s reduces from 21 to 8, and the number of arguments of *action*s from 29 to 6.

4.5   Scripting Agents Based on Virtual Space Ontologies

In summary, application designers can *sketch* scenarios with *virtual space ontologies*. The arguments of *cue*s and *action*s could be specified qualitatively, including positions and orientations. Agents choose target points by the intersection of the point set inferred from *virtual space ontologies* and the point set computed from tactical analysis. *Abstract actions* could be used to control agents due to the improvement of agents' autonomy. Consequently, the length of scenarios is decreased. Advantages obtained from *virtual space ontologies* are listed in Table 3. The one for agent *John*, as shown in Fig. 4, exemplifies scenario length. Application users can use *abstract actions* and *qualitative arguments of actions* to control agents in real time, because agents could interpret the intent of region and orientation in *action*-like commands.

Table 3. Advantages obtained from virtual space ontologies

	Action Number		Argument Number		Scenarios
	Primit ive Action	Abstract Action	Primitiv e Action	Abstract Action	Length(in lines)
Without virtual space ontologies	21		29		324
With virtual space ontologies	21	8	29	6	75

5   Applications of Virtual Space Ontologies in COMMANDER

We develop a multi-agent simulation system *COMMANDER* for training army leaders of squads, platoons, companies and battalions. Model creators construct various virtual spaces according to the requirement of combat simulation, and mark up *virtual space ontologies*, including entity name and entity property of traffic ability, visibility, cover grade, etc. Super-ordinate commanders (trainers) set enemy's arrangement including formation, marching route and weapons in scenarios. Sub-ordinate commanders (trainees) accept the task, make tactical decisions and plan agents in scenarios. Trainees test their plans through simulation. Trainees change scenarios in real time according to combat situation in *action*-like sentence. After various scenarios for the same task have been experimented, trainees' skill for tactical analysis and decision-making are improved.

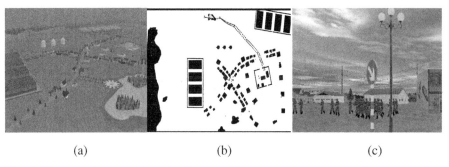

(a)   (b)   (c)

Fig. 8. The virtual space (a) and grid array (b) of a small town as well as agents being scripted (c)

Given as an example, a small town for combat simulation is designed. Its grid array for agents is shown in Fig. 8(b). The scope of the town is about 1200m×800m, and the resolution of grid array for agents is 1m×1m. Black color pixels imply impassable grids, and passable grids are illustrated in white color. Agents being scripted are shown in Fig. 8(c).

6   Related Work

Ontology has become popular in almost every area of information processing in recent years. In the context of information systems, *ontology refers to a precise specification of the meanings and inter-dependencies of a set of concepts.* The specification can be used to check and maintain the integrity of a database, and also to facilitate integration and inter-operation between different databases. It may also be used as a basis for implementing functionality for querying and presenting information, which requires flexible, multi-perspective access to data.

The spatial and geographical ontologies involve a rich and highly interdependent conceptual structure. Some kind of ontology specifying meanings and logical connections between concepts is essential to supporting applications to access data in flexible way. *OWL-Space* effort provides a way for different spatial reasoning engines and spatial resources to communicate with each other, as well as a way for people to mark up spatial information on their web sites. The goals of this effort inlude: 1) produce an ontology that would enable general, though not necessarily efficient, reasoning about spatial concepts and link with various standards for geographical information, such as *GML* (http://www.opengis.net/gml/index.htm); 2) link with more efficient specialized reasoning engines for spatial reasoning; 3) link with the numerous databases that exist containing a wealth of specific geographical and spatial information e.g., *OpenCyc* (http://www.cyc.com/cycdoc/vocab/spatial-vocab.html), *SUMO* (http://ontology.teknowledge.coml); 4) support convenient query capabilities for spatial information.

Discussion on the nature and efficacy of ontologies in geographical information (*GI*) has featured strongly across the *GI* science community over the past few years. Motivation for advancement of *GI* ontologies is soundly grounded in some key and distinct problems facing the advancement of *GI* content, service and application development. Improving the meaning of *GI* to the end user, interoperability of *GI* data, internet-based data mining and knowledge discovery, are all areas where applications of an ontological approach could aid both the user and *GI* industry.

We exemplify spatial and geographical ontologies by *OWL-Space*, which include the following topics: **1) Topology**. Points, arcs, regions, volumes, closed loops and surfaces, ordering relations, directions on lines and loops, connectedness, continuity, boundaries and surfaces, interior and exterior, directed boundaries, disjoint, touching, bordering, overlapping, containing regions, location at, holes, etc. **2) Orientation**. Frames of reference (including earth-based, person-based, vehicle-based, force-based, …), relative orientations (parallel and perpendicular), Cartesian and polar coordinate systems, bearing and range, transformations between coordinate systems, degrees of freedom, qualitative trigonometry (granularities on orientations), 2 1/2 dimensions, elevation from sea level versus ground level, planar versus spherical geometry, etc. **3) Shape**. 2D (two-dimensional) versus 3D (three-dimensional) shapes, shape descriptors (round, tall, narrow, convex, …), relative shapes (rounder, sharper, …), same shape as, negative shape, fits-in, etc. **4) Size**. Length, distance, area, volume, precise measures, alternate descriptions of size, English-metric conversions, coarse granularities (order of magnitude, half order of magnitude), implied precision, qualitative measures (large, medium, small, …), encoding uncertainty, uncertainty of location versus imprecise regions, etc. **5) Granularity**. A city can be viewed as a point (1D, one-dimensional), a region (2D), or a volume (3D). **6) Spatial aggregates**. What are the most common ways of describing spatial aggregates? **7) Geologic/geopolitical regions**. Natural geographical regions include land masses (continent, island, …), bodies of water (ocean, lake, river, …), terrain features (mountain, valley, forest, desert, …). Political regions include countries, political subdivisions (state, province, county, …), municipalities (city, town, village, …), residences and street addresses, etc.

While it would be wrong to claim that *virtual space ontologies* are uniquely different from other domain ontologies, it does seem that virtual space concepts present some fundamental problems for ontology construction. We take *OWL-Space* as an example and the following differences are noticed: **1) Motivation**. *OWL-Space* aims to increase the interoperability among various resources and applications, whilst *virtual space ontologies* aim to facilitate interaction between humans and agents. **2) Sharing**. *OWL-Space* are shared among different communities or within a large community, such as geographical information community, whist *virtual space ontologies* are shared by a group of humans who are organized for special tasks, such as designing multi-agent system. **3) Potential application**. *OWL-Space* has vast applications in flight map system, *COA* (Course Of Action) planning, traffic ability, travel system, political divisions, weather, geologic and space applications, cell biology, image interpretation and description as well as robotics, whilst *virtual space ontologies* find applications in computer graphics, virtual realities, video games and synthetic battlefields, where both the interaction between agents and environments, as well as the interaction between humans and agents are emphasized.

7   Conclusion

We facilitate scripting massive multi-agents by introducing *virtual space ontologies*. Application designers use *qualitative* arguments of *action*s and *abstract actions* to *sketch* scenarios for units of agents. Application users communicate their intent better with agents in *meta-level*. Advantages obtained from *virtual space ontologies* are: **1) Qualitative arguments of actions**. Positions and orientations are reasoned by hybrid approach of integrating qualitative with quantitative spatial reasoning. Firstly, a grid array is computed from *virtual space ontologies*. Then, entities are queried from *virtual space ontologies*, and a candidate point set is calculated by qualitative reasoning about region, position and orientation. Agents do tactical analysis and compute tactical candidate point set. At last, one target point is chosen from the intersection of this two candidate point sets. **2) Abstract actions**. Agents can interpret qualitative region and orientation. This provides the possibility for *abstract actions* to be used by application designers to *sketch* scenarios for units of agents. As a result, the number of arguments, the number of *action*s and the length of scenarios are decreased. **3) Better communication of intent between humans and agents**. Application users can use *qualitative arguments* of *action*s and *abstract actions* to modify scenarios and control agents in *action*-like commands at *meta-level*.

Acknowledgement

This paper is partly supported by JSNSF with grant number BK2003001, Ministry of Education of PRC with grant number 6809001001.

References

[1] Akin M. S., Westbrook D. L., and Cohen P. R.: Domain-general simulation and planning with physical schemas. In *Proceedings of the 2000 Winter Simulation Conference*, 2000
[2] Berners Lee T., Hendler J. and Lassila O.: The Semantic Web: A new form of Web content that is meaningful to computers will unleash a revolution of new possibilities. *The Scientific American*, 2001

[3] Dale, J., Willmot, S., Burg, B.: Agentcities: Challenges and Deployment of Next-Generation Service Environments. *Pacific Rim International Workshop on Multi-Agents (PRIMA 2002)*, Tokyo, Japan, 2002

[4] DAML+OIL Revised Language Specification, march 2001. http://www.daml.org/2001/03/daml+oil-index/

[5] Dill S., Eiron N. and Gibson D.: SemTag and Seeker: Bootstrapping the Semantic Web via Automated Semantic Annotation, In *Proceedings of the 121th International World Wide Web Conference,* 2003

[6] Doyle P.: Believability through Context: Using "knowledge in the world" to create intelligent characters. *AAMAS02*, Bologna, Italy, pp342-349, 2002

[7] Fortune S. J.: A sweepline algorithm for Voronoi diagrams, http://netlib.bell-labs.com/cm/cs/who/sjf/index.html

[8] Gao Z. Q., Kawasoe T., Yamamoto, A., and Ishida, T.: Meta-Level Architecture for Executing Multi-agent Scenarios. *Lecture Notes in Artificial Intelligence*, 2413, Springer-Verlag, pp163-177, 2002

[9] Gao Z Q.: Designing Interactive Multi-agent Systems with Semantic 3D Environments. *In Proceedings of International Workshop on Semantic Web Technologies and Application Technologies,* Nara, Japan, 2003

[10] Goldberg A.: IMPROV: A system for real-time animation of behavior-based interactive synthetic actors. *Lecture Notes in Computer Science*, 1195, 1997.

[11] Handschuh S., Staab S., and Volz R.: On Deep Annotation. In *Proceedings of the 121th International World Wide Web Conference, WWW 2003*

[12] Horrocks I., Patel-Schneider P. F.: Three Theses of Representation in the Semantic Web. In *Proceedings of the 12th International World Wide Web Conference, WWW 2003*

[13] Ishida, T.: Q: A scenario Description Language for Interactive Agents. *IEEE Computer*, Vol. 35, No 11, pp54-59, 2002

[14] Ishida, T.: Digital City Kyoto: Social Information Infrastructure for Everyday Life. *Communications of the ACM (CACM)*, Vol. 45, No. 7, pp76-81, 2002

[15] Martinez J.: "Overview of the MPEG-7 Standard (version 5.0)". *ISO/IEC JTC1/SC29/WG11 N4031*, Singapore, March 2001

[16] Murakami Y., Ishida T., Kawasoe T. and Hishiyama R.: Scenario Description for Multi-agent Simulation, *AAMAS'03*, Melbourne, Australia. pp369-376, 2003

[17] Wang Z. J., Sheng H. Y., Ding P.: A Q-Based Architecture for Semantic Information Interoperability on Semantic Web, *International Semantic Web Conference*, LNCS 2870, pp. 722-737, 2003

Challenges in Building Very Large Teams

Paul Scerri and Katia Sycara

Carnegie Mellon University,
{pscerri, katia}@cs.cmu.edu

Abstract. When agents coordinate according to the principles of teamwork they can flexibly, robustly and reliably achieve complex goals in complex, dynamic and even hostile environments. An emerging standard for building such teams is via the use of *proxies*, which encapsulate domain independent teamwork algorithms in a software module that works closely with a domain specific person, agent or robot and other proxies to create a team. Succesful, previous generations of proxies and teamwork algorithms were limited to small teams because of their reliance on accurate models of the team and task state. By developing new algorithms that rely on probabilistic models we have been able to build teams that are orders of magnitude larger than before. However, key challenges remain before such teams can be deployed in real-world environments, including the need for languages to specify plans for such teams and ways of modeling and predicting team performance in new domains.

1   Introduction

Teamwork allows intelligent, heterogeneous actors (robots, agents and people) to cooperate flexibly, robustly, cohesively and efficiently to achieve complex goals in complex environments. Very large teams are needed for domains such as the military, space operations[12], disaster recovery and commerce, where there are many inter-related, complex activities to be performed by many actors. Typically, the problems for which such teams are most applicable do not require optimal behavior, but require reliably "good" behavior despite an uncertain, complex and potentially hostile environment.

The key technical difference between teamwork and other forms of coordinated behavior is the use of an explicit model of teamwork and an explicit representation of the current team status maintained by each team member. Each team member uses their model of teamwork and the team status to reason about the actions, both actions in the environment and communication acts, that will lead to the best expected outcome for the team. Early work on the logic of teamwork[6, 13] proscribed the reasoning an agent performs from these models. More recent, practical implementations[36, 16] relax some of the requirements of the logical formulation. Once coordination algorithms have been developed they can be reused in a variety of domains. The key to building large teams is to find ways to scale up the maintainance of agents' models of team state and reasoning with those models.

T. Ishida, L. Gasser, and H. Nakashima (Eds.): MMAS 2004, LNAI 3446, pp. 86–103, 2005.

The central abstraction used in our teamwork models is a *team oriented plan* (TOP). A TOP describes the individual activities, *roles*, that must be performed to achieve team objectives and any constraints between those individual activities. The team starts with a library of *TOP templates* that are dynamically instantiated when preconditions for the TOP are fulfilled. For example, a TOP template for rescuing an injured civilian in a disaster response domain may have two roles: one for bringing the civilian to safety; and another for administering first aid. A *constraint* would require that the latter role be performed *after* the former. Typically, a large team will be simultaneously executing many TOPs at once, with only a small number of team members directly involved in any particular TOP. Using the TOP abstraction, the task of coordination via teamwork is to determine what action a team member should take, given the current TOPs and what each team member should communicate about the TOPs. In practice, scalable teamwork requires that each team member does not need to reason and communicate about each TOP, but only some subset.

The "backbone" of our scalable team is an *associates network*, which statically and logically arranges the team into a scale-free network[39]. The team uses the associates network to intelligently share information and dramatically limit the amount of communication required for cohesive activity. The agents exploit the *small-worlds property* of a scale-free network which is that any two agents are separated by a relatively small number of links[39]. Team members can leverage the network to make coordinated decisions by making part of a decision then pushing the decision to its neighbor in the network most likely to be able to continue making the decision. This allows team members to act despite having very limited models of the status of the rest of the team, reducing the need to communicate state information. However, as a consequence the logical guarantees provided by previous teamwork algorithms are replaced by algorithms that have high probability of working correctly. We have developed probabilistic algorithms that leverage the associates network for distributed plan instantiation, role allocation, information sharing and adjustable autonomy within a team.

Our approach to teamwork has been implemented in domain independent software proxies, called Machinetta[30]. Software proxies, which are becoming the standard means for creating heterogeneous teams, are semi-autonomous coordination modules, one for each team member[37]. Each proxy encapsulates the team work algorithms and works closely with an individual team member and with other proxies to implement the teamwork. Our implementation of the coordination algorithm utilizes the abstraction of a mobile agent for robustness and ease of development. We have used Machinetta proxies in several domains, including for coordination of large groups of unmanned aerial vehicles.

2 Team Oriented Plans

Team Oriented Plans (TOPs) are the abstraction that constrain team activities allowing it to achieve specific goals. The TOPs provide the mapping from team level goals to individual *roles* that are performed by individual team members. Roles are lowest level of abstraction in a team plan and are simple goals, activities or responsibilities that will most often be performed by a single team member. Often several roles will be required for a particular task. For example, in a disaster response domain, a patient rescue task may have roles for carrying the front of the stretcher, the back of the stretcher and a role for administering first aid. It is possible (even likely in some domains) that a single team member takes on multiple roles, e.g., one of the stretcher bearers might also administer first aid, but a role is only ever taken on by a single team member at a particular point in time.[1]

Importantly, while TOPs describe the breakdown of team activities into individual activities, they do not describe what coordination is required to execute the plan. A TOP does not describe which team member will perform which role or exactly how the role should be performed. This allows the team maximum flexibility to deploy its available resources to execute the current plans. For example, the stretcher bearing roles described above might be filled by robots or humans, depending on their availability and the path taken from the location of the patient to the ambulance will depend on whether robots or humans are carrying the stretcher. However, typically individual roles are not completely decoupled from other roles. The interactions between the roles are represented with *constraints* on the TOP. The team members that are assigned to the roles are informed of the constraints and must coordinate with the team members executing roles with which their roles are constrained to ensure constraints are not violated. These closely coordinating agents form a *sub-team* (see next Section).

The TOP templates typically have open parameters which are instantiated with specific domain level information at run time. For example, we can write one template to represent a generic plan of "Fight a fire at building x", rather than writing hundreds of plans of the form "Fight a fire at building 1", "Fight a fire at building 2", "Fight a fire at building 3", etc. When the preconditions of a plan template match the proxy's current state of beliefs, a new plan belief is instantiated with the specific details of the particular precondition match. The TOP includes each plan's termination conditions, under which a team plan is achieved, irrelevant or unachievable. Such explicit specification ensures common knowledge of such conditions, so that the team can terminate the goal coherently.

3   The Associates Network: The Backbone of a Large Scale Team

To provide structure to the team, we connect all team members via a static, task independant, logical network. Neighbors in this network are called *associates*. Team members are required to keep their neighbors in the associates network

---

[1] If a task requires multiple team members doing the same thing, there are multiple roles.

informed of their current activities, including which TOPs they are working on. This requirement leads to knowledge about ongoing activities being spread across the team. The associates network can then be used as a backbone for the key coordination algorithms.

Since agents also keep their neighbors in the associates network informed of their current activities, the group of agents with up-to-date knowledge of progress on a specific TOP consists of the agents actually performing roles in the plan and their neighbors in the associates network. Because the agents performing roles in a particular plan can change over time, the members of the subteam change over time. Moreover, since agents can perform multiple roles and have multiple neighbors, they can be part of several subteams at once. Thus, we can view the structure of the team as a set of dynamic, overlapping subteams. A snapshot of the resulting dynamic, structure is shown in Figure 1. This *dynamic, partial centralization* is often a feature of large scale coordination infrastructure,[24] likely because it balances the need for flexibility against the structure required for effective coordination though it is not exactly clear why this structure is a consistent feature of large scale teams. By not imposing any particular structure, we allow the team to allocate resources most flexibly to the current situation. Although some structure might lead to some efficiency gains, it is our research hypothesis that eventually no imposed structure will yield the best results. Scalability is possible, because the number of agents needing to know about the plan is a function of the complexity of the TOP, rather than the size of the team.

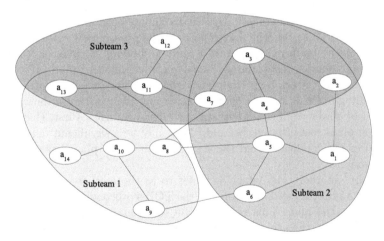

Fig. 1. Relationship between subteams and the associates network

The associates network is specially designed to be a *scale-free network*, which is a type of *small worlds network*[39]. In a small worlds network there is a low *degree of separation* between group members, i.e., a message can be passed between any two agents via a small number of the point-to-point connections. Such networks exist among people and are popularized by the notion of "six degrees of separation"[1]. We have developed a number of key coordination algorithms, leveraging the associates network for scalable teamwork. (See [28, 42, 31, 21] for more details.)

3.1   Plan Instantiation with the Associates Network

Notice that this approach to plan instantiation is completely decentralized; there is no imposed hierarchy or centralization. Once TOPs are instantiated, subteams develop around the TOP resulting in a type of structure, however this structure emerges from the interaction with the team and the environment.

While the distributed plan instantiation process allows the team to instantiate plans efficiently and robustly, two possible problems can occur. First, the team could instantiate different plans for the same goal, based on different preconditions detected by different members of the team. For example, two different plans could be instantiated by different team members for fighting the same fire depending on what particular team members know or sense. Second, the team may initiate multiple copies of the same plan. In a large team, it is infeasible to require all agents to agree on the plan before execution of the plan can commence, since this may take a long time. Instead, we use a two pronged approach, leveraging the associates network of minimizing the number of conflicting plans created, detecting and then removing the ones that are[21].

Avoiding Conflicting Plans. We use two different algorithms for minimizing instantiations of conflicting plans depending on the situation.

First, we have a probabilistic rule that requires no information about other team members. This rule, which we refer to as the *probabilistic instantiation rule*, requires that the team member wait a random amount of time, to see whether another team member instantiates that plan (or a conflicting plan.) If it does not hear from its associates about the plan within the time, it instantiates the plan. The advantage of this rule, is that by spreading plan instantiations over time there will be fewer conflicts. There are two disadvantages. First, there may be conflicting plans instantiated. Second, there may be a significant delay between detection of pre-conditions and the instantiation of the plan depending on the random wait.

Secondly, another rule, which we refer to as the *local information rule*, requires that a proxy must detect some of the TOP's preconditions locally, in order to instantiate the plan. This rule is useful when many agents are likely to be able to instantiate the same plan. Specifically, at least one of the TOPs preconditions must have come into the team member directly from the environment, rather than from a an associate. Although this will lead to conflicting plans when multiple proxies locally sense preconditions, it is easier to determine where the conflicts might occur and resolve them quickly. Specifically we can look for proxies with the ability to locally sense information, e.g., those in a specific part of the enviornment. The major disadvantage of this rule is that when a TOP has many preconditions the team members that locally detect specific preconditions may never get to know all the preconditions and thus not instantiate the plan.

Removing Conflicting Plans. While the instantiation rules limit the number of duplicate plans, some remain, thus requiring a deconfliction phase. As described above, agents are obliged to inform their associates of plans they are currently working on. It turns out that if any two plans conflict with each other (or are duplicates) there is very high probability that at least one agent will get to know of both plans. Assume that $subteam_i$ is executing $plan_i$. If plans $plan_i$ and $plan_j$ have some conflict or potential synergy, some agent can detect that conflict or synergy iff $subteam_i \cap subteam_j \neq \emptyset$. A simple probability calculation reveals that the probability of overlap between subteams is:

$$Pr(overlap) = 1 - \frac{(n-k)C_m}{nC_m}$$

where where n = number of agents, k = size of subteam A, m = size of subteam B and $_aC_b$ denotes a combination. For example, if $|subteam_i| = |subteam_j| = 20$ and $|A| = 200$, then $P(overlap) = 0.88$, despite each subteam involving only 10% of the overall team. Since, the constituents of a subteam change over time, this is actually a lower bound on the probability that a conflict is detected because over time more agents are actually involved. Once a conflict (or duplicate) is detected a simple negotiation is used to either remove a duplicate or change conflicting plans[2].

4   Scalable Coordination Algorithms

A variety of algorithms, each targeting specific issues, need to work together for effective coordination. We have developed new algorithms for several key problems, because existing algorithms were not able to scale to the large numbers of actors we were dealing with. Specifically, we have developed new algorithms for role allocation, information sharing and adjustable autonomy.

Two key principles underly each of the algorithms. First, we note that because coordination is in the context of a team, individuals will have broad knowledge of the state of the team. Technically, this knowledge can be gleaned either from observation or via inference from ongoing coordination. For example, in a disaster response domain when there is a major earthquake, a team member can reasonably assume that response resources will be stretched, either by seeing the amount of damage or noticing the number of roles the team is attempting to allocate. When using heuristics this broad, probabilistic knowledge is invaluable in making appropriate decisions.

4.1   Allocating Roles to Team Members

Role allocation is the problem of assigning roles to agents so as to maximize overall team utility[23, 38, 40]. Large-scale teams emphasize key additional requirements in role allocation: (i) rapid role allocation as domain dynamics may

---

[2] A more efficient way of doing this is an area for future work.

cause tasks to disappear; (ii) agents may perform one or more roles, but within resource limits; (iii) many agents can fulfill the same role; (iv) inter-role constraints may be present. This role allocation challenge in such teams will be referred to as E-GAP, as it subsumes the generalized assignment problem (GAP), which is NP-complete[34].

We have adapted ideas from Distributed Constraint Optimization (DCOP) [22, 11] for role allocation, as DCOP offers the key advantages of distributedness and a rich representational language which can consider costs/utilities of tasks. Despite these advantages, DCOP approaches to role allocation suffer from three weaknesses. First, complete DCOP algorithms[22] have exponential run-time complexity, partially due to the purely local view of the team that each agent has. Using probabilistic models we can estimate properties of good allocations and use this information to focus the search. While relying on such estimates prevents guarantees of optimality, they can dramatically reduce the search space. Second, similar agent functionality within extreme teams results in dense constraint graphs increasing communication within a DCOP algorithm. Third, DCOP algorithms do not address the additional complications of constraints *between* roles.

For large scale teams, we have developed a novel DCOP algorithm called LA-DCOP (Low communication Approximate DCOP)[10]. LA-DCOP uses a representation where agents are variables that can take on values from a common pool, i.e., the pool of roles to be assigned. The mechanism for allocating values to variables encapsulates three novel ideas. First, LA-DCOP improves efficiency by not focusing on an exact optimal reward; instead by exploiting the likely characteristics of optimal allocations, given the available probabilistic information, it focuses on maximizing the team's expected total reward. In particular, the agents *compute* a minimum threshold on the expected capability of the agent that would maximize expected team performance. If the agent's capability to perform a role is less than the threshold capability, the agent does not consider taking on the role, channeling the role towards more capable agents. Second, to reduce the significant communication overheads due to constraint graph denseness, *tokens* are used to regulate access to values. Only the agent currently holding the token for a particular value can consider assigning that value to its variable. The use of tokens removes the possibility of several agents taking on the same role, thus dramatically reducing the need to communicate about and repair conflicts. Third, to deal with groups of tightly constrained roles, we introduce the idea of allowing values to be represented by *potential tokens*. When groups of roles must be simultaneously performed, instead of committing to a role by assigning the value represented by a token, a team member accepting a potential token simply indicates that it will accept the role (i.e., assign the value, only when all simultaneous roles can be assigned. While team members are being found to fill the other simultaneous roles, a team member with a potential token can perform other roles. Only when team members have been found for all roles will the holders of the potential tokens actually take on the roles. This technique frees team members up for other roles when not all roles in a constrained set can be filled. More detail can be found in [28].

4.2   Information Sharing

Information or events sensed locally by an agent will typically not be sensed by other agents in the team. In some cases, however, that information will be critical to other members of the team and hence, should be communicated to them. For example, consider the case of a large scale rescue response. Some fire fighter learns from a civilian that a certain building, far across the city, has large amounts of flammable chemicals stored in the basement. The fire fighter should inform his co-workers fighting any fires in or around that building, but he will likely not know who those co-workers are.

Previous algorithms for sharing information in a multiagent system have made assumptions that do not hold in very large teams. Specifically, previous algorithms either assume that centralization is possible[33] or assume that agents have accurate models of other members of the group[36]. Often techniques for communication assume that an agent with some potentially relevant information will have an accurate model of the rest of the group[36, 25].

We are developing new communication reasoning that reduces the need to know details about other team members by exploiting the small worlds property of the associates network. The intuition behind our approach is that agents can rapidly get information to those requiring it simply by "guessing" which acquaintance to send the information to. The agent attempts to guess which of its neighbours either require the information or are in the best position to get the information to the agent that requires it. In a small worlds network, an agent only needs to guess correctly slightly more often than it guesses wrong and information is rapidly delivered. Moreover, due to the low degree of separation, there only needs to be a small number of correct "guesses" to get information to its destination. Since the agents are working in a team, they can use information about the current state of the coordination to inform their guesses. While members of large teams will not have accurate, up-to-date models of the team, our hypothesis is that they will have sufficiently accurate models to "guess" correctly often enough to make the algorithm work.

The models of its neighbors that an agent uses to make decisions about where to forward information are created using previously received messages. When an agent has a piece of information to forward, it looks at that piece of information's relationship to information previously received from each of its neighbors. The probability that a neighbor is the best to pass a piece of information to is computed, using a variation of Bayes' Rule, from the relationships between the current piece of information and the messages received from that neighbor. For example, if agent A has recieved a message about a fire in Newell Simon Hall (location of the Robotics Institute) from agent B, then when it has information about flammable chemicals in the basement of Newell Simon Hall, agent B is likely to either want the information or be well positioned to pass that information to someone who does. Technical details of this approach can be found in [32, 42].

4.3   Adjustable Autonomy via Meta-reasoning

When teams are used in domains where mistakes can cause physical, psychological or financial harm, for systems to be acceptable to users, humans must be allowed to make critical decisions if they desire. Humans may have better models of preferences or experience that means their decisions are more appropriate than even the best autonomous system. To allow humans to make these critical decisions in the context of coordination is an interesting challenge. First, it is infeasible for humans to monitor ongoing coordination and intervene quickly enough to make the critical decisions unless the team explictly transfers control of the decision to the human. Since the coordination is distributed, the complete state of the team will typically not be completely known by any individual member of the team. Moreover, in a sufficiently large team or sufficiently dynamic domain, it will be infeasible to continually present an accurate picture of the team to any observer. Thus, the team must proactively transfer control of key decisions to human experts. Second, even when decision-making control is explicitly given, in a dynamic domain, with many possible decisions to make, human decision-making will not always be available or cannot be made quickly enough to allow the team to continue to operate correctly. It should not be the case that delays in making decisions intended to improve coordination end up causing miscoordination. Thirdly, there may be multiple human experts who can make decisions and the decisions should be sent to the expert in the best position to make them in a timely manner. In previous work, these three problems have not been adequately addressed by a complete solution. An effective solution must identify decisions where human input is necessary or useful in a distributed way then transfer control of those decisions to humans capable and available to make those decisions without compromising ongoing coordination with decision-making delays.

Our approach to this problem embodies two key ideas[31]. To allow the team to identify critical decisions to be made by humans, we use *coordination meta-reasoning* which uses heuristics to find coordination phenomena that may indicate problems. For example, when there are two high risk alternative courses of action that the team cannot autonomously distinguish, humans may draw on additional experience to choose between. We explicitly represent coordination tasks, such as initiating a team plan or allocating a resource, explicitly via *coordination roles* allowing meta-reasoning to simply identify cases where role performance is poor. Critically, the meta-reasoning is performed "out in the team", based on local information of individual team members and hence does not rely on an aggregation of coordination information at some central point. However, distributed identification of decisions for potential human input is a double edged sword: on the one hand it removes the need to generate and maintain a centralized state, but on the other it means that identification must be performed with only local knowledge, resulting in less accurate identification of key decisions.

The second part of our approach is that when a decision is to be made by a human, a *transfer-of-control* strategy is used to ensure that lack of a timely response does not negatively impact the performance of the team[29]. A transfer-of-control strategy is a pre-planned sequence of actions that are designed to balance the benefits of getting human input against the costs of that input not coming in a timely manner. Each action in a transfer-of-control strategy either transfers decision-making control to some entity, human or agent, or takes an action to buy more time for the decision to be made. Previously, a mathematical model of transfer-of-control strategies was presented and operationalized via Markov Decision Processes[30]. In that work, although the mathematical model supported the possibility of having multiple humans available to give input, experimental results used only one human expert. In this work, we make multiple human experts available to the agent team and allow the transfer-of-control strategies to reason about transferring control to each. People are modelled by the types of meta-reasoning they can perform and the agents maintain models of what tasks each person is currently performing, in order to create appropriate transfer-of-control strategies.

5   Machinetta

A number of algorithms work together to achieve the teamwork, given the framework described above. There are algorithms for allocation roles[10], instantiating plans[21], sharing information[42], human interaction[31] and resource allocation. To avoid requiring a reimplementation of the algorithms for each new domain, the coordination algorithms are encapsulated in a *proxy*[15, 37, 25, 30]. Proxies are becoming a standard mechanism for building heterogeneous teams. Each team member works closely with a single proxy that coordinates with the other proxies to implement the teamwork. The basic architecture is shown in Figure 2. The proxy communicates via a high level, domain specific pro-

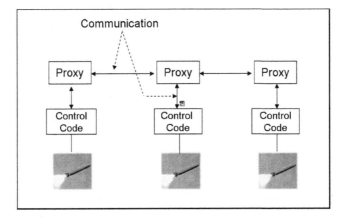

Fig. 2. The basic system architecture showing proxies, control code and Unmanned Aerial Vehicles (UAVs) being controlled

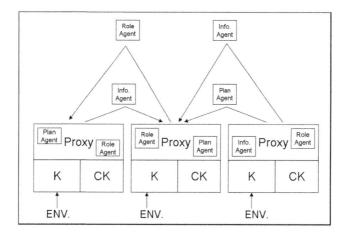

Fig. 3. High level view of the implementation, with coordination agents moving around a network of proxies

tocol with the robot, agent or person it is representing in the team. Most of the proxy code is domain independent and can be readily used in a variety of domains requiring distributed control. Our current proxy code, known as Machinetta, is a substantially extended and updated version of the TEAMCORE proxy code[37]. Machinetta proxies are in the public domain and can be downloaded from http://teamcore.usc.edu/doc/Machinetta.

Coordination Agents. In a dynamic, distributed system, protocols for performing coordination need to be extremely robust. When we scale the size of a team to hundreds of agents, this becomes more of an issue than simply writing bug-free code. Instead we need abstractions and designs that promote robustness. Towards this end, we are encapsulating "chunks" of coordination in *coordination agents*. Each coordination agent manages one specific piece of the overall coordination. When control over that piece of coordination moves from one proxy to another proxy, the coordination agent moves from proxy to proxy, taking with it any relevant state information (see Figure 3). We have coordination agents for each plan or subplan (PlanAgents), each role (RoleAgents) and each piece of information that needs to be shared (InformationAgents). For example, a RoleAgent looks after everything to do with a specific role. This encapsulation makes it far easier to build robust coordination. Coordination agents manage the coordination in the network of proxies. Thus, the proxy can be viewed simply as a mobile agent platform that facilitates the functioning of the coordination agents. However, the proxies play the additional important role of providing and storing local information.

6   Results

The algorithms described in this chapter and encapsulated in the Machinetta software have been extensively tested in several domains. In this section, we present key results showing the utility and generality of the approach. In Figures 4 and 5, we show the results of an experiment using 200 Machinetta proxies. These experiments represent high fidelity tests of the coordination algorithms and illustrate the overall effectiveness of the approach. In the first experiment, the proxies control fire trucks responding to an urban disaster. The trucks must travel around an environment, locate fires (which spread if they are not extinguished) and extinguish them. The top level goal of the team, G, was to put out all the fires. A single plan requires that an individual fire be put out. In this experiment, the plan had only one role which was to put out the fire. We varied the sensing range of the fire trucks ("Far" and "Close") and measured some key parameters. The most critical thing to note is that the approach was successful in coordinating a very large team. The first column compares the number of fires started. The "Close" sensing team required more searching to find fires, and as a result, unsurprisingly, the fires spread more. However, they were able extinguish them slightly faster than the "Far" sensing team, partly because the "Far" sensing team wasted resources in situations where there were two plans for the same fire (see Column 3, "Conflicts"). Although these conflicts were resolved it took a non-trivial amount of time and slightly lowered the team's ability to fight fires. Resolving conflicts also increased the number of messages required (see Column

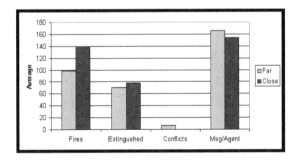

Fig. 4. Coordinating 200 agents in disaster response simulation (average on y-axis, fires, extinguished, conflicts and messages per agent on x-axis)

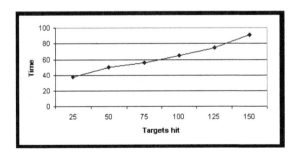

Fig. 5. Coordinating 200 simulated UAVs in a battlespace (time on y-axis, targets hit on x-axis)

4), though most of the differences in the number of messages can be attributed to more fire fighters sensing fires and spreading that information. The experiment showed that the overall number of messages required to effectively coordinate the team was extremely low, partially due to the fact that no low level coordination between agents were required (since there was one fire truck per plan). Figure 5 shows high level results from a second domain using exactly the same proxy code. The graph shows the rate at which 200 simulated unmanned aerial vehicles, coordinated with Machinetta proxies, searched a battle space and destroyed targets. Taken together, the experiments in the two domains show not only that our approach is effective at coordinating very large teams but also suggests that it is reasonably general.

To better understand the information sharing algorithm, we looked in detail at exactly how many messages must be propagated around the network to make the routing efficient (Figure 6). Using 8000 agents we varied the number of messages the eventual recipient agent would send before the source of some information sent that information onto the network. Notice that only a few messages are required to dramatically affect the average message delivery time.

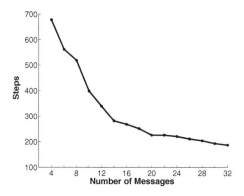

Fig. 6. Association between number of relative messages and delivery time. The y-axis shows the number of agents the message passed through before reaching the recipient agent. The x-axis shows the strength of relationship between the messages used to train the network and the test message

To understand the functionality of the associates network on conflict resolution, simulations were run to see the effect of having associates on a dynamically changing subteam. We wanted to demonstrate that if the subteams have common members (associates), then conflicts between subteams can be detected more easily. Two subteams, each composed of 1-20 members, were formed from a group of 200. For each subteam size, members were chosen at random and then checked against the other subteam for any common team members. Figure 7a shows the calculated percentage of team member overlap when the subteam are initially formed during the simulation, closely matching the calculated probability. To simulate the effect of dynamic subteams, in the case that both initial subteams are mutually exclusive, a team member outside of the existing subteams was chosen at random to replace a current subteam member. Figure 7b shows the average number of times that team members needed to be replaced before a common team member was found.

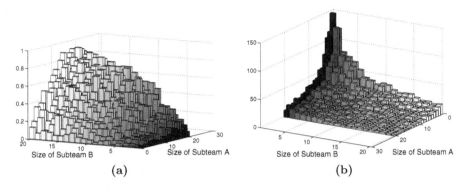

(a)   (b)

Fig. 7. (a) The probability of having at least one common agents vs. subteam size (b)The average number of times that agents need to be replaced in order to have at least one common agents

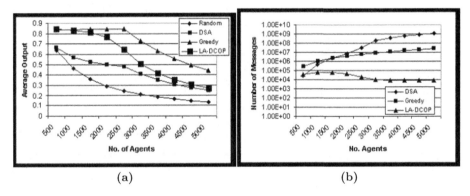

(a)   (b)

Fig. 8. (a) comparing the average output per agent versus the number of agents. (b) the number of messages sent versus the number of agents

Our first experiments tests LA-DCOP against three competitors. The first is DSA, which is shown to outperform other approximate DCOP algorithms in a range of settings [22, 11]; we choose optimal parameters for DSA [43]. DSA does not easily allow multiple roles to be assigned to a single agent so our comparison focuses on the case where each agent can take only one role. As a baseline we also compare against a centralized algorithm that uses a "greedy" assignment[3] and against a random assignment. Figure 8(a) shows the relative performance of each algorithm. The experiment used 2000 roles over 1000 time steps. The y-axis shows the total reward per agent, while the x-axis shows the number of agents. Not suprisingly, the centralized algorithm performs best and the random algorithm performs worst. LA-DCOP is statistically better than DSA. However, the key is the amount of communication used, as shown in Figure 8(b). Notice that the y-axis is a logaritmic scale, thus LA-DCOP uses approximately three orders of magnitude fewer messages than the greedy algorithm and four orders of magnitude less messages than DSA. Thus, LA-DCOP performs better than DSA despite using far less communication and only marginally worse than a centralized approach, despite using only a tiny fraction of the number of messages.

7   Related Work

Coordination of distributed entities is an extensively studied problem[6, 5, 17, 20, 35]. A key design decision is how the control is distributed among the group members. Solutions range from completely centralized[9], to hierarchical[8, 14] to completely decentralized[41]. While there is not yet definitive, empirical evidence of the strengths and weaknesses of each type of architecture, it is generally considered that centralized coordination can lead to behavior that is closer to optimal, but more distributed coordination is more robust to failures of communications and individual nodes[2]. Creating distributed groups of cooperative autonomous agents and robots that must cooperate in dynamic and hostile environments is a huge challenge that has attracted much attention from the research community[18, 19]. Using a wide range of ideas, researchers have had moderate success in building and understanding flexible and robust teams that can effectively act towards their joint goals[4, 7, 15, 27].

Tidhar [38] used the term "team-oriented programming" to describe a conceptual framework for specifying team behaviors based on mutual beliefs and joint plans, coupled with organizational structures. His framework also addressed the issue of team selection [38] — team selection matches the "skills" required for executing a team plan against agents that have those skills. Jennings's GRATE* [15] uses a teamwork module, implementing a model of cooperation based on the joint intentions framework. Each agent has its own *cooperation level* module that negotiates involvement in a joint task and maintains information about its own and other agents' involvement in joint goals. The Electric Elves project was the first human-agent collaboration architecture to include both proxies and humans in a complex environment[4]. COLLAGEN [26] uses a proxy architecture for collaboration between a single agent and user. While these teams have been successful, they have consisted of at most 20 team members and will not easily scale to larger teams.

8   Conclusions

In this paper, we have presented an approach to developing very large teams that overcomes the limitations of previous team work algorithms via the use of an associates network. The algorithms we have developed for scalable team-work are encapsulated in domain independant proxies that have been used to demonstrate effective teamwork with 500 team members in two distinct domains. While progress has been made, significant challenges must be overcome before large teams can be reliably deployed. If these challenges can be overcome, large scale teamwork will revolutionize the way some very complex tasks will be completed, improving efficiency, safety and robustness.

Acknowledgments

This research was supported by AFSOR grant F49620-01-1-0542 and AFRL/MNK grant F08630-03-1-0005. Many people have contributed to this work including Milind Tambe, David Pynadath, Nathan Schurr, Steven Okamoto, Alessandro Farinelli, Mike Lewis, Yang Xu, Elizabeth Liao and Bin Yu.

References

1. Albert-Laszla Barabasi and Eric Bonabeau. Scale free networks. *Scientific American*, pages 60–69, May 2003.
2. Johanna Bryson. Hierarchy and sequence vs. full parallelism in action selection. In *Intelligent Virtual Agents 2*, pages 113–125, 1999.
3. C. Castelpietra, L. Iocchi, D. Nardi, M. Piaggio, A. Scalzo, and A. Sgorbissa. Co-ordination among heterogenous robotic soccer players. In *Proceedings of IROS'02*, 2002.
4. Hans Chalupsky, Yolanda Gil, Craig A. Knoblock, Kristina Lerman, Jean Oh, David V. Pynadath, Thomas A. Russ, and Milind Tambe. Electric Elves: Agent technology for supporting human organizations. *AI Magazine*, 23(2):11–24, 2002.
5. D. Cockburn and N. Jennings. *Foundations of Distributed Artificial Intelligence*, chapter ARCHON: A Distributed Artificial Intelligence System For Industrial Applications, pages 319–344. Wiley, 1996.
6. Philip R. Cohen and Hector J. Levesque. Teamwork. *Nous*, 25(4):487–512, 1991.
7. K. Decker and J. Li. Coordinated hospital patient scheduling. In *Proceedings of the 1998 International Conference on Multi-Agent Systems (ICMAS'98)*, pages 104–111, Paris, July 1998.
8. Vincent Decugis and Jacques Ferber. Action selection in an autonomous agent with a hierarchical distributed reactive planning architecture. In *Proceedings of the Second International Conference on Autonomous Agents*, 1998.
9. T. Estlin, T. Mann, A. Gray, G. Rapideau, R. Castano, S. Chein, and E. Mjolsness. An integrated system for multi-rover scientific exploration. In *Proceedings of AAAI'99*, 1999.
10. Alessandro Farinelli, Paul Scerri, and Milind Tambe. Building large-scale robot systems: Distributed role assignment in dynamic, uncertain domains. In *Proceedings of Workshop on Representations and Approaches for Time-Critical Decentralized Resource, Role and Task Allocation*, 2003.

11. Stephen Fitzpatrick and Lambert Meertens. *Stochastic Algorithms: Foundations and Applications, Proceedings SAGA 2001*, volume LNCS 2264, chapter An Experimental Assessment of a Stochastic, Anytime, Decentralized, Soft Colourer for Sparse Graphs, pages 49–64. Springer-Verlag, 2001.

12. Dani Goldberg, Vincent Cicirello, M Bernardine Dias, Reid Simmons, Stephen Smith, and Anthony (Tony) Stentz. Market-based multi-robot planning in a distributed layered architecture. In *Multi-Robot Systems: From Swarms to Intelligent Automata: Proceedings from the 2003 International Workshop on Multi-Robot Systems*, volume 2, pages 27–38. Kluwer Academic Publishers, 2003.

13. Barbara Grosz and Sarit Kraus. Collaborative plans for complex group actions. *Artificial Intelligence*, 86:269–358, 1996".

14. Bryan Horling, Roger Mailler, Mark Sims, and Victor Lesser. Using and maintaining organization in a large-scale distributed sensor network. In *In Proceedings of the Workshop on Autonomy, Delegation, and Control (AAMAS03)*, 2003.

15. N. Jennings. The archon systems and its applications. Project Report, 1995.

16. N. R. Jennings. Specification and implementation of a belief-desire-joint-intention architecture for collaborative problem solving. *Intl. Journal of Intelligent and Cooperative Information Systems*, 2(3):289–318, 1993.

17. David Kinny. The distributed multi-agent reasoning system architecture and language specification. Technical report, Australian Artificial intelligence institute, Melbourne, Australia, 1993.

18. Hiraoki Kitano, Minoru Asada, Yasuo Kuniyoshi, Itsuki Noda, Eiichi Osawa, , and Hitoshi Matsubara. RoboCup: A challenge problem for AI. *AI Magazine*, 18(1):73–85, Spring 1997.

19. John Laird, Randolph Jones, and Paul Nielsen. Coordinated behavior of computer generated forces in TacAir-Soar. In *Proceedings of the fourth conference on computer generated forces and behavioral representation*, pages 325–332, Orlando, Florida, 1994.

20. V. Lesser, M. Atighetchi, B. Benyo, B. Horling, A. Raja, R. Vincent, T. Wagner, P. Xuan, and S. Zhang. The UMASS intelligent home project. In *Proceedings of the Third Annual Conference on Autonomous Agents*, pages 291–298, Seattle, USA, 1999.

21. E. Liao, P. Scerri, and K. Sycara. A framework for very large teams. In *AAMAS'04 Workshop on Coalitions and Teams*, 2004.

22. P. J. Modi, W. Shen, and M. Tambe. Distributed constraint optimization and its application. Technical Report ISI-TR-509, University of Southern California/Information Sciences Institute, 2002.

23. R. Nair, T. Ito, M. Tambe, and S. Marsella. Task allocation in robocup rescue simulation domain. In *Proceedings of the International Symposium on RoboCup*, 2002.

24. Regis Vincent Paul Scerri and Roger Mailler, editors. *Proceedings of AAMAS'04 Workshop on Challenges in the Coordination of Large Scale MultiAgent Systems*, 2004.

25. David Pynadath and Milind Tambe. Multiagent teamwork: Analyzing the optimality and complexity of key theories and models. In *First International Joint Conference on Autonomous Agents and Multi-Agent Systems (AAMAS'02)*, 2002.

26. C. Rich and C. Sidner. COLLAGEN: When agents collaborate with people. In *Proceedings of the International Conference on Autonomous Agents (Agents'97)"*, 1997.

27. P. Rybski, S. Stoeter, M. Erickson, M. Gini, D. Hougen, and N. Papanikolopoulos. A team of robotic agents for surveillance. In *Proceedings of the fourth international conference on autonomous agents*, pages 9–16, 2000.

28. P. Scerri, A. Farinelli, S. Okamoto, and M. Tambe. Allocating roles in extreme teams. In *Proceedings of AAMAS'04, Poster Presentation*, 2004.

29. P. Scerri, D. Pynadath, and M. Tambe. Towards adjustable autonomy for the real world. *Journal of Artificial Intelligence Research*, 17:171–228", 2002.

30. P. Scerri, D. V. Pynadath, L. Johnson, P. Rosenbloom, N. Schurr, M Si, and M. Tambe. A prototype infrastructure for distributed robot-agent-person teams. In *The Second International Joint Conference on Autonomous Agents and Multiagent Systems*, 2003.

31. P. Scerri, K. Sycara, and M Tambe. Adjustable autonomy in the context of coordination. In *AIAA 3rd "Unmanned Unlimited" Technical Conference, Workshop and Exhibit*, 2004. Invited Paper.

32. P. Scerri, Yang. Xu, E. Liao, J. Lai, and K. Sycara. Scaling teamwork to very large teams. In *Proceedings of AAMAS'04*, 2004.

33. Daniel Schrage and George Vachtsevanos. Software enabled control for intelligent uavs. In *Proceedings of the 1999 IEEE International Symposium on Computer Aided Control System Design*, Hawaii, August 1999.

34. D. Shmoys and E. Tardos. An approximation algorithm for the generalized assignment problem. *Mathematical Programming*, 62:461–474, 1993.

35. Munindar Singh. Developing formal specifications to coordinate hetrogeneous agents. In *Proceedings of third international conference on multiagent systems*, pages 261–268, 1998.

36. Milind Tambe. Agent architectures for flexible, practical teamwork. *National Conference on AI (AAAI97)*, pages 22–28, 1997.

37. Milind Tambe, Wei-Min Shen, Maja Mataric, David Pynadath, Dani Goldberg, Pragnesh Jay Modi, Zhun Qiu, and Behnam Salemi. Teamwork in cyberspace: using TEAMCORE to make agents team-ready. In *AAAI Spring Symposium on agents in cyberspace*, 1999.

38. G. Tidhar, A.S. Rao, and E.A. Sonenberg. Guided team selection. In *Proceedings of the Second International Conference on Multi-Agent Systems*, 1996.

39. Duncan Watts and Steven Strogatz. Collective dynamics of small world networks. *Nature*, 393:440–442, 1998.

40. B. B. Werger and M. J. Mataric. Broadcast of local eligibility for multi-target observation. In *Proc. of 5th Int. Symposium on Distributed Autonomous Robotic Systems (DARS)*, 2000.

41. Tony White and Bernard Pagurek. Towards multi swarm problem solving in networks. In *Proceedings of the International conference on multi-agent systems*, pages 333–340, Paris, July 1998.

42. Y. Xu, M. Lewis, K. Sycara, and P. Scerri. Information sharing in very large teams. In *In AAMAS'04 Workshop on Challenges in Coordination of Large Scale MultiAgent Systems*, 2004.

43. W. Zhang and L. Wittenburg. Distributed breakout revisited. In *Proceedings of AAAI'02*, 2002.

Maximal Clique Based Distributed Coalition Formation for Task Allocation in Large-Scale Multi-agent Systems

Predrag T. Tošić and Gul A. Agha

Open Systems Laboratory, Department of Computer Science,
University of Illinois at Urbana-Champaign,
Mailing address: Siebel Center for Computer Science,
201 N. Goodwin Ave., Urbana, IL 61801, USA
{p-tosic, agha}@cs.uiuc.edu

Abstract. We present a fully distributed algorithm for coalition formation among autonomous agents. The algorithm is based on two main ideas. One is a distributed computation of maximal cliques (of bounded sizes) in the underlying graph that captures the interconnection communication topology of the agents. Hence, given the current configuration of the agents, the coalitions that are formed are characterized by a high degree of connectivity, and therefore a high fault tolerance with respect to the subsequent node and/or link failures. The second idea is that each agent chooses its most preferable coalition based on how highly the agent values each such coalition in terms of the coalition members' combined resources or capabilities. Coalitions with sufficient resources for fulfilling highly desirable tasks are preferable to the coalitions with resources that suffice only for completing less valuable tasks. We envision variants of our distributed algorithm presented herein to prove themselves useful coordination subroutines in many massively multi-agent system applications where the agents may repeatedly need to form temporary groups or coalitions of modest sizes in an efficient, online and fully distributed manner.

Keywords: distributed algorithms, large-scale multi-agent systems, distributed group formation, agent coalitions.

1 Introduction and Motivation

Agent coordination poses a number of challenges to a designer of a large-scale *multi-agent system (MAS)*. In particular, in order to be able to effectively coordinate, agents need to be able to *reach consensus* on various matters of common interest. The two particularly prominent distributed consensus problems that often arise in *MAS* applications are those of *leader election* (e.g., [7, 18]) and *coalition formation*. Group or coalition formation is an important issue in distributed systems in general (e.g., [7]), and *MAS* in particular (e.g., [29, 25]). Given a collection of communicating agents, the goal in distributed coalition formation is that these agents, based on their local knowledge only, decide how to effectively self-organize into coalitions, so that each agent knows which coalition(s) it belongs to.

There are several critical issues that the *MAS* designer needs to address in the context of distributed coalition formation. First, what is the desired notion of a coalition

T. Ishida, L. Gasser, and H. Nakashima (Eds.): MMAS 2004, LNAI 3446, pp. 104–120, 2005.

in a given setting? Second, a distributed coalition formation mechanism - that is, a distributed algorithm that enables the agents to effectively form coalitions - needs to be provided. Third, coalitions and each agent's knowledge about its coalition membership need to be maintained and, when needed, appropriately updated. Fourth, are the coalitions to be allowed to overlap, so that an agent may simultaneously belong to two or more coalitions? These and other challenges related to autonomous agents forming coalitions have been extensively studied in the literature on multi-agent systems, e.g., [8, 10, 11, 14, 15, 29]. They have also arisen in our own recent work on parametric models and a scalable simulation of the large scale ($10^3 - 10^4$ agents) ensembles of autonomous unmanned vehicles on a multi-task mission [5, 6, 19, 20].

Herein, we restrict our attention to the second issue above. We propose a particular mechanism (distributed algorithm) for an effective coalition formation that ensembles of autonomous agents can use as one of their basic coordination subroutines. A need for a dynamic, fully distributed, efficient and online coalition formation may arise due to a number of different factors, such as geographical dispersion of the agents, heterogeneity of tasks and their resource requirements, heterogeneity of agents' capabilities, and so on [20]. While for the small- and medium-scale systems of, e.g., robots or unmanned vehicles, a fully or partially centralized approach to coalition formation and maintenance may be feasible, the large scale systems (with the number of agents of orders of magnitude $10^3 - 10^4$ or higher) appear to necessitate a genuinely distributed approach.

The proposed algorithm is a graph algorithm. The underlying undirected graph captures the communication network topology among the agents. Each agent is a node in the graph. As for the edges, the necessary requirement for an edge between two nodes to exist is that the two nodes be able to directly communicate with one another. That is, an unordered pair of nodes $\{A, B\}$ is an edge of the underlying graph if and only if A can communicate messages to B, or B can communicate messages to A, or both.

The basic idea is to efficiently and in a fully decentralized manner partition this graph into (preferably, *maximal*) *cliques* of nodes. These coalitions are then maintained until they are no longer useful or meaningful. For instance, the coalitions should be transformed, or else simply dissolved, when the interconnection topology considerably changes, either due to the agents' mobility, or because many old links have died out and perhaps many new, different links have formed, and the like. Another possible reason to abandon the existing coalition structure is when the agents determine that the coalitions have accomplished the set of tasks that these coalitions were formed to address. Thus, in an actual *MAS* application, the proposed coalition formation algorithm may need to be invoked a number of times as a coordination subroutine.

The rest of the paper is organized as follows. The preliminaries are covered in Section 2. We include in this section some examples of large-scale multi-agent systems that are characterized by the *sparse communication network topologies,* as well as a brief overview of the most relevant related work. In Section 3, we succinctly state the problem addressed, the approach taken, and the critical assumptions that need to hold in order for our approach to be applicable. Section 4 is the central part of the paper: we first outline our *Maximal Clique-based Distributed Coalition Formation (MCDCF)* algorithm, and then provide a simple yet illustrative toy-size example of how the algorithm works. Section 5 includes an outline of the cost analysis of the algorithm, and some discussion. Finally, we summarize in Section 6.

2   Coalition Formation in Large-Scale Multi-agent Systems

Large ensembles of autonomous agents provide an important class of examples where the agents' capability to coordinate and, in particular, to self-organize into groups or coalitions, is often of utmost importance.

We propose herewith a distributed coalition formation algorithm based on the idea that, in peer-to-peer (in particular, *leaderless*) *MAS*, an agent would prefer to form a coalition with those agents that it can communicate with directly, and, moreover, where every member of such a potential coalition can communicate with any other member directly. That is, the preferable coalitions are *(maximal) cliques*. It is well-known that finding a maximal clique in an arbitrary graph is **NP**-hard in the centralized setting [3, 4]. This implies the computational hardness that, in general, each node faces when trying to determine the maximal clique(s) it belongs to. However, if the degree of a node is sufficiently small, then finding all maximal cliques this node belongs to may become computationally feasible. If one cannot guarantee that, or *a priori* does not know if, all the nodes in a given underlying *MAS* interconnection topology are of a small degree, then one has to impose additional constraints in order to ensure that the agents are not attempting to solve an infeasible problem.

We describe our distributed maximal clique based coalition formation algorithm in Section 4. Variations of this basic algorithm can be designed to meet the needs of various types of agents, such as, to give some examples, the following:

- the classical cooperative *distributed problem solving (DPS)* agents [8, 9, 14, 15];
- different kinds of self-interested, strictly competing or competing-and-cooperating agents [11, 20] where concepts, paradigms and tools from the *N-person game theory* have found many applications; and, more generally,
- various bounded-resource, imperfect-knowledge agents acting in complex environments [20, 26] that are only *partially accessible* to any agent; such autonomous agents are thus characterized by the *bounded rationality* [16].

One may ask, why would this, maximal-clique based approach be promising for the very large scale (or *massive*) multi-agent systems (*MMAS*) that may contain ensembles of anywhere from thousands to millions of agents? The underlying network of such *MMAS* is bound to be very large, thus rendering even many typically feasible (i.e., polynomial-time in the number of agents) graph algorithms obsolete due to their prohibitive cost - let alone allowing distributed coordination strategies that are based on the graph theoretic algorithms that are, in the centralized setting, **NP**-hard in general.

However, there is one critical observation that saves the day of our approach: even if the underlying graph is indeed very large, in many important *MMAS* applications this graph will also tend to be *very sparse*. That is, a typical node in such a graph will tend to have only a handful of neighbors. Therefore, a distributed algorithm where agents reason and communicate strictly locally, where no *flooding* of the network is ever performed (or needed), and where each agent needs to store and work with only the data pertaining to its near-by agents, can still be designed to be sufficiently efficient.

Some examples of the engineering, socio-technical and socio-economic systems and infrastructures that can be modeled as *MMAS* and that are also characterized by the aforementioned *sparseness* of the underlying network topology, include the following:

(i) *Large-scale* ($10^3 - 10^4$) *ensembles of micro-UAVs* or other similar autonomous unmanned vehicles deployed, for example, in a surveillance or a search-and-rescue mission over a sizable geographic area. Unlike the scenarios where dozens of *macro UAVs* are deployed, where a centralized control and/or one human operator per UAV are affordable and perhaps the most efficient and robust way of deployment, in a very large scale system of autonomous *micro UAVs* no central control is feasible or even possible, and the run-time human intervention is either minimal or nonexistent. Such micro-UAV ensembles need to be able to coordinate, self-organize, and self-adapt to the changing environments in a truly decentralized, dynamic and autonomous manner. For more on the design and simulation challenges of such large-scale ensembles of micro-UAVs, see [5, 19, 20].

(ii) *Smart sensor networks* that include anywhere from thousands to millions of tiny sensors, each of which often of only a few millimeters in size, and of a rather limited computational power and communication range and bandwidth. Such smart sensors usually communicate via *local broadcasts* with very limited ranges. The main "communication mode" of the agents in our algorithm in *Section 4* are precisely the local broadcasts. Due to their small memory capacities and low power consumption requirements, smart sensors need to simultaneously minimize both the amount of local processing, and the amount of communication.

(iii) Various *social networks*, and, in particular, various variants of the *'small-world' networks* where, in addition to the strictly local connectivity in the communication network topology, a relatively few long-range connections are also present [23, 24]. A typical node in such a network will have only a handful of neighbors it can directly communicate with, and, moreover, most or nearly all of these neighbors in the network will also tend to be the neighbors in the usual, physical proximity sense.

(iv) Various *socio-technical infrastructures*, such as, e.g., various transportation systems, power grids, etc. An ambitious project on realistic, large-scale modeling and simulation of infrastructures such as the city traffic systems, called *TRANSIMS*, is described at [22] and in the documents found therein.

2.1   Related Work

A variety of coalition formation mechanisms have been proposed in the *MAS* literature both in the context of DPS agents that are all sharing the same goal (as, e.g., in [15]) and in the context of self-interested agents where each agent has its own individual agenda (as, e.g., in [14, 29]). In particular, the problem of distributed task or resource allocation, and how is this task allocation coupled to what coalition structures are most desirable in a given scenario [8, 15], are also of central importance in our own work on a concrete *MAS* application, namely, a scalable parametric model and software simulation of unmanned aerial vehicles (UAVs) that are residing and acting in bounded resource multi-task environments [5, 19, 20].

Another body of MAS literature highly relevant to the distributed coalition formation and task and/or resource allocation, casts the distributed resource allocation problems into the distributed constraint satisfaction and/or optimization (DCS/DCO) terms
[8, 9, 10]. Of a particular relevance to our work herein and other possible extensions of
the original maximal clique based coalition formation algorithm presented in [21] are
the references [15] and [9]. While Modi et al. in [9] offer the most complete formalization of various distributed resource and/or task allocation problems, as well as general
mappings to the appropriate types of *(dynamic) distributed constraint satisfaction or
optimization* problems, their approach is not suitable for a direct application to our
modeling framework of massively multi-agent systems in general (see, e.g., [20]), and
the application domains we had in mind when devising the algorithm presented herein,
in particular. Namely, the agents in [9] are strictly cooperative, share the same goals,
and, as such, are not endowed with any notion of individual utilities or preferences.
While we have studied cooperative *MAS* in [20] and elsewhere, as well, one of our
main assumptions is that, due to a large scale of the system and a high dynamism and
unpredictability of the changes in the environment, no shared or global knowledge about
the environment is maintained. In particular, each agent has its own individual preferences over the possible (local) states of the world. The collaboration is then achieved
through "encoding" incentives into the individual agents' *individual behavior functions*
[19], and thus using the *incentive engineering* approach [2] to enable the agents to
cooperatively coordinate with one another.

The importance of DCS in *MAS* in general is discussed, e.g., in [28]. However,
further discussion of DCS based approaches to distributed resource or task allocation
and coalition formation is beyond the scope of this paper.

3   Problem Statement and Main Assumptions

The main purpose of this work is a fully distributed, scalable and efficient algorithm
for ensembles of autonomous agents to use as a subroutine within their coordination
strategy, with the purpose of efficiently forming temporary coalitions of modest sizes.

Each agent is equipped with a tuple of its internal resources or *capabilities* [15].
Each entry in the capability tuple of any agent is a nonnegative real number. Likewise,
each task requires a certain nonnegative amount of each of the individual resources
from this tuple in order to be serviced. A single agent, or a coalition of two or more
agents, can service a given task if and only if their joint capabilities suffice with respect
to that task's resource consumption requirements. That is, for each component of the
capability vector, the sum of the corresponding values taken over all the agents in the
coalition has to be greater than, or equal to, the value of the corresponding component
of the chosen task's resource consumption vector.

Our distributed maximal clique based coalition formation algorithm is described in
the next section. For this algorithm to be applicable, the following basic assumptions
need to hold:

- Agents communicate with one another by exchanging messages either via local broadcasts, or in a peer-to-peer fashion.

- Communication bandwidth availability is assumed sufficient.

- Each agent has a sufficient local memory (including the message buffers) for storing all the information received from other agents.

- Communication is reliable during the coalition formation, in the following sense: if an agent, A, sends a message to another agent B, then either agent B gets *exactly* the same message that A has sent, or else the communication has failed, so that B does not receive anything from A at all. In particular, we assume no *scrambled* or otherwise modified messages are ever received by any agent. Of course, once the coalitions have been already formed, the above assumption on communication reliability need no longer hold[1].

- Each agent has a unique global identifier, 'UID', and the agent knows its UID.

- There is a total ordering, $\prec$, on the set of UIDs, and each agent knows this ordering.

- Each agent has, or else can efficiently obtain, a reliable knowledge of which other agents are within its communication range.

- The *veracity* assumption holds, i.e., an agent can trust the information received from the neighboring agents.

On the other hand, an agent need not *a priori* know the UIDs of any of the other agents, or, indeed, how many other agents are present in the system at any time.

4   *MCDCF* Algorithm

After the preliminaries and the clear statement of the problem addressed and the assumptions made, we now present, analyze and discuss our distributed coalition formation algorithm. The *Maximal Clique based Distributed Coalition Formation (MCDCF)* algorithm will be presented in subsection 4.1. An example of a simple network of agents, and how the algorithm works when applied to this network, is given in subsection 4.2. An outline of the algorithm's cost analysis will follow in Section 5.

4.1   Algorithm Description

We approach distributed coalition formation for task allocation as follows. The candidate coalitions are required to be cliques of uniformly bounded sizes. That is, the system designer, based on the application at hand and the available system resources (local computational capabilities of each agent, bandwidth of the agent-to-agent communication links, etc.), *a priori* chooses a threshold, $K = K(n)$, such that only the coalitions of sizes up to K are considered. Agents themselves subsequently form coalitions in a fully distributed and online manner, as follows. Each agent (i) first learns of

---

[1] As this requirement is still restrictive, and considerably limits the robustness of our algorithm, we will try to relax this assumption in our future work, and enable the agents to effectively form coalitions even in the presence of some limited amount of communication noise during the coalition formation process itself.

who are its neighbors, then (ii) determines the appropriate *candidate coalitions,* that the agent hopes are (preferably maximal, but certainly of sizes bounded by K) cliques that it belongs to, then (iii) evaluates the utility value of each such candidate coalition, measured in terms of the joint resources of all the potential coalition members, then (iv) chooses the most desirable candidate coalition, and, finally, (v) sends this choice to all its neighbors. This basic procedure is then repeated, together with all agents updating their knowledge of (a) what are the preferred coalitions of their neighbors, and (b) what coalitions have already been formed.

In addition to its globally unique identifier UID, which we assume is a positive integer, and the vector of capabilities, each agent also has two local flags that it uses in communication with other agents. One of the flags is the binary "decision flag", which indicates whether or not this agent has already joined some coalition. Namely, $decision \in \{0, 1\}$, and the value of this flag is 0 as long as the agent still has not irrevocably committed to what coalition it is joining. The second flag is the "choice flag", which is used to indicate to other agents, how happy is the agent with its current tentative choice or proposal of the coalition to be formed. That is, the choice flag indicates the level of an agent's urgency that its proposal for a particular coalition to be formed be accepted by the neighbors to whom this proposal is being sent. If an agent v_i sends to its neighbors the choice flag value $choice(i) = 0$, that means that this agent has no satisfactory alternatives to its currently proposed coalition. The choice flag value of 1 indicates that an agent can afford to change its coalition choice, but that each of the available alternative coalitions is strictly less preferred than the current proposal. Finally, $choice(i) = 2$ indicates that agent v_i has alternative choices that are of equal preference as the currently proposed coalition.

We remark that any *candidate coalition,* that is, a subset of the set of all neighbors of an agent, such that the agent currently considers this subset to be a possible choice of the coalition this agent would like to form, need not be a clique, let alone a *maximal clique.* Indeed, based on its strictly local knowledge, the agent in general does not know which of its candidate coalitions are cliques, if any. However, only those candidate coalitions that indeed *are cliques* will ever be agreed upon by the participating agents, and therefore have a chance of possibly becoming the *actual* coalitions. This observation justifies the name of our algorithm.

We split the *MCDCF* algorithm into six stages. Four of these six are iteratively repeated until the consensus on coalition formation is reached. We point out, however, that *each agent executes these stages asynchronously and in parallel with the other agents.* The only assumption about the synchronization among the agents is that an agent does not begin another iteration of *Stages 2 - 5* before its neighbors are done with the previous iteration. Should an agent fail to receive the update from one of its neighbors within the pre-specified time slot, the agent assumes that its neighbor is no longer available for the coalition formation, and deletes this neighbor's UID from all the appropriate lists. In the sequel, we won't bother distinguishing between an agent or a communication network node, v_i, and this agent's (alternatively, node's) UID, i; the intended meaning in any given situation will be clear from the context.

Stage 0: Each agent, asynchronously and in parallel with all other agents, broadcasts a four-tuple to all its immediate neighbors. The entries in this tuple are (i) the agent's

UID, (ii) the agent's list of immediate neighbors, L(i), that includes i, (iii) the value of the choice flag that indicates that the list sent is the neighborhood list, and (iv) the value of the decision flag. Each agent also receives the corresponding tuples from all of its neighbors. Those neighbors whose messages have not been received within the allotted time are discarded from the future coalition considerations.

Stage 1: Each agent i locally computes the overlaps of its neighborhood list with the neighborhood lists that it has received from its neighbors, $C(i,j) \leftarrow L(i) \cap L(j)$. These list intersections are then ordered with respect to the list size.

Each agent repeats *Stages 2 - 5* until it either reaches a consensus on what coalition it is joining, or else is left with no choice but to form the trivial single-member coalition.

Stage 2: Agent i looks for information from its neighbors, whether they have joined a coalition "for good" during the previous round. Those neighbors that have are deleted from the neighborhood list $L(i)$; the intersection lists $C(i,j)$ and the candidate coalition lists $C(i)$ are also updated accordingly, and those $C(i,k)$ for which k is deleted from the neighborhood list $L(i)$ are also deleted. Likewise, the coalition values $val[C(i,k)]$ are updated as appropriate.

Stage 3: Agent i picks one of the most preferable lists $C(i,j)$; let $C(i) \leftarrow chosen [C(i,j)]$. If the group or coalition size is the main criterion, then one of the lists of maximal length is chosen. If the combined *capabilities* of each tentative coalition for servicing various tasks are the main criterion, then each agent first evaluates or estimates the *coalition value* with respect to its local knowledge of the existing tasks and their demands in terms of the coalitional capabilities. To evaluate these coalition values, agent i needs to obtain information about other, near-by agents' capabilities. The agent then orders possible future coalitions based on these estimated coalition values, and picks as its current coalition proposal one of the possible coalitions with the highest coalition value. Since the assumption is that the capability vector of each agent has all entries nonnegative, this *monotonicity property* ensures that no proper subset of a candidate maximal clique coalition is ever chosen - except in the cases when the clique size exceeds the threshold, $K(n)$.

Stage 4: Each agent sends its tuple with its UID, the tentatively chosen list $C(i)$, the value of the choice flag, and the value of the decision flag, to all its neighbors. Likewise, each agent receives the corresponding 4-tuples from its current neighbors.

Stage 5: Agent i compares its chosen list $C(i)$ with the lists $C(j)$ received from its neighbors. If a satisfactory clique that includes the node i exists, and all members of this clique have selected it at this iteration as their current coalition of choice (that is, if $C(i) = C(j)$ for all $j \in C(i)$), this will be efficiently recognized by the agents that are forming this particular clique. The decision flag of each agent $j : j \in C(i)$ is then set to 1, the coalition is formed, and this information is broadcast to all of the neighbors. In particular, agent i locally broadcasts its agreed-upon coalition, and decision flag $decision(i) = 1$, to all of its still remaining neighbors. Else, if no such agreement is reached, then agent i, based on its UID and priority, and its current value of the *choice flag*, either does nothing, or else changes its mind about its current coalition of choice, $C(i)$.

Each agent uses *time-outs* in order to place an upper bound on for how long it may be waiting to hear from any other agent during any stage of the algorithm. If agent v_p has sent a message to agent v_q, and the latter is not responding, then there are four possibilities: (i) agent v_q has failed; (ii) the communication link from v_q to v_p has failed; (iii) while v_q is in v_p's communication range, the converse does not hold (but v_p may not know it), and (iv) either the agent v_q, or the communication link from v_q to v_p, is too slow. In each case, once v_p has waited sufficiently long to hear from v_q, v_p will simply consider v_q unavailable for the joint coalition formation, and will delete v_q from its candidate coalition lists. Thus, case (iv) will be treated by agent v_p in exactly the same way as the other three cases.

In order to ensure that the algorithm avoids cycling in every possible scenario, once an agent, v_i, changes its mind about the preferred coalition $C(i)$, it is not allowed through the remaining rounds of the algorithm to go back to its old choice(s). Once no other choices are left, this particular agent sticks to its current choice, and waits for other agents to settle to their choices. This requirement ensures the ultimate convergence to a coalition structure that all agents (locally) agree on. That is, under the assumptions stated in the previous section, the agents will reach consensus on the coalition structure after a finite number of iterations through the *Stages 2 - 5.*

Once all the agents exit the iterated execution of the *Stages 2 - 5,* each formed coalition will indeed be a clique. Moreover, those agent coalitions whose sizes do not exceed the pre-specified threshold, K, are also maximal in a sense that, given such a coalition C, no agent(s) outside of this coalition can be added to it, so that the following requirements simultaneously all hold: (i) each of the new agents is already adjacent to all the "old" coalition members of C, (ii) if more than one new agent is added, then all the added agents are also pairwise neighbors to each other, (iii) the newly added agent(s) do not already belong to a coalition (or coalitions) that have already been formed, and (iv) the new size of the augmented coalition C is still at most K.

However, it is easy to construct examples of the underlying graphs and the particular runs of the algorithm such that, once every agent joins a coalition and the algorithm terminates, several agents end up in trivial coalitions. It is therefore reasonable, in many application contexts, to introduce an *optional Stage 6* of the algorithm during which some of these small and, therefore, potentially not sufficiently useful coalitions, may be merged together. Thus, if some two small coalitions, or one small and one bigger coalition, are adjacent to each other[2], they can be merged together. For an illustration, we refer the reader to the worked out example in subsection 4.2.

4.2   How MCDCF Algorithm Works: A Simple Example

To show how the *MCDCF* algorithm works, we use a simple example. The interconnection topology of a group of agents is given in *Figure 1.* For simplicity, we assume that the only value associated with each coalition is the coalition's size. We also assume that no agent falls behind others by too much, i.e., that all agents complete each iteration of *Stages 2 - 5* within the allotted time.

---

[2] That is, if there exist node x in the first coalition and node y in the second such that x and y are adjacent in the underlying graph.

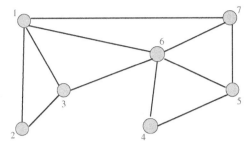

Fig. 1. An example: the agents' starting communication topology

We notice that the largest clique that any agent in this example belongs to is a 3-clique. However, several agents belong to multiple triangles, so this toy example is instructive insofar as how the agents break ties, avoid deadlocks, and reach consensus on the coalition structure.

First, the initialization stage takes place, during which each agent locally broadcasts its list of neighbors to each of its neighboring agents. Then each agent, asynchronously and in parallel with the other agents, forms the initial candidate coalitions by computing the pairwise neighborhood list intersections. However, not all of thereby formed coalitions are *reachable*: if $C(i,k) \subsetneq C(i,j)$ then there exists a (maximal reachable) candidate coalition $C(i,\cdot)$, $C(i,k) \subseteq C(i,\cdot) \subsetneq C(i,j)$, such that for some agent $v_p : p \in C(i,\cdot)$, there exists an agent v_q such that $q \in C(i,j)$, and v_p and v_q are not adjacent to each other. Clearly, this agent v_p will never agree on forming the bigger coalition $C(i,j)$, since this coalition would include at least one agent that v_p cannot directly communicate with. Hence, all such sets $C(i,j)$ that *properly include* other prospective coalitions can be safely deleted from the list of candidate coalitions.

In our example, agent v_1 can safely delete the set $\{1, 3, 6, 7\}$, as this coalition can never be agreed upon by all four agents. Concretely, v_3 will never agree to form a coalition that includes v_7 (and vice versa). Furthermore, based on the information received from v_3 and v_7, agents v_1 and v_6 can readily and safely *infer* that the coalition $\{1, 3, 6, 7\}$ cannot be agreed on.

Once all such *unreachable coalitions* are deleted, the column denoted *"candidate coalitions $C(i,j)$"* in *Table 1* is obtained. After that, each agent picks one of the available choices. Under the *monotonicity assumption* discussed earlier, each agent will select one of the *maximal sets (potential cliques)* that it belongs to. Each agent also appropriately sets the value of its *choice flag*. When the coalition size is the criterion of that coalition's value, agent v_1, for example, would set its *choice flag* to 2, since it has more choices that are just as preferable as the selected candidate coalition, the set $\{1, 2, 3\}$. Once this step is completed by all agents, the overall configuration is reached as depicted in *Table 1*, where each row represents the corresponding agent's current local knowledge of the neighborhood structure and of its choice of a tentative coalition.

For simplicity, we have assumed in this example that, in case of a tie, each agent picks the lexicographically lowest coalition. Hence, the agents v_1, v_2 and v_3 immediately reach the agreement on forming the coalition $\{1, 2, 3\}$. The other four agents, however, do not reach an agreement after the first iteration. Let us assume that, among sev-

Table 1. State of each agent v_i at the end of first iteration

Node	neighborhood $L(i)$	nbhd. overlaps $L(i) \cap L(j)$	candidate coalitions $C(i,j)$	chosen $C(i)$	choice flag
v_1	$\{1,2,3,6,7\}$	$\{1,2,3\}$, $\{1,2,3,6\}$, $\{1,3,6,7\}$, $\{1,6,7\}$	$\{1,2,3\}$, $\{1,3,6\}$, $\{1,6,7\}$	$\{1,2,3\}$	2
v_2	$\{1,2,3\}$	$\{1,2,3\}$	$\{1,2,3\}$	$\{1,2,3\}$	0
v_3	$\{1,2,3,6\}$	$\{1,2,3,6\}$, $\{1,2,3\}$, $\{1,3,6\}$	$\{1,2,3\}$, $\{1,3,6\}$	$\{1,2,3\}$	2
v_4	$\{4,5,6\}$	$\{4,5,6\}$	$\{4,5,6\}$	$\{4,5,6\}$	0
v_5	$\{4,5,6,7\}$	$\{4,5,6\}$, $\{4,5,6,7\}$, $\{5,6,7\}$	$\{4,5,6\}$, $\{5,6,7\}$	$\{4,5,6\}$	2
v_6	$\{1,3,4,5,6,7\}$	$\{1,3,6\}$, $\{1,3,6,7\}$, $\{4,5,6\}$, $\{1,5,6,7\}$, $\{4,5,6,7\}$,	$\{1,3,6\}$, $\{1,6,7\}$, $\{4,5,6\}$, $\{5,6,7\}$	$\{1,3,6\}$	2
v_7	$\{1,5,6,7\}$	$\{1,6,7\}$, $\{1,5,6,7\}$, $\{5,6,7\}$	$\{1,6,7\}$, $\{5,6,7\}$	$\{1,6,7\}$	2

eral agents with the same value of the choice flag, $choice > 0$, the ones with the lowest index among their neighbors are required to change their proposed coalitions. In our example, this means that, in the second iteration, v_5 drops $\{4,5,6\}$ and selects $\{5,6,7\}$ instead. Upon doing so, agent v_5 also adjusts its value of the choice flag, and broadcasts these changes to agents v_4, v_6 and v_7. Also, since agents v_1 and v_3 are no longer available, agents v_6 and v_7 delete v_1, v_3 from their neighborhood lists, and update the candidate coalitions accordingly.

After each of the agents v_5, v_6 and v_7 performs the described updates, and then locally broadcasts its new configuration to all of the remaining neighbors, the overall configuration at the end of the second round is as in *Table 2*.

Table 2. Coalition configuration at the end of the second iteration

Node	candidate coalitions $C(i,j)$	chosen $C(i)$	choice flag	decision status
v_1	$\{1,2,3\}$, $\{1,3,6\}$, $\{1,6,7\}$	$\{1,2,3\}$	...	done
v_2	$\{1,2,3\}$	$\{1,2,3\}$	...	done
v_3	$\{1,2,3\}$, $\{1,3,6\}$	$\{1,2,3\}$	...	done
v_4	$\{4,5,6\}$	$\{4,5,6\}$	0	busy
v_5	$\{5,6,7\}$	$\{5,6,7\}$	0	busy
v_6	$\{4,5,6\}$, $\{5,6,7\}$	$\{4,5,6\}$	2	busy
v_7	$\{5,6,7\}$	$\{5,6,7\}$	0	busy

After the second round is completed, the only agent that still has some "maneuvering room" is v_6; since there is still no agreement, and $choice(v_6) > 0$, whereas $choice(i) = 0$ for all $i \neq 6$ such that v_i is not done yet, in the next round v_6 changes its coalition proposal to $\{5,6,7\}$, thereby reaching the consensus with v_5 and v_7, and yielding the final configuration as in *Table 3*.

Table 3. The final coalition configuration; the only unhappy node is v_4

Node	candidate coalitions $C(i, j)$ at the time of agreement	chosen $C(i)$	choice flag	decision status
v_1	$\{1, 2, 3\}$, $\{1, 3, 6\}$, $\{1, 6, 7\}$	$\{1, 2, 3\}$	...	done
v_2	$\{1, 2, 3\}$	$\{1, 2, 3\}$	...	done
v_3	$\{1, 2, 3\}$, $\{1, 3, 6\}$	$\{1, 2, 3\}$	...	done
v_4	$\{4\}$	$\{4\}$	0	doomed
v_5	$\{5, 6, 7\}$	$\{5, 6, 7\}$	0	done
v_6	$\{5, 6, 7\}$	$\{5, 6, 7\}$	0	done
v_7	$\{5, 6, 7\}$	$\{5, 6, 7\}$	0	done

Thus, in the end, each of the agents, except for v_4, has joined (one of) the coalition(s) optimal for it. Since agent v_4 has ended up left out, and since it is adjacent to the coalition $\{v_5, v_6, v_7\}$, it can be merged with this coalition to form a larger coalition $\{v_4, v_5, v_6, v_7\}$ in the optional *Stage 6* (see discussion in subsection 4.1). Given the assumed *monotonicity* and (locally constrained) *super-additivity* of the multi-agent environment, any coalition arising from such a merger clearly cannot be a clique.

5   Algorithm Cost Analysis and Discussion

We now outline the cost analysis of the *MCDCF* algorithm. We will focus on the main resource requirements *per agent*. We analyze under what assumptions will the required amounts of computation time, memory storage and communication be feasible so that an agent would want to venture into participating in the coalition formation based on our algorithm. However, we do not address the issues of, e.g., communication reliability, network delays, and similar.

The first and foremost cost requirement is that the algorithm be of a feasible computational complexity when it comes to its overall worst-case running time. At the very least, this running time needs to be *polynomial in the number of agents, n*. Moreover, for *MMAS* of up to 10^6 agents, the upper bound on the total number of elementary computational steps better be a polynomial of a low degree. We show that, under a restrictive yet reasonable assumption on the sparseness of the underlying network of agents, this goal can be attained. Due to the space constraints, we limit our complexity analysis to that pertaining to *the execution time,* i.e., to the number of elementary computation steps carried out by each agent. We will assume that the time to send and receive messages is not increasing the asymptotic upper bounds on local computations. Since the amount of data that the agents locally broadcast in the algorithm is fairly small (namely, *linear* in the size of the largest list used by an agent), our assumption boils down to assuming a sufficient available bandwidth, sufficiently big buffers for the arriving messages, and no excessive network delays.

We shall split the time complexity analysis into two parts. First, we will estimate the maximum number of rounds, i.e., how many times an agent may need to iterate through the *Stages 2 - 5* (see subsection 4.1). Second, we will show that the amount of computation per agent within a single iteration is relatively small.

Let $K = K(n)$ be a nonnegative, monotonically nondecreasing function of n, and let the class of the underlying graphs of agents be such that, for any positive integer n (except possibly for the first $O(1)$ of them), the size of any clique in the graph is bounded by $K(n)$. To show under what conditions is our algorithm going to iterate at most polynomially many times, we establish the following result:

Proposition 1. *Let an undirected graph with n nodes be such that the bound on the maximum node degree in this graph is given by $K(n) \leq c \cdot \log n$, for some positive constant c. Let's assume each node in the graph is an agent with sufficient computational and communication resources. Then the maximum number of iterations of the algorithm described in Section 4, when executed by the agents, will be polynomial in the number of agents, n.*

Proof. Let $K(n) \leq c \cdot \log n$. Let v_i be an arbitrary agent. Since v_i has at most $K(n)$ neighbors, the maximum number of candidate coalitions that would include agent v_i is at most $2^{K(n)+1}$, which is bounded from above by $2 \cdot 2^{c \log n} = 2n^c$. Since, during a single round of the algorithm, at least one agent has to change its current choice of the proposed coalition, and since the old choice is permanently discarded, at each round the total number of the remaining candidate coalitions in the entire system is reduced by at least one. Since there are at most $n \cdot 2^{K(n)+1} \leq 2n \cdot n^c$ possible coalitions at the beginning, the total number of rounds is $O(n^{c+1})$.

Hence, if the underlying network topology of a *MAS* is such that $K(n) = O(\log n)$, then our algorithm will run in time polynomial in n. Moreover, if $K(n) \leq c \log n$ holds for $c = 1$, then the number of rounds is at most quadratic in n. We shall assume that the bound $K(n) \leq c \log n$ holds for some positive, real constant c close to 1. We shall also assume that, whatever the criteria of "goodness" for these clique-based coalitions may be, given the necessary data about its neighbors, an agent can efficiently compute the candidate coalition's *value*, $val[C(i)]$, for any such potential coalition $C(i)$. In particular, we shall assume in the sequel that, for any agent v_i, a single evaluation or value estimation of any coalition $C(i)$ of size at most m takes $O(m^2)$ steps.

Proposition 2. *Let the assumptions from the discussion above hold. Then the amount of local computation that any agent has to perform during any iteration of our MCDCF algorithm is polynomial in the size of the data structures involved (cf. lists $L(i), C(i)$ and $C(i,j)$). In particular, assuming that the encoding of all information about a single agent (its UID, list of available resources, etc.) is bounded by $O(\log n)$, the total number of elementary bitwise operations of our algorithm is bounded by $O((\log n)^4)$.*

Proof. Under the stated assumptions, $K(n) \leq c \cdot \log n$, and therefore for any agent v_i, any of the lists $C(i), L(i), C(i,j)$ that this agent operates with are also of sizes bounded by $O(\log n)$. Since *Stages 0 - 1* are executed only once, and *Stage 4* includes communication *only*, we just need to estimate the amounts of local computation during *Stages 2, 3 and 5*. During *Stages 2 - 3*, a number of operations on individual lists and pairs of lists are performed. Sorting a list with K elements takes time $O(K \log K)$.

Finding an element and deleting it from a list with at most K elements takes time $O(K)$. When both lists are of size $O(K)$, comparing two sorted lists, computing their intersection, or testing if one sorted list is a subset of the other, each takes at most $O(K \cdot \log K)$ operations. An agent v_i may need to perform up to K such pairwise list comparisons, intersections and similar list operations - one for each $j \in L(i)$, where $|L(i)| \leq K$. Each of these operations is done at the granularity level of a single list element, which we have assumed is encoded by $O(\log n)$ bits. Hence, the total number of list operations at the bit level is bounded by $O(K^2 \log K \log n)$, which, given our assumptions, is just $O((\log n)^3 (\log \log n))$.

Let's assume that the time to evaluate any $val[C(i)]$ is bounded by some function $T(m)$, where $m = |C(i)|$ is the size of coalition $C(i)$. Let's also assume that, at each node, the candidate coalitions are *sorted* in a non-increasing order with respect to their values $val[C(i)]$. Then evaluating the coalitional values takes at most $O(\log n) \cdot (T(c \cdot \log n) + c \cdot \log(c \log n) + O(1))$ elementary steps. When $T(m) = O(m^2)$, this simplifies to $O((\log n)^3)$. Since each step is assumed to require no more than $O(\log n)$ bit operations, we arrive at $O((\log n)^4)$ bitwise operations overall. As updating and maintaining the coalition values during the subsequent iterations is no costlier than originally computing them from the scratch at the first iteration, the upper bound of $O((\log n)^4)$ remains valid.

Similar analysis applies to *Stage 5*, where the costliest operations are the pairwise list comparisons. Thus *Stages 2 - 5* together take the number of elementary bitwise steps per iteration that is $O((\log n)^4)$.

5.1   Discussion

The proposed distributed coalition formation algorithm is based on two main ideas. One idea, familiar from the literature (see, e.g., [15] and references therein), is to formulate a distributed task and/or resource allocation problem as a *(distributed) set covering problem, (D)SC,* in those scenarios where the coalition overlaps are allowed, or a *(distributed) set partitioning problem, (D)SP,* when no coalition overlaps are allowed. Two (or more) coalitions overlap if there exists an element that belongs to both (all) of them. It is well-known that the decision versions of the classical, centralized versions of the *SC* and *SP* problems are **NP**-complete [4]. Consequently, what is needed are efficient distributed heuristics so that the agents can effectively apply *DSC-* or *DSP-based* strategies for coalition formation. Fortunately, some such efficient heuristics are already readily available [15].

The second main idea is to ensure that the formed coalitions of agents meet the robustness and fault tolerance criteria, which are particularly important in applications where there is a high probability of the subsequent node and/or communication link failures. The most robust coalitions of agents of a particular size are those that correspond to *maximal cliques* in the underlying interconnection topology of the agents' communication network. Alas, the *Maximal Clique* problem is also well-known to be **NP**-hard [3, 4]. This hardness stems from the fact that an agent may need to test for the "cliqueness" exponentially many candidate subsets that it belongs to. However, in those graphs where the maximum degree of each node is bounded by $c \log n$, the number of subsets that each node belongs to is $O(n^c)$, i.e., *polynomial in the total number* *of agents.* Moreover, in those graphs where the node degrees are uniformly bounded by some (small) constant, $K = O(1)$, since 2^K is presumably still sufficiently small, finding maximal cliques becomes not only tractable in theory (i.e., solvable in polynomial time) but also practically feasible in the online, real-time and bounded-resource scenarios that are of the main interest in many *MMAS* applications.

What are the main properties of the coalition structures likely to arise when our algorithm is invoked on an arbitrary large but sufficiently sparse graph that satisfies the aforementioned assumptions? Once the coalitions are formed according to the algorithm, these coalitions of agents will be tight (as everyone in the coalition can communicate with everyone else *directly*), and therefore as robust and fault-tolerant as possible. This is a highly desirable property involving the coalitions or teams of agents operating in the environments where both the agent failures and the agent-to-agent communication link failures can be expected once these agent coalitions are deployed to service their appropriate tasks. One example of such a *MMAS* application domain and, in particular, some coordination strategies in that domain, are studied in [5, 6, 19, 20].

The proposed algorithm can be used as a subroutine in many multi-agent system scenarios where, at various points in time, the system needs to reconfigure itself, and the agents need to form new coalitions (or transform the existing ones) in a fully distributed manner, where each agent has to reason, act and coordinate with other agents *strictly locally,* and where it is important for the agents to be able reach consensus on these coalitions efficiently.

Our final observation is that the proposed algorithm can be expected to be useful only when the time scale of significant changes in the inter-agent communication topology is much coarser than the time scale for the coalitions of agents, first, to form according to the algorithm, and, second, once formed, to accomplish something useful in terms of the agents' ultimate goals (see, e.g., [20, 21]).

6   Conclusion

We propose in this paper an algorithm for distributed coalition formation based on a distributed computation of (maximal) cliques of modest sizes in the underlying communication network of agents. We hope that this algorithm, or its appropriately fine-tuned variants, will turn out to be a potentially useful subroutine in many multi-agent system applications, where the interconnection topology of the agents may often change, so that the system needs to dynamically reconfigure itself *repeatedly,* yet where these topology changes are at a time scale that allows agents to (i) form their coalitions, and (ii) do something useful while participating in such coalitions, before the underlying communication topology of the system changes so much as to render the formed coalitions either obsolete or ineffective.

As for the future work, we plan a detailed comparative analysis of the approach presented herein on one, and the well-known coalition formation approaches from the MAS literature, on the other hand. In particular, we would like to compare and contrast the purely peer-to-peer, genuinely "democratic" approaches to multi-agent coordination, where *all agents are made equal* (except possibly for the different capability vectors), with the asymmetric, less democratic and more leader-based coordination approaches (such as, e.g., various automated dynamic auctions). Intuitively, the genuinely leaderless mechanisms for coalition formation, such as our maximal clique based approach, are less prone to "bottlenecks" and single points of failure than the coordination strategies where certain agents are given special roles or the "leader" status. However, this intuition needs to be both further theoretically investigated and experimentally validated via appropriate comparative simulations and performance measurements.

Acknowledgment. Many thanks to Myeong-wuk Jang, Nirman Kumar and Reza Ziaei for many useful discussions. This work was supported in part by the *DARPA IPTO TASK Program,* contract # *F30602-00-2-0586.* The first author would also like to acknowledge the travel grant from the MMAS'04 conference organizers.

References

1. N. M. Avouris, L. Gasser (eds.), "Distributed Artificial Intelligence: Theory and Praxis", Euro Courses Comp. & Info. Sci. vol. 5, Kluwer Academic Publ., 1992
2. D. H. Cansever, "Incentive Control Strategies For Decision Problems With Parametric Uncertainties", Ph.D. thesis, Univ. of Illinois Urbana-Champaign, 1985
3. T. H. Cormen, C. E. Leiserson, R. L. Rivest, "Introduction to Algorithms", MIT Press, 1990
4. M. R. Garey, D. S. Johnson, "Computers and Intractability: a Guide to the Theory of NP-completeness", W. H. Freedman & Co., New York, 1979
5. M. Jang, S. Reddy, P. Tosic, L. Chen, G. Agha, "An Actor-based Simulation for Studying UAV Coordination", Proc. 15th Euro. Symp. Simul. (ESS '03), Delft, Holland, 2003
6. M. Jang, G. Agha, "On Efficient Communication and Service Agent Discovery in Multi-agent Systems," 3rd Int'l Workshop on Software Engineering for Large-Scale Multi-Agent Systems (SELMAS '04), pp. 27-33, May 24-25, Edinburgh, Scotland, 2004
7. N. Lynch, "Distributed Algorithms", Morgan Kaufmann Publ., Wonderland, 1996
8. P. J. Modi, H. Jung, W. Shen, M. Tambe, S. Kulkarni, "A dynamic distributed constraint satisfaction approach to resource allocation", in Proc. 7th Int'l Conf. on Principles & Practice of Constraint Programming, 2001
9. P. J. Modi, H. Jung, W. Shen, "Distributed Resource Allocation: Formalization, Complexity Results and Mappings to Distributed CSPs", technical report, Nov. 2002
10. P. J. Modi, W. Shen, M. Tambe, M. Yokoo, "An asynchronous complete method for distributed constraint optimization", Proc. 2nd AAMAS '03, Melbourne, Australia, 2003
11. J. Rosenschein, G. Zlotkin, "Rules of Encounter: Designing Conventions for Automated Negotiations among Computers", The MIT Press, Cambridge, Massachusetts, 1994
12. T. Sandholm and V. Lesser, "Issues in automated negotiation and electronic commerce: Extending the contract net framework", in 1st Int'l Conf. on Multiagent Systems, pp. 328-335, San Francisco, 1995
13. T. Sandholm, V. Lesser, "Coalitions among Computationally Bounded Agents", *Artificial Intelligence,* spec. issue on "Principles of MAS", 1997
14. O. Shehory, S. Kraus, "Coalition formation among autonomous agents: Strategies and complexity", Proc. MAAMAW'93, Neuchatel, Switzerland, 1993
15. O. Shehory, S. Kraus, "Task allocation via coalition formation among autonomous agents", Proc. 14th IJCAI-95, Montreal, August 1995
16. H. A. Simon, "Models of Man", J. Willey & Sons, New York, 1957
17. R. G. Smith, "The contract net protocol: high-level communication and control in a distributed problem solver", IEEE Trans. on Computers, 29 (12), 1980

18. G. Tel, "Introduction to Distributed Algorithms", 2nd ed., Cambridge Univ. Press, 2000

19. P. Tosic, M. Jang, S. Reddy, J. Chia, L. Chen, G. Agha, "Modeling a System of UAVs on a Mission", Proc. SCI '03 (invited session), Orlando, Florida, 2003

20. P. Tosic, G. Agha, "Modeling Agents' Autonomous Decision Making in Multiagent, Multi-task Environments", Proc. 1st Euro. Workshop on MAS (EUMAS '03), Oxford, 2003

21. P. Tosic, G. Agha, "Maximal Clique Based Distributed Group Formation Algorithm for Autonomous Agent Coalitions", Proc. Workshop on Coalitions & Teams, within AAMAS '04, New York City, July 19-23, 2004

22. For more on the *TRANSIMS* project at the Los Alamos National Laboratory, go to http://www-transims.tsasa.lanl.gov/ (The *'Documents'* link includes a number of papers and technical reports for the period 1995 - 2001)

23. D. J. Watts, "Small Worlds: The Dynamics of Networks Between Order and Randomness", Princeton Univ. Press, Princeton, N. Jersey, 1999

24. D. J. Watts, S. H. Strogatz, "Collective dynamics of 'small-world' networks", *Nature* 393, 1998

25. G. Weiss (ed.), "Multiagent Systems: A Modern Approach to Distributed Artificial Intelligence", The MIT Press, Cambridge, Massachusetts, 1999

26. M. Wooldridge, N. Jennings, "Intelligent Agents: Theory and Practice", Knowledge Engin. Rev., 1995

27. M. Yokoo, K. Hirayama, "Algorithms for Distributed Constraint Satisfaction: A review", AAMAS, Vol. 3, No. 2, 2000

28. M. Yokoo, "Distributed Constraint Satisfaction: Foundation of Cooperation in Multi-agent Systems", Springer, 2001

29. G. Zlotkin, J.S. Rosenschein, "Coalition, cryptography and stability: Mechanisms for coalition formation in task oriented domains", Proc. AAAI'94, Seattle, Washington, 1994

Quantitative Organizational Models for Large-Scale Agent Systems*

Bryan Horling and Victor Lesser

University of Massachusetts,
Amherst, MA 01003-9264
{bhorling, lesser}@cs.umass.edu

Abstract. As the scale and scope of multi-agent systems grow, it becomes increasingly important to manage the manner in which the participants interact. The potential for bottlenecks, intractably large sets of coordination partners, and shared bounded resources can make individual and high-level goals difficult to achieve. To address these problems, many large systems employ an additional layer of structuring, known as an organizational design, that assigns agents particular and different roles, responsibilities and peers. These additional constraints can allow agents to operate effectively within a large-scale system. In this paper, we will introduce a domain-independent organizational design representation capable of modeling and predicting the quantitative performance characteristics of agent organizations. This representation supports the selection of an appropriate design given a particular operational context. We will demonstrate how the language can be used to represent complex interactions, and show modeling techniques that can address the combinatorics of large-scale agent systems.

1 Introduction

Many of the decisions made in multi-agent system design, and in computational systems in general, are predicated on the idea that one wishes to minimize the "bad" characteristics of the system while maximizing the "good". This practice manifests itself in blanket, axiomatic objectives such as "minimizing communication", "reducing uncertainty", and "maximizing profit". While these are worthy, abstract goals that have critical practical and research importance, when a system is deployed and situated in context such ideals may no longer have the same level of relevance. Consider the underlying issues that drive these objectives. Why should communication be minimized? Why do we care about the combinatorics of a particular technique? Why should centralization be avoided? In each case, we presume the existence of some limiting factor,

---

* This material is based upon work supported by the National Science Foundation under Grant No. IIS-9988784. This material is also based upon work supported by the National Science Foundation Engineering Research Centers Program under NSF Award No. EEC-0313747. Any opinions, findings, conclusions or recommendations expressed in this material are those of the author(s) and do not necessarily reflect the views of the National Science Foundation.

T. Ishida, L. Gasser, and H. Nakashima (Eds.): MMAS 2004, LNAI 3446, pp. 121–135, 2005.

some bounded resource which motivates these objectives. However, when the system is placed in a particular context where these bounds can be quantified, the intangible nature of these blanket statements is no longer sufficient. For example, if ample communication bandwidth is available and additional utility may be derived by using it, then a strategy which always minimizes communication may lead to a solution which fails to reach its potential. If a particular resource is bounded, and the qualitative side effects of using some or all of that resource are the same, then the system should exploit it as best it can in service of satisfying or maximizing the system's specified goals.

Because of this, it our belief that any real-world system must be tailored to the environment in which it exists, if it is to make effective use of the resources and flexibility available to it. We will explore this tailoring through the system's *organizational design*. The notion of an organizational design is used in many different fields, and generally refers to how members of a society act and relate with one another. This is true of multi-agent systems, where the organizational design of a system can include a description of what types of agents exist in the environment, what roles they take on, and guide how they act both independently and with one another. More generally, if we assume an entity has a set of possible choices to make during its operation, the organizational design will identify a particular subset of those choices that should actually be considered at runtime. By working with this typically smaller set, the entity's decision process is facilitated. This additional structure becomes increasingly important the system scales in number and scope [1]. Imagine how difficult it would be for a large human organization, such as a corporation or government, to function if individuals lacked job descriptions and long-term peer relationships. Agents in large and massively-scaled systems face similar challenges, and can derive similar benefits from an explicit organizational design.

In previous work, we demonstrated that the organizational design of a multi-agent system has a measurable, quantifiable effect on the performance of the system as a whole [2]. Intuitively, changing the manner in which agents interact or the pattern that those interactions take on can change how the system behaves from both global and local perspectives. We also demonstrated that it was possible to analytically model and predict those effects in a realistic, complex domain. In this paper, we will continue with this line of reasoning, and present a generic, domain-independent language capable of capturing these types of organization effects. This organizational design modeling language (ODML) incorporates quantitative information in the form of mathematical expressions, which are used to predict the characteristics of an organization.

The immediate benefits of such a language are twofold. First, by incorporating quantitative information about the environment, resources, agents, tasks, goals, or any other object relevant to the system's performance, candidate organizations may be tailored and evaluated in a context-specific way. Second, once a suitable model has been found, it can serve as an explicit organizational representation, guiding agents' local decisions in a manner consistent with global objectives. The longer-term benefits of the organizational model include being able to make predictions about runtime performance, which can be used to isolate and diagnose system failures and deficiencies. This same information can also be used to support adaptation of the system, by incorporating learned knowledge into the existing model and analyzing the resulting structure.

In the following section, we will provide an example of the type of organizational decisions we are concerned with, and how they can affect system performance. We will continue by introducing ODML, and show how it can be used to model those decisions and support organizational reasoning. We will conclude by discussing strategies that can be used to cope with the combinatorics inherent in the models of large-scale systems.

2   Information Retrieval Domain

We will frame our discussion within an information retrieval domain, inspired by work presented by Zhang in [3]. A general peer-to-peer information retrieval system is composed of a number of interconnected databases, controlled by entities which we will refer to as agents. Queries are first received by individual members of the network. An appropriate set of information sources must then be discovered that can address the query, after which the query is routed and processed to produce a response for the user. The information necessary for responding to a particular query may be distributed across the network, which can cause an undirected retrieval process to be time consuming, costly, or ineffective, particularly when the number of sources is large.

Zhang proposes that a structured, hierarchical organization can be used to address this problem. Content in the network is arranged in hierarchies, allowing queries to quickly propagate to data sources, and results be efficiently routed and incrementally aggregated back to a single agent in the network. At the top level of the hierarchy are a set of mediators. Each mediator is responsible for providing a concise and accurate description, known as a collection signature, of the data available in its hierarchy. A hierarchy forms below an mediator, which manages a collection of information sources. An information source may be an individual database, or an aggregator agent which manages other sources. Mediators are also responsible for handling the user queries, by first using the collection signatures of other mediators to compare data sources, and then routing the query to those sources that seem most appropriate. A graphical depiction of a simple organization in this style will be seen later in Figure 1b.

This organizational design provides several advantages. The use of collection signatures to model the contents of a number of individual sources can dramatically reduce the number of agents that must be searched and queried. The use of hierarchies introduces an element of parallelism into the query distribution process. These same hierarchies also distribute the communication and processing load of the response through the use of information aggregation and consolidation.

At the same time, if the structures are poorly designed, they can also lead to inefficiencies. A single collection signature, which must be bounded by size to be efficiently used, can become unacceptably imprecise if the set of sources it models is large or extremely diverse. This can cause data sources to be overlooked, potentially reducing the response quality. Whenever a hierarchy is used, there also exists a tension between the width and height of the structure. Very wide structures can lead to bottlenecks, as particular individuals with high in-degree may become overwhelmed by the number of interactions. Very tall structures can be slow or unresponsive, as the long path length from root to leaf increases latency. The collection signature generation process may also be affected by the tree height, as when abstraction is used at intermediate nodes, causing the signatures of tall hierarchies to incur additional imprecision.

Additional constraints and characteristics exist in the system that exist independent of the organization that is employed, but are relevant to the organization selection process. The communication and processing loads of individual agents are bounded. There may be quality or response time constraints imposed at a high level by the designer. Queries may arrive at regular rate, or at least be probabilistically predictable. Individual databases will vary in size, scope and content. Each of these aspects may affect performance in a non-trivial way.

The problem then, is to determine the most appropriate organization of agents and databases, given the desired characteristics of the system, the provided characteristics of the environment and the tradeoffs we have presented here. For example, how tall should the aggregation hierarchies be? How many nodes should be searched to answer a query? How many mediators should be created? How should these various roles be mapped to actual agents? In the following section, we will introduce our organizational modeling language, and show how these questions can be answered by embedded the relationships described above in such an organizational model.

3   Organizational Representation

The organizational model, as we have described it, must serve in several different capacities. At design time, it should be possible to use the structure to create and evaluate not just a single organizational instance, but an entire family of organizational possibilities. At runtime, it should accurately describe the current organization. In both cases, the model must be sufficiently descriptive and quantitative that one can evaluate the organization, and rank alternatives according along some specified criteria. Below, we enumerate the desired capabilities and characteristics the modeling language should possess to satisfy these requirements:

1. Represent the scope of organizational possibilities, by identifying general classes of organizations and the parameters which influence their behavior.
2. Represent the current organizational structure. This would include roles, interactions and associations (e.g. coalitions, teams). Different flows in the organization, such as communication and resources, should be represented.
3. Allow deductive analysis by quantitatively describing the relevant characteristics exhibited by the structure, and the manner in which those characteristics interact. For example, both communication overhead and the effect that overhead has on work load should be representable.
4. Identify which parameters and characteristics are under deliberate control, and which are derived from external factors.
5. Define thresholds and constraints, and the possible consequences of exceeding those thresholds.

Several different organizational representation schemes have been developed by researchers in the past [4, 5, 6, 7, 8, 9], however none of these meets all the requirements outlined above. Consequently, we have designed the Organizational Design Modeling Language (ODML) to meet our needs. Conceptually, ODML models exist in two distinct forms that share a common representational definition. The first acts as a template, that expresses the range of organizational possibilities by explicitly encoding the organizational decisions that must be made. The second is an organizational instance, created from the template by making specific choices for those decisions. Because the instance form is an instantiation of the template, individual entities in the instance are related to their original abstract specification. This relationship allows one to explore the space of changes that might be made to an organization at runtime.

Formally, an ODML template specification $\mathcal{O}$ is defined as follows:

$$\mathcal{O} = \{\mathcal{N}, H, C, K, M, V\}$$
$$\mathcal{N} = \{N_0, N_1, \ldots, N_n\}$$
$$N = \{t, \bar{p}, I, H, C, K, M, V\}$$

The foundation of the ODML template specification is the set $\mathcal{N}$ of *node templates*, each of which corresponds to a particular physical or logical entity which might exist in the organization. For example, in our information retrieval scenario there would be nodes corresponding to mediators, aggregators, databases, agents and the environment, among other things. Each node N contains a number of elements, defined below:

t The node's *type*. This label must be unique within the set of template nodes that make up the organization.

$\bar{p}$ A list of *parameters* which must be passed to the node's template when an instance of the node is created. These are analogous to the parameters one might pass to an object constructor. Each parameter is specified with a type and local name.

I The set of node types that this node has an *is-a* relation with, with the conventional object-oriented inheritance semantics. If we assume that a node's $I = \{a, b\}$, an instance of the node will also be an instance of a and b, possessing the characteristics of all three node type.

H The set of node types that this node has a *has-a* relation with. If we assume that $H = \{a, b\}$, an instance of the node will possess some number of instances of both a and b. It is through this type of relationship that the primary organizational decomposition is formed.

C A set of *constants*, which represent quantified characteristics associated with the node. Constants may be defined with numeric constants (e.g. 42), or mathematical expressions (e.g. $x + y$).

K A set of *constraints*. An organization is considered valid if all of its constraints are satisfied.

M A set of *modifiers*, which can affect (e.g. mathematically change) a value contained by a node.

V A set of *variables*, representing decisions that must be made when the node is instantiated. Each variable is associated with a range of values it can take on.

The top-level organization node $\mathcal{O}$ also contains the elements H, C, K, M, V, providing a location for the designer to embed global information and constraints. Collectively, we will refer to H, C, K, M as a node's *fields*, and the quantitative state of a

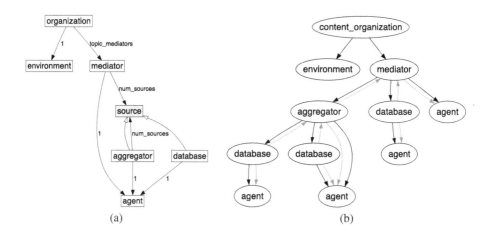

(a)   (b)

Fig. 1. a) An ODML template structure for the information retrieval domain. Vertices represent nodes. Solid edges are has-a relations, and hollow edges are is-a relations. Edge labels reflect the magnitude of the has-a relation. b) A small organizational instance produced from that template. Black edges indicate has-a relationships, gray edges reflect value modifiers that span nodes

field as its *value*. For example, the constant field *total_load* might be defined with the expression *total_load = work_load + communication_load* and have a value of 0.9 for an agent in a particular organization. Note that the term "constant" may be misleading. While the expression defining *total_load* is fixed, the value for *total_load* produced by that equation may change through the application of modifiers or due to changes in fields or values that the expression is dependent on.

The different aspects of ODML are best explained with an example. For clarity, we will represent particular nodes, or fields that reside the nodes, in italics. Space precludes showing the raw, textual model constructed for the information retrieval environment, however, a graph showing some aspects of the model can be seen in Figure 1a. Vertices in the graph, such as *mediator* and *database*, represent nodes. Directed edges with a solid arrow represent has-a relations, and the corresponding label indicates the magnitude of that relation. For example, each *aggregator* node has a single *agent*, while *organization* has a number of *mediators* specified by the variable *topic_mediators*. A hollow-arrow edge represents an is-a relation, so both *aggregator* and *database* are instances of *source*. Shaded nodes, such as *source* are abstract, and cannot be instantiated. This particular template also demonstrates the ability to design recursive models in ODML, because *aggregator* has both is-a and has-a relationships with *source*.

The heart of any ODML model exists in the expressions encoded within nodes' fields. A portion of the fields contained by the *aggregator* node are shown in Table 1. Each field may contain an arbitrary mathematical equation, combining local and nonlocal information to calculate new local values. These expressions provide a way for the designer to represent how different characteristics of the node may be computed. For example, the *data_size* of an aggregator is the sum of the *data_size* values for each of its

Table 1. A portion of the *aggregator* node's fields

Constants	$query\_rate = manager.query\_rate$
	$response\_time = max(sources.response\_time) + agent.work\_load$
	$data\_size = forallsum(sources.data\_size)$
	$communication\_load = query\_rate \times env.query\_communication\_load$
	$work\_load = query\_rate \times env.query\_work\_load$
Constraints	None (modeled by corresponding agent node)
Modifiers	$manager.response\_rate += response\_rate / num\_sources$
	$agent.communication\_load += communication\_load$
	$agent.work\_load += work\_load$
Variables	$num\_sources = \{2, 3, 4\}$

sources. Similarly, the aggregator's *agent.work_load* is affected by the aggregator role's *work_load*, which is itself derived from the local *query_rate* that models how frequently the aggregator is asked to retrieve information. In this way, the characteristics of one node may affect or be affected by those of another. The resulting web of equations allows one to model important concepts such as information flow, control flow, and the effects of interactions. By propagating data through these expressions, the model can predict the characteristics of both individual nodes and the organization as a whole.

As mentioned earlier, ODML templates can describe a family of organizations, where individual members of such a family represent different decision paths through the template. For example, *topic_mediators* is a variable in this template. It can be assigned different values, which will result in organizations that have different numbers of mediators. In addition, because both *aggregator* and *database* are possible instances of *source*, mediators with the same number of sources can be further differentiated by the types of sources they manage. A complete set of decisions applied to the template will produce a particular organizational instance, such as the one shown in Figure 1b. Again, space precludes showing the complete specification for the instance, which includes much more quantitative information, but the graph depicts the relationship between entities in the structure. In this example, a single mediator manages two sources, one of which is an aggregator hierarchy, while the other is a simple database. The example instance also shows a single agent taking on two different roles, as both an aggregator and database in the left subtree. The environment node is used to capture information outside of the scope of other nodes, such as the query rate expected by the system, or the communication bandwidth available to the participants.

Like the working system it represents, there are many facets to the model we present here. Although each can be modeled as a particular, distinct characteristic of the system, they may interact through coexistence in nodes' fields. The tensions that arise in the resulting object embody the tradeoffs and decisions that must be made when designing the organization. We will discuss some of the interesting aspects below in more detail.

Roles. The main portion of the organization is divided into mediator, aggregator and database nodes. In this model, these nodes do not represent particular agents by themselves. Instead, each represents a role that may exist in the organization, that is assigned a particular agent through a has-a relationship. Separating these two concepts allows the creation of more complex organizations, where agents may be assigned multiple roles, possessing the capabilities, constraints and responsibilities of each. We also believe this separation facilitates the modeling process, by clearly identifying the individual factors which contribute to (in this case) an agent's overall place in the organization [10].

Constraints. The notion of bounded rationality manifests itself in this domain within the agents. Specifically, each agent has a finite amount of processor cycles and bandwidth at its disposal. There are both "soft" effects caused by increased load, and "hard" load constraints that may not be violated. An example of the former is the increased time needed to finish any individual task as the local processing load increases. The latter occurs when the agent can no longer keep up with the requests it receives. In this case, the local work queue will grow without bound, causing an untenable situation.

Both these effects are present in the model. The relevant high level metric is the mediator's *response_time*, which represents the average length of time from query to response. As mentioned above, each role has a set of responsibilities which affect the agent it is assigned to. The model specifies the *work_load* and *communication_load* incurred by the role, which are then propagated to the agent with a pair of modifiers. During instantiation, the agent will then receive the cumulative effects of each of its roles. To model the soft effect of work delay, the *response_time* for each role is dependent on its agent's *work_load*. As the load increases, so will the delay for that particular agent. Because the response rate for an aggregator or mediator is dictated by its slowest source, this can potentially affect the performance of the entire hierarchy. The hard constraint is modeled solely within the agent, which has a pair of constraints that ensure a satisfying agent will not be assigned too much work (on average).

Task Environment. The load incurred by a mediator at runtime, and by relation any sources beneath it, will be dependent on the number of queries that mediator is asked to service. This value depends on a number of factors, including the mediator's perceived value, the average number of queries arriving in the system, the number and value of competing mediators, and how many mediators are used to answer the query. To estimate this probability, we first determine the *rank* of each mediator. This ranking reflects the relative *perceived_response_size* of the mediator, which is an estimate of how good a response the mediator is expected to return based on its collection signature. For example, a mediator with many sources of information will have a higher rank than one with just a few, because its "larger" signature will cause it to be selected more frequently to answer queries. We distinguish this perceived size from the mediator's *actual_response_size*, the true quality of its response, to model the effect that signature imprecision can have on search efficiency, as mentioned in Section 2. By this definition, a mediator with higher rank will be selected over those with lower, so by determining the rank we can begin to determine the individual mediator's *query_probability*. With this, that mediator's *query_rate* can be determined, which is propagated to its *sources* so that they may estimate their individual work loads.

Utility Function. A key evaluation criteria used by [3] is information recall. This metric, defined as the ratio of relevant documents retrieved to the total number of relevant documents available, objectively quantifies the quality of the query response. The mediators' *query_probability* and *actual_response_size*, along with the total amount of relevant information in the environment, can be used to determine the average information recall for the organization. A secondary metric, the response time, gives the average amount of time the system requires to answer a query. We have previously implied how the response time of an individual agent is determined, by incorporating work load data from the roles it has been assigned. The response time of an individual mediated hierarchy ties these values together, along with the number of queries received by the mediator, the height of the tree and communication latency. The value is generated incrementally, and propagated up the tree to the mediator.

These two metrics are combined by the *organization* node in its *utility* field, which is typically used to compare and rank candidate instances. In this case, recall is more important than response time, so a multiplicative factor is applied to the recall value, after which the response time is subtracted out. This will generally favor quality over speed, but instances with equal recall will be differentiated by their response time. An arbitrary utility function could be substituted here as needs dictate.

Together, the decisions paths embodied in the template represent a wide range of possible organizations. The characteristics we have described above capture the distinguishing features that allow instances generated from the template to accurately predict how that organization will behave at runtime. We can therefore define the search space of an ODML template as the ranked set of possible organizations it produces. An appropriate organization can be found by finding the valid instances in this set (i.e. those with no unsatisfied constraints), and selecting one with sufficient utility. The optimal organization can be found be selecting the one with the highest utility.

4   Coping with Scale

As noted earlier, structured organizations become increasingly important as the number of participants grows, because of increased difficulty when coordinating, forming consensus, managing shared resources and discovering appropriate partners, among other things. It is therefore critical that any organizational representation be able to model the relevant effects of larger systems. Unfortunately, finding valid organizations from an ODML template can be very difficult, as the search space can be multiply-exponential in the template size. If we are to design organizations for hundreds, thousands or even millions of agents, different modeling techniques must be employed.

The complexity of an ODML template is derived from the number of decisions that must be made when using the structure to generate organizations, which determines the number of candidate organizations that may be derived from that template. When the number of agents that can be in the final organization increases, the number of agent-role assignments will usually increase accordingly, as may the size and number of the less tangible organizational structures such as hierarchies, teams, resource pools, etc. This potentially large number of candidate organizations can make finding the optimal, or even an appropriate, organization a difficult process.

We can begin to address the scale problem through changes to the model itself. By altering the template, one can limit the number of decisions that must be made when interpreting the template, thereby making the number of decisions less dependent on the

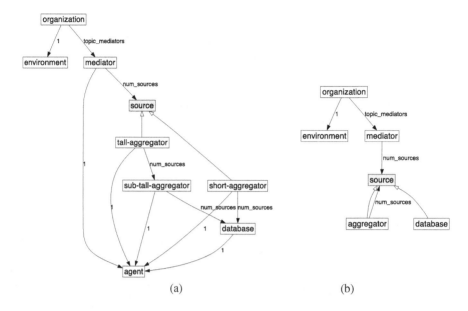

Fig. 2. Two information retrieval templates, derived from Figure 1a. a) Incorporates homogeneity, by limiting aggregator selection to two distinct choices. b) Incorporates abstraction, by eliminating the assignment of roles to distinct agents

number of agents in the system. This will reduce the number of candidate organizations, which will shrink the organizational space that must be searched.

4.1   Homogeneity

Enforcing a certain amount of homogeneity, or at least similarity, within an organizational structure can dramatically reduce the number of decisions which must be made by eliminating organizational choices. For example, we might change our template such that all of a mediator's sources must have the same form, e.g. that they are all single level aggregators. We can improve on this strategy by exploiting ODML's inheritance rules to embed multiple distinct alternatives, rather than providing only a single choice. For example, consider the template in Figure 2a. In this model, we have defined two distinct source types, a *tall-aggregator* that has two levels, and a *short-aggregator* that has just one. Both contain a total of four databases, but they will have different performance characteristics because of their different structure. In this new template, candidate organizations may contain either or both alternatives, while other permutations of the aggregator hierarchy have been eliminated.

We view the use of homogeneity as an iterative process best exploited during the design phase. Typically, one would begin by creating a very general template, capable of producing almost all feasible organizations. As variations are generated and compared, it is common that particular organizational characteristics will define certain classes of structures or substructures. Simple examples of this include the "tall" and "short" varieties we have identified in the information retrieval domain. The members of a particular variety may be similar enough that a single representative structure can stand in for the entire class with only minimal loss of utility. For example, there are a vast number of short and wide aggregator hierarchies that have only minor differences in form and function. In Figure 2a we replaced this large number of choices with a single *short-aggregator*, which will certainly reduce the organizational search space, and hopefully not limit the quality of the final organization. Such classes can serve as the foundation for a reduction process that captures the notion of homogeneity, by replacing a potentially complicated set of decisions with a set of predefined structures. Optimally, one could incorporating a representative from each distinguished class, producing a template with a smaller candidate search set but negligible loss of potential utility.

4.2   Abstraction

A different way to reduce the decision complexity of a model is to use abstraction to reduce elements of the structure to their simplest form. Unnecessary or optional details may be removed or captured with a probabilistic representation to eliminate branches of the template which would otherwise add to the decision process. As with homogeneity, this practice can potentially lead to an undesirable loss of expressivity in the model, but with care an appropriate compromise can usually be found.

An example of this approach, particularly relevant to decomposition-based representations such as ODML, is to truncate the model at some point higher than the level actually used by the running system. This is already used in the example models in some respects because the internal decision making processes of agents are not represented. A more typical example of this technique is to not model down to the level of assigning roles to individual entities or agents, as shown in Figure 2b. Organizations derived from this template will specify what roles exist, and where they are located in the organizational structure, but leave them otherwise unbound. This technique is analogous to those presented by Durfee in [11], which used team-level abstraction to leave specific agent assignments unbound during coordination, also to reduce complexity. If agents were heterogeneous or permitted to take on multiple roles, this can reduce the search space exponentially. Even if agents were homogeneous, in a hierarchical structure this can cut the size of instances in half, which simplifies analysis and reduces memory consumption. The precision lost in this instance stems from the details that were previously stored within individual agent nodes. For example, it is more difficult to validate an individual agent's communication or work loads. Generic agent nodes can be retained to compensate for this loss of detail, but one will not be able to predict how the combined effects of multiple roles affect the agent or its performance within the organization.

The further implication of using this technique arises from the fact that the resulting organizational instance will no longer completely specify how it should be applied to a set of resources and agents. Decisions that were previously made during the design process must now be made by an axillary process or at runtime. In the example above, roles must be assigned to specific agents before the system can function. A second process must take the agent population and map them to the nodes proscribed by the selected organizational instance, which is itself a search process [12]. Although this late binding requires additional analysis after the design phase, our belief is that it also fosters increased context-sensitivity by providing a framework to support dynamic allo-

Table 2. Results from organizational search in small-scale information retrieval templates. Number of agents and utility are given for the optimal found organization

Template	Decisions	Valid Organizations	Agents	Utility
Baseline	14,380,508	8539	9	6.978
Homogeneous	2,329,951	6785	9	6.978
Abstract	4947	15	9	6.978
Homogeneous + Abstract (a)	1309	6	9	6.978
Homogeneous + Abstract (b)	1050	4	8	6.975

cation. For example, assume that the *mediator* role not been bound to a particular agent at design time. At runtime, when the actual number and types of databases are known (as opposed to the statistical averages used in our models), the organizational design can be inspected to determine what resources that role requires and what burdens it will place on the agent it is assigned to. That entity model, coupled with the new information obtained at runtime can be used to select an appropriate agent to fill that role.

4.3   Scalability Technique Examples

The exact amount of search space reduction that is observed using these techniques is dependent on the particular manner in which the template changes are carried out. Some approaches will clearly be better than others in terms of space complexity and achievable utility, and we have shown how hybrid strategies that use a limited set of decisions can help offset the drawbacks associated with model reduction.

To demonstrate the effectiveness of these techniques, we created two sets of templates for the information retrieval domain. The small set allowed up to five databases, up to two mediators, and the aggregators could have two, three or four sources. The larger design allowed up to 100 databases, with up to five mediators, each of which could have one to four sources. The number of agents was unbounded. The source node types are the same hierarchies discussed in Section 2, with a single level height restriction in the small scenario, and a three-level restriction in the large (i.e. up to two aggregators with a database leaf). Five templates were created for each scenario. The baseline template is shown in Figure 1a. The second template, using the homogeneous technique, is similar to that shown in Figure 2a. The third employs abstraction, by not assigning a particular agent to each role. Alternatively, one could also view this model as creating a new agent for each role. The fourth and fifth templates incorporate both the homogeneous and abstract techniques. Slightly different modeling changes were made in each, to demonstrate how the search space may be affected by these techniques.

Node constraints specify a maximum communication and work load for individual agents, as well as a minimum average response recall for the organization as a whole. All valid structures must satisfy those constraints. Utility was calculated primarily with the response recall, with ties broken by the average expected response time. Other environmental and behavioral values were the same between templates. A complete, depth-first search was performed for each template, and the optimal instances generated compared. Although the structures themselves are different, the expressions

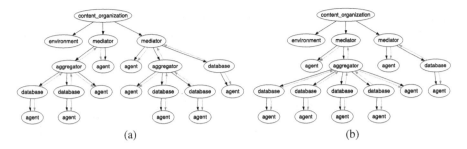

Fig. 3. Optimal organization instances produced by the Homogeneous + Abstract (a) and (b) templates for the small-scale scenario

underlying the utility function they employ are the same, therefore the computed utility of the structures the different templates produce remain directly comparable.

The results from the small scenario are shown in Table 2. The table shows the number of decisions made during the entire search, the number of valid organizations that were found, and the number of agent and utility of the optimal structure. The most dramatic reductions in search space occurred using abstraction, which reduced the number of valid organizations by two orders of magnitude. The reduction in decisions that were made was even greater. As we will discuss below, the number of possible assignments of agents to roles can be quite large even for small organizations, so avoiding this process results in a tremendous savings in complexity. Because there was no predefined limit on the number of agents used, and no additional costs were incurred by using more agents, the optimal organizations for both the small and large scenarios use as many agents as possible. This distributes the load, which in turn decreases the time needed to answer a query, which ultimately causes such organizations to have higher utility.

The organizations produced by the two Homogeneous + Abstract templates in the small scenario can be seen in Figure 3. Template (a) allowed single hierarchies of two databases, while (b) used hierarchies of four. Although both structure have the same information recall, the optimal organization arising from template (b) had slightly lower utility. As seen in in Figure 3, the mediators in (a) are more evenly balanced than those in (b). This imbalance lead to an increase in average response time, which resulted in the slightly lower expected utility. This demonstrates the intuitive fact that different modifications will result in different search space modifications, and it is possible to lose an optimally valued solution in the process. Template (a) retained an optimally valued organization, while it was lost through the modifications to (b).

The optimal organization for three of the five large-scale database scenarios were simply too difficult to compute. Consider that, if agents may take on multiple roles, a single candidate structure containing 100 roles has 100^{100} possible assignments of agents to those roles. Even if agents may take on only a single role, there may be 100! permutations if the agents are distinguishable. Organizations produced from the structures used in this scenario may contain more than 100 roles, and there are billions of possible structures. Finding the optimal structure in such a large space is intractable. However, by incorporating the concepts of homogeneity and abstraction into the original model, we were able to design valid organizations in a reasonable amount of time. A

Table 3. Results from organizational search in large-scale information retrieval templates. Number of agents and utility are given for the optimal found organization

Template	Decisions	Valid Organizations	Agents	Utility
Baseline	Intractable, $\approx 7.4 \times 10^{301}$ candidates			
Homogeneous	Intractable, $\approx 2.2 \times 10^{108}$ candidates			
Abstract	Intractable, $\approx 7.4 \times 10^{201}$ candidates			
Homogeneous + Abstract (a)	52,792,143	473	135	14.561
Homogeneous + Abstract (b)	44,057,638	264,293	116	10.489

quantitative summary of the search process for the remaining structures which employ both the abstraction and homogeneity techniques is shown in Table 3. Lacking a baseline comparison, we cannot state that the optimal organizations that were found had the optimal utility originally achievable. However, many different organizations were found, all of which meet or exceed the constraints specified by the original model.

The particular organizations obtained by the two remaining templates are of minor significance here, more important is the fact that we were able to use generic models to find appropriate organizations for systems incorporating more than 100 agents. These results demonstrate how generic modeling techniques can be used to reduce the complexity of an organizational search process. If suitable modifications are made, one can vastly reduce the search space with minimal reduction to utility, although the amount of reduction is clearly affected by the skill of the expert making the changes.

5   Conclusions and Future Work

All of the organizational characteristics described in Section 3 have been implemented in models created with ODML's domain-independent language. In doing so, we have produced an artifact that both describes the breadth of possible organizational alternatives, and gives the tools necessary to evaluate and compare those alternatives in a concrete, quantifiable manner. This provides the foundation upon which automated organizational design technology can be built.

We have also demonstrated how relatively simple optimizations to organizational models can be used to make organizational design for large scale multi-agent systems more realistic. Unfortunately, despite such modifications, the search space of organization models remains generally intractable with scale, and the exhaustive search approach we used quickly becomes inappropriate. Because of this, it is important to couple techniques such as those presented here with better search strategies that can make more effective decisions during the analysis. We are currently exploring the use of equivalence classes and gradient estimation as a way of bounding the search. We intend to pursue other techniques in future work.

ODML models have been used to design organizations for the information retrieval domain presented here, as well as a distributed sensor network domain described in [2]. Our hope is that the flexibility and generality of the language will allow it to be suitable for many other types of agent systems. We have tested the organizations produced by such models, and shown that the predictions they make correspond correctly to observed behaviors. A rigorous empirical comparison currently underway.

We believe that structured, explicit organization design will be a critical element in large-scale multi-agent systems. In practice, implicit organizations already exist in almost all agent systems – it is common for agents to take on different roles, interact with only a subset of the population, and have a variety of different interrelationships. By making the construction and representation of the organization an explicit, principled act it is possible to make hidden inefficiencies apparent and take full advantage of the resources at hand.

References

1. Corkill, D.D., Lander, S.E.: Diversity in Agent Organizations. Object Magazine **8** (1998) 41–47
2. Horling, B., Mailler, R., Lesser, V.: A Case Study of Organizational Effects in a Distributed Sensor Network. In: Proceedings of the International Conference on Intelligent Agent Technology (IAT 2004), Beijing, China (2004)
3. Zhang, H., Lesser, V.: A Dynamically Formed Hierarchical Agent Organization for a Distributed Content Sharing System . Proceedings of the International Conference on Intelligent Agent Technology (IAT 2004) (2004)
4. Decker, K., Lesser, V.R.: Quantitative Modeling of Complex Environments. International Journal of Intelligent Systems in Accounting, Finance and Management. Special Issue on Mathematical and Computational Models and Characteristics of Agent Behaviour. **2** (1993) 215–234
5. Fox, M.S.: Organization structuring: Designing large complex software. Computer Science Technical Report CMU-CS-79-155, Carnegie-Mellon University (1979)
6. Pattison, H.E., Corkill, D.D., Lesser, V.R.: Instantiating Descriptions of Organizational Structures. Distributed Artificial Intelligence, Research Notes in Artificial Intelligence **I** (1987) 59–96
7. DeLoach, S.: Modeling organizational rules in the multi-agent systems engineering methodology. In: Proceedings of the 15th Conference of the Canadian Society for Computational Studies of Intelligence on Advances in Artificial Intelligence, Springer-Verlag (2002) 1–15
8. Hübner, J.F., Sichman, J.S., Boissier, O.: A model for the structural, functional, and deontic specification of organizations in multiagent systems. In: Proceedings of the Brazilian Symposium on Artificial Intelligence (SBIA'02). (2002) 118–128
9. Dignum, V., Vazquez-Salceda, J., Dignum, F.: A model of almost everything: Norms, structure and ontologies in agent organizations. In: Proceedings of the Third International Joint Conference on Autonomous Agents and Multi-agent Systems. (2004)
10. Horling, B., Mailler, R., Shen, J., Vincent, R., Lesser, V.: Using Autonomy, Organizational Design and Negotiation in a Distributed Sensor Network. In Lesser, V., Ortiz, C., Tambe, M., eds.: Distributed Sensor Networks: A multiagent perspective. Kluwer Academic Publishers (2003) 139–183
11. Durfee, E.H., Montgomery, T.A.: Coordination as distributed search in a hierarchical behavior space. IEEE Transactions on Systems, Man, and Cybernetics **21** (1991) 1363–1378
12. Sims, M., Goldman, C., Lesser, V.: Self-Organization through Bottom-up Coalition Formation. In: Proceedings of Second International Joint Conference on Autonomous Agents and MultiAgent Systems (AAMAS 2003), Melbourne, AUS, ACM Press (2003) 867–874

Adaptive Modeling: An Approach and a Method for Implementing Adaptive Agents[1]

Reza Razavi[1], Jean-François Perrot[2], and Nicolas Guelfi[1]

[1] Software Engineering Competence Center University of Luxembourg,
6, rue Richard Coudenhove-Kalergi Luxembourg,
L-1359 – Luxembourg
{reza.razavi, nicolas.guelfi}@uni.lu
[2] Laboratoire d'Informatique de Paris VI (LIP6),
Université Pierre et Marie Curie – CNRS Paris – France
jean-francois.perrot@lip6.fr

Abstract. This paper describes the fundamentals of a research project which is being launched in the emerging field of *Ambient Intelligence* as defined by the European Union's 6th Research Program on Information Society. Massively multi-agent systems is the natural technique for implementing Ambient Intelligence. Adaptivity is one of the key features of ambient systems. Ensuring that the evolution of an ambient system is predictable and desirable is a challenging open design issue. We propose a user-driven approach to adaptation. We call it "Adaptive Modeling" because it relies on the architectural style known as Adaptive Object-Models. This provides us with a design method and tool for agents to be used in this context. Systems built with this method allow non-programmer domain experts to locally modify the structure and behavior of agents at runtime, and thus obtain system-level adaptation. Expert-driven adaptation should ensure the appropriateness of the system's behavior with respect to its requirements. We illustrate our method with an existing multi-agent system. Work is under way for extending it with other features, notably fault-tolerance, as well as "agent-driven adaptation" by replacing expert users with monitoring agents endowed with the same expertise.

Keywords: Massively Multiagent Systems, Adaptive Object-Models, Ambient Intelligence, Adaptive Agent.

1 Introduction and Problem Statement

1.1 Massively Multi-agent Systems and Ambient Intelligence

The specific features of Multi-Agent Systems that are due to their size are now attracting attention. Having to deal with very many agents distributed on a very large network brings to the forefront problems like scalability, control and adaptivity. The

---

[1] The work communicated in this paper has been conducted while the first author doing his PhD at Laboratoire d'Informatique de Paris 6 (LIP6), Université Paris 6 - CNRS, Paris, France.

T. Ishida, L. Gasser, and H. Nakashima (Eds.): MMAS 2004, LNAI 3446, pp. 136–148, 2005.
© Springer-Verlag Berlin Heidelberg 2005

design of such systems calls for disciplined production techniques and tools. This paper proposes to attack the problem of adaptivity with tools that were created for a specific class of object-oriented applications.

We are interested in the particular sort of Massively Multi-Agent Systems that go under the name of *Ambient Intelligence*. As stated by I. Satoh in his invited talk at the MMAS Workshop [1], *Ambient intelligence enables us to be surrounded by electronic environments that are sensitive and responsive to people. Ambient intelligence technologies are expected to combine concepts of intelligent systems, perceptual technologies, and ubiquitous computing*. Not all MMAS will be in this category, but clearly any Ambient Intelligence system will have its software built as a MMAS.

Ambient Intelligence (AmI) was selected by the European Union's *Information Society Technologies Advisory Group* (ISTAG) as a vision of Information Society for the 6th Framework Program. As a new class of distributed, adaptive systems that is expected to operate in extremely dynamic configurations, it aims at greater user-friendliness, more efficient services support, user-empowerment, and support for human interactions. The mission of this EU-funded initiative is to examine how information technology can be diffused into everyday objects and settings, and how this can lead to new ways of supporting and enhancing people's lives - ways that go above and beyond what is possible with computers today (see the various documents issued by ISTAG or directly inspired by it [2, 3]).

In this framework, for instance, the EU *e-Health program* aims at applying the AmI vision to the general problem of Healthcare. The program will bring about a thorough follow-up of the patient's state, thus increasing her security. It will allow patients to follow a medical treatment at home, thereby freeing hospital space. The program will also foster the development of "personalized e-Health services and individualization of diagnoses and treatment", as formulated in a seminar sponsored by EU [4].

Several important research projects are launched on similar pursuits, for example:

– AIR-D Consortium (INRIA, Philips and Thomson multimedia), and OZONE, New Technologies and Services for Emerging Nomadic Societies [5],
– Context-Aware Computing project at MIT Media Lab [6],
– Berkeley Webs (Wireless Embedded Systems) [7],
– Center for Embedded and Networked Sensing at UCLA [8],
– The TASK [9] and NEST [10] projects at UIUC,
– The Cyber Assist Consortium projects relevant to ambient intelligence and ubiquitous computing [11]

An integrated system conforming to the AmI vision will be made up of a set of material, tangible everyday artifacts that incorporate specific software and/or hardware components and interact in a loosely-coupled way. Let us call such an everyday artifact an *ambient object*, and the system itself an *ambiance*. Within an ambiance, ambient objects work together in order to provide a behavior or functionality that exceeds the sum of their parts and that dynamically adapts to the environment or requirements changes. The phrase "ambient intelligence" qualifies this global behavior. The ambiance itself as a global system with its emergent behavior may be seen as a community in the sense of Ishida [12].

As an example consider a patient to whom is given a heavy medical treatment made up of various pills and injections. The patient's state must be continuously monitored. A dedicated "healthcare ambiance" assists her as well as her doctor. It is composed of ambient objects like a) sensors to retrieve data, e.g., heart rhythm, blood pressure, movement indications; b) pumps to administer some injections such as insulin for diabetes; c) devices to remind the patient to take in time her medications whose application cannot be automated; d) communication devices for regularly transmitting data to a doctor, and receiving instructions from him; e) cameras to capture images; f) monitors for checking if the devices are functioning properly and reporting faults or dealing with them, etc.

Multi-agent systems are the obvious implementation technology for ambiances. The number and variety of agents involved, their distribution and adaptivity, all these characteristics clearly put ambiances within the emerging domain of massively multi-agent systems [1, 11, 13]. Additionally, ambiances are representative of a paradigm shift that fits especially well the vision of MMAS proposed by Ishida [14].

1.2 The Adaptivity Issue

Some of the quality attributes that are expected of MMAS and especially of ambiances, like modularity, openness, learning, reasoning and mobility, have been already treated for multi-agent systems [15, 16, 17]. Rigorous and stepwise development of these systems has been studied e.g. by Lucena, Romanovsky *et al* [18]. This paper concentrates on adaptivity, which we propose to address from an architectural perspective.

We refer here to the notion of *architectural style*, e.g. layered or client-server styles. An architectural style defines a family of architectures that satisfy a given set of constraints [19]. Styles allow one to apply specialized design knowledge to a particular class of systems, and to support this class of system design with style-specific tools, analysis, and implementations. In our view, architectural styles are keys to rigorous and stepwise development of software systems, especially because they lend themselves to the production of software tools.

However, there is currently no architectural style for developing MMAS and particularly ambiances. For instance, the Telemedicine Systems Interoperability Alliance is specifying an architecture for e-Health systems of the kind we outlined in 1.1. They state that: "There are already a lot of useful components out there for building tele-medicine systems; however, none will already support the full vision of what we want to achieve." [20]. Our work aims at contributing to this effort.

One of the major open issues with engineering of adaptive systems is ensuring that all adaptations of the system are predictable and desirable (*meaningful-adaptivity*). For instance, the healthcare ambiance of our example should allow adaptation of prescriptions and follow-up procedures at virtually any time, to take into account the evolutions of the patient status and of the environment. For obvious reasons such evolutions should happen in a safe and meaningful manner.

Ideally, the system should adapt in an automatic way, without human interference. But the state of the art (e.g. Z. Guessoum [21]) shows that this is far from being achieved. We propose to concentrate on *user-driven adaptation*, where knowledgeable end-users, in particular non-programmer domain experts, are empowered to issue instructions at runtime that result in structure and behavior modification for some agents in a given ambient object. This local modification is "instantaneously" taken into account by the running ambient object and they result in a meaningful adaptation of the object. It may also result in a global adaptation of the system's behavior at the ambiance level.

As a second step, expert users will be replaced by monitoring agents endowed with the same expertise. For instance in the "morphological" MMAS conceived by Campagne & Cardon [13] to simulate emotions in a robot, so-called *analysis agents* are expected to control a population of subordinate (and massively multiple) *aspectual agents*. These analysis agents are supposed to possess cognitive capacities and to modify the behavior of aspectual agents. For this purpose, the structure of aspectual agents is designed to be changeable at runtime: in the paper [13], their behavior is "governed by some sort of augmented transition network (ATN) that can be parameterized by a set of values". This is precisely where our proposed architecture would be employed, as we shall explain later.

Our proposal described in the following sections is to implement user-driven adaptivity by means of the architectural style called *Adaptive Object-Models* (AOMs) [22]. This architectural style proved effective for implementing user-driven adaptation in object-oriented software. Our aim is to apply it to the design of ambiances, as part of two research projects: one called *Åmbiance*[2], funded by the University of Luxembourg (2005-2006), the other called *e-Care*[3], funded by the Luxembourg National Research Fund (2005-2007).

1.3 Adaptive Object Models and the Design of Ambiances

The concept of Adaptive Object-Model was born recently from research aiming at discovering and documenting the design principles of a particular class of software with complex behavior that emerged from industry and proved most useful for businesses that are rapidly changing. Adaptive Object-Models have been also called in the past "User Defined Product architecture" [23], "Active Object-Models" [24] and also "Dynamic Object Models" [25].

AOMs are a sophisticated way of building object-oriented systems that let non-programmers customize the behavior of the system. The aim is to take advantage of the competence of a category of end-users, namely domain experts. Indeed, as it is observed by Bonnie A. Nardi [26], "domain experts have the detailed task knowledge necessary for creating the knowledge-rich applications they want and the motivation to get their work done quickly, to a high standard of accuracy and completeness". Usually, an AOM-based system includes a Domain Specific Language (DSL). This language is tailored to meet the expressive needs of the domain experts who are to use it for customizing the system. In our view, the adequate design of this language is the key toward user-driven adaptivity.

The AOM architectural style is classically described by means of a composition of several design patterns [22]. Our previous contribution to the subject is an architecture

---

[2] Åmbiance: from Adaptive Object-Models to Meta-tool Support for Ambient Dependable Intelligence Systems.
[3] e-Care: Towards a Secured, Efficient Platform for the e-Commerce of Personalized Health Products.

for designing AOMs, based on the spreadsheet approach to programming advocated by Nardi [26]. This architecture is called *Dycra*. It is currently implemented as an object-oriented framework programmed in Smalltalk [27, 28].

The heart of our proposal here is to apply our architecture to the implementation of ambiances. As a first step, we show how it applies to the explicit modeling of agents for user-driven adaptivity. We call *adaptive modeling* this way of designing agents. One of the goals of our current projects is to exploit the explicit representation of agents for automating the generation of deployable ambiances, by model-to-code transformations. We also plan to integrate our architecture into the Campagne-Cardon framework [13], as stated above. In order to be more precise, we need some material.

We first explain the principles of our Dycra architecture (section 2), then we sketch its application to the adaptive modeling of agent systems through the example of the Mobidyc multi-agent simulation system (section 3).

2 The Dycra Architecture

2.1 Dycra = Darc + Dart

Dycra, *DYnamic Class Refinement Architecture*, is an abstract design created with reuse and extension as primary considerations, and rigorously documented by means of design patterns (the classical reference is [29]), the UML modeling notation, and textual descriptions. Dycra was developed by the first author in the course of his doctoral thesis [28]. It is made up of two main interconnected parts:

- *Darc* that corresponds to the "core of Adaptive Object Models" following the terminology of [25],
- *Dart* that corresponds to a generic model for describing computation processes.

Roughly speaking, Darc takes care of the evolving structure of objects, whereas Dart deals with their behavior. Dycra is implemented as a set of Smallalk classes and metaclasses (in several versions, using various Smallatlk dialects: VisualWorks, Squeak, and Metaclasstalk by N. Bouraqadi [27]). This implementation is called *Dyctalk*[4].

Since behavior modeling is the most interesting part from the design of adaptive agents, we focus in the following subsection only on Dart. In section 3 we illustrate the use of the Dycra architecture in a multi-agent simulation system.

2.2 Dart: A Model for Computation Processes

Describing behavior is always a difficult problem. In the AOM perspective, the most advanced work in this direction is Manolescu's micro-workflow architecture [30].

A process model (i.e., key process abstractions and their relationships) constitutes the core of an architecture for behavior modeling. As Manolescu observes [31], there are three types of process models: activity-, artifact-, or communication-based (a combination of these - i.e., a hybrid model - is also possible). For his architecture,

---

[4] For more information please point to the URL: http://www-poleia.lip6.fr/~razavi/Dyctalk/

Manolescu preferred the activity-based process model. Our model conforms to the artifact-based process model, hence its name Dart for *Dynamic ARTifact-driven* class specialization.

The main quality of Dart is its ease of use by non-programmers. The basic inspiration comes from the computational model of spreadsheets, advocated by B. Nardi [26]. The main assumption is that complex behavior can be modeled by:

1. Associating operations to cells,
2. Relating together those cells as "operation result holders" that provide the argument to new operations,

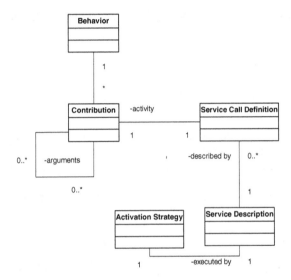

Fig. 1. The core design of the Dart model for computation processes

One of the main characteristics of Dart is its interoperability with dynamically defined data structures, or the structure of individual types, in the sense that these structures can be read/write accessed by automatically generated *setters* and *getters* (as specific types of services). This feature relates it to Darc, the other part of our AOM tool.

As is depicted by Figure 1 above, the core of Dart is composed of only four concepts: *Contribution, Service Call Definition, Activation Strategy,* and *Service Description*. This design allows representing a behavior with a finite directed acyclic graph, called π-graph. Each node of a π-graph represents a *Contribution*, that is, the artifact that the expert is concerned with. It may also serve as a cache for an object in the object memory space. Two types of *Contributions* are distinguished: *Given value* and *Computed Contribution*. *Computed Contributions* are described by *Service Call Definitions*. Each *Service Call Definition* can have N other *Contributions* as arguments. The operational semantics of a *Service Call Definition* is determined by its associated *Activation Strategy*. When activated, the nodes of this graph are run in parallel, and linked to their data dependencies. Programmers can implement different execution semantics by extending *Activation Strategy*.

Dart supports also late value and method binding. In addition, π-graphs are recursive and reflective. They are recursive since the content of every node of a π-graph can be itself a π-graph. They are reflective since some of the underlying concepts are themselves used for extending this syntax. For instance, adding conditional and iteration constructs does not require adding new concepts to Dart: they can be implemented by programmers as an extension of the *Computed Contribution* concept.

In short, Dart allows to make domain processes explicit, by reifying those concepts that are required for their definition and interpretation. A detailed example of its functioning will be given in subsection 3.2.

3   Adaptive Modeling with Dycra: The Mobidyc Example

We present here a view of the Mobidyc simulation system to illustrate our *adaptive modeling* approach. This will give us the necessary context for a detailed example showing how our architecture functions.

3.1   The Mobidyc Project

Mobidyc [32, 33] is an acronym for *Modelling Based on Individuals for the Dynamics of Communities*[5]. This project promotes a framework approach for developing *Individual-Based Modeling* (IBM) simulation software. Emphasis is put on the ease of learning and using by non-programmer ecologists.

A simulation experiment with Mobidyc consists in the creation of an initial agent population (often a large one: up to 100 000 agents), which is then activated and evolves as a consequence of the interactions between individual agents. This evolution is monitored and the collected data constitute the result of the experiment. Mobidyc implements three kinds of agents: *Animats*, *Cells*, and *Non-Located Agents*. It includes tools for the creation of cell agents (squared or hexagonal lattices, or obtained from ASCII contour files describing any shape of cells), tools to display or save results such as a video recorder, a system to manage the units of the user, tools to automatically generate initial agent populations, etc. Simulation experiments may be linked in order to test the sensitivity of the model to parameter values.

The essential point is the definition of the various types of agents that will be instantiated to make up the initial population. This fundamental task is entirely in the hands of expert ecologists. Ecologists are provided with a user-friendly editor (called the *Agent Type Editor*) to produce the specifications, which are saved in a repository

---

[5] The Mobidyc system has been developed by teams from the French National Institute for Agricultural Research (INRA), University Paris-VI (LIP6), the French Institute of Research for Development (IRD), and the French Centre for International Cooperation in Agronomy Research for Development (CIRAD-Tera/Ere). Mobidyc project has been supported by the French National Centre for Scientific Research (CNRS), section "Biodiversitas" of the "Environment Life and Societies" program, through the thematic action of the Public Group of Interests Hydro Systems entitled: "the fish in its environment". A research prototype of the Mobidyc platform is freely available in French and English. A tutorial in French is also provided. It uses the Smalltalk VisualWorks environment developed by the Cincom company. This environment is free for non commercial use and runs on almost all platforms. For more information the reader may visit the sites http://www.avignon.inra.fr/mobidyc.

(the *Meta-data Repository*). As expressed in fig. 2 below, the Mobidyc system dynamically changes its behavior, by loading from the repository the corresponding set of agent types, instantiating them, and running their behavior. In this way the same running software serves to simulate different ecosystems (known in the literature as *DeAngelis*, *Wolf&Goat*, etc.).

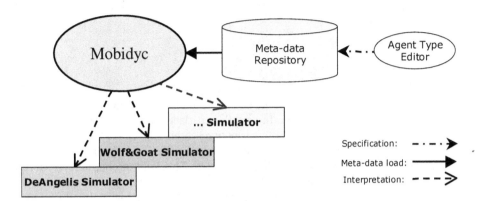

Fig. 2. Mobidyc dynamically loads and interprets the object-models of different agent types

3.2   An Example of Explicit Behavior Modeling Using Dart

Complex individual behavior is defined from more "primitive" behavior. Mobidyc assumes that each elementary task that forms the behavior of an individual follows the same pattern: first, an individual must locate and select information, then he must update his state, the state of other individuals, or the state of the rest of the 'world' [36]. Experience shows that only 25 primitives, split into 6 groups (*locate*, *select*, *translate*, *compute*, *end*, and *workflow control*) are enough to build quite complex models.

As a very simple example, consider an ecologist willing to define the following behavior for an agent:

1. Select one of the other agents in my immediate neighborhood under the age of three,
2. Move to the cell to which the selected agent is bound.

This behavior can be implemented by the following algorithm, expressed in the domain-specific language of the ecologist:

1. A List of Cells = Select all cells in my immediate neighborhood containing another agent,
2. 1st List of Agents = Collect all agents associated to (A List of Cells),
3. 2nd List of Agents = Select all agents (1st List of Agents) with (age) less than 3,
4. Selected Agent = Random Select (2nd List of Agents),
5. Destination = Find the Cell associated to (Selected Agent),
6. Move to (Destination).

Those 6 lines will be entered *verbatim* by the ecologist through the GUI of the *Agent Type Editor*. Here is now a somewhat detailed account of how the Dart framework interprets them.

Dart represents this algorithm as a set of seven *Contributions*. Six of them are instances of *Computed Contribution* and may be named as follows:

1. A List of Cells,
2. 1st List of Agents,
3. 2nd List of Agents,
4. Selected Agent,
5. Destination,
6. No name.

where each *Contribution* bears the name of the value resulting from the corresponding computation in the above algorithm. In workflow parlance this approach is called artifact-driven process modeling. The last contribution is arbitrarily called "No name" since it represents a call to the procedure *Move*, whose return value is not significant here.

A seventh *Getter Contribution* is further needed. This kind of contribution serves to specify a read access to the value of an agent's attribute, here *age*, which is one of the attributes of this class of agent, as specified by the same ecologist also at runtime. Its initial value is zero. This value is augmented during the course of the simulation by means of another algorithm which is also defined by the ecologist, much in the same way. The value of *age* is needed here for computing the value of the "2nd List of Agents" contribution as further explained below. This case illustrates an example of the dynamic co-evolution of structure and behavior in Dycra since the dynamically defined behavior refers to an attribute that is also defined at runtime.

Furthermore, each of these contributions points to an instance of a primitive function, through its instance variable named *serviceCall*. It should be noted that each primitive is reified and implemented as a class according to the Strategy design pattern. Instantiating a primitive then corresponds to creating an instance of the associated class. Configuring such an instance corresponds to valuating its instance variables by means of a GUI. In Dart terminology, a primitive instance is called a *service call*. Service calls are however not limited to primitive instances. For example, instances of getters and setters are also *service calls*.

In our example, each of the first six *Computed Contributions* points to an instance of one of the 25 "hard coded" primitives of Mobidyc as follows:

1. "A List of Cells" points to an instance of "Neighborhood". This primitive serves to compute the collection of cells that are in the neighborhood of the cell associated to an agent, and contain another agent. This instance is configured for selecting the most immediate neighbors of the current agent, i.e., those attached to its adjacent cells,
2. "1st List of Agents" points to an instance of "From Cells to Agents". This primitive returns systematically for each cell received as argument the agent that is attached to it. It has no specific configurations,
3. "2nd List of Agents" points to an instance of "Select". This primitive serves to filter a collection of agents according to a given criteria. This instance uses "age" of the agent as selection criteria. It is configured to select all agents under the age of three years,

4. "Selected Agent" points to an instance of "Final Selection". This primitive serves to reduce a collection of agents to only one agent. This instance is configured for a randomized selection,
5. "Destination" points to an instance of "From Agents to Cells". This primitive return systematically for each agent received as argument its corresponding cell. It has no specific configurations. In this case it returns a unique cell since it receives as argument a unique agent (value of the "Selected Agent" contribution),
6. "No name" points to an instance of "Move to New Cell". This primitive attaches the current agent to the "Destination" cell. It has no specific configurations.

The seventh *Getter Contribution* points to an instance of an auto-generated service called "Get Age", whose function is fetching the current value of a dynamically added attribute, here *age*.

Each of these *service calls* points, on the one hand, to an ordered collection referring to its arguments (other *contributions*), and on the other hand, to one *service description* object that provides metadata about the called service, i.e., the number, order and type of the arguments (which is needed at behavior definition time), as well as the associated activation strategy for that call (which is needed for behavior execution).

Further, each contribution *A* needing the result of the computation of another contribution *B* as argument is said to be *dependent* of *B*. Following the Observer design pattern, this dependency is implemented as a pointer to *A* through the `Dependents` collection of *B*. This relationship is established automatically, when the expert chooses *B* as an argument for *A*. For instance, here is the dependency relationship among the contributions of our current example:

1. "A List of Cells" depends on nothing,
2. "1st List of Agents" depends on "A List of Cells",
3. "2nd List of Agents" depends on "1st List of Agents" and "Age",
4. "Selected Agent" depends on "2nd List of Agents",
5. "Destination" depends on "Selected Agent",
6. "No name" depends on "Destination",
7. "Age" depends on nothing.

The dependency relationship provides major information for the execution mechanism of such behavior definitions. Indeed, the execution starts in parallel with all *service calls* associated to those contributions that depend on no other contribution, here instances of "Neighborhood" and "Get Age", respectively associated to "A List of Cells" and "Age" contributions. At the end of the execution of its service, each *contribution* sends an `update` message (according to the Observer design pattern) its dependents. This launches the computation of all dependent contributions. For instance, as soon as "1st List of Agents" has finished, "2nd List of Agents" is launched. However, each contribution starts its evaluation with that of all its arguments. Its execution will be paused until the values of all arguments will be computed. Therefore, in our example, the computation of "2nd List of Agents" can be paused until the end of the computation of "Age".

With this lengthy explanation we hope to show the usefulness of an elaborate architecture for designing systems like Mobidyc. The design of larger-scale software like MMAS will require more sophisticated tools, for which we suggest that Dycra could be a starting point.

We are now capable of stating what "integrating Dycra into the Campagne-Cardon framework" would mean:

1. *Aspectual agents* are built with Dycra in the same way as Mobidyc agents. In particular, their behavior is described with Dart equipped with a set of primitives which depends on the domain.
2. *Analysis agents* issue behavior modifications for aspectual agents as Dart objects like the one shown here. That is, the result of their reasoning on morphological data is a Dart object.

4 Conclusions and Perspectives

We propose here an approach to the design of software intensive systems for Ambient Intelligence that we call ambiances, which are typical instances of Massively Multi-Agent Systems. Adaptivity being a key characteristic, we suggest to concentrate on user-driven adaptivity, with the aim of keeping the evolution of the system both desirable and predictable.

Our main idea is to embed in the system a Domain Specific Language allowing a knowledgeable user to modify the behavior of some of the agents involved.

The architectural style known as Adaptive Object-Models offers a design technique that has been successfully applied to conventional distributed object-oriented software. We have given here an outline of its extension to agent systems, as a first step toward using it in the design of ambiances. This extension uses a rather complex architecture of which we gave an illustrative excerpt. What we call adaptive modeling is the disciplined use of this technique.

We see the architecture of AOMs as an appropriate starting point for ambiance design methodology. It provides generic and industrially-proven models and tools for controlled and expressive adaptivity, giving domain experts (non-programmers) access to agent behavior programming and adaptation. By adopting a particular vision of software development, built on the basis of explicit modeling of domain knowledge (competence) for specifying the functionality of the system, it ensures relevance and acceptability of the software.

However, it does not address other requirements of ambiances, like fault-tolerance, availability and proactivity. In the above-mentioned *Åmbiance* and *e-Care* research projects (end of subsection 1.2), we are currently engaged in extending Dycra with characteristics borrowed form agent architectures. Specifically, our work on fault-tolerance is based on work by Ch. Dony *et al* on fault-tolerance in multi-agent systems [34], and a work under progress in Luxembourg by the *Correct*[6] project (2004-2006) in collaboration with Romanovsky *et al* [35].

Finally, in the setting of autonomous adaptive agents, knowledgeable end-users should be emulated by learning capacities (e.g. evolutionary computing techniques [36, 37]) that would deliver the same customizing instructions as domain experts. This remains to be explored.

---

[6] CORRECT – rigorous stepwise development of complex fault tolerant distributed systems: from architectural description to Java implementation.

Acknowledgments

The authors gratefully acknowledge the support of Vincent Ginot at INRA. Ch. Dony and A. Karageorgos provided valuable feedback and comments on preliminary versions of this paper. This research benefited also from a UIUC-CNRS exchange program, directed by Gul Agha and J.-P. Briot, and from the Luxembourg National Research Fund (FNR/04/MA2/43).

References

1. Satoh, I.: Mobile Agents for Ambient Intelligence. To appear in *Postproceedings of International Workshop on Massively Multi-Agent Systems (MMAS'2004),* Lecture Notes in Computer Science (LNCS), Springer (2005)
2. IST Advisory Group: Ambient Intelligence: from vision to reality - For participation in society & business (2003)
3. Ducatel, K., Bogdanowicz, M., Scapolo, F., Leijten, J. & Burgelman, J-C. (eds.): ISTAG, Scenarios for Ambient Intelligence in 2010. IPTS-ISTAG, EC: Luxembourg (2001)
4. Olsson, S.: European Commission activities in the area of eHealth. European Commission. Directorate General Information Society. eHealth, ICT for Health Unit. EU R&D Seminar Stockholm, 26 April (2004)
5. Philips Research, OZONE: New Technologies and Services for Emerging Nomadic Societies (2004)
6. Media Lab MIT: Context-Aware Computing Project (2004)
7. Berkeley Webs: Wireless Embedded Systems. URL: http://webs.cs.berkeley.edu/
8. Center for Embedded and Networked Sensing at UCLA. URL: http://cens.ucla.edu/
9. TASK Project: A Parametric Model for Large-Scale Agent Systems. Open Systems Lab., UIUC
10. NEST Project. Customizable Real-Time Coordination Services for Large-scale Network Embedded Systems. Open Systems Lab., UIUC
11. *Proceedings of the Third Cyber Assist Consortium International Symposium,* Yokohama Symposia, November 5, Japan (2004)
12. Ishida, T. (ed.) *Community Computing and Support Systems,* LNCS n° 1519, Springer (1998)
13. Campagne, J. C., Cardon, A.: Artificial emotions for robots using massive multi-agent systems. SID2003, London (2003)
14. Ishida, T.: Concluding remarks at the International Workshop on Massively Multi-Agent Systems, Kyoto (2004)
15. Varela, C., Agha, G.: Programming dynamically reconfigurable open systems with SALSA. SIGPLAN Not., ACM Press, volume 36, n° 12, pages 20-34 (2001)
16. Agha, G.: Abstracting Interaction Patterns: A Programming Paradigm for Open Distributed Systems. In: E. Najm and J.-B. Stefani, editors, *Formal Methods for Open Object-based Distributed Systems* IFIP Transactions. Chapman and Hall (1997)
17. Maciuszek, D., Shahmehri, N., Aberg, J.: Dependability requirements to aid the design of virtual companions for later life, HEAT 2004: The Home and Electronic Assistive Technology, A Workshop Organised by the Interdisciplinary Research Collaboration in Dependability of Computer-Based Systems (DIRC) (2004)
18. Lucena, C., Garcia, A.-F., Romanovsky, A., Castro, J., Alencar, P.S.C. (eds.): *Software Engineering for Multi-Agent Systems II, Research Issues and Practical Applications.* Lecture Notes in Computer Science (lncs 2940). Springer-Verlag, ISBN 3-540-21182-9 (2004)

19. Clements, P., Bachmann, F., Bass, L., Garlan, D., Ivers, J., Little, R., Nord, R., Stafford, J.: Documenting Software Architectures: Views and Beyond. Released: 26 September, ISBN: 0201703726 (2002)
20. Telemedicine Systems Interoperability Alliance (TIA), Telemedicine System Interoperability Architecture - Concept Description and Architecture Overview. Version 0.9
21. Guessoum, Z.: Adaptive Agents and Multi-Agent Systems. In: Distributed Systems Online Journal, IEEE Computer Society (2004)
22. Yoder, J.W., Johnson, R.E.: The Adaptive Object-Model Architectural Style. *3rd IEEE/IFIP Conference on Software Architecture (WICSA3)*, pp.3-27, Montréal, Canada, (2002)
23. Johnson, R.E., Oakes, J.: The User-Defined Product Framework (1998)
24. Foote, B., Yoder, J.: Metadata and active object-models, *Conference on Pattern Languages of Programming (Plop98)*, Washington University Department of Computer Science (1998)
25. Riehle, D., Tilman, M., Johnson, R.E.: Dynamic Object Model. *Conference on Pattern Languages of Programming (PLoP 2000)*, Washington University, Washington University (2000)
26. Nardi, B.A.: *A Small Matter of Programming: Perspectives on End User Computing*, MIT Press, Cambridge (1993)
27. Razavi, R., Bouraqadi, N., Yoder, J.W., Perrot, J.F., Johnson, R.: Language Support for Adaptive-Object Models using Metaclasses. *Proceedings of the ESUG Research Track*, Köthen, Germany, Sept. 2004. Also published in a special issue of the Elsevier international journal Computer Languages, Systems and Structures (to appear in 2005)
28. Razavi, R.: "Outils pour les Langages d'Experts --- Adaptation, Refactoring et Réflexivité". Ph.D. Thesis, LIP6-OASIS, Université Pierre et Marie Curie (Paris 6), Paris (2001)
29. Gamma, E., Helm, R., Johnson, R., Vlissides, J.: *Design Patterns - Elements of Reusable Object-Oriented Software*, Addison-Wesley (1995)
30. Manolescu, D.: Micro-Workflow: A Workflow Architecture Supporting Compositional Object-Oriented Software Development. PhD Thesis, University of Illinois at Urbana-Champaign, Illinois (2000)
31. Manolescu, D.: Workflow enactment with continuation and future objects. *Proceedings of the 17th ACM SIGPLAN conference on Object-oriented programming, systems, languages, and applications.* ACM Press, ISBN 1-58113-471-1. Pages 40 – 51. Seattle, Washington, USA (2002)
32. Ginot, V., Le Page, C.: Mobidyc, a generic multi-agents simulator for modeling communities dynamics. IEA-98-AIE, Lecture Notes in Artificial Intelligence n°1416: 805-814. Springer (1998)
33. Ginot, V., Le Page, C., Souissi, S.: A multi-agents architecture to enhance end-user individual-based modelling, Ecological Modeling 157 pp. 23-41 (2002)
34. Souchon, F., Dony, Ch., Urtado, C., Vauttier, S.: Improving exception handling in multi-agent systems. In Lucena *et al* [18] (2004)
35. Romanovsky, A., Dony, Ch., Knudsen, J.L., Tripathi, A. (eds.): *Advances in Exception Handling Techniques.* Lecture Notes in Computer Science (lncs 2022). Springer-Verlag (2001)
36. Kaelbling, L.P., Littman, M.L., Moore, A.W.: Reinforcement Learning: A Survey, Journal of Artificial Intelligence Research (1996)
37. Sutton, R.S., Barto, A.G.: *Reinforcement Learning, an introduction.* MIT press (1998)

Multi-agent Based Participatory Simulations on Various Scales

Paul Guyot and Alexis Drogoul

LIP6, boîte 169,
Université Pierre et Marie Curie - Paris VI,
4, place Jussieu, F-75252 Paris Cedex 05
{paul.guyot, alexis.drogoul}@lip6.fr

Abstract. In this paper we present a framework called Simulación designed to drive multi-agent based participatory simulations on various scales. Such simulations are defined as simulations where human actors and autonomous agents play similar roles. With Simulación, each participant sits at a computer and interacts with an agent running on it. Humans and agents are paired and the agents can be considered as gates to the simulation, interacting together.

Using Simulación, we were able to conduct experiments over both local area networks and wide area networks. We were thus allowed to measure the requirements for participatory simulations led across laboratory and local area network boundaries. We also present how we started making the agents within these simulations as autonomous as possible, targeting large-scale and wide area experiments.

1   Introduction

Among experiments involving human actors and software agents, the specificity of multi-agent based participatory simulations is that humans and agents play similar roles.

These particular simulations inherit from multi-agent based simulations and role playing games. As multi-agent systems, they include agents capable of playing a role within a complex system, designed through the participation of experts. They can also be seen as an evolution of the RPG/MAS approach as described by Olivier Barreteau, François Bousquet, Stanislas Boissau et al. [1, 2, 3].

Unlike traditional multi-agent systems [4], though, agents in multi-agent based participatory simulations are cognitive agents. Indeed, the experiments can be seen as role playing games where humans play through semi-autonomous assistant agents. The agents are paired with humans tutors. The design of these simulations [5] consists in two steps. First, we bootstrap assistant agents from participatory simulations. Then, agents are taught by their human counterparts who correct their mistakes or completely take control.

Because they rely on assistant agents, multi-agent based participatory simulations are intrinsically highly scalable participatory simulations. Besides, the

T. Ishida, L. Gasser, and H. Nakashima (Eds.): MMAS 2004, LNAI 3446, pp. 149–160, 2005.

models considered often require the simulations to be scalable for both wide area and large-scale experiments. Consequently, we performed local area and wide area experiments and this paper relates our experience.

In order to conduct our experiments, we built a framework called Simulación. In the first part, we will present its architecture and especially its networking architecture, and the models we worked on. The second part will be devoted to the specificity of wide area participatory simulations including the requirements of such simulations we became aware of through our experiments. Finally, we will present how we started to design assistant agents. We will stress automatic extraction of interaction patterns. We will conclude with future directions towards large-scale multi-agent based participatory simulations.

2   Architecture and Experiments

2.1   The Simulación Framework

The Simulación framework currently consists of about 200 classes and 30,000 lines of code, mostly in Java. Java was chosen for portability, maintenance and efficiency in networking code. Indeed, applications based on Simulación ran on many platforms during the experiments : MacOS X, FreeBSD, Solaris, Linux and Windows. The C++ code is limited to ZeroConf support on MacOS X and players using other platforms only need to download a simple jar file that they can click from Windows explorer or launch easily on unices.

The atom in experiments conducted with Simulación is a network entity that can send and receive messages. Being proactive, these entities can be considered as agents in the traditional meaning of the term. Each entity is a Java process that can run on any machine on the network. Typically, the Simulación-based applications run on the user's desktop computer, although some experiments were conducted where they did run on a central server using an exported display to the user's desktop. The network entities communicate through unicast messages with XML-RPC types (integers, strings, dictionaries, etc.). Any entity can communicate with another entity, although the underlaying implementation may use a server to relay the messages.

Thanks to the discovery service, players can join or leave the game at any time. The model may require some players to always be present, however, or it could suspend the game until some players logs in. For example, SimBar requires the bar agent to be there for players to decide to go to the bar or not. Still, they are able to interact even if the bar agent did not log in.

2.2   Models and Experiments

Two sets of experiments were conducted with two different models, SimCafé and SimBar, and the adaptation of a third model is in progress.

SimCafé is centered on the coffee market of the state of Veracruz, Mexico. Coffee production consists in growing the fruit (cereza), transforming it into an

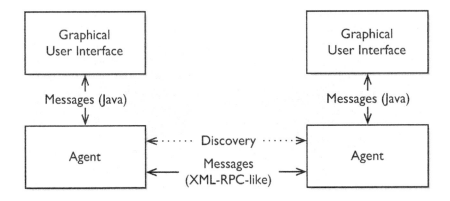

Fig. 1. Simulación's Networking Architecture

intermediary product (pergamino) and then into the final product (oro). Some coffee producers in the state of Veracruz buy cereza coffee and transform it into pergamino. These producers own a factory, called beneficio humido, where the transformation process takes place. The size of the factory determines the throughput of the production. Producers get offers from buyers and they have a certain amount of time to fulfill these contracts and deliver the coffee.

It is believed that coffee producers accept offers even if they cannot provide the buyers with the amount of coffee from their own stocks and production. When this happens, producers actually negotiate with fellow producers and a coalition is formed to supply the demand. One of the motivation for the SimCafé experiment was to confirm a typology of coalitions between producers. Consequently, in this model, producers can discuss together and exchange money and coffee. Their stocks were visible to the buyer so he was able to ask for more coffee than what the target producer was able to provide in order to trigger the formation of coalitions. The exact analysis of the results of the validation can be found in a previous report [6].

SimBar, the second model used with Simulación, is based on the El Farol bar problem as described by Brian Arthur [7]. This problem was also studied by Bruce Edmonds who used a multi-agent system approach with genetic programming to simulate it [8]. The El Farol bar problem is a repeated economic game where players should decide whether they go to the bar or not. If more than 60% of players go to the bar, then the bar is considered to be crowded and players who went did not enjoy it. In Economics terms, going to the bar when less than 60% of players did go has the highest utility, staying home comes next and going with more than 60% of players go to the bar has the smallest utility. Players have to guess what the majority of other players will do and do the contrary.

Bruce Edmonds added simple communications between players : they mention simultaneously if they will go to the bar or not. In a second step, players can decide to go or to stay. Therefore, they could decide differently from what they announced based on what fellow players said. In our experiment, players could ask each other whether they intended to go and decide what to do on the basis of the answers they got. Unlike Bruce Edmonds' simulation, the communications are private.

The SimCafé experiments were led in a single, large room where each player sat at a computer with SimCafé running on it. Players did not really communicate directly but used the SimCafé interface instead. The SimBar experiments were led in various rooms, first with players being in various offices of the laboratory, then with some participant playing from home across the Internet.

2.3   Networking, Ease of Use and Scalability

The Simulación Framework includes two networking methods to connect players together.

The original version used with SimCafé was based on ZeroConf multicast-dns service discovery protocol. The rationale was to have a very simple way to connect computers together with a setup phase as short as possible. This networking architecture worked fairly well in the LANIA laboratory, in Xalapa, Veracruz. Each Simulación entity consisted in a multicast-dns responder advertising the service and an XML-RPC HTTP server running on a random free port selected by the Java virtual machine. This code allowed us to run several instances of the program on the same computer.

The first SimBar experiments also used ZeroConf networking code. However, while no setup was required indeed, some problems started to arise with wireless networks and network address translation performed by the wireless access points. Indeed network address translation is incompatible with a TCP/IP server running on each computer. UDP servers using the reverse UDP technique as used by peer-to-peer networking architectures was considered but nowadays system administrators in laboratories often block peer-to-peer protocols and consequently we were led to use another approach more compatible with wide area experiments.

The second networking method is based on HTTP. Each entity within the network is an HTTP client performing HTTP requests to a central server. These requests could be made via a proxy or directly. These requests actually are XML-RPC based and encapsulate the Simulación discovery and communication messages. Entities connect to a server that handles discovery and dispatches messages to the various entities.

The big advantage of HTTP is that it works everywhere there is something called an internet access. Our architecture uses HTTP 1.1 basic features and would work even if there were transparent proxies or firewalls.

The drawback of HTTP is, however, that the underlaying networking architecture is asymmetrical. As a multi-agent system, the Simulación framework requires entities to be able to receive messages at any time and using TCP/IP

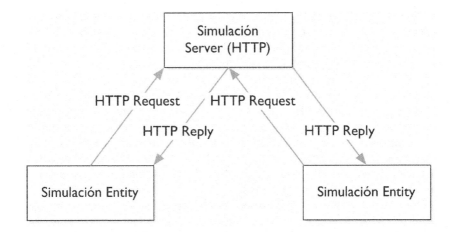

Fig. 2. Simulación's HTTP Networking Architecture

clients with a single request protocol seems incompatible with this requirement. To overcome this difficulty, the client sends a request to the server to wait for an incoming message. When a message arrives, the server returns this information to the client. If no message arrives and an HTTP-timeout expires, the server returns a message to mention that there is nothing new and the client should send another HTTP request to wait for an incoming message. This architecture allows immediate transmission of messages without much expensive polling since the timeout is 10 seconds and during a game, the frequency of messages is much higher.

3 Specificity of Wide Area Participatory Simulations

Some specificities of wide area participatory simulations could probably not be forecast. With our experiments, we realized the software has to be robust in order to cope with bugs and networking problems. The applications also have to be easy to use and some channels have to be reserved for online technical support. Finally, since the players are not in a specific room for the experiments, the interface must be designed in such a way that the game will not be interrupted and the game must be set in such a way that players should not be too distracted from activities in their own offices or places.

3.1 Robustness

The key requirement of wide area participatory simulations is the robustness. In local experiments, the designers and the animators are able to fix last-minute bugs or networking problems. Bugs actually had to be fixed during the first experiment conducted with the Simulación framework. But in wide area participatory simulations, the bugs cannot be fixed during the simulation. Additionally, there may be exogenous networking problems. Consequently, the framework and the model must be designed in a robust way.

The first key element of robustness is exception handling. Exceptions can typically occur within Java code because of bugs or because of networking problems. The Simulación framework is very robust to exceptions and these are caught to prevent them to propagate where they should not. When an exception occurs, the operation is considered to have failed and the user is warned about it. For example, a networking problem may prevent a user to send a message and the interface will blink to mention the problem. The exception may actually happen after the message was actually sent.

The second element to robustness is transactions. When players exchange money or coffee or when they decide to go to the bar or not, these operations are transactional and the local agent must get a confirmation from the other end. The transactional approach ensures that the coffee is not subtracted from the sender's stock and never added to the receiver's stock for example. Transactions are also used to ensure that two players cannot select the same role within the simulation.

The third element to robustness is the symmetry. Players can join or leave the game at any time and there is no special order or requirement so each entity is independent from the others. Additionally, with the ZeroConf-based networking code, all entities are equal network-wise, being both a server and a client. This changed with the HTTP code since the HTTP server has to remain online. To ensure a good robustness, there is a Java process dedicated to the server task and additional agents on the same computer run in different processes.

The fourth element to robustness is duplication. In both SimBar and SimCafé, except one player (coffee buyer or bar tenant) who counted points or sent offers, all players had the same role (coffee producer or bar regular). In SimBar, the bar agent kept a record of the points of the bar regulars. Consequently, when some bar regular did quit and join the game, it downloaded its record from the bar agent and the game could continue as though it never left it.

All these elements allowed us to successfully run experiments in spite of inherent problems due to the wide area networking architecture or to the lack of prior large-scale testing.

3.2   Ease of Use and Support

Another requirement for wide area participatory simulations is the ease of use of the application. In local participatory simulations, one usually teaches the players how to play to the game and one can reply to questions during the simulation and stop the experiment to explain some elements again. This is not possible when players are all around the world.

For this reason, a particular care was brought to make the interface as simple as possible and as easy to use as possible. Some tests were conducted before the experiment to make sure the interface was easy enough to use and the interface was improved from comments that we got during these tests.

Additionally, in the case of SimBar, a player was added to the model. This player is the bar tenant. This role is linked with the bar agent counting points. Its role was played by the animator of the simulation and during the experiment, players could ask questions to the tenant which could then reply individually or collectively and thus give information about the interface or the game model.

3.3   Attractiveness and Timing

In addition to robustness and ease of use with online technical support, successful wide area participatory simulations require the interface to be attractive and the timing to be properly set in order to motivate players to play and avoid distractions that could hinder the game.

Great care was taken to provide the user with a friendly interface. Both Sim-Café and SimBar benefitted from beautiful graphics designed by Michael Vacík which made the game appealing to the users. We got many comments on the animated characters in the game and their expressions. Additionally, applications using the Simulación framework can be written in several languages and the framework itself detects the user's preferred language and displays the interfaces in this language (provided that the applications were translated). SimCafé did run in English, French and Spanish and SimBar did run in English and French.

In both cases, the interface was improved between experiments in order to make the game easier to play and more attractive. One of the key element to these experiments is the timing. In SimCafé, the simulation time is a fraction of real time because of the transformation process which takes some time (three days in reality). We did change the time scale between two experiments in order to make the game easier to play. This kind of settings is in an XML file in order to be easily changed within a single experiments session.

The SimBar game does not have a fixed time scale. Instead, the week is over when all players cast their decision to go or to not go to the bar. In order to improve the experience of players, and as suggested during the first experiment, a sound is emitted when the turn is over. Additionally, if some players do not make their decision, after a while, the system considers that they are out of the game and proceeds to the next turn without them.

Finally, the attractiveness problem is a key element for experiments with assistant agents. The agents need to be credible in order for human experts to accept to teach them and play with them.

4   Towards Assistant Agents

The participatory simulations that we conducted are also the first step towards the design of multi-agent based participatory simulations with assistant agents.

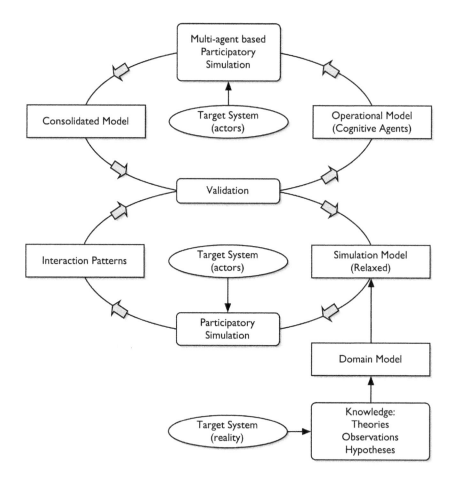

Fig. 3. Multi-agent based participatory simulation design process (detail)

4.1   Design of Multi-agent Based Participatory Simulations

The process of designing multi-agent based participatory simulations is iterative like all role playing game and multi-agent systems processes.

The first iterations are made of participatory simulations. The model is modified to make it playable. This includes adding a role for online help. Most importantly, the model is relaxed in order to let the players behave differently from what they are expected to do. For example, in the SimCafé model, players could send coffee to other players without any money exchange. They could also exchange money and coffee without any prior offer from the buyer. This extension is required for model validation.

The second step of the first iterations consist in automatic extraction of interaction patterns. These patterns are then validated by the domain expert (a.k.a.

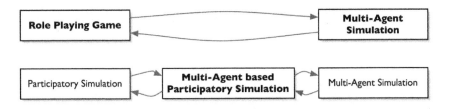

Fig. 4. RPG/MAS and MABS iterations

thematician). Further iterations can be performed if the interaction patterns are not found valid by the expert.

Multi-agent based participatory simulations actually consist in the second set of iterations. The proto-agents are designed from the interactive patterns and are taught by the players. Once the assistant agents become autonomous, they form a consolidated multi-agent model and can be used in multi-agent simulations with no participation. The consolidated model can then be validated by the expert.

The design of multi-agent based participatory can be compared with the Role Playing Game/Multi-Agent System approach. While multi-agent based participatory simulations can be used to design multi-agent systems, the outcomes of such simulations mostly consist in multi-agent based participatory experiments themselves. These experiments combine the outcomes of both role playing games and multi-agent systems in the RPG/MAS paradigm.

4.2   From Participatory Simulations to Multi-agent Based Participatory Simulations

The transformation of participatory simulations into multi-agent based participatory simulations lie in the design of assistant agents. Our approach is to bootstrap the agents with an automatic processing of the log of the participatory simulations. This processing is an extraction of interaction patterns written in a superset of the Q Language [9].

```
(guard
((?hear ''Hello'' :from Jerry)
 (!speak ''Hello'' :to Jerry) ... )
((?see railway_station :direction ''south'')
 (!walk :from bus_terminal :to railway_station) ... )
(otherwise
 (!send ''I am still waiting'' :to Tom) ... ))
```

Fig. 5. Example of a Lisp counterpart of a card in the Q Language

```
(guard
((?hear ''Hello'' :from $X)
 (!speak ''Hello'' :to $X) ... )
((?see $Y :direction ''south'')
 (!walk :from bus_terminal :to $Y) ... )
(otherwise
 (!send ''I am still waiting'' :to $Z) ... ))
```

Fig. 6. Q Scenario with variables

The reasons why we chose Q as the language to describe the interactions include the need for a readable representation of the patterns in order to validate them with the domain experts.

Indeed, scenarios in Q are isomorphic to what Toru Ishida calls Interaction Patterns Cards which are cards that can be edited in a spreadsheet program by experts with no programming skill.

The extraction consists of first using logging agents to log all the interactions and then processing the logs to generate interaction patterns which are Q scenarios.

While logging agents are needed in the case of a symmetric networking architecture, their use could be questioned in the case of a central server, since all the messages exchanged between entities are sent to the server. However, the log agents also allow us to log interactions between human players with their own agents. The architecture is such that several log agents can be used at the same time in order to ensure that the log is complete in spite of networking hazards.

The Q Language is a subset of the Lisp language (Fig. 5), and considering the small amount of data collected with the simulations, we chose genetic programming to build Q scenarios. The fitness function simply consists in the ability of programs to generate logs similar to the real logs.

Strongly-typed genetic programming [10] allow us to force the structure of the programs in order to get Q scenarios. Indeed, we can associate the guard node with a given type and force all the members of the genetic population to be of this type. This method reduces the size of the exploration set by limiting it to programs having a given form.

Unsurprisingly, standard genetic programming yield to poor results. We decided to create generic interaction pattern cards by adding variables that can be instantiated with any value within an enumerated set (typically the set of players). Indeed, matching the log is much easier when we introduce variables into the cards the way they could be used in generic Q scenarios (Fig. 6).

However, variables are a problem in genetic programming [11]. Unlike regular variables approaches [12], our fitness function consisted in an unification engine to match the variables with the values of the log, and our variables turned out to be prolog-like. This mechanically produced much better results for our own problem than with regular variables (Fig. 7). Moreover, the scope of variables, limited to a single guard closure, improves the meaningfulness of extracted patterns.

Analysis of the results showed that this algorithm was able to extract synchronous interactions. However, the synchronicity of the Q language does not allow extraction of asynchronous interactions and we consequently started working on an extension of the Q language and on adding support for parallel interactions to the unification engine.

5   Conclusion

The cards that are automatically extracted will be used as the basis of the assistant agents within scalable participatory simulations. Extraction of these cards is improved by using parallel nodes in the genetic programming algorithm together with backward chaining in the unification engine. The assistant agents will then have to choose instantiation of variables in cards as well as which card to execute and when. They will be corrected by their human tutors who will also be able to take full control over their agents. Taking full control is indeed required for validation purposes and to avoid frustration on the human players' part.

Moreover, semi-autonomous assistant agents is a path towards wide area and large-scale participatory experiments : the players may let the assistants play when they are away from the computer and hence experiments may be easier to set up with assistant agents than without.

Future work also includes integration with Cormas multi-agent system designing tool around a new model with both local area and wide area experiments and design of the assistant agents from the automatically extracted patterns.

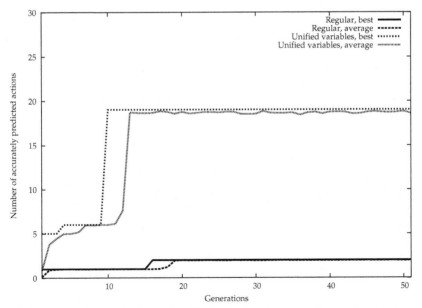

Fig. 7. Use of regular variables and unified variables to generalize Abelardo's behavior during a SimCafé experiment

Acknowledgments

The SimCafé experiments were conducted within a project funded by Le Labora-toire Franco-Mexicain d'Informatique (LAFMI) and directed by Amal El Fallah Seghrouchni and Christian Lemaître Léon. We also would like to thank the fellow members of le Laboratoire d'Informatique de Paris 6 who agreed to participate to the SimBar experiments and who gave us an extremely valuable feedback.

References

1. Barreteau, O., Bousquet, F., Attonaty, J.M.: Role-playing games for opening the black box of multi-agent systems: method and lessons of its application to senegal river valley irrigated systems. Journal of Artificial Societies and Social Simulation **4** (2001)
2. Bousquet, F., Barreteau, O., d'Aquino, P., Etienne, M., Boissau, S., Aubert, S., Le Page, C., Babin, D., Castella, J.C.: Multi-agent systems and role games: Collective learning processes for ecosystem management. In Janssen, M., ed.: Complexity and Ecosystem Management: The Theory and Practice of Multi-agent Approaches. Edward Elgar Publishers (2002) 248–285
3. Boissau, S., Lan Anh, H., Castella, J.C.: The samba role play game in northern vietnam : An innovative approach to participatory natural resource management. Mountain Research and Development **24** (2004) 101–105
4. Drogoul, A., Meurisse, T., Vanberge, D.: Multi-agent based simulations: Where are the agents? In Sichman, J.S., Bousquet, F., Davidsson, P., eds.: Multi-Agent-Based Simulation, Third International Workshop, MABS 2002, Bologna, Italy, July 15-16, 2002, Revised Papers. Volume 2581 of Lecture Notes in Computer Science., Springer (2002) 1–15
5. Guyot, P., Drogoul, A.: Designing multi-agent based participatory simulations. In Coelho, H., Espinasse, B., eds.: Proceedings of 5th Workshop on Agent Based Simulations, Erlangen, San Diego, SCS Publishing House (2004) 32–37
6. Guyot, P.: Simulations multi-agents participatives: Vers une méthode de validation et de consolidation des modèles de pratiques collectives. Master's thesis, Université Pierre et Marie Curie (2003)
7. Arthur, B.: Inductive reasoning and bounded rationality. American Economic Review **84** (1994) 406–411
8. Edmonds, B.: Gossip, sexual recombination and the el farol bar: modelling the emergence of heterogeneity. Journal of Artificial Societies and Social Simulation **2** (1999)
9. Ishida, T.: Q: A scenario description language for interactive agents. IEEE Computer **35** (2002) 54–59
10. Montana, D.J.: Strongly typed genetic programming. BBN Technical Report #7866, Bolt Beranek and Newman, Inc. (1993)
11. Kirshenbaum, E.: Genetic programming with statically scoped local variables. In: Proceedings of the Genetic and Evolutionary Computation Conference (GECCO) 2000, Morgan Kaufmann (2000) 459–468
12. Koza, J.R.: Genetic Programming: On the Programming of Computers by Means of Natural Selection. MIT Press, Cambridge, MA, USA (1992)

A Massively Multi-agent System for Discovering HIV-Immune Interaction Dynamics

Shiwu Zhang[1,2] and Jiming Liu[1]

[1] Hong Kong Baptist University, Kowloon Tong, Hong Kong
[2] University of Science and Technology of China, Anhui, China
{swzhang, jiming}@comp.hkbu.edu.hk

Abstract. In MMAS-based biological system simulation, it is a challenging task to deal with numerous interactions among a vast number of autonomous agents. In our work, a hybrid massively multi-agent systems (MMAS) model is developed, and it incorporates the characteristics of cellular automaton (CA) and system-level mathematical equation modeling to simulate HIV-immune interaction dynamics. The mathematical equations are adopted within the site of a two-dimensional lattice. As the average high density, agent interactions can be calculated according to the equations without significantly affecting the performance of the systems studied. In the mean time, the CA model keeps the spatial characteristics of HIV evolution among the sites. The simulation based on the implemented MMAS discovers the dynamics of HIV evolution over different temporal and spatial scales, and reproduces the typical three-stage dynamics of HIV infection.

1   Introduction

There are plenty of biological systems involving multi-entity interactions. The goal of studying such systems is twofold [1]: (1) we can gain a better understanding of the working mechanisms underlying complex behaviors (e.g. mass extinction [2] and epidemic spreading [3]), (2) we can derive new methods for solving hard computational problems (e.g. genetic algorithm [4] and ant colony optimization [5][6]). Our objective of developing a new hybrid MMAS model is to demonstrate and understand the dynamics in complex biological systems. Human immune system is a typical example of a highly sensitive, adaptive and self-regulated complex system involving numerous interactions among a vast number of cells that belong to different types. Immune response is an emergent phenomenon from the interactions of numerous entities, which protects the human body from invaders such as bacteria, virus and other parasites.

In order to deal with numerous interactions among a vast number of autonomous agents in MMAS-based simulation, here we present a hybrid MMAS model that incorporates the characteristics of CA and system-level mathematical equation modeling to simulate the complex interactions in the process of human immune response to HIV. CA and system-level equation models are often used to simulate complex interactions in the immune system. CA allows for

T. Ishida, L. Gasser, and H. Nakashima (Eds.): MMAS 2004, LNAI 3446, pp. 161–173, 2005.
© Springer-Verlag Berlin Heidelberg 2005

spatial structure analysis and emphasizes the emergence from individual interactions. However, CA dealing with separate reactions and components consumes
too much CPU time. Modeling based on system-level equations is a top-down
method to simulate biological systems, while the model ignores the spatial structure and non-homogeneous characteristics of the systems which are the most
important factors in emergence. In our hybrid MMAS model, the mathematical
equations are used within a single site and agents can diffuse among different
sites. This reserves the spatial characteristics of the system and reduces the
heavy computational cost of the CA model as well.

The remainder of the paper is organized as follows. Section 2 surveys related
simulation work on the immune system. Section 3 introduces HIV-immune interaction dynamics according to clinical discoveries. Section 4 provides details
on the hybrid MMAS model. Section 5 describes and analyzes the experimental
results. Section 6 concludes the paper by summarizing the features of the model.

2   Related Work

Although modern experimental techniques are able to isolate the human immune
system into comprehensible parts, the immune response that emerges from the
interactions among immune cells still cannot be completely understood. An alternative way is to study the whole integrated system through the use of mathematical models.

Till now, there have been some mathematical models used to simulate HIV-
immune interaction dynamics, and they can be classified into three categories:
cellular automata, system-level equations and agent-based models.

2.1   Cellular Automaton

Cellular automaton is a discrete dynamical system that is often used to simulate some natural phenomena. It contains an n-dimensional lattice and identical
cells. The cells on the sites of the lattice have variable states, which can change
according to particular rules in the simulation. The self-organization and life-like
behaviors in the CA model have been researched in depth. CA models have been
applied in many areas to explore the emergent behaviors in complex systems.

As for the immune system, Santos et al. have pointed out that CA is a
good tool to study the adaptation and self-regulation properties in the immune
system [7]. They have illustrated some clauses on how to understand the immune system with CA [8]. CA models for HIV-immune dynamics in physical
space or "shape space" are also developed by Santos et al. [9] and Hersberg
et al. [10] respectively. In the immune system, different strains of the immune
cells, antibodies and antigens are distinguished based on the shape of molecules
on their surface. Accordingly, the "shape space" means space consisting of different strains of elements in the immune system. However, both models have
shortcomings for unreasonable simplifications in CA.

The advantages of CA lie in their capabilities to allow for spatial structure
analysis and to emphasize the emergence from individual interactions. This is the

most important issue in exploring HIV-immune dynamics [11][12][13]. However, CA also has shortcomings. For example, the rules are too simple to represent the complex interactions within most biological systems, CA dealing with each separate reaction and component consumes too much CPU time, CA views each cell or entity as being identical, which often does not reflect the reality.

2.2 System-Level Equation

System-level equation modeling is a traditional top-down method for analyzing systems with differential equations. Nowak et al. have presented a differential equation model based on the understanding of the interactions among immune cells and antigens [14]. The model simplifies the interactions in the process of the immune response and discusses the relations among virus load, immune responsiveness, antigenic diversity and infection progress. The simulation results indicate that virus diversity often increases virus load and speeds up infection progress [14]. Kirsher et al. also presented several differential equation models accounting for HIV infection and discovered some important issues in HIV-immune interaction dynamics [15][16][17].

The reason why system-level equations are frequently applied in the immune system lies in the particular characteristics in describing key mechanisms and simplifying implementation. The system-level equations view the elements in the system as being homogeneous, and ignore the spatial structure of the biological system in the microscopic scale. This allows for extensive mathematical analysis and reduces the computational cost of simulation. However, the models often fail to account for the large-scale emergence from local interactions and individual diversity [13].

2.3 Agent-Based Model

In recent years, multi-agent theories have been applied in many areas to simulate, understand and predict the complex behaviors emerging from complex adaptive systems including the immune system. In a multi-agent system, entities are viewed as agents with internal contents, which can sense their environment, alter their internal states and act on the environment. The agent-based simulation is more closer to the real interactions among entities than that based on CA [18]. However, the deficiency in handling massive agents limits agent-based modeling applications.

In order to explore the emergence of complex deterministic macroscopic functions out of stochastic microscopic interactions, a hybrid MMAS model is developed to simulate HIV-immune interaction dynamics. In the model, HIV and immune cells are denoted by the agents of different types. A two-dimensional lattice provides an environment for HIV and the immune cells to live and interact. In order to reduce the computational cost of simulation, the concepts of mathematical equation models are adopted within the site, which views components of the same type within the same site as being homogenous and uses mathematical equations to describe their interactions. Because of the high-density distribution of agents in a single site, the formulation is reasonable and does not significantly affect the performance of the system [10].

3   HIV-Immune Interaction Dynamics

HIV invasion, erosion and eventual crash on the immune system is a very complex process. However, most microscopic interactions among HIV and the immune cells have been revealed by modern instrumentations. Generally, the process can be stated as the following.

HIV virion is a type of retrovirus. It has a selective tropism to the CD4+ T cells, which are the most important cells in the immune response. After a virion binds to a cell, it will enter the cell and reproduce copies with the same "gene". HIV also infect other cells, such as B cells and monocytes too. Because of the cytopathic effect or other indirect mechanisms, the population of the CD4+ T cell will decrease sharply in the initial stage of infection, and simultaneously HIV population will increase rapidly.

The CD4+ T cells play a central role in the immune system, because they can detect invaders, and initiate an immune response. In the immune response, the immune system will be stimulated to produce more CD4+ T cells of the same type and activate the CD8 T cells, another type of T cells, as the killer T cell. The CD8 T cell will seek and kill cells infected by the invaders. The CD4+ T cell can also stimulate B cells to create antibodies, which serve as antigen killing devices. Virus with the same gene as the recognized virion are eliminated by the corresponding T cells and antibodies. Thus the density of HIV decreases sharply and that of T cell refreshes suddenly. It is the typical dynamics of the immune response like that of other diseases. However, HIV have a much higher mutation rate than other antigens for inaccurate RNA replication processes in the virus proliferation. Because of the fast mutation rate, HIV of other strains cannot be annihilated completely. HIV will remain in the peripheral tissue with low density for a long period depending on different human individuals, which means that the illness comes into the clinical latency period. In the latency period HIV-immune dynamics demonstrate a steady state in which the HIV population and the immune cells population are in balance [19]. However, HIV still destroy the immune system gradually until the immune system cannot control virus load finally, which comes the onset of AIDS. More details about the mechanisms of how HIV destroy the immune system can be found in [20][21][22][23].

4   MMAS Design

4.1   Interactions in the MMAS

In the developed MMAS model, there are three types of agents involved in interactions according to the above description on HIV-immune dynamics. They are T cells (immune cells), O cells (other cells) and HIV. More than 90% immune cells are located in an organism and few immune cells circulate in the peripheral blood. Cells in the human organism cannot flow and interact everywhere as those in the peripheral blood. Most cells can only play their role in their local environment, so the assumption that the agents only interact in a two-dimensional lattice is reasonable. However, the agents not only live in the physical space, but also live in a "shape space". "Shape space" is the space constructed by "genes" of HIV and T cells. Here a gene is used to represent the strain of HIV or T cells. Each virion or T cell has its own gene. HIV mutation means HIV diffusion in the "Shape space".

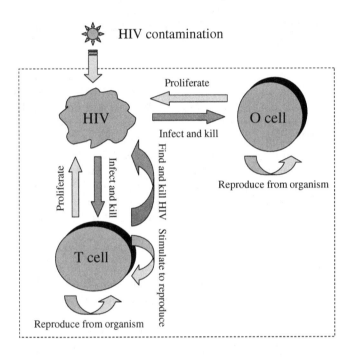

Fig. 1. The interactions among different types of agents: O cells, T cells and HIV. After HIV enter the human organism, the process of HIV destroying the immune system is triggered

In the simulation, if a T cell meets and recognizes a virion with the same gene at a site, it will kill the virion and stimulate the neighboring sites to create more T cells of the same type. The new T cells can kill virus with the same gene as the recognized virion at the same site. HIV can infect and kill cells at the same site. Simultaneously HIV can also proliferate and mutate. HIV and the immune cells will diffuse from high-density sites to less-crowded sites. The interactions among the three types of agents are shown in Fig. 1.

4.2   Rules and Reactions

According to the above description, the rules and reactions of the hybrid MMAS model are listed below. We use mathematical equations as rules to calculate interactions within a site.

- **Rule 1:** *The environment* is an $N \times N$ two-dimensional lattice that is circular. $D_{hiv}^t(i,j), D_{tcell}^t(i,j), D_{ocell}^t(i,j), D_{cell}^t(i,j)$ denotes the density of HIV, T cells, O cells and all cells at time t at site $[i,j]$ respectively. The gene of an agent is denoted by an integer.
- **Rule 2:** *T cell recognizing HIV and stimulating to reproduce itself.* At the site $[i,j]$, if a T cell finds HIV with the same "gene" as that of itself, the cell will kill HIV and stimulate four neighboring sites to produce new T cells with the same "gene".
- **Rule 3:** *HIV infecting and killing cells.* At site $[i,j]$, a virion can infect a cell (T cell or other cell) with a probability P_{inf}. If a cell is infected by virus, it will die and produce $N_{cellhiv}$ virus with the same gene as that of the infecting virion. If there exist k HIV virus and one cell, the probability for the cell to be infected is $1 - (1 - P_{inf})^k$.
- **Rule 4:** *HIV mutation.* HIV mutation rate is set as $P_{mutation}$, which means that when a virion is reproduced, the probability that the virion mutates is $P_{mutation}$. Once a virion mutates, its gene will be an integer randomly selected from a gene space. Here the gene space is $[0 \sim 1024]$.
- **Rule 5:** *HIV and cells diffusion.* HIV and the immune cells can diffuse from high-density sites to low-density sites according to the diffusion equation:

$$D^{t+1}(i,j) = D^t(i,j) + (\sum_{k=neighbors} D^t(k)/m - D^t(i,j)) * C_{diffusion}$$

In the above equation, $D^{t+1}(i,j)$ means the density of HIV or cells at time $t+1$ at site $[i,j]$. $C_{diffusion}$ is the diffusion constant. m denotes the number of the site's neighbors.
- **Rule 6:** *Cell natural creation by an organism.* When the density of cells at a site is lower than threshold T_{cell} and the density of HIV at the site is lower than T_{hiv} respectively, the system will produce cells (T cells or Other cells) at the site. The equation is described as follows:

$$\text{IF} \quad D_{hiv}^t < T_{hiv} \& D_{cell}^t < T_{cell}$$
$$D_{cell}^{t+1} = D_{cell}^t + 1$$
$$\text{ELSE}$$
$$D_{cell}^{t+1} = D_{cell}^t$$
$$\text{END}$$

The type of the produced cell is controlled by P_{type}, which means that when a cell is generated by an organism, it will be a T cell with the probability P_{type}, and be an O cell with the probability $1 - P_{type}$. If the new cell is a T cell, its gene will be randomly produced by the system. The rule mimics the high ability of the immune system recovering from the immunosuppression generated by the infection.

- **Rule 7:** *Natural death of HIV and cells.* Besides being killed in the interactions among agents, the agents also die for other reasons such as ageing. The probability of cell death at each step at site $[i, j]$ is $P_{cellnd} = D_{cell}(i, j)/T_{cellnd}$. Similarly, the probability of HIV natural death is $P_{hivnd} = D_{hiv}(i, j)/T_{hivnd}$. Here T_{cellnd} and T_{hivnd} are all constants, which means the number of HIV and the immune cells is limited. The rule reflects the competitive relations within the same groups of agents partly.

4.3   Simulation Process

The whole system updates in a synchronized parallel way according to the above rules. The simulation starts with the cell natural creation and death. After a certain number of steps, the contamination, HIV, is added into the system. Simultaneously HIV-immune interaction dynamics begin to be recorded. Below is the simulation process:

> **Initialize** the system
> **Add** the contamination
> **For** each step
>> **For** each site
>>> Cells natural creation according to Rule 6
>>> T cell killing HIV and reproduction according to Rule 2
>>> HIV infection and reproduction according to Rule 3
>>> HIV mutation according to Rule 4
>>> HIV and cells diffusion according to Rule 5
>>> Cells and HIV natural death according to Rule 7
>> **End**
> **End**

5   Experimentation and Discussion

In the simulation, HIV dynamics over different temporal and spatial scales are observed. The experiment is conducted on a two-dimensional lattice with the size of 20×20, and the number of running steps is 4000. After ten steps of the natural creation and death, ten virus with the same gene are added into a randomly selected site, and HIV-immune interaction dynamics begin to be recorded. The experimental parameters are listed in Table 1.

5.1   Temporal Emergence

The common pattern of HIV dynamics in infected patients is the three-stage dynamics of HIV infection, which has been proven by many researchers. The three-stage dynamics include the primary response, the clinical latency and the onset of AIDS. The details of the three-stage dynamics can be found in [24][10].

Table 1. The parameters in the experiment

LatticeSize	20	*m*	4
GeneSpace	1024	T_{hiv}	6
P_{inf}	0.2	T_{cell}	2
$N_{cellhiv}$	10	T_{cellnd}	4
$P_{mutation}$	0.05	T_{hivnd}	12
P_{type}	0.3	$C_{diffusion}$	0.4

Figure 2 shows the dynamics of the HIV population in the experiment. It can be concluded that the typical three-stage dynamics of HIV infection is well reproduced in the simulation, which means that the temporal pattern emerges from the local interactions between HIV and the immune system. A similar conclusion can be obtained from Fig. 3. The observations also validate the model.

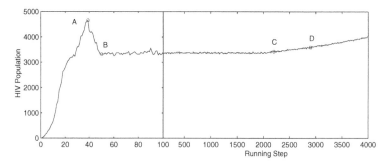

Fig. 2. HIV population dynamics in the experiment. The three-stage dynamics of HIV infection is emerged. Before B: the primary response, $B \sim C$: The clinical latency, After D it is the onset of AIDS. At A, the HIV population reaches a maximum. From C, the mechanism that decreases the natural ability of an organism in producing T cells is incorporated

In Fig. 2, the HIV population increases and decreases sharply in the first 50 steps which accounts for the primary immune response. After the primary response there is a long period with the virus population keeping stable and increasing slowly. However, HIV and the immune cells are still active with very high death and reproduction rates. Coffin has pointed out that in the clinical latency stage, the HIV death rate is approximately equal to the HIV reproduction rate [19]. At C in Fig. 2, we assume that the natural ability of an organism in producing T cells becomes weaker. The assumption is reasonable as McCune has pointed out that HIV destroys mature cells and reduces the ability of the body to replace cells from immature progenitors [22]. Therefore after C, the HIV population increases and the T cell population decreases quickly. After D,

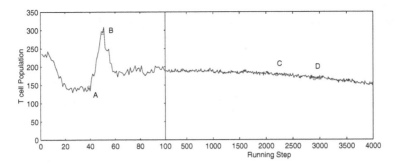

Fig. 3. T cell population dynamics in the experiment. In the figure, points A, B, C and D are selected as the same as those in Figure 2

it comes the period of AIDS onset. The comparison on the HIV population before C and after C indicates that without decreasing the natural ability of an organism in creating T cells, the immune system can still control the HIV level even after many steps in the clinical latency period. The result also means that decreasing the natural ability of the immune system in creating T cells is a fatal factor for HIV to destroy the immune system, although we do not know how HIV weaken the immune system's ability for self-recovery.

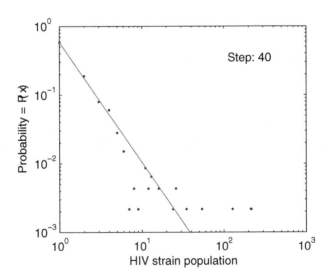

Fig. 4. HIV strain population distribution in the experiment at step 40, which follows a power law. X axis is the size of HIV strain, Y axis displays the probability of a special HIV strain size

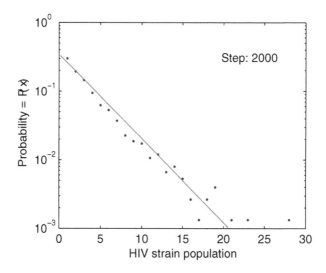

Fig. 5. HIV strain population distribution in the experiment at step 2000, which follows an exponential distribution. X axis is the size of HIV strain, Y axis displays the probability of a special HIV strain size

5.2   "Shape Space" Emergence

Besides the temporal dynamics of the HIV population, HIV distribution in "Shape Space" is also very important in understanding HIV infection, HIV therapy and vaccine. Because of the rapid mutation rate, HIV gene sequences change a lot even in a single infected patient. Pennisi discussed viral diversity and pointed out that the viral diversity is difficult to tackle for the immune system in traditional views [24]. However, it is easy to observe the dynamics of HIV strain distribution along with the time (HIV strain Dynamics) in the MMAS simulation.

The most interesting result, "shape space" emergence, is shown in Fig. 4 and Fig. 5. Two special scenes at step 40 and step 2000 in the experiment are selected and the HIV strain population distributions are shown. Figure 4 illustrates the HIV distribution in the "shape space": HIV strain population distribution at step 40, at which the HIV population is the largest in the primary response according to Fig. 2. The distribution of the HIV strain population follows a power law, which means that HIV can self-organize into a special structure in the "shape space". The phenomenon originates from the positive feedback that exists in many complex systems, such as the distribution of web sites [25]. However, from Fig. 5 it can be found that the HIV strain distribution at step 2000 changes to an exponential distribution, which means that the probability of the appearance of HIV strains of large size decreases. At the same time, more HIV strains of small size appear, which means HIV diversity becomes large. The reason is that the HIV strain size is larger, the probability of HIV being found and killed is greater. Thus after the primary immune response, the HIV strain size is difficult to become large under the control of the immune system. Another reason why the HIV strain size cannot become larger is the HIV high mutation rate. Therefore, the HIV strain population distribution becomes more and more average. Size of HIV strains that are found and killed by the immune cells becomes smaller, which reveals the reason why the immune system cannot eradiate HIV eventually.

Till now, there are no specific literatures explaining the quantitative population dynamics of HIV strains. The reason is that it is difficult to examine the relative large proportion of HIV in the human body and the whole sequence of HIV genes. However, there are still many studies on the HIV diversity to explore its causes, development and therapy means [14][19][26][27][28][29]. In [29], Wolinsky analyzed the development of the gene sequence similarity in six patients and indicated that the HIV diversity becomes large along with the HIV evolution and the immune response selective pressure, which is also consistent with our results.

6   Conclusion

In the hybrid MMAS model, the characteristics of CA and system-level equation modeling are utilized to simulate HIV-immune interaction dynamics. The model emphasizes the inhomogeneity among different sites and the homogeneity within sites. The characteristics of the model that are different from other models are as follows:

- The model is based on a massively multi-agent system. Entities in the system are viewed as agents that can sense and act on their environment. This makes the model closer to a real situation. The model incorporates the characteristics of CA and system-level equations. It not only keeps the spatial characteristics of the local interactions, but also reduces the computational cost of the simulation.
- The temporal emergence validates our model. Moreover, it reveals that AIDS cannot break out if HIV only destroy T cells without weakening the T cell reproduction mechanism. The emergence in "shape space" indicates that it is because the HIV's fast mutation that the immune system cannot eradicate HIV as easily as it does to other invaders. The discoveries help researchers to understand HIV-immune interaction dynamics more comprehensively.
- The concepts of "shape space" and the physical space are incorporated into the model simultaneously, which are also not found in the previous models.

Our results have indicated that the hybrid MMAS model incorporating the characteristics of CA and mathematical equations is effective in simulating and characterizing biological systems.

Acknowledgements

The authors of this work would like to acknowledge the support of the following research grants: (1) Hong Kong Research Grant Council (RGC) Central Allocation Grant (HKBU 2/03/C) and Earmarked Research Grants (HKBU 2121/03E)(HKBU 2040/02E), (2) Major State Basic Research Development Program of China (973 Program) (2003CB317001), (3) Open Foundation of Beijing Municipal Key Laboratory for Multimedia and Intelligent Software Technology (KP0705200379), and (4) Hong Kong Baptist University Faculty Research Grants (FRG).

References

1. Liu, J., Jin, X.L., Tsui, K.C.: Autonomy Oriented Computing (AOC): From Problem Solving to Complex Systems Modeling. Springer, (2004)
2. Newman, M.E.J.: A Model of Mass Extinction. Santa Fe Institute Working Papers, (1997) http://ideas.repec.org/p/wop/safiwp/97-02-013.html
3. Romualdo, P.S., Alessandro, V.: Epidemic Spreading in Scale Free Networks. Physical Review Letters, (2001) 3200–3203
4. Holland, J.H.: Genetic Algorithm and the Optimal Allocations of Trials. SIAM Journal of Computing, Vol. 2 (1973) 88–105
5. Dorigo, M., Caro, G.D.: The Ant Colony Optimization Meta-Heuristic. New Ideas in Optimization. McGraw-Hill, (1999) 11–32
6. Dorigo, M., Caro, G.D., Gambardella, L.M.: Ant Algorithms for Discrete Optimization. Artificial Life, Vol. 5(2) (1999) 137–172
7. Bernardes, A.T., Santos, R.M.: Immunization and Aging: A Learning Process in the Immune Network. Physical Review Letters, Vol. 81 (1998) 3034–3037
8. Santos, R.M.: Immune Responses: Getting Close to Experimental Results with Cellular Automata Models. Annual Reviews of Computational Physics VI, (1999) 159–202
9. Santos, R., Coutinho, S.: On the Dynamics of the Evolution of HIV Infection. (2000) http://arxiv.org/abs/cond-mat/0008081
10. Hershberg, U., Louzoun, Y., Atlan, H., Solomon, S.: HIV Time Hierarchy: Winning the War while, Loosing all the Battles. Physica A, Vol. 289 (2000) 178–190
11. Morel, P.A.: Mathematical Modeling of Immunological Reactions. Frontiers in Bioscience 3, (1998) 338–347
12. Louzoun, Y., Solomon, S., Atlan, H., Cohen, I.R.: The Emergence of Spatial Complexity in the Immune System, (2000) http://xxx.lanl.gov/abs/nlin.AO/0008133
13. Louzoun, Y., Solomon, S., Atlan, H. ,Cohen, I.R.: Microscopic Discrete Proliferating Components Cause the Self-organized Emergence of Macroscopic Adaptive Features in Biological Systems, (2000) http://xxx.lanl.gov/abs/nlin.AO/0006043
14. Nowak, M.A., Bangham, C.R.M.: Population Dynamics of Immune Responses to Persistent Viruses. Science, Vol. 272 (1996) 74–79
15. Kirschner, D.E., Webb, G.F.: A Mathematical Model of Combined Drug Therapy of HIV Infection. Journal of Theoretical Medicine, Vol. 1 (1997) 25–34
16. Kirschner, D.E., Mehr, R., Perelson, A.S.: Role of the Thymus in Pediatric HIV-1 Infection. Journal of Acquired Immune Deficiency Syndromes and Human Retrovirology, Vol. 18 (1998) 95–109

17. Kirschner, D.E.: Using Mathematics to Understand HIV Immune Dynamics. Notices of the American Mathematical Society, (1996) 191–202

18. Liu, J., Zhang, S.W., Yang, J.: Characterizing Web usage regularities with information foraging agents. IEEE Transactions on Knowledge and Data Engineering. Vol. 16(5) (2004) 566–584

19. Coffin, J.M.: HIV Population Dynamics in Vivo: Implications for Genetic Variation, Pathogenesis, and Therapy. Science, Vol. 267 (1995) 483–489

20. Perelson, A.S., Newmann, A.U., Markowitz, M., Leonard, J.M., Ho, D.D: HIV-1 Dynamics in Vivo: Virion Clearance Rate, Infected Cell Life-span, and Viral Generation Time. Science, Vol. 271 (1996) 1582–1586

21. Fauci, A.S.: The Immunodeficiency Virus: Infectivity and Mechanisms of Pathogenesis. Science, Vol. 239 (1988) 617–622

22. McCune, J.M.: The Dynamics of CD4+ T-cell Depletion in HIV Disease. Nature, Vol. 410 (2001) 974–979

23. Wei, X., et al.: Viral Dynamics in Human Immunodeficiency Virus Type 1 Infection. Nature, Vol. 373 (1995) 117–122

24. Pennisi, E., Cohen, J.: Eradicating HIV from a Patient: Not Just a Dream? Science, Vol. 272 (1996) 1884

25. Adamic, L.A., Huberman, B.A.: Technical Comment to "Emergence of Scaling in Random Networks". Science, Vol. 286(15) (1999) 509–512

26. Nowak, M.A., Anderson, R.M., Boerlijst, M.C. Bonhoeffer, S., May, R.M., McMichal, A.J.: HIV-1 Evolution and Disease Progression. Science, Vol. 274 (1996) 1008–1010

27. Rodrigo, A.G.: HIV Evolutionary Genetics. Proceedings of the National Academy of Sciences, Vol. 6 (1999) 10559–10561

28. Bonhoeffer, S., Holmes, E.C., Nowak, M.A.: Causes of HIV Diversity. Nature, Vol. 376 (1995) 125

29. Wolinsky, S.M. et al.: Adaptive Evolution of Human Immunodeficiency Virus-Type 1 During the Natural Course of Infection. Science, Vol. 272 (1996) 537–542

A Massive Multi-agent System for Brain MRI Segmentation

Radia Haroun[1], Fatima Boumghar[2], Salima Hassas[3], and Latifa Hamami[4]

[1] Signal and Image Processing Post-Graduation,
Electronics & Computing Faculty, USTHB, Algiers, Algeria
rd_haroun@yahoo.fr
[2] LRPE, Electronics & Computing Faculty, USTHB,
Algiers, Algeria
fboumghar@usthb.dz
[3] LIRIS, Claude Bernard University-Lyon 1, France
hassas@liris.cnrs.fr
[4] Signal and Communications Laboratory,
Electronic Department, ENP, Algiers
l_hamami@hotmail.com

Abstract. There are several image segmentation algorithms; each one has its advantages and its limits. In this work, we aim to use the advantages of two algorithms, in a massive multi-agents environment. We use the FCM (Fuzzy C-Mean) algorithm, to manage uncertainty and imprecision and the Region Growing algorithm, to act locally on the image. The massive multi-agents paradigm is then introduced into the region growing process in order to improve the segmentation quality. However in some cases some defaults appear in the segmented image, we propose then the use of a double predicate for the Region Growing algorithm, through a massive cooperative process, in order to improve the quality of the segmented image. Massiveness of the system allows for a better quality analysis.

1 Introduction

To diagnose certain diseases related to internal lesions, the clinician must analyze medical images. To study a tumor evolution, it is necessary to know with exactitude the changes that have occurred. However the visual interpretation of the medical images is not always reliable. Moreover, it is sometimes necessary to analyze several images before reaching the final decision. Consequently, one needs decision support systems that allow the clinicians to get information about the characteristics of the elements composing the image being analyzed. These systems also offer to clinicians the possibility to navigate in an organ through a 3D space or even a 4D space by adding the temporal axis.

For a reliable diagnosis, in the medical field, the precision is important. In terms of image analysis, it is necessary to get the segmentation precise.

T. Ishida, L. Gasser, and H. Nakashima (Eds.): MMAS 2004, LNAI 3446, pp. 174–186, 2005.

Most of the medical images contain several artifacts that make the segmentation process difficult. These artifacts are mainly due to noise or even to perturbations introduced by the patient motion during the examination. In particular, Magnetic Resonance Images (MRI) are characterized by *the partial volume effect* [14], which is found when a voxel having a certain gray level (that is also the case with pixels in 2D images) actually corresponds to a mixture of two or several tissues. In this case, pixels are called *mixels*. This artifact is mainly met at the borders separating tissues.

The aim of our work is to design an image segmentation system by focusing on its high quality. This is important because further processing strongly depends on the segmentation result. The processing objective could be the study of a tumor evolution or even a non-pathological change of state.

In this paper we are in the particular case of the brain MRI. Our segmentation extracts the three principal tissues composing the brain: White Matter (WM), Grey Matter (GM) and the Cerebro-Spinal Fluid (CSF). We compare our method with a classical one and motivate choices we have made on the adopted methods and the used tools.

There are several image segmentation algorithms, following cases to be solved. However each method has its advantages and its limits. In this work, we use a segmentation method that uses the whole image to segment it (the FCM), combined with an algorithm that makes it possible to take into account local image characteristics (region growing). The region growing algorithm is widely used in image segmentation works; in the case of brain MRI, it effects some wrong segmentation. In the proposed approach, we aim to improve the region growing segmentation quality by building it on a Massive Multi Agents System which allows for a strategy of balancing exploration and exploitation in the segmentation process. This strategy makes the system provide results with better quality than classical methods, due to the large exploration, of the environment, balanced with an efficient exploitation of useful encountered information.

This article is organized as follows: After an introduction, we present a state of the art about image segmentation methods and related works using mono and multi-agents frameworks. The segmentation by clustering and the segmentation by region growing are described in sections 3 and 4. We present the global segmentation method in section 5. In section 6 we describe the massive multi-agents system architecture and some implementation issues. Our results and a discussion are then presented in section 7 before concluding the paper.

2   State of the Art

2.1   Image Segmentation

Segmentation subdivides an image into its constituents regions or objects, and labels each part. In our case, it makes it possible to characterize the pixels belonging to the same cerebral tissue. The existing segmentation algorithms are based on one of the two basic properties of the intensities values [10]: *discontinuity* and *similarity*. In the first category, the approach is to partition an image based on abrupt changes in intensity, such as edges in an image. Principal approaches in the second category are based on partitioning the image into regions that are similar according to a set of predefined criteria. Thresholding and Region Growing are examples of methods from this category.

2.2 Related Works

Much work has been done in medical images segmentation field, either based on sequential approaches or using the multi-agents paradigm. In [18], Stao and al. study the atrophy evolution of the frontal lobe. They use fuzzy method to segment the brain on three cerebral tissues. They use then, volumes measurement and the fractal dimension measurement of each tissue and study the relation between these characteristics and the atrophy evolution. The fuzzy segmentation is here used alone, however, the FCM does not give well segmentation in all images; we show in section 6 comparison of our approach with the classical fuzzy segmentation. Jaggi [12] propose an approach based on Markov fields, that allows taking into account the partial volume effect. Geraud [7] introduces contextual information with the help of different formalisms. With Markovian regularization, he shows that energetic terms of localization permit the separation of two grey classes, and with mathematical morphology, he proposes chains processing dedicated to several cerebral objects. J. Liu and al. in [15] propose an autonomous agent-based approach to image features extraction. Agents operate in a two-dimensional lattice of a digital image, and exhibit a number of reactive behaviors. Agents sense the local stimuli from their image environment by means of evaluating the gray-level intensity of locally connected pixels, and accordingly activate their behaviors. The agents behavioral repository consists of : 1) feature-marking at local pixels and self-reproduction of offspring agents in the neighboring regions if the local stimuli are found to satisfy feature conditions, 2) diffusion to adjacent image region if the feature conditions are not held, or 3) death if agents exceed their life span. Germond and al. [8] propose to mix, in a cooperative framework, several information and knowledge types provided and used by complementary individual systems: a multi-agent system, a deformable model and an edge detector. The outcome is a cooperative segmentation performed by a set of region and edge agents constrained automatically and dynamically by specific grey levels in the considered image, statistical models of the brain structures and general knowledge about MRI brain scans. This work uses an *a priori* knowledge that can not be verified on some pathological cases. In the work of Richard and al. [16] situated agents cooperate to segment brain MRI. Many categories of agents are defined: a global control agent, several local controls agents and at the lowest level, segmentation agents, specialized in the detection of the three tissues (GM, WM and CSF) in 3D brain MRI. Duchesnay [5] uses a multi-agents system, where agents are organized on an irregular pyramid and cooperate to aggregate regions. Porquet and al. [15] propose to implement a multi-agents platform that allows to carry out a region-region cooperation. In this work regions and edges are agents that cooperate and negotiate to optimize the image segmentation. Cooperation/negotiation strategies are implemented as automata that use several image processing criteria. The experimentation field of this work is the breast scanner, but he done some tests on brain MRI. Our approach is different from the existing work at two levels: it combines both global (FCM) and local (RG) methods. By making a coarse grain analysis, FCM provides global information that is used at a local level, through a massive multi-agents processing.

3 Segmentation by Clustering

In segmentation by clustering, the image is divided into several clusters in such a way that, the more similar elements aggregate to form a cluster. Thus different clusters are distinguished by their very different composing elements. This approach makes it possible to gather samples in subpopulations, according to any similarity criterion.

According to the wanted classification certainty, and the relation between the clusters, we distinguish two classification types: *Crisp classification* and *Fuzzy classification* [4]. In our work, we use a fuzzy classification algorithm: the fuzzy C-Mean (FCM), in order to manage data uncertainty and its imprecision. The imprecision management is done through the consideration of gradual borders [17] between clusters, rather than crisp ones. Uncertainty is expressed in the fact that a pixel has attributes that assign it to several different clusters. Thus fuzzy classification does not assign to a pixel a label related to one cluster, but its uncertain membership to each one. The membership values are taken in [0, 1] interval and the intersection of obtained clusters is not empty:

$$\forall \ Ci, Cj \in C, \ i \neq j \ Ci \cap Cj \neq \emptyset. \tag{1}$$

Where C is a set of clusters.

The FCM algorithm tends to minimize the objective function J [1]:

$$J(X, U, V) = \sum_{i=1}^{c} \sum_{k=1}^{n} u_{ik}^{\ m} d^2(x_k, v_i) \tag{2}$$

Where:

- c *a priori* known, represents the number of clusters;
- n represents the data size (number of image pixels);
- m (≥ 1) is a parameter determining the amount of fuzziness of the clustering results. If m tends to 1, the classification becomes crisp and u_{ik} approaches 0 or 1. Conversely when m becomes too great, there is less tolerance to noise, and the distribution of the membership value tends to concentrate around 1/c;
- d is the Euclidian distance between the observed data and the class prototype.

The objective function minimization is done in an iterative way. At each iteration the membership values and prototype are updated. They are expressed as [1], [9]:

$$u_{ik} = \frac{(d(x_k, v_i))^{\frac{2}{1-m}}}{\sum_{j=1}^{c} (d(x_k, v_j))^{\frac{2}{1-m}}} \qquad v_i = \frac{\sum_{k=1}^{n} u_{ik}^{\ m} x_k}{\sum_{k=1}^{n} u_{ik}^{\ m}} \tag{3}$$

Where u_{ik} is the membership value of the pixel x_k to the cluster i known by its prototype v_i.

4 Segmentation by Region Growing

Region Growing is a method that repeatedly increases pixels or regions in more and more large regions according to a double criterion: similarity (*Predicate*) and adjacency [3]. The algorithm begins with the whole set of points called *seeds*. The growth is carried out first, by adding to each seed, neighboring pixels that have similar properties to those of the initial seed, and then, by adding those of the region. The process of region growing terminates when a specified stop criterion is reached.

The criterion can relate to the region size (it should not exceed a certain number of pixels). The process continues until the region border is not able to find any more pixels that satisfy the predicate. The choice of the termination criterion is application dependant.

In the following section we compare the described segmentation methods, and motivate our choices.

5 Description of Our Approach

Classification systems generate pixels clusters without taking into account neither their position in the image, nor their topological relations. Classification is made in the same way for whole data that is positioned in a random way. The region growing takes into account simultaneously the topological relations and the homogeneity of regions. In the majority of cases, choice of seeds is not obvious.

MRI images are often characterized by uncertain data. This is mainly due to the partial volume effect. To take into account this artifact, it is necessary to do not associate to pixels, the label of their single cluster, but to express their membership to each one. To do so, we adopt the fuzzy classification method which also allows us to handle the imprecision caused by noise and unhomogenousness present in images. To mitigate the limits of classification systems, without loosing their advantages, we moreover, choose to use the Region Growing method, jointly with the FCM. On another hand, and to be able to use Region Growing effectively, we design the system in a *massive multi-agents* environment. Indeed, this allows us to carry out the Region Growing process associated with several seeds, in a simultaneous way.

5.1 Use of the Multi-agent Paradigm

In multi-agents literature, there are several definitions of an agent. We admit the general definition proposed by M. Wooldridge [13], "an agent is a computer system situated in some environment, and that is capable of *autonomous action* in this environment in order to meet its design objectives".

The multi-agents paradigm permits to handle problems that need multiple solvers. In the multi-agents paradigm, agents have the possibility to interact between them and to act on their environment. The current situations of interaction include [2]:.

- Cooperation: work together for the solution of a common goal;
- Coordination: organize the solution of a problem so that the harmful interactions are prevented and the beneficial interactions are exploited;
- Negotiation: reach an acceptable agreement for all the concerned parts.

With regard to our application, the agents *are situated* in the image; this one represents the environment in which they are distributed and act in a simultaneous way. We use the multi-agents paradigm for the potential it offers, in making different segmentation methods cooperate, and improve notably the segmentation quality.

5.2 Description of Our Segmentation System

In our work, we aim to extract the WM, GM and CSF. The use of the region growing, through a sequential mono-agent processing, often leads to overflow. This is due to the continuous growing of a region, during the processing, making the invasion of not yet explored regions possible. To tackle this problem, the growth is carried out in a simultaneous way for the three classes. Several agents are situated on the image. Each agent is associated with one region or one seed. Thus, by growing, each agent protects its region against other agents. Consequently, the first preoccupation is the positioning of seeds on the image.

5.3 Seeds Selection by FCM

If we look at any point as being a seed, the segmentation process just provides homogeneous regions without giving any information about the tissue corresponding to this region. Moreover, data uncertainty (essential characteristic of the MRI because of the partial volume effect) will not be taken into account. Steps of our method are as follow:

- We carry out the FCM to obtain membership values. Some pixels have a great membership value. We admit that for $u_{ik} > 0.8$ these pixels belong to the cluster.

- We position points on the image in a regular way with a step of 7 pixels. This choice was done after experiments held on a 256*256 sized image. These points are positioned only in the brain zone. They are potential seeds. If their membership values are higher than the fixed threshold then they are taken as seeds, else they are rejected. For each one of these seeds an agent called **RegionAgent** is created to initiate the **Growing Region** algorithm.

5.4 Choice of the Tools

In a multi-agents system, processes are carried out in a parallel way; each agent has its own thread. The Java language provides the class "Thread" which allows multi-threads computing. Java is also secure and portable which makes it possible to work on any type of system or machine and even in a heterogeneous way in the case of multiprocessors. We thus choose to use Java language for our implementations [6], [19].

There are several multi-agents platforms. In our work the platform to use must offer certain requirements and a certain number of services. The *Madkit[1]* platform implemented in Java is appropriate for our application. It is based on a micro-kernel architecture type and offers the possibility of parallel computing. Moreover, it does not require a specific kind of agent model.

---

[1] http://www.madkit.org

5.5 The Massive Multi-agents System Architecture and Some Implementations Issues

Our system is a massive multi-agents system making use of two kinds of agents: **RegionAgent** and **ImaAgent.** A **RegionAgent** exists in the system in many instances (one for each seed). It has several different roles that achieve the **Region Growing** process, in a distributed cooperative way. We have defined mainly 3 major roles:

- The "growth" role corresponds to the region growing process.
- The "negotiate" role consists in negotiating a possible fusion with another agent.
- The "merge" role consists in carrying out a merging with another agent.

Moreover **RegionAgent** can be either in "operating", "waiting" or "suspended" state.

An **ImaAgent**, exist in the system as one instance. It is aimed to offer some management facilities, such as launching **RegionAgents** and allowing them to change their roles.

These two kinds of agents are implemented as Java classes, using each, specific variables (class members) namely *RoleList* and *SuspList* for the **ImaAgent**, and *Seed position, SeedType, AssignList, BordList* and *State* for the **RegionAgen**t.

The *RoleList* variable is a table which size is equal to the number of agents of **RegionAgent** kind. All the cells of this list are set to zero except those corresponding to the next agent that must make the growth. The *SuspList* variable informs the system about agents which had reached the stop criterion of the region growing and are waiting for a possible fusion with another agent. *SeedType* variable concerns the cerebral tissue corresponding to this seed. *AssignList* variable concerns pixels already assigned to the agent region. *BordList* variable concerns pixels belonging to the region border. Candidate pixels are known to the agent at each time. *State* variable represents the agent state.

5.6 Agents Behaviors

A previous version of this work was implemented in an asynchronous way without attributing priorities to different threads sharing the machine clock cycle. At each time, we do not know which agent will work. This has the advantage to optimize the processing time, because no control on the time-sharing exists and communications with agents are reduced. However this asynchronous system operates randomly and the processing is non deterministic, since it depends on the machine on which the threads are launched. Moreover, we encountered some management problems, for example: more than two agents meet at the same time and announce this meeting in an almost instantaneous way. Before the end of the suitable treatment and data update, another meeting occurs between other agents or with negotiating agents. To avoid this lack of coordination between the different agents behaviors, we made the system synchronous.

In the following, we present the different phases occurring during the processing evolution and governing agents behaviors.

The Initialization Phase
ImaAgent behavior:

    ImaAgent is constantly listening to its messages.

    ImaAgent launches a **RegionAgent** relating to the first seed.

    When **ImaAgent** knows that the first **RegionAgent** was put in the "waiting" state it launches the second **RegionAgent** and updates its data.

RegionAgent behavior:

    RegionAgent that has been just launched takes the "growth" role and goes to the "operating" state.

    RegionAgent begins its growth starting from its seed.

    It observes its neighborhood pixels

    It adds to its region, pixels that satisfy the Predicate,

    It increments the iterations number and updates the lists: *AssignList* and *BordList*.

    It goes to the "waiting" state. This state will allow **ImaAgent** to launch a second **RegionAgent** relating to the second seed.

The Region Growing Phase
When **ImaAgent** perceives that **RegionAgent** is in the "waiting" state: It analyzes RoleList and launches the next RegionAgent.

    When a **RegionAgent** satisfies the stop criterion it does not die, because it may be requested for merging with another agent. This agent goes to the "suspended" state. During the region growing process, if a **RegionAgent** wants to add to its region a pixel that already belongs to another region, a negotiation phase starts.

The Negotiation Phase
ImaAgent makes the two concerned agents in the "negotiate" role.

    As long as the negotiation is not finished, **ImaAgent** does not launch another agent. If the two **RegionAgent** agents have the same seeds type then they merge: In this case **ImaAgent** creates a new **RegionAgent** and kills the two merged ones. The new created **RegionAgent** recovers all the data of its two parent agents.

    We call this phase "negotiation" because two agents discuss on the possibility of there merging.

Remark 1: With the process progression, the agents number falls and the processing speed increases.

Remark 2: The stop criterion is the non-existence of pixels that could be added to the region that is growing. The adopted predicate expresses the fact that the difference between the grey level of the inspected pixel and the average of the grey levels of the current region is lower than a prefixed threshold. This threshold depends on a precision that we assert ourselves. To improve the segmentation, we add another predicate that expresses the fact that the membership value obtained from the FCM of the current pixel is greater than 70%.

ImaAgent controls the system but it does not control all the RegionAgent actions, RegionAgents are capable of autonomous actions, at any time we do not know if a RegionAgent will meet other, we do not know if it will merge or not, agents decide of this action alone.

6 Results and Discussion

The original images, we used for our experiments, are obtained from the McConnell Brain Imaging Centre[1] of the Montreal Neurological Institute (McGill University, Canada). These images are generated using a simulator of Magnetic Resonance Images. Visualized images depend on the acquisition parameters and are built starting from an image model.

6.1 Skull Striping

Before beginning the image segmentation into three classes, it is necessary to make a skull striping to eliminate the pixels relating to the cranium, the skin and surrounding tissues. To do so, we use some mathematical morphology techniques (see Fig 1). More details are given in [11].

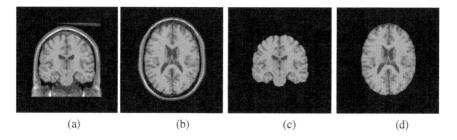

(a)   (b)   (c)   (d)

Fig. 1. Skull striping: (a) coronal original slice (b) axial original slice, ((c), (d)) isolated brains

6.2 Brain Segmentation

In the following images, we will present segmentation results obtained with the classical algorithm FCM and those obtained with our MMAS approach with 352 agents. In figures a and c, there are three grays, each one corresponds to one region, in figures b the black edge corresponds to the boundary between regions.

6.3 Results Comparisons

The following figures give some comparisons and permit to discuss the results.

We first compare our method with a classical one (see Fig. 4). Then we show the contribution of the adding of a second predicate of the region growing (see Fig. 5). We present after that, results obtained with our method, considering different sizes of agent populations (see Fig 6).

---

[1] HTTP://www.bic.mni.mcgill.ca/brainweb

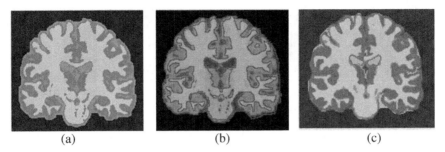

(a)   (b)   (c)

Fig. 2. Segmentation of the coronal slice (a) Result by the FCM (regions visualizations), (b) Result by the FCM (boundaries visualizations) and (c) Result of the segmentation by our MMAS approach

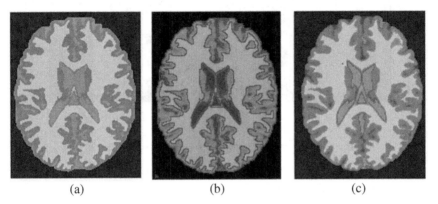

(a)   (b)   (c)

Fig. 3. Segmentation of the axial slice: (a) Result by the FCM (regions visualizations), (b) Result by the FCM (boundaries visualizations) and (c) Result of the segmentation by our MMAS approach

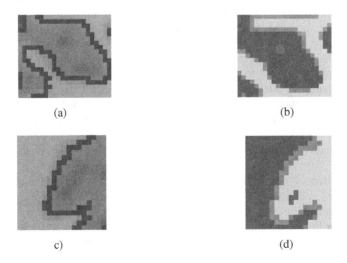

(a)   (b)

c)   (d)

Fig. 4. (a) and (c) results with FCM, (b) and (d) results with our MMAS approach

(a)   (b)

Fig. 5. (a) Result with only one predicate and (b) Result with two predicates

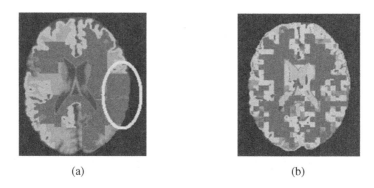

(a)   (b)

Fig. 6. (a) Result with only 15 agents and (b) Result with 128 agents

6.4   Discussion

Images of Fig.4 represent a zoom of certain parts segmented by the two approaches: simple FCM and our method. On Fig.4.a,c. pixels surrounded by black edge are considered by the FCM segmentation, as belonging to the same region. This is due to the fact that this algorithm uses the whole image to segment it. In this case, each pixel is a lonely point, and the grey level is the only exploited information. Region Growing takes into account image local characteristics. We see on Fig.4.b, Fig.4.d, that, pixels which are badly segmented by the FCM are neither taken as pertaining to the region in light gray, nor to the region dark gray. There are nevertheless some pixels that are badly segmented. This is due to the value of the Region Growing predicate. In Fig.5.a there is an overflow between WM and GM, in Fig.5.b The overflow disappears with the use of two predicates rather than one, the second was obtained from the FCM. The Fig.6 shows that with a great number of agents the segmentation quality is improved, there is much less overflow in Fig.6.b that in Fig.6.a.

The contribution of our MMAS method compared to classical ones is twofold. First we can act simultaneously both locally and globally on the image, while managing data uncertainty and imprecision. Second, Region Growing as we presented it can avoid overflows, in comparison to sequential methods. The approach presented in [8] makes use, as we do, of several agents to achieve Region Growing. Agents are positioned in the image after the skull stripping step as we do, but here Germond uses an a priori knowledge that consists of a brain model: the GM is in the periphery of the brain and the CSF is in the center. However this knowledge could be useless in certain pathological images where the GM and the WM are not positioned in this arrangement in the entire image (in certain cases the GM can be found in the WM region). Our method does not use such an a priori knowledge. The only external information used, is that the CSF is the darker and the WM is the lighter. This information does not require any knowledge about the pathologic state of the image.

7   Conclusion and Future Works

In this paper we have presented a new approach based on massive multi-agents method that aims to improve the image segmentation quality. It consists in cooperation between the FCM classification with the region growing algorithm. Indeed, the region growing is based on a massive multi agents system and is initialized by FCM. We applied the segmentation to two-dimensional cerebral MRI. In the preceding sections we explained the massive multi-agents environment contribution for the region growing.

The use of several segmentation algorithms working in cooperation makes it possible to mitigate the problems caused by using only one algorithm, and this by exploiting only the advantages of each one. The MMAS enabled us to carry out segmentation by region growing distributed on the image while acting on all surface in a simultaneous way; this processing prevents the pixels of a region from being added to the region of the first seed which begins the growth. We have demonstrated in Fig 6. that the number of agents is important to improve the segmentation quality.

We begin our work by using phantom images, but very recently we work with clinicians in radiology who gave us real medical images. Our first results on real medical images have been evaluated visually by doctor.

The future works consist in an optimization of this method by using another cooperation type; the use of the asynchronous mode, an extension towards three-dimensional MRI, the choice of the threshold relating to the predicate of the region growing will be done after study of the image characteristics. We propose also to add another negotiation between agents concerning the peripheral regions pixels. It could be interesting to re implement the system without MadKit or on an image processing plate-form as proposed in [16].

References

1. Ahmed, M.N., Yamany, S.M., Farag, A.A., Moriarty, T.: A modified fuzzy c-means algorithm for bias field estimation and segmentation of MRI data. IEEE Transactions on medical imaging, Vol.21, No.3 (2002) 193-199
2. Chaib-draa, B.: Systèmes multi-agents principes généraux et applications, cours notes, computer department, Laval University, Canada, (2001). http://www.damas.ift.ulaval.ca/~coursMAS/
3. Coquerez, J-P., Philipp, S.: Analyse d'images: filtrage et segmentation, Masson (1995)
4. Dimitriadou, E., Barth, M., Windischberger, C., Hornik, K., Moser, E.: A quantitative comparison of functional MRI cluster analysis. Artificial Intelligence in Medicine, Vol. 20, (2003)

5. Duchesnay, E.: Agents situés dans l'image et organisés en pyramide irrégulière : contribution à la segmentation par une approche d'agrégation coopérative et adaptative, PHD thesis of the Rennes-1 University (2001)
6. Efford, N.: Digital image processing a practical introduction using Java, Addison Wesley, (2000)
7. Géraud, T.: Segmentation des structures internes du cerveau en imagerie par résonance magnétique, PHD thesis of the ENST Paris (1998)
8. Germond, L., Dojat, M., Taylor, C., Garbay, C.: A cooperative framework for segmentation of MRI brain scans. Artificial Intelligence in Medicine. Vol. 20 (2000) 77-94
9. Grekovs, R.: Methods of fuzzy pattern recognition. Scientific proceeding of RIGA technical university, Computer Science, Information Technology and Management Science (2002)
10. Gonzalez, R.C., Woods, R.E.: Digital image processing, Addison-Wesley (2002) 613
11. Haroun, R., Hamami, L., Boumghar, F.: Segmentation d'images médicales IRM par un système hybride flou - croissance de régions, dans un système multi agents, Journées d'ETudes algéro-françaises en Imagerie Médicale (2004) 21-30
12. Jaggi, C.: Segmentation par méthode markovienne de l'encéphale humain par résonance magnétique: théorie, mise en oeuvre et évaluation. PHD thesis of the Caen University (1998)
13. Jennings, N.R., Wooldridge, M.: Applications of Agent Technology. Agent Technology: Foundation Applications and Markets, Springer-Verlag (1998)
14. Kastele, B., Vetter, D., Patay, Z., Germain, P.: Comprendre l'IRM, Masson (2001)
15. Liu, J., Y. Y, Tang., Y. C. Cao. : An evolutionary autonomous agents approach to image feature extraction. IEEE Trans. on Evolutionary Computation, Vol. 1, No. 2 (1997) 141-158.
16. Porquet, C., Settache, H., Ruan, S., Revenu, M.: Une plate-forme multi-agent pour la segmentation d'images. Etude des stratégies de coopération contour-région, ORASIS Géradmer, (2003) 413-422
17. Richard, N., Dojat, M., Garbay, C.: Multi-Agent approach for image processing for MRI human brain scans interpretation. 9th Conference on Artificial Intelligence in Medicine Europe (2003)
18. Rick, A.: Représentation de la variabilité dans le traitement d'images flou application à la mammographie numérique, PHD thesis of the Paris 6 University (1999)
19. Stao, K., Sugawara, K., Narita, Y., Namura, I.: Consideration of the method of image diagnosis with respect to frontal lobe atrophy. IEEE Transactions on nuclear science, Vol.43, No.6 (1996) 3230-3239
20. Wooldrige, M.: Agent-based computing. Interoperable Communication Networks. Vol. 1 (1998) 71-97

Mobile Agents for Ambient Intelligence

Ichiro Satoh

National Institute of Informatics,
2-1-2 Hitotsubashi, Chiyoda-ku, Tokyo 101-8430, Japan
Tel: +81-3-4212-2546   Fax: +81-3-3556-1916
ichiro@nii.ac.jp

Abstract. This paper presents a mobile agent-based framework for ambient intelligence. The goal of the infrastructure is to provide people, places, and objects with computational functionalities to support and annotate them. Using location-tracking systems the infrastructure can navigate Java-based mobile agents to stationary or mobile computers near the entities and places to which the agents are attached, even when the locations change. The infrastructure enables application-specific functionalities to be implemented within mobile agents instead of the infrastructure itself. It maintains the locations of people and objects, including computing devices, and allows mobile users to directly access their personalized services from stationary computing devices in the environment or from their portable computing devices. This paper presents the rationale, design, implementation, and applications for our prototype infrastructure.

1   Introduction

Ambient intelligence enables us to be surrounded by electronic environments that are sensitive and responsive to people. Ambient intelligence technologies are expected to combine concepts of intelligent systems, perceptual technologies, and ubiquitous computing. Perceptual technologies have made it possible to measure and track the locations of people, computers, and practically any other object of interest. For example, indoor location systems, such as RFID (radio frequency identification) tags, detect the locations of physical entities in a building and enable applications to respond to these locations.

Location awareness is becoming an essential feature of services targeted at ambient intelligence. Several researchers have explored such location-aware services. Existing services can be classified into two approaches. The first concern is to make the computing devices that move with the user. It often assumes that such devices are attached to positioning systems, such as GPS receivers, which enable them to determine their own locations. For example, in HP's Cooltown project [5], mobile computing devices such as PDAs and smart phones are attached to GPSs to provide location-awareness for web-based applications running on the devices. The second approach assumes that a space is equipped with tracking systems which establish the location of physical entities, including people and objects, within the space so that application-specific services can be provided to appropriate computers. A typical example of this is the so-called follow-me application, which was a study by Cambridge University's Sentient Computing project

T. Ishida, L. Gasser, and H. Nakashima (Eds.): MMAS 2004, LNAI 3446, pp. 187–201, 2005.

[3], to support ubiquitous and personalized services on computers located near users. The two approaches are posed as polar opposites, although their final goals seem to coincide.

This paper presents a mobile agent-based framework for integrating the two approaches to support their advantages. The framework does not distinguish between mobile and stationary computing devices. It can permit tracking sensors to be moved with the user and dynamically added to and removed from a space it does this, because it dynamically creates a world model when detecting the appearance and movement of sensors and physical entities including people, objects, and computing devices. Moreover, it is unique among other existing location-aware systems in that it uses mobile agent technology. It enables these agents to be spatially bound to people, places, and objects, which the agents then support and annotate. Using mobile agents makes the framework application-independent, application-specific services are implemented within mobile agents instead of the infrastructure. Therefore, the framework enables various location-aware or personalized services to be constructed.

In the remainder of this paper, we describe our design goals (Section 2), the design of our approach, called SpatialAgent, and a prototype infrastructure (Section 3), and programming models for mobile agents (Section 4). We describe the current implementation of the framework (Section 5) and present how to bridge the gap between the physical world and cyberspace (Section 6) and discuss our experience with several applications, which we developed with the infrastructure (Section 7). We briefly review related work (Section 8). We also provide a summary and some future issues (Section 9).

2   Approach

The framework presented in this paper aims to enhance the capabilities of users, particularly mobile users, things, including computing devices and non-electronic objects, and places, such as rooms, buildings and cities, that have the computational functionalities to support and annotate them.

2.1   Location-Sensing Systems

Our goal is to provide a location-aware system in which spatial regions can be determined within a few square feet, so that one or more portions of a room or building can be distinguished. The current implementation uses RFID tag technology to locate objects. An RFID system uses RF (radio frequency) readers, which detect the presence of small RF transmitters, often called *tags*. The framework assumes that physical entities, including people and computing devices, and places are equipped with these tags so that they are automatically locatable. It spatially binds software for information-based services to an RFID tag attached to a person, place, or thing in the physical world. The framework also provides a symbolic location model to hide the differences between the underlying location-sensing systems from applications as much as possible. This is because the framework aims at building location-aware applications for annotating and supporting people, objects, and places and such applications are often associated with semantic and structural spaces, such as buildings, rooms, and portions of a room or building, rather than geometric locations.

2.2   Location-Based Services

A ubiquitous computing environment consists of many computing devices, which may have only limited resources, such as restricted levels of CPU power and limited amounts of memory. As a result, even if a device is at a location suitable for providing a wanted service, the device may not be able to do so due to a lack of capabilities, such as input or output facilities. To overcome this limitation, the framework introduces mobile agent technology each agent only needs to be present at the computer during the time the computer needs the services provided by that agent. Mobile agent technology also has the following advantages.

- Various kinds of infrastructures have been used to construct and manage location-aware services. However, such infrastructures have mostly focused on a particular application, such as user navigation. By separating application-specific services from the infrastructure, our framework provides a general infrastructure for a variety of location-aware services, enabling application-specific services to be implemented within mobile agents.
- Each mobile agent can dynamically be deployed at and locally executed within computers near the position of the user. As a result, the agent can directly interact with the user, whereas RPC-based approaches, on which other approaches are often based, must have network latency between the local computer and remote servers. The agent also can directly access various equipment belonging to that device as long as the security mechanisms of the device permit this.
- After arriving at its destination, a mobile agent can continue working without losing any previous results of working, e.g., the content of instance variables in the agent's program, at the source computers. Thus, the technology enables us to easily build follow-me applications as proposed in [3].

The framework presented in this paper enables a physical entity and place to spatially bind with one or more mobile agent-based services. These services annotate and support the entities or places in the sense that the services can be dynamically deployed at stationary and mobile computing devices that are near or within the locations of the entities and places.

3   Design and Implementation

This framework provides the middleware infrastructure for managing location-sensing systems and deploying mobile agents at suitable computing devices according to the locations of users and objects, including computing devices. It consists of three parts: (1) location information servers, called LISs, (2) service-provider mobile agents, and (3) agent hosts, as we can see in Figure 1. The first part manages more than one location-sensor and recommends destinations to mobile agents. The second offers application-

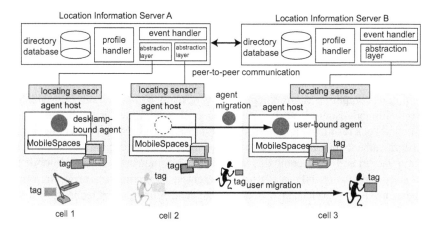

Fig. 1. Architecture of the SpatialAgent framework

specific services, which are attached to physical entities and places. The third consists of computing devices that can execute mobile agent-based applications.

3.1   Location Information Server

LISs are responsible for managing location sensing systems and recommending agents devices at which the agents provide their services. They can run on a stationary or mobile computer and provide all LISs that can run on a stationary or mobile computer and that have the following functionalities:

RFID-Based Location Model: This framework represents the locations of objects with a symbolic names to specifying the sensing ranges of RFID readers, instead of geographical models. Each LIS manages more than one RFID reader that detects the presence of tags and maintains up-to-date information on the identities of those that are within the zone of coverage. This is achieved by polling the readers or receiving events issued by the readers. An LIS does not require any knowledge on other LISs, but it needs to be able to exchange its information with others through multicast communication. To hide the differences between the underlying locating systems, each LIS maps low-level positional information from the other LISs into information in a symbolic model of location. An LIS represents an entity's location in symbolic terms of the RFID reader's unique identifier that detects the entity's tag. We call each RFID reader's coverage a *cell*, as in the models of location reported by several other researchers [7]. Multiple RFID readers in the framework do not have to be neatly distributed in spaces such as rooms or buildings to completely cover the spaces; instead, they can be placed near more than one agent host and the reader coverage can overlap.

Location Management: Each LIS is responsible for discovering mobile agents bound to tags within its cells. Each maintains a database in which it stores information about

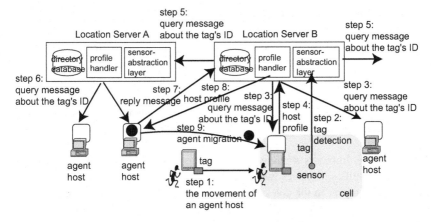

Fig. 2. Agent discovery and deployment

each of the agent hosts and each of the mobile agents attached to a tagged entity or place. When an LIS detects a new tag in a cell, the LIS multicasts a query that contains the identity of the new tag and its own network address to all the agent hosts in its current sub-network. It then waits for reply messages from the agent hosts. Here, there are two possible cases: the tag may be attached to an agent host or the tag may be attached to a person, place, or thing other than an agent host.

- In the first case, the newly arriving agent host will send its network address and device profile to the LIS; the profile describes the capabilities of the agent host, e.g., input devices and screen size. After receiving a reply message, the LIS stores the profile in its database and forwards the profile to all agent hosts within the cell.
- In the second case, agent hosts that have agents tied to the tag will send their net-work addresses and the requirements of acceptable agents to the LIS; requirements for each agent specify the capabilities of the agent hosts that the agent can visit and perform its services at.

The LIS then stores the requirements of the agents in its database and moves the agents to appropriate agent hosts in a manner we will discuss later. If the LIS does not have any reply messages from the agent hosts, it can multicast a query message to other LISs. When the absence of a tag is detected in a cell, each LIS multicasts a message with the identifier of the tag and the identifier of the cell to all agent hosts in its current sub-network. Figure 2 shows the sequence for migrating an agent to a suitable host when an LIS detects the presence of a new tag.

Location/Personal-Aware Deployment of Mobile Agents: We will now explain how the framework deploys agents at suitable agent hosts. When an LIS detects the move-ment of a tag attached to a person or thing to a cell, it searches its database for agent hosts that are present in the current cell of the tag. It also selects candidate destinations from the set of agent hosts within the cell, according to their respective capabilities. The framework offers a language based on CC/PP (composite capability/preference profiles) [16]. The language is used to describe the capabilities of agent hosts and the requirements of mobile agents in an XML notation. For example, a description contains information on the following properties of a computing device: vendor and model class of the device (i.e, PC, PDA, or phone), its screen size, the number of colors, CPU, memory, input devices, secondary storage, and the presence/absence of loudspeakers. The framework also allows each agent to specify the preferable capabilities of agent hosts that it may visit as well as the minimal capabilities in a CC/PP-based notation. Each LIS is able to determine whether or not the device profile of each agent host satisfies the requirements of an agent by symbolically matching and quantitatively comparing properties.

The LIS then unicasts a navigation message to each of the agents that are bound to the tagged entities or places, where the message specifies the profiles of those agent hosts that are present in the cell and satisfy the requirements of the agent. The agents are then able to autonomously migrate to the appropriate hosts. When there are multiple candidate destinations, each of the agents that is tied to a tag must select one destination based on the profiles of the destinations. When one or more cells geographically overlap, a tag may be in multiple cells at the same time and agents tied to that tag may then receive candidate destinations from multiple LISs. However, since the message includes the network address of the LIS, the agents can explicitly ask it about the cell ranges. Our goal is to provide physical entities and places with computational functionality from locations that are near them. Therefore, if there are no appropriate agent hosts in any of the cells at which a tag is present but there are some agent hosts in other cells, the current implementation of our framework forces agents tied to the tag to move to hosts in different cells.

3.2   Service-Provider Mobile Agent

The framework encapsulates application-specific services into mobile agents so that it is independent of any applications and can support multiple services. In the appendix of this paper, each mobile agent is constructed as a collection of Java objects and is equipped with the identifier of the tag to which it is attached.[1] Each is a self-contained program and is able to communicate with other agents. An agent that is attached to a user always internally maintains that user's personal information and carries all its internal information to other hosts. A mobile agent may also have one or more graphical user interfaces for interaction with its users. When such an agent moves to other hosts, it can easily adjust its windows to the new host's screen by using the compound document framework for the MobileSpaces system that was presented in our previous paper [10].

3.3   Agent Host

Each agent host must be equipped with a tag. It has two forms of functionality: one for advertising its capabilities and the other for executing and migrating mobile agents. The current implementation assumes that LISs and agent hosts can be directly connected through a wired LAN such as Ethernet or a wireless LAN such as IEEE802.11b. When a host receives a query message with the identifier of a newly arriving tag from an LIS,

---

[1] Appendix describes programming interfaces of agents.

it replies with one of the following three responses: (i) if the identifier in the message is identical to the identifier of the tag to which it is attached, it returns profile information on its capabilities to the LIS; (ii) if one of the agents running on it is tied to the tag, it returns its network address and the requirements of the agent; and (iii) if neither of the above cases applies, it ignores the message.

The current implementation of this framework is based on a Java-based mobile agent system called MobileSpaces [9].[2] Each MobileSpaces runtime system is built on the Java virtual machine, which conceals differences between the platform architecture of the source and destination hosts, such as the operating system and hardware. Each of the runtime systems moves agents to other agent hosts over a TCP/IP connection. The runtime system governs all the agents inside it and maintains the life-cycle state of each agent. When the life-cycle state of an agent changes, e.g., when it is created, terminates, or migrates to another host, the runtime system issues specific events to the agent. This is because the agent may have to acquire various resources or release them, such as files, windows, or sockets, which it had previously captured. When a notification on the presence or absence of a tag is received from a LIS, the runtime system dispatches specific events to the agents that are tied to that tag and these run inside it.

4   Service-Provider Mobile Agent Program

Services are implemented in mobile agents instead of the MobileSpaces runtime systems. Each mobile agent is executed in the MobileSpaces runtime system and migrated between the runtime systems running on different computers. It is constructed as a collection of Java objects and is equipped with the identifier of the tag to which it is attached. Every agent program must be an instance of a subclass of the abstract class TaggedAgent as follows:

```
class TaggedAgent extends MobileAgent
implements Serializable {
    void go(URL url) throws NoSuchHostException { ... }
    void duplicate() throws IllegalAccessException { ... }
    void destroy() { ... }
    void setTagIdentifier(TagIdentifier tid) { ... }
    void setAgentProfile(AgentProfile apf) { ... }
    URL getCurrentHost() { ... }
    boolean isConformableHost(HostProfile hpf) {...}
    ....
}
```

Here are some of the methods defined in the TaggedAgent class. An agent executes the go(URL url) method to move to the destination host specified as the url by its runtime system.[3] The setTagIdentifier method ties the agent to the identity of

---

[2] The framework itself is independent of the MobileSpaces mobile agent system and can thus work with other Java-based mobile agent systems.

[3] In MobileSpaces, agents can have higher-level routings among multiple hosts [12].

the tag specified as `tid`. Each agent can specify a requirement that its destination hosts must satisfy by invoking the `setAgentProfile()` method, with the requirement specified as `apf`. The class has a service method called `isConformableHost()`, which the agent uses to decide whether or not the capabilities of the agent hosts specified as an instance of the `HostProfile` class satisfy the requirements of the agent. Each agent can have more than one listener object that implements a specific listener interface to hook certain events issued before or after changes in its life-cycle state or the movements of its tag.

5   Current Status

The framework presented in this paper was implemented in Sun's Java Developer Kit, version 1.1 or later versions, including Personal Java. This section discusses some features of the current implementation.

5.1   Location-Sensing Systems

The current implementation supports four commercial RFID systems: RF Code's Spider system, Alien Technology's 915Mhz RFID-tag system, Philips' I-Code system, and Hitachi's mu-chip system. The first system provides active RF-tags, which periodically emit an RF-beacon that conveys their unique identifier (every second) via 305 MHz-radio pulse. The system allows us to explicitly control the omnidirectional range of each of the RF readers to read tags within a range of 1 to 20 meters. The Alien Technology system provides passive RFID-tags and its readers periodically scan for present tags within a range of 3 meters by sending a short 915 MHz-RF pulse and waiting for answers from the tags. The Philips and Hitachi RFID systems are passive RFID tag systems that can sense the presence of tags within a range of a few centimeters. Although there are many differences between the four, the framework abstracts these.

5.2   Performance Evaluation

Although the current implementation of the framework was not built for performance, we measured the cost of migrating a 3-Kbytes agent (zip-compressed) from a source host to the destination host recommended by the LIS. This experiment was conducted with two LISs and two agent hosts, each of which was running on one of four computers (Pentium III-1GHz with Windows 2000 and JDK 1.4), which were directly connected via an IEEE802.11b wireless network. The latency of an agent's migration to the destination after the LIS had detected the presence of the agent's tag was 410 msec and the cost of agent migration between two hosts over a TCP connection was 42 msec. The latency included the cost of the following processes: UDP-multicasting of the tags' identifiers from the LIS to the source host, TCP-transmission of the agent's requirements from the source host to the LIS, TCP-transmission of a candidate destination from the LIS to the source host, marshaling the agent, migrating the agent from the source host to the destination host, unmarshaling the agent, and security verification. We believe that this latency is acceptable for a location-aware system used in a room or building.

5.3   Security and Privacy

Security is essential in mobile agent computing. The framework can be built on many Java-based mobile agent systems with the Java virtual machine. Therefore, it can directly use the security mechanism of the underlying mobile agent system. The Java virtual machine can explicitly restrict agents so that they can only access specified resources to protect hosts from malicious agents. To protect against the passing of malicious agents between agent hosts, the MobileSpaces system supports a Kerberos-based authentication mechanism for agent migration. It authenticates users without exposing their passwords on the network and generates secret encryption keys that can selectively be shared between mutually suspicious parties.

The framework only maintains per-user profile information within those agents that are bound to the user. It promotes the movement of such agents to appropriate hosts near the user in response to his/her movement. Since agents carry their users' profile information within them, they must protect such private information while they are moving over a network.[4] The MobileSpaces system can transform agents into an encrypted form before migrating them over the network and decrypt them after they arrive at their destinations. Moreover, since each mobile agent is just a programmable entity, it can explicitly encrypt its particular inner fields and migrate itself with the fields along with its own cryptographic procedure, except for its secret keys.

6   Discussions

The framework does not have to distinguish between mobile and stationary computing devices and between mobile and stationary location-sensing systems. It can inform mobile agents attached to tags about their appropriate destinations according to the current positions of the tags. It supports four types of linkages between a physical entity such as a person, thing, or place, and one or more mobile agents, as shown in Fig. 3.

- The first type of linkage assumes that a moving entity carries more than one tagged agent host and that a space contains a place-bound tag and sensor (Fig. 3 a). When the sensor detects the presence of a tag that is bound to one of the agent hosts, the framework instructs the agents attached to the tagged place to migrate to the visiting agent hosts to offer location-dependent services.
- The second type of linkage assumes that tagged agent hosts and sensors have been allocated (Fig. 3 b). When a tagged moving entity enters the coverage area of one of the sensors, the framework instructs the agents attached to the entity to migrate to the agent hosts within the same coverage area to offer the entity-dependent services of the entity.
- The third type of linkage assumes that an entity carries a sensor and more than one agent host and that a space contains more than one place-bound tag (Fig. 3 c). When the entity moves near a place-bound tag and the sensor detects the presence of the

---

[4] The framework itself cannot protect agents from malicious hosts, because this problem is beyond the scope of this paper.

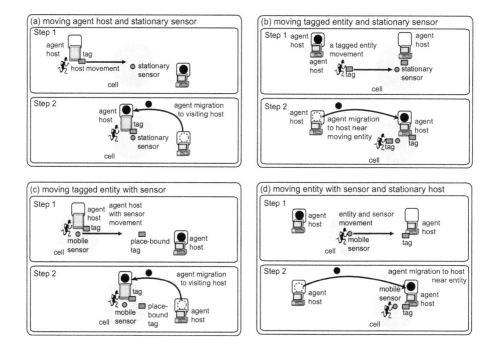

Fig. 3. Four types of linkages between physical and logical entities

tag within its coverage area, the framework instructs the agents attached to the tagged place to migrate to the visiting agent hosts to offer the location-dependent services of the place.

- The fourth type of linkage assumes that an entity carries a sensor and a space contains a place-bound tag and more than one tagged agent host (Fig. 3 d). When the entity moves and the reader detects the presence of an agent host's tag within its coverage area, the LIS instructs the agents attached to the moving entity to migrate to the agent host within the same coverage area to offer services dependent on the entity.

Note that the above linkages are independent of the underlying locating systems. Therefore, they are available in various source of location information, e.g., GPS, local wireless networks, and cellular networks. Existing location-aware systems can only support each of the above linkages, whereas our infrastructure does not have to distinguish between them and can synthesize them seamlessly. For example, the linkage shown in Fig. 3 (a) corresponds to *person tracking display* approach in the EasyLiving project [1], the linkage shown in Fig. 3 (b) corresponds to *Follow-me applications* approach in the Sentient Computing project [3] and the linkage shown in Fig. 3 (c) corresponds to services on location-aware portable devices studied in the Cooltown [5] and NEXUS [4] projects.

7   Applications

This section presents several typical location-based and personalized services that were developed through the framework. Note that these services can be executed at the same time, since the framework itself is independent of any application-specific services and each service is implemented within mobile agents.

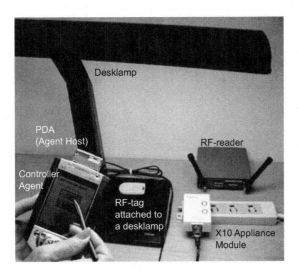

Fig. 4. Controlling desk lamp from PDA

7.1   Location-Bound Universal Remote Controller

The first example corresponds to Figure 3 (a) and allows us to use a PDA to remotely control nearby electric lights in a room. Each light was equipped with a tag and was within the range covered by an RFID reader in the room. We controlled power outlets for lights through a commercial protocol called X10. In both approaches described here, the lights were controlled by switching their power sources on or off according to the X10 protocol. In this system, place-bound controller agents, which can communicate with X10-base servers to switch lights on or off, are attached to locations with room lights. Each user has a tagged PDA, which supports the agent host with WindowsCE and wireless LAN interface. When a user with a PDA visits a cell that contains a light, the framework moves a controller agent to the agent host of the visiting PDA. The agent, now running on the PDA, displays a graphical user interface to control the light. When the user leaves that location, the agent automatically closes its user interface and returns to its home host.

7.2   Mobile Personal Assistance

The second example corresponds to Figure 3 (b) and offers a user assistant agent that follows its user and maintains profile information about him/her inside itself, so that

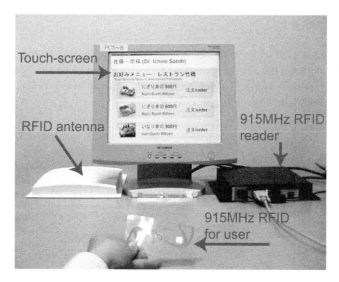

Fig. 5. Screenshot of follow-me user assistant agent for selecting its user's favorite sushi from the menu database of a restaurant that the user is in front of

he/she can always assist the agent in a personalized manner anywhere. Suppose that a user has a 915MHz-RFID tag and is moving on front of a restaurant, which offers an RFID reader and an agent host with a touch-screen. When the tagged user enters inside the coverage area of the reader, the framework enables his/her assistant agents to move to the agent host near his/her current location. After arriving at the host, the agent accesses a database provided in the restaurant to obtain a menu from the restaurant. [5] It then selects appropriate meal candidates from the menu according to his/her profile information, such as favorite foods and recent experiences, stored inside it. It next displays only the list of selected meals on the screen of its current agent host in a personalized manner for him/her. Figure 5 shows that a user's assistant agent runs on the agent host of the restaurant and seamlessly embeds a list of pictures, names, and prices of selected meal candidates with buttons for ordering them into its graphical user interface. Since a mobile agent is a program entity, we can easily define a more intelligent assistant agent.

7.3   User Navigation System

We developed a user navigation system that assists visitors to a building. Several researchers have reported on other similar systems [2, 4]. In our system, tags are distributed to several places within a building, such as its ceilings, floors, and walls. As we can see from Figure 3 (c), each visitor carries a wireless-LAN enabled tablet PC, which is equipped with an RFID reader to detect tags, and includes an LIS and an agent

---

[5] The current implementation of the database maintains some information about each available food, such as name and price, in an XML-based entry.

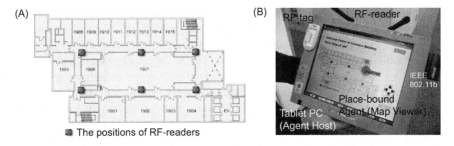

Fig. 6. A) Positions of RF-tags in floor and B) screen-shot of map-viewer agent running on table PC

host. The system initially deploys place-bound agents to invisible computers within the building. When a tagged position is located by a cell of the moving RFID reader, the LIS running on the visitor's tablet PC detects the presence of the tag. The LIS detects the place-bound agent that is tied to the tag. It then instructs the agent to migrate to its agent host and provide the agent's location-dependent services at the host. The system enables more than one agent tied to a place to move to the table PC. The agents then return to their home computers and other agents, which are tied to another place, may move to the tablet PC. Fig. 6 shows a place-bound agent to display a map of its surrounding area on the screen of a tablet PC.

8 Related Work

Research on ambient intelligence or smart spaces has become common at many universities and corporate research facilities. For example, Cambridge University's Sentient Computing project [3] provides a platform for building location-aware applications by using locating systems. Unlike our framework, the management of the the platform is centralized and cannot dynamically reconfigure itself. The project uses CORBA-based middleware can move CORBA objects to hosts according to the location of tagged objects [8]. However, CORBA objects are not well suited for implementing user interface components and migrating between heterogeneous platforms. Microsoft's EasyLiving project [1] provides context-aware spaces, with a particular focus on home and office. This project can dynamically aggregate network-enabled input/output devices, such as keyboards and mice, even when they belong to different computers in a space. However, its management is centralized, and it does not dynamically migrate software to other computers according to the location of users. Both projects assume that locating sensors have initially been allocated in the room, and that dynamically reconfiguring the platform is difficult when sensors are added to or removed from the environment. In contrasts, our framework permits sensors to be mobile and scattered throughout a space.

Several studies have focused on enhancing context-awareness in mobile computing, for example HP's Cooltown [5] and the NEXUS system [4]. These projects assume that each user has a notebook PC, tablet PC, or PDA, equipped with GPS-based positioning sensors and wireless communication. Applications that run on such devices access resources stored on the web via a browser by using standard HTTP communication.

Although user familiarity with web browsers is an advantage in these systems, the services available are constrained by the limitations of web browsers and HTTP. In contrast, our framework can dynamically deploy mobile agents, which are autonomous programmable entities, to mobile computing devices. Unlike our approach, neither Cooltown nor NEXUS can support mobile users through stationary computers distributed in a smart environment.

While many researchers have explored mobile agent technology, no attempts have been made to integrate the mobility of physical objects with the mobility of agents in a ubiquitous computing setting. We previously presented an early prototype of the present framework [11] that did not support the mobility of sensors and agent hosts, so that the three linkages described in the second section of this paper were not available in that previous version of the framework.

9   Conclusion

We presented a mobile agent-based infrastructure for managing location-sensing systems and dynamically deploying services at suitable computing devices. Using location-tracking systems the infrastructure provides entities, e.g. people and objects, and places, with mobile agents to support and annotate them and migrate agents to stationary or mobile computers near the locations of the entities and places to which the agents are attached. It is a general framework in the sense that it is independent of any higher-level applications and location-sensing systems and supports a variety of spatial linkages between the physical mobility of people and things and the logical mobility of services. Furthermore, we designed and implemented a prototype system of the infrastructure and demonstrated its effectiveness in several practical applications.

Finally, we would like to point out further issues to be resolved. Since the framework presented in this paper is general-purpose, in future work we need to apply it to specific applications as well as the three applications presented in this paper. The location model of the framework was designed for operating real location-sensing systems in ubiquitous computing environments. We plan to design a more elegant and flexible world model for representing the locations of people, things, and places in the real world by incorporating existing spatial database technologies. We have developed an approach to testing context-aware applications on mobile computers [13, 14]. We are interested in developing a methodology that would test applications based on the framework. We have also constructed a general location model for ambient intelligence [15]. We plan to integrate the model into the location-aware deployment of services presented in the paper.

References

1. B. L. Brumitt, B. Meyers, J. Krumm, A. Kern, S. Shafer: EasyLiving: Technologies for Intelligent Environments, Proceedings of International Symposium on Handheld and Ubiquitous Computing, pp. 12-27, 2000.

2. K. Cheverst, N. Davis, K. Mitchell, and A. Friday: Experiences of Developing and Deploying a Context-Aware Tourist Guide: The GUIDE Project, Proceedings of Conference on Mobile Computing and Networking (MOBICOM'2000), pp. 20-31, ACM Press, 2000.

3. A. Harter, A. Hopper, P. Steggeles, A. Ward, and P. Webster: The Anatomy of a Context-Aware Application, Proceedings of Conference on Mobile Computing and Networking (MOBICOM'99), pp. 59-68, ACM Press, 1999.

4. F. Hohl, U. Kubach, A. Leonhardi, K. Rothermel, and M. Schwehm: Next Century Challenges: Nexus - An Open Global Infrastructure for Spatial-Aware Applications, Proceedings of Conference on Mobile Computing and Networking (MOBICOM'99), pp. 249-255, ACM Press, 1999).

5. T. Kindberg, et al: People, Places, Things: Web Presence for the Real World, Technical Report HPL-2000-16, Internet and Mobile Systems Laboratory, HP Laboratories, 2000.

6. B. D. Lange and M. Oshima: Programming and Deploying Java Mobile Agents with Aglets, Addison-Wesley, 1998.

7. U. Leonhardt, and J. Magee: Towards a General Location Service for Mobile Environments, Proceedings of IEEE Workshop on Services in Distributed and Networked Environments, pp. 43-50, IEEE Computer Society, 1996.

8. D. Lopez de Ipina and S. Lo: LocALE: a Location-Aware Lifecycle Environment for Ubiquitous Computing, Proceedings of Conference on Information Networking (ICOIN-15), IEEE Computer Society, 2001.

9. I. Satoh: MobileSpaces: A Framework for Building Adaptive Distributed Applications Using a Hierarchical Mobile Agent System, Proceedings of Conference on Distributed Computing Systems (ICDCS'2000), pp. 161-168, IEEE Computer Society, 2000.

10. I. Satoh: MobiDoc: A Framework for Building Mobile Compound Documents from Hierarchical Mobile Agents, Proceedings of Symposium on Agent Systems and Applications / Symposium on Mobile Agents (ASA/MA'2000), LNCS, Vol. 1882, pp. 113-125, Springer, 2000.

11. I. Satoh: SpatialAgents: Integrating User Mobility and Program Mobility in Ubiquitous Computing Environments, Wireless Communications and Mobile Computing, vol.3, no.4, pp.411-423, Wiley, June 2003.

12. I. Satoh: Building Reusable Mobile Agents for Network Management, IEEE Transactions on Systems, Man and Cybernetics, vol.33, no. 3, part-C, pp.350-357, August 2003.

13. I. Satoh: A Testing Framework for Mobile Computing Software, IEEE Transactions on Software Engineering, vol. 29, no. 12, pp.1112-1121, December 2003.

14. I. Satoh: Software Testing for Wireless Mobile Computing, IEEE Wireless Communications, vol. 11, no. 5, pp.58-64, IEEE Communication Society, October 2004.

15. I. Satoh: Location Model for Pervasive Computing Environments, to appear in Proceedings of IEEE 3rd International Conference on Pervasive Computing and Communications (PerCom'05), IEEE Computer Society, March 2005.

16. World Wide Web Consortium (W3C): Composite Capability/Preference Profiles (CC/PP), http://www.w3.org/TR/NOTE-CCPP, 1999.

Himalaya Framework: Hierarchical Intelligent Mobile Agents for Building Large-Scale and Adaptive Systems Based on Ambients

Amal El Fallah Seghrouchni and Alexandru Suna

LIP6, University of Paris 6, CNRS-UMR 7606,
8, Rue du Capitaine Scott, 75015, Paris, France
{Amal.Elfallah, Alexandru.Suna}@lip6.fr

Abstract. This paper presents a framework called Himalaya that allows to design mobile multi-agent systems (MMAS) deployed on several computers. An MMAS is a set of connected hierarchies of intelligent agents. Every agent (*i.e.* a node) contains cognitive elements (*e.g.* knowledge, goals, capabilities), processes and sub-agents. An agent is also mobile, he can move inside his hierarchy or to a remote one. In addition, an agent can dynamically acquire (kind of inheritance) intelligent and computational components from his sub-agents. The mobility and the inheritance as defined in our framework favor a dynamic adaptability and reconfiguring of systems in order to face the increasing complexity of distributed and cooperative applications.

1 Motivations for the Himalaya Framework

The main motivation of this work is to provide a framework enabling to build large-scale and adaptive systems as mobile multi-agent systems (MMAS).

Large-scale system means open system which could be deployed on several computers and could involve a big number of heterogenous agents (*e.g.* agents endowed with different skills) or a system to be deployed in open environments such as the Internet.

An adaptive system means a system which can adapt its structure (*e.g.* its number of agents, its organization, the location of its components, etc.) and can improve the services it offers, *i.e.* new services can be created dynamically from other elementary or composite services.

Scalability and adaptability raise at least two questions: which structure should be flexible enough to enable this dynamics and which kind of operations should make easy and effective the composition of services? To answer these questions, we developed the Himalaya framework (Hierarchical Intelligent Mobile Agents to build Large-scale and Adaptive sYstems based on Ambients) as an approach based on three fundamental concepts: mobility, hierarchical representation of agents and mechanisms of inheritance as allowed by the underlying representation.

T. Ishida, L. Gasser, and H. Nakashima (Eds.): MMAS 2004, LNAI 3446, pp. 202–216, 2005.

The Himalaya framework is built on:

- a high-level declarative agent-oriented programming language that allows the designer to develop MMAS. Called CLAIM (Computational Language for Autonomous, Intelligent and Mobile Agents) [6], this language combines cognitive elements (*e.g.* knowledge, goals, capabilities) and computational aspects such as mobility and enables to define agents or classes of agents. It also allows to deal with hierarchy and inheritance. The language has operational semantics [7] useful for the verification of the built MMAS.
- a distributed platform that supports the deployment of MMAS designed thanks to CLAIM. Called SyMPA (SYstem Multi-Platforms of Agents) [22], this platform offers all the necessary mechanisms for a secure execution of a distributed MMAS.

This paper is organized as follows. The next section presents the related work. Section 3 introduces an e-libraries network application as a case study that will illustrate the concepts and the mechanisms brought out along the paper. Section 4 summarizes the key concepts of the language, while the fifth section focuses on the MMAS reconfiguring and adaptation using mobility, inheritance and agents' creation and removal primitives. Section 6 briefly describes the platform which supports both the language and the reconfiguring mechanisms. Some implementation aspects of these mechanisms are given in section 7. Section 8 highlights the hierarchy and the inheritance aspects through the e-libraries case study. Section 9 presents the performed tests and the results we obtained. Finally, the last section concludes the paper and outlines our future work.

2   Related Work

The work presented in this paper tackles several domains: agent-oriented programming languages, concurrent languages and mobile agent platforms.

On one hand, the agent-oriented programming (AOP) languages, such as *AGENT-0* [21], *AgentSpeak* [23] or *3APL* [11] allow representing the mental state of the agents, containing beliefs, goals, intentions or abilities; these languages offer reasoning capabilities and communications primitives, but do not support agents' mobility. On the other hand, concurrent languages such as the *ambient calculus* [3], the *safe ambients* [16] or *Klaim* [4] have been proposed to formalize concurrent processes, that can communicate and migrate in a distributed environment. Several have well defined operational semantics, but in none of these languages it is possible to represent intelligent agents, with explicit believes, plans, goals or reasoning. *Telescript* [24] and *April* [17] are focused on the agents' mobility; nevertheless, they have neither the expressiveness and the reasoning capabilities of the AOP languages nor the formal solidity of the concurrent languages. A detailed presentation of all these languages can be found in [6].

Quantum [19] is a language for controlling the resource consumption of distributed computations, proposing a hierarchical representation of agents, similar to Himalaya. In the same spirit, the *CyberOrgs* [12] is a hierarchical model for resource sharing between agents running on a network of computers, with primitives similar to our framework, including mobility. However, these approaches focus on the resource consumption and do not treat intelligent aspects of agents.

Several platforms supporting mobile agents exist nowadays, such as *Aglets* [1], *D'Agents* [8] or *Grasshopper* [10]. All of them offer mechanisms for the agents' creation, communication, migration and management, while insuring a high level of security, which is a vital element in the context of mobile agents travelling around the insecure Internet. However, the supported agents are implemented mainly using Java, and so the agents are actually mobile objects. The reader can find in [22] a more detailed presentation of the mobile agent platforms.

The *MobileSpaces* [20] platform uses a hierarchical representation of agents, inspired from the ambient calculus and similar to our approach. However, the agents are Java objects. *Jason* [2] is another platform that has common elements with our approach; it contains an interpret implemented in Java for agents designed in AgentSpeak.

Considering the existing languages, it is not easy to design intelligent and mobile agents. Consequently, we have been led to develop the CLAIM language and the SyMPA platform to support the design and the deployment of MMAS.

3   Case Study: An e-Libraries Network

This section presents an application we developed[1] in order to emphasize the main features of the Himalaya framework, such as the utility of the hierarchical representation of agents and the dynamic reconfiguring of the system using mobility operations and inheritance.

This application is a collection of digital libraries, whose services are used by customers' agents searching various documents. Several libraries are distributed on several computers connected through a network. Every library has a main site, where a *Librarian* agent is deployed, managing the clients' inscriptions, the index of documents and the sections (one for each important category of documents). This agent also has pieces of information about the other libraries' content, as the main goal of our application is to satisfy the subscribers, even if this means to redirect them towards other libraries. For each section, there is a *Section librarian* agent (sub-agent of the main librarian agent) that manages the documents in his category and has qualitative information about these documents. This network of libraries is used by customers that are searching documents following various criterions (*e.g.* category, authors, keywords). For every customer there is a corresponding *Client* agent that will dynamically create a new *Search* agent for every category of documents concerned by a request. Afterwards, the *Client* will migrate with the current sub-agents to the libraries he knows, where the *Search* agents go to the concerned sections, request infor-

---

[1] Application designed together with Gilles Klein, University of Paris Dauphine.

mation about the quality and the disposability of the documents that match their request and return to the client with the gathered pieces of information. The *Client* uses this information to choose the documents to borrow (or to go to other library) and afterwards goes back to his initial site. When there are too many clients on a library site, some of the sections migrate with all their clients to other computers less charged.

4   Key Concepts of Himalaya

4.1   MMAS in Himalaya

An MMAS in Himalaya is a set of hierarchies of agents running on computers connected via a network. An agent is a node in a hierarchy and contains other agents, running processes and reasoning elements.

Figure 1 presents an intuitive graphical representation of a part of the MMAS of our application sketched in the previous section. In this figure, we have four hierarchies, two of them composed of *Librarian* agents containing sections and clients, one containing a section that migrated later to another site and the forth hierarchy (up, left) having as root a *Client* that created two *Search* agents for two different requests.

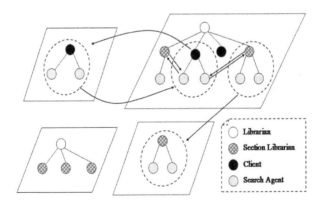

Fig. 1. An MMAS in Himalaya: Application's schema

4.2   Agents in Himalaya

An agent in Himalaya is an autonomous, intelligent and mobile entity, uniquely identified in the MMAS. He can be seen as a bounded place where computation happens, belonging to a hierarchy. Thus, an agent has a parent and may have several sub-agents.

The intelligent components of an agent are the *knowledge* base, the *goals* and the *capabilities*; together, these elements allow an autonomous, reactive or goal-driven behavior.

The *knowledge* base (noted K_α, α being the name of the agent) contains pieces of information about the other agents' classes and capabilities or about the environment he is acting in. The knowledge about other agents has a standard format, containing the name of the concerned agent and his class or capability. In addition, the user can define his own ontology of information about the world, represented as propositions containing a name and a list of arguments.

Agent's behavior is triggered either by the received messages, or by his goals. An agent α can have several goals (noted G_α), represented as propositions. In order to achieve a goal, an agent tries to execute capabilities whose effects (seen as post-conditions) match the current goals.

Therefore, the capabilities (noted C_α) are the main elements of an agent. A capability has a message of activation, a condition, the process to be executed and eventual effects. After receiving a message, in order to execute a capability, the agent must verify the associated condition. A condition can be a Java function that returns a *boolean*, or a condition about the agent's knowledge, sub-agents or about his achieved effects. A capability may have a *null* message and in this case the capability is executed whenever the condition is verified; the condition can also be *null*, and the capability is executed when the message is received.

Once a capability is activated, the corresponding processes are executed (concurrently with the already running processes of the agent). So an agent α contains a set of concurrent running processes, $P_\alpha = p_i \mid p_j \mid ... \mid p_k$. One of these concurrent processes can be a (possibly empty) sequence of processes, a message transmission, the creation of a new agent, a mobility operation, a variable instantiation, a function defined in another programming language (*e.g.* Java methods), or an instruction (for executing a process for all the agent's elements from the knowledge base or sub-agents that verify certain criterions).

$p_i ::= 0 \mid p_j.p_k \mid send(\alpha, m) \mid$
$\qquad newAgent\ \alpha(K, G, C, P) \mid$
$\qquad in(\beta) \mid out(\beta) \mid move(\beta) \mid$
$\qquad open(\beta) \mid acid \mid kill(\beta) \mid$
$\qquad ?x = (value \mid Java(object.method(args))) \mid$
$\qquad Java(object.method(args)) \mid$
$\qquad forAllKnowkedge(k)\{p_j\} \mid$
$\qquad forAllAgents(\alpha_i)\{p_j\}$

The *send* primitive transmits a message to another agent, to all the agents belonging to a class (multicast) or to all the agents in the system (broadcast). There are pre-defined messages, with a specific treatment, used during the mobility protocols for asking and granting permissions, or used by agents to exchange information about their capabilities and knowledge bases. The users can also define their own messages, represented as propositions.

An agent, *e.g.* α, is noted as $\alpha(G_\alpha, K_\alpha, C_\alpha, P_\alpha)$, for denoting his goals, knowledge base, capabilities and his concurrent running processes.

The previous elements allow two types of reasoning for the Himalaya agents: *forward reasoning* (or reactive behavior): an agent activates capabilities when the corresponding messages arrive and the capabilities' conditions are verified; and *backward reasoning* (or goal-driven behavior): an agent executes capabilities in order to achieve goals.

5   Adaptive MMAS Through Reconfiguring Operations

This section focuses on the key operations for an MMAS reconfiguring. With respect to the hierarchical representation of agents, these operations allow flexible reconfiguring of systems and dynamic gathering of capabilities and knowledge. We distinguish three kinds of primitives: for mobility, for inheritance and for dynamic creation and removal of agents. They are briefly described below and represented in a graphical manner. The hierarchies' modifications will be obvious on the figures and the agents' components that change will be explicitly represented. For readability reasons, an agent will be represented only by his name but he will contain all his components; *i.e.* an agent α will be read as $\alpha(G_\alpha, K_\alpha, C_\alpha, P_\alpha)$. For a detailed presentation, in particular concerning the operational semantics of these primitives, the reader is invited to see [7].

5.1   Mobility Primitives

The mobility primitives are inspired by the ambient calculus [3]. Thus, an agent moves as a whole, with all his components (intelligent elements, running processes and sub-agents). Using *in* (figure 2), an agent can enter another agent from the same level in the hierarchy (*i.e.* having the same parent) and using *out*, an agent can exit his parent (figure 3). Unlike the ambient calculus, where there is no control, we added an asking/granting permission mechanism. By default, a Himalaya agent will receive these permissions, unless another agent is explicitly programmed to refuse to give them. The *move* mobility operation is a direct migration into another agent, without verifying a structure condition (figure 4). Nevertheless, the *move* operation is subject to permissions using a specific protocol (see [6]).

5.2   Inheritance Primitives

The inheritance primitives are inspired by the ambient calculus, but they have been adapted to suit our goal: dynamic reconfiguring of intelligent MMAS. Tak-

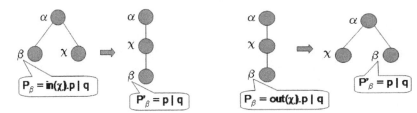

Fig. 2. In operation   Fig. 3. Out operation

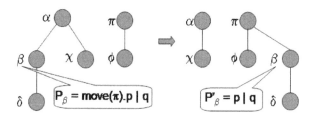

Fig. 4. Move operation

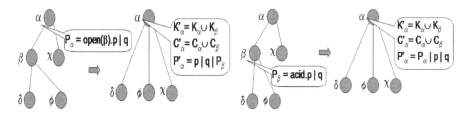

Fig. 5. Open operation (absorption)   **Fig. 6. Acid** operation (dissolution)

ing full advantage of the hierarchical representation of the agents and using the *open* primitive, an agent can open the boundaries of one of his sub-agents, thus inheriting the latter's running processes and sub-agents, as in the ambient calculus, but also the knowledge and capabilities (figure 5). In this case, the sub-agent is absorbed by his parent. The *acid* primitive (figure 6) is similar to *open*, but it is an agent who decides to open his own boundaries, and as a consequence, his components are inherited by his parent. In this case, the sub-agent dissolves himself into his parent.

Thence, both in absorption and in dissolution situations, an agent dynamically gathers new capabilities and enriches his knowledge base; it is what we call inheritance in our framework.

5.3   Dynamic Creation and Removal of Agents

Another important element towards the system's adaptability is the possibility to create and remove agents dynamically. New agents are created using the *newAgent* primitive (figure 7) and an agent can completely remove (without

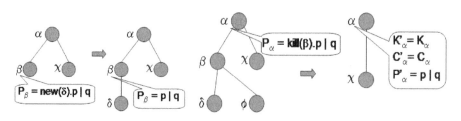

Fig. 7. New Agent operation   **Fig. 8. Kill** operation

inheriting his cognitive components) one of his sub-agents using the *kill* (figure 8) primitive.

6   The Platform at a Glance

The Himalaya framework is supported by a distributed platform implemented in Java [13] that offers all the necessary mechanisms for agents' management, communication, mobility, security and fault-tolerance. The main difference and advantage with respect to other mobile agent platforms is that our platform supports agents implemented in a high-level agent-oriented programming language while other platforms support agents implemented using mainly object-oriented languages (*e.g.* Java in most cases). In addition, a Himalaya agent can use Java methods for computation purposes. The platform's architecture is compliant with the specificatsions of the MASIF [18] standard from the OMG.

Himalaya is deployed on a set of connected computers. The platform's architecture is presented in the figure 9. There is a central system providing management functions. An agent system is deployed on each computer connected to the platform. It provides a graphical interface for defining and creating agents and for visualizing their execution, a compiler, mechanisms for agents' deployment, communication, migration and management (conf. figure 10), all of these in a secure and fault tolerant environment. The compiler was implemented using JavaCC (Java Compiler Compiler) [14]. The agent system is also in charge of the communication with other agent systems or with the central system and of the mobility. The communication and the mobility are implemented using Java on top of the TCP/IP protocol.

6.1   Mobility in Himalaya

Due to the hierarchical representation of the agents and the distributed deployment of an MMAS, we distinguish local and remote migrations. The local migra-

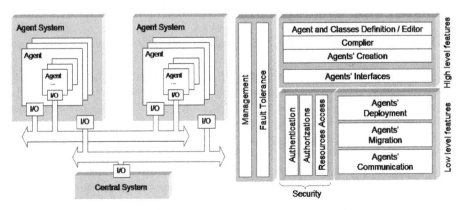

Fig. 9. Platform's Architecture   **Fig. 10.** Platform's Features

tion takes place inside a hierarchy, while the remote migration is the migration between hierarchies, using the *move* primitive.

The remote mobility in Himalaya can be considered at two levels. First, there is a strong migration at the language level, because, before the migration, the state of an agent is saved and then transferred to the destination. The agent's language-specific processes are resumed from their interruption point. An agent can be at any moment saved in a format similar to the definition, containing the current state (*e.g.* knowledge, messages, running processes). This representation is sent via network to the destination agent system, in an encrypted format and the agent's execution is resumed from the saved state.

At the Java level, we use its mobility facilities, so there is a weak migration. A Java method begun before the migration will be reinvoked after the arrival at the destination. Since the migration is achieved using the language's primitives, unlike in other platforms, where there are Java objects that migrate during their execution, a solution can also be to let all the agent's running Java methods terminate before his migration.

6.2   Security in Himalaya

The mobile agents are programs running in a distributed and insecure environment (*e.g.* the Internet) where there are possible different attacks from the agents against the host agent system or attacks against an agent during the migration or during his execution. Several solutions exist to these attacks [9], but they are outside the scope of this paper. Therefore, for the agent systems' protection, we are using agents' authentication, the control of the access to the system's resources in accordance with a set of permissions given to agents with regard to their authority, and audit techniques. For the agents' protection, we are using encryption during the migration and during the execution on a agent system (when the agent is stored on the disk), and also fault-tolerance mechanisms. The reader can find in [22] a detailed description of these security aspects.

7   The Implementation of the Reconfiguring Operations

In this section we present in an intuitive manner how the reconfiguring operations are implemented in Himalaya.

We have seen that on each site there is an Agent System that offers mechanisms for agents' creation, management, communication and mobility by launching a process that we call *PSystem*. Also, for each agent, there is a corresponding process (called *PAgent*) that executes the agent (both the reactive and the proactive behaviors) and offers a graphical interface. The operations that involve only the current agent are treated by the *PAgent* process. However, all the reconfiguring operations involve more than one agent and are managed by *PSystem*.

As we have already specified, all these operations can be classified in operations having as result a dynamic change in the system's structure and hierarchy (actually all the presented operations modify the hierarchies) and operations having as result a dynamic gathering of cognitive elements, processes, etc. (in this category we have the inheritance primitives: *open* and *acid*).

For the hierarchy change, if it is an operation requiring a structure condition (i.e. *in*, *out*, *open*) *PSystem* must verify first this condition. If the condition is verified, the protocol for asking/granting permissions begins. Since the current structure must not be changed during the execution of an operation, the involved agents are not allowed to treat other mobility messages. Then *PSystem* updates the hierarchy and the MMAS goes on with its execution.

Here is a pseudo-code of the operation $in(B)$ executed by an agent A:

```
Algorithm in {
  if neighbors(A,B){ // verify the structure condition
    A.blockMessagesTreatment(); // A blocks the mobility messages' treatment
    A.askInPermission(B); // A asks enter permission from B
    if(A.receiveInPermission(B)) { // If B gives the permission,
      B.blockMessagesTreatment(); // B blocks the mobility messages' treatment
      A.parent ← B; // B becomes the parent of A
      B.addAgent(A); // A is added in B's list of sub-agents
      A.resume(); // the two agents unblock the messages' treatment
      B.resume(); // and resume their execution
    } else {A.postponeProcess(in); A.resume(); } // If A does not receive
      // the permission, he unblocks the mobility messages' treatment,
      // postpones the in operation and resumes the execution
  } else {A.postponeProcess(in);} // A postpones the in operation
}
```

For the inheritance operations there are both a change in the agents' structure and a change in the internal states of the agents. For *open* (in the pseudo-code bellow, A is opening B), there is first a structure condition to be verified, followed by a permission asking (*acid* is similar, without verifying a structure condition and without permission asking). If these requirements hold, *PSystem* updates the hierarchy, the intelligent aspects are inherited by the parent agent and the MMAS resumes its execution.

```
Algorithm open {
  if A.hasAgent(B){ // verify the structure condition
    A.blockMessagesTreatment(); // A blocks the mobility messages' treatment
    A.askOpenPermission(B); // A asks open permission from B
    if(A.receiveOpenPermission(B)) {// If B gives the permission,
      B.blockMessagesTreatment(); // B blocks the mobility messages' treatment
      forAll(ag ∈ B.agents) {A.addAgent(ag)}
      forAll(p ∈ B.processes) {A.addProcess(p)}
      forAll(k ∈ B.knowledge) {A.addKnowledge(k)}
      forAll(c ∈ B.capabilities) {A.addCapability(c)}
      // the agents, processes, knowledge and capabilities are inherited by A
      stop(B); // B stops his execution and disappears from the MMAS
      A.removeAgent(B); // B is eliminated from the list of A's sub-agents
      A.resume();// A unblocks the messages' treatment and resumes his execution
```

```
    } else {A.postponeProcess(open); A.resume();} If A does not receive
    // the permission, he unblocks the mobility messages' treatment,
    // postpones the open operation and resumes the execution
  } else {A.postponeProcess(open);} // A postpones the open operation
}
```

8   Hierarchy and Inheritance Through the Case Study

This section emphasizes the interest of the main features of Himalaya through the e-libraries network application presented in the section 3. Pieces of CLAIM code will also be given.

8.1   Dynamic MMAS Reconfiguring and Structure Change

We have seen that the network of libraries is used by clients that are searching documents in function of different criterions (*e.g.* category, authors, keywords). In the following code, the client searches for SF novels written by Asimov and funny books. A first reconfiguring of the system occurs when a *Client* agent dynamically creates new *Search* agents in accordance with the current requests (one for each concerned category of documents) using the *newAgent* primitive. Thus, these agents become sub-agents of the *Client*. Using the *move* primitive he will migrate (with his sub-agents) to one of the known libraries (where he is registered). The code of this capability of the client is presented below.

```
Agent C:Client() {
  knowledge={search(S1,SF,<Asimov>,<>);search(S2,Various,<>,<funny>);
    registered(Lib1);}
  ...
  capabilities {
  search {
  message=search();
  condition=hasKnowledge(search(?n,?d,?a,?kw));
  do{forAllKnowledge(search(?n,?d,?a,?kw)){newAgent ?n:Search(?d,?a,?kw)}.
    forAllKnowedge(registered(?l)){ move(?l) }. ...}
  effects=null;
  } ... } ...
  }
```

Another adaptation is done when there are too many clients on a library site. Taking benefit from the hierarchical representation, some of the sections migrate as a whole (*i.e.* with all their clients) to other computers less charged. In this case we are using results from our resource sharing mechanism [15], where computers are classified using Galois lattices in function of their technical characteristics gathered by mobile agents. Using this classification, the tasks will be executed on computers with available resources.

8.2   Dynamic Inheritance

Once inside the destination library, the *Search* agents will exit the *Client* (*out* operation) and will enter the corresponding *Section librarian* (*in* operation). They request information about the quality and the availability of the documents that match their requests. They enrich their knowledge base with the references of interesting documents for their requests. If there are no matching documents in the current library, maybe the *Section librarian* agents know other libraries holder of interesting documents. After gathering information, the *Search* agents exit the sections and enter their *Client* agent where they open their own boundaries (using the *acid* operation). Hence, the *Client* inherits the knowledge bases of these agents (together with their capabilities) and can use these pieces of information to decide what documents borrow or in which library search for documents. After borrowing the documents, the *Client* agent can move with them back to his site.

The CLAIM code bellow corresponds to two of the capabilities of a *Search* agent. The first one allows the migration to the section and the demand for information about documents matching the request. The second one is used, after receiving this information from the *Section librarian* agent, to go to the client and to open his own boundaries allowing in this way the inheritance of his cognitive elements by the client.

```
AgentClass Search(?section,?authors,?keywords) {
  ...
  capabilities {
  goToSection {
  message=go();
  condition=null;
  do{ out(parent).in(?section).
     send(?section,wantInformations(?authors,?keywords)) }
  effects=null;
  }
  returnToClient {
  message=receivedInformation();
  condition=null;
  do{ out(?section).in(authority).acid }
  effects=null;
  } ... }
  }
```

9   Tests and Results

The classes of agents of the application were implemented using our language. The platform was installed on a set of computers with different technical characteristics, connected at a local network. On some of these computers we deployed several libraries, with their sections and their knowledge about docu-

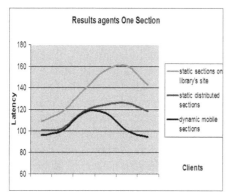
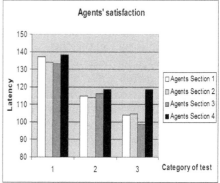

Fig. 11. Results clients one section   **Fig. 12.** Clients' satisfaction

ments, clients and other libraries. A big number of clients, with different research criterions, were started on all the available computers. They dynamically create *Search* agents in function of their requests and migrate to the libraries; next, the *Search* agents go to the corresponding sections. When a site is overloaded, some sections migrate to other computers from the network, with sufficient resources.

The expressiveness of the language and the dynamic adaptability and reconfiguring was proved by the application itself and by the dynamic behavior of the MMAS during execution. In addition, in order to prove the efficiency of the dynamic distribution of sections and the advantage of the mobility we performed three types of tests. First, all the sections of a library will stay on the library's computer. In the second type of tests, half of the sections of some libraries will be deployed from the beginning on different computers than their library, but will not migrate next. Finally, we allow the dynamic migration of sections. As shown in figure 11 (where we represent the average waiting time of different clients' agents arriving to one particular section of a library in our three cases), the best results are obtained when the mobility is allowed as the libraries transfers other sections on another computers letting the overloaded section run alone while the other can run more freely altogether. In fact, the figure 12 (presenting the average latency time in the four sections of one of the libraries) shows that dynamic load distribution reduces the waiting time for every agent whatever their section of interest.

10   Conclusion and Future Work

In this paper, we argued that MMAS could be useful to build large-scale and adaptive distributed systems. To implement this idea, we developed the Himalaya framework, that offers a hierarchical representation of agents and reconfiguring operations (mobility or inheritance primitives) allowing a dynamic adaptability of MMAS.

The Himalaya environment has been used for developing several complex applications that proved the expressiveness of the language and the robustness and the strength of the platform: an application for information research on the Web [5], an electronic commerce application [6], a load balancing and resource sharing application using mobile agents [15] and an application of a digital libraries network. All the results were very promising.

Our short term future work is three-folds. First, we would like to experiment our framework in more open environments, and on a bigger number of computers connected through the Internet. Secondly, we intend to develop a planner for new systems' reconfiguring. The designer should specify the initial configuration of his application/system and the target configuration that fulfills his requirements; the system should be able to reconfigure itself even if the execution environment changes. This is particulary useful in dynamic and open environments. Finally, today our framework meets the requirements of mobile computation reinforced with intelligent skills. We would like to deploy Himalaya on mobile devices in order to fulfill also the ambient intelligence requirements.

Acknowledgement. The authors would like to thank David Kinny for the interesting discussions during the ProMAS workshop at AAMAS 2004 conference about the reconfiguring of complex distributed systems.

References

1. Aglets Workbench: http://www.trl.ibm.co.jp/aglets
2. Bordini R.H., Hubner J.F.: Jason, A Java-based agentSpeak interpreter used with saci for multi-agent distribution over the net. On-line at http://jason.sourceforge.net/Jason.pdf,
3. Cardelli L., Gordon A.D.: Mobile Ambients. Foundations of Software Science and Computational Structures, Maurice Nivat (Ed.), LNCS, **1378**, (1998) 140-155
4. deNicola R., Ferrari G.L., Pugliese R.: Klaim: a Kernel Language for Agents Interaction and Mobility. IEEE Transactions on Software Engineering (1998) 315-330
5. El Fallah Seghrouchni A., Suna A.: An Unified Framework for Programming Autonomous, Intelligent and Mobile Agents. Proceedings of CEEMAS'03, LNAI, **2691** (2003) 353-362
6. El Fallah Seghrouchni A., Suna A.: CLAIM: A Computational Language for Autonomous, Intelligent and Mobile Agents. Proceedings of ProMAS'03, LNAI, **3067** (2004) 90-110
7. El Fallah Seghrouchni A., Suna A.: Programming Mobile Intelligent Agents: an Operational Semantics. Proceedings of IEEE IAT'04 conferece, IEEE Press, Beijing, China, (2004)
8. Gray R.S., Kotz D., Cybenko G., Rus D.: D'Agents: Security in a multiple-language, mobile-agent system. Mobile Agents and Security, LNCS, **1419** (1998) 154-187
9. Greenberg M.S., Buyington J.C., Harper D.G.: Mobile Agents and Security. IEEE Comunications Magazine, (1998) 76-85
10. Grasshopper on-line at http://www.grasshopper.de
11. Hindriks K.V.,deBoer F.S., van der Hoek W., Meyer J.J.Ch.: Agent Programming in 3APL. Intelligent Agents and Multi-Agent Systems, **2** (1999) 357-401

12. Jamali N., Agha G.A.: CyberOrgs: A Model for Decentralized Resource Control in Multi-Agent Systems. Proceedings of Workshop on Representations and Approaches for Time-Critical Decentralized Resource/Role/Task Allocation of AAMAS, (2003)

13. Java on-line at http://java.sun.com

14. JavaCC on-line at https://javacc.dev.java.net/

15. Klein, G., Suna A., El Fallah Seghrouchni A.: Resource sharing and load balancing based on agent mobility. Proceedings of ICEIS '04 (2004)

16. Levi F., Sangiori D.: Controlling Interference in Ambients. Proceedings of the 27th ACM SIGPLAN-SIGACT symposium on Principles of programming languages (2000) 352-364

17. McCabe F.G., Clark K.L.: April Agent PRocess Interaction Language. Intelligent Agents: Theories, Architectures, and Languages, LNAI, **890** (1994)

18. Milojicic D., Breugst M., Busse I., Campbell J., Covaci S., Friedman B., Kosaka K., Lange D., Ono K., Oshima M., Tham C., Virdhagriswaran S., White J.: MASIF, The OMG Mobile Agent System Interoperability Facility. Proceedings of Mobile Agents, LNAI, **1477** (1998) 50-67

19. Moreau L., Queinnec C.: Design and Semantics of Quantum: a Language to Control Resource Consumption in Distributed Computing. Usenix Conference on Domain-Specific Languages (DSL'97), (1997) 183-197

20. Satoh Ichiro: MobileSpaces: A Framework for Building Adaptive Distributed Applications Using a Hierarchical Mobile Agent System. Proceedings of IEEE International Conference on Distributed Computing Systems, (2000) 161-168

21. Shoham Yoav: Agent Oriented Programming. Artifficial Intelligence, **60** (1993) 51-92

22. Suna A., El Fallah Seghrouchni A.: A mobile agents platform: architecture, mobility and security elements. Proceedings of ProMAS'04, Workshop of AAMAS'04, New-York, (2004)

23. Weerasooriya D., Rao Anand S., Ramamohanarao K.: Design of a Concurrent Agent-Oriented Language. Intelligent Agents. Proceedings of First International Workshop on Agent Teories, Architectures and Languages (ATAL'94), LNAI, **890** (1994)

24. White J.: Mobile agents. Software Agents, Bradshaw, J. Ed., MIT Press, (1997)

Multi-agent Human-Environment Interaction Framework for the Ubiquitous Environment

Satoshi Kurihara[1], Kensuke Fukuda[2], Toshio Hirotsu[3], Shigemi Aoyagi[4],
Toshihiro Takada[4], and Toshiharu Sugawara[4]

[1] ISIR, Osaka University, 8-1, Mihogaoka, Ibaraki, Osaka 567-0047, Japan
`kurihara@ist.osaka-u.ac.jp`
`http://www.ai.sanken.osaka-u.ac.jp`
[2] NTT Network Innovation Labs., Tokyo, Japan
[3] Toyohashi University of Technology, Aichi, Japan
[4] NTT Communication Science Labs., Nara, Japan

Abstract. We discuss how humans interact with the environment like mental and physical harmonization. Keyword is "resonance". Each human has his own natural frequency, which is a metaphor for personality or daily habitual behaviors. In the proposed framework, each human behavior reacts the environment and the environment performs sensor-data mining and extracts each human's natural frequency. The environment constructed from a multi-agent system is always watching humans, and when there is information to give one particular human, the environment interacts with him by using his natural frequency, so he can spontaneously and efficiently get the information from the environment. To achieve this, we set up several interaction devices between humans and the environment as well as various kinds of many sensors.

1 Introduction

In recent years, progress in computer technology, the appearance of IPv6, the development of various radio technology including IEEE 802.11, and the practical use of radio-tags like RFID have greatly activated studies of ubiquitous computing like sensor-network [1]. But, the purpose of many proposed ubiquitous systems is to present information of the virtual-world like the Internet to humans living in the real-world by using physical properties like monitors and loudspeakers, etc [2], [3]. On the other hand, our purpose is to construct a framework to enable flexible and real-time interaction between humans and the real-world. Keyword is resonance. Resonance is a well-known phenomenon in the real-world. Consider that a certain vibration *source-A* wants to resonate with a vibration *target-B*. At this point, A does not have to interact with B directly. A only has to start vibrating with the natural frequency of B. Then the vibration is transmitted to B through the air, regardless of A's intention, and as the result, B starts to vibrate. In this paper, we propose a methodology for applying resonance to the interaction between humans and the real-world.

T. Ishida, L. Gasser, and H. Nakashima (Eds.): MMAS 2004, LNAI 3446, pp. 217–223, 2005.

The real-world that we assume in this study is homes and offices, etc., where daily habitual behaviors of humans are easy to extract. Hereinafter we call the real-world as "the environment." The environment learns the daily habitual behaviors of each human, and performs the most suitable interaction to whoever should receive it. To embody this interaction framework, the environment must be an autonomous action entity, and it is necessary to construct this entity as a massively multi-agent system to enable management and control of various broadly dispersed sensors and physical properties for interaction and to enable real-time interaction with humans. We placed many sensors which acquire daily habitual human behaviors as well as several physical properties like liquid crystal projectors which displays information onto a wall and a floor, a loudspeaker array system which can construct a sound field, an autonomous moving robot as many interaction channels.

2   Human-Environment Interaction

2.1   From Humans to the Environment

Each human's behavior wakes up the various kinds of sensors buried in the environment, then the environment performs sensor-data mining and extracts daily

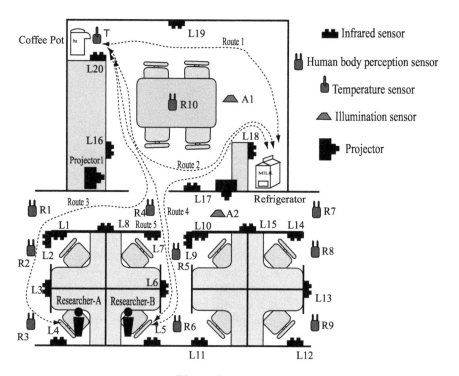

Fig. 1. Sensor map

habitual behaviors of each human. Consider figure 1 (our working and meeting rooms) and figure 2. Infrared sensors ($L1$ ...$L20$) detect humans passing in front of these sensors. Temperature sensor (T) measures temperature of the pot for making a coffee. Human body perception sensors ($R1$ ...$R10$) detect infrared rays emitted from human bodies. Illumination sensors ($A1$ and $A2$) measure the brightness of these rooms. Moreover, we placed several sensors that sense the opening and shutting of the meeting room and refrigerator doors, and a smell sensor to sense the smell of coffee or tea near the pot. Each sensor is controlled by each individual agent (*sensor-agent*). Consider that *researcher-A* in the figure 1 usually moves along the route 3 from his seat to the pot to make a coffee. Then the following habitual infrared sensor reaction sequence is extracted and learned: $L4 \rightarrow L3 \rightarrow L2 \rightarrow L8 \rightarrow L16 \rightarrow L20$. And this reaction sequence and the following three sets of data: "output value of each sensor", "the time when the behavior started", "the time needed for the behavior" are described as one "*action-series*" as follows. For example, if *researcher-A* started this behavior at *August 20 10:00 a.m. 23 minutes* and took 1 minute, then the *action-series* of *researcher-A* is described as follows:

Action-series1:
$\langle \{L4, L3, L2, L8, L16, L20\}(8/20/10/23, 1) :$
$T(high)\{L20\}, A_1(on)\{L16, L20\}, A_2(on)\{L4, L3, L2, L8\}\rangle$

In this description, four position sensors $\{L4, L3, L2, L8\}$ are related to illumination sensor A_2, two position sensors $\{L16, L20\}$ are related to illumination sensor A_1, and position sensor $\{L20\}$ is related to temperature sensor T^1. Each acquired *action-series* is managed by each "*action-monitor-agent*". *Action-monitor-agents* always watch human behaviors and perform real-time planning for interaction.

2.2   From the Environment to Humans

If the environment could automatically switch on the lights of the meeting room, like $A_1(off) \rightarrow A_1(on)$, it might be good for *researcher-A* always arriving to the working room first and making some coffee. And if the environment could notify *researcher-B*, who always secondarily arrives, that coffee is not made this morning on account of that *researcher-A* could not make some coffee for some reasons when *researcher-B* starts his daily habitual behavior to drink coffee always made by *researcher-A*, he could avoid wasting effort on useless actions.

When a certain person starts one of his *action-series*, an *action-monitor-agent*, which manages this *action-series*, senses his behavior and begins planning to achieve strategy 1 of 2 below at first and tries to perform strategy 2 when strategy 1 is judged to be impossible.

Strategy 1: Let the *action-series* complete safely.

---

[1] To propose a methodology for extracting and learning the relationships between position sensors like the infrared sensor and state sensors like the illumination sensor is also one of our goal.

Strategy 2: Notify him immediately and effectively that this *action-series* cannot be achieved. In other words, the environment tries to stop this action which has a high probability of being wasteful.

Strategy 1: *Action-monitor-agent* performs interaction that allows a person to complete its managing *action-series* safely. For example, consider that the infrared sensors reacted as $L4 \rightarrow L3 \rightarrow L2$ when *researcher-A* started one of his habitual behaviors. Then several *action-monitor-agents*, each of which manages *action-series* including the reaction time order of $L4 \rightarrow L3 \rightarrow L2$, begin checking possibility of that *researcher-A* can perform their managing *action-series* safely or not. To make this, each *action-monitor-agent* acquires the state of each sensor at the present and then performs STRIPS-like planning. For example, suppose that the illumination of a meeting room is off due to some troubles, so it is assumed that it was A_1 *(off)*. In this case, since the current environment state becomes $\{T(high), A_1(off), A_2(on)\}$, certain *action-monitor-agent* managing *action-series1* in section 2.1 lets the environment change the current environment state to the following goal state $\{T(high), A_1(on), A_2(on)\}$.

As I mentioned in section 2.1, many physical properties for various kinds of interaction actions from environment to humans are prepared. Each action is described as an *unit-action*. For example, a *unit-action* "*meeting_room_lights_on*" to switch on the lights of the meeting room becomes follows.

$\langle meeting\_room\_lights\_on$:
$preconditions : \{A_1(off)\}$
$add\_list : \{A_1(on)\}$
$delete\_list : \{A_1(off)\}$
$time : 1.0$
effectiveness: 1.0
$area : \{L16, L17, L18, L19, L20\}\rangle.$

The *action-monitor-agent* selects certain *unit-action* which can change the current state to the goal state[2], and selected *unit-action* executes its action. At this point, the important elements of *unit-action* are "*time*" and "*effectiveness*". *Time* shows necessary time for *unit-action* to execute its action, and *effectiveness* shows effectiveness of *unit-action* (*effectiveness* is real number from 0 to 1). For example. when a *unit-action* of controlling power of room light is an extremely effective action for changing an existing state into the goal state, so, the *effectiveness* of the *unit-action* is set to 1.0, because state of the light can change in a twinkle. And since this action can complete instantly, *time* can be expressed with the fixed number (in *unit-action:meeting_room_lights_on*, *time* was set to 1 second). But in some cases, it is necessary to describe *time* as a formula. For example, for the *unit-action* which controls power of the pot, the state of temperature sensor T cannot become *high* immediately even if it is switched on,

---

[2] *Unit-action* of that the element of *preconditions* is included in the current state and the element of *add_list* is included in the goal state is selected.

because the water takes several minutes to boil. The time taken for the water to boil depends on the pot's temperature when it is switched on. Therefore, in this case, *time* must be expressed by a function like $func(temp)$, (*temp* shows the temperature of water in the pot), and this function can be found by analyzing sensor data of T.

Strategy 2: In the above case, it is a good strategy that *researcher-A* does not begin the *action-series* for making a coffee until $T(low)$ becomes $T(high)$. Therefore, the environment needs to recommend *researcher-A* to stop the execution of this *action-series* immediately. If the *time* value of *unit-action* is bigger than the *time* value of *action-series*, the *action-monitor-agent* managing this *action-series* decides that accomplishment of the *action-series* is impossible, and adds the item *"impossible"* to the current state. Then, several *unit-actions* whose *preconditions* is set to *impossible* start their actions to stop the current behavior of *researcher-A*. We placed several liquid crystal projectors at some locations where corridors or passages seemed to intersect (see figure 1), and they can display various kinds of information onto the floor (see figure 2 (f)). For example, a *unit-action* of *projector1* is described as follows:

$\langle projector1 : preconditions : \{impossible\}$
$add\_list : \{null\}$
$delete\_list : \{null\}$
$time : 1.0$
effectiveness: 0.9
$area : \{L16\}\rangle$

When the temperature of the pot is still low, certain *action-monitor-agent* decide to stop moving of researcher-A toward the pot, and executes *unit-action: projector1* to display "water is still cold", because *preconditions* of *projector1* is *impossible*.

3   Initial Experiment

First, we checked whether *action-monitor-agents* could extract series of our daily habitual behaviors from sensor data of about a month. As I mentioned before, buried position sensors are "infrared sensor" and "human body perception sensor", and state sensors are "door opening and shutting detection sensor", and "the temperature and smell sensor" of the pot (see figure 2). Currently, we have been adopting the following simple strategy. If sensor-A and sensor-B react during very short period, we think that the sensor-A and sensor-B may be located closely. As a result, the route1 - 5 in figure 1 could be acquired distinctly without any problems. Figure 3 shows the acquired infrared-sensor graph of our working and meeting rooms, in which each node shows the infrared sensor.

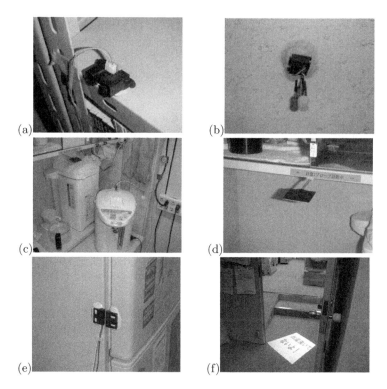

Fig. 2. (a) Infrared sensor, (b) Human body perception sensor, (c) Temperature sensor, (d) Smell sensor, (e) Door opening and shutting detection sensor, (f) Liquid crystal projector to reflect information to the floor

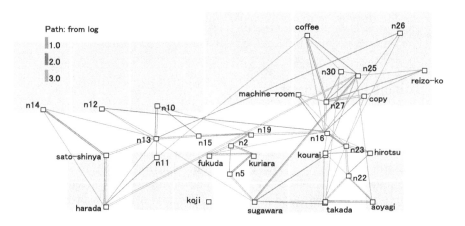

Fig. 3. Acquired infrared-sensor graph

4   Discussion

As I mentioned in the section 1, the proposed framework assumes homes or offices, where the environment may be able to extract habitual behaviors of humans. Currently we have no plan to use tag system like RFID to identify each person. It may be difficult to extract an individual movement trace only from sensor reaction time order without tag system under the following situations where a lot of people temporarily gather like station, park, conference, etc. Of course, we also guess that tag system will be used in almost every place in a future. However, tag coverage will probably not be 100%, so we think it will be necessary for our interaction model to be able to work even in an environment not existing tag system.

In figure 2 (f), the projector displays the text "Water has not boiled" to show the state of temperature sensor $T(low)$, but if we make this, the *unit-action: projector1* needs to know that "Water has not boiled" has the same meaning as $T(low)$, and this knowledge cannot be extracted only from sensor-data, so we need to give one by one when we implement this interaction system. For this problem, we considered the following methods: Output value of the temperature sensor is just shown. This methodology may be hard to understand at beginning, but it may be able to work if persons related to this information become be able to recognize that output value means water has not boiled through daily habitual behaviors or interaction between humans. So, it is necessary to design a framework that positively uses human perception abilities, which does not depend on the detailed information presented by the environment based on the affordance theory. And this strategy corresponds better to the framework of the resonance effect between humans and the environment.

5   Conclusion

In this paper, we proposed a new interaction framework between humans and the environment based on resonance. This framework uses the metaphor that different natural frequencies can be considered as different daily habitual behaviors of each person. As for controlling the movement of people in the situation like a station, conference and theme-park, where an unspecified number of people are gathering and moving, it may be good to regard the habitual group behavior of a certain large number of people as one natural frequency.

References

1. Anind K. D, Albrecht Schmidt, and Joseph F. M (Eds.), *Proceedings of 5th International Conference of Ubiquitous Computing (UbiComp2003)*, LNCS 2864, 2003.
2. Krumm. J, Cermark, G, and Horvitz. E: RightSPOT: A Novel Sense of Location for a Smart Personal Object, *5th International Conference of Ubiquitous Computing (UbiComp2003)*, pp. 90 – 106, 2003.
3. Koile. K, Tollmar. M, Demirdjian. D, Shrobe. H, and Darrell. T: Activity Zones for Context-Aware Computing, *5th International Conference of Ubiquitous Computing (UbiComp2003)*, pp. 36 – 43, 2003.

Agent Server for a Location-Aware Personalized Notification Service

Teruo Koyanagi[1], Yoshiaki Kobayashi[2], Sachiko Miyagi[3], and Gaku Yamamoto[1]

[1] IBM Research, Tokyo Research Laboratory,
1623-14 Shimotsuruma, Yamato-shi, Kanagawa-ken, Japan
{teruok, yamamoto}@jp.ibm.com
[2] IBM Software Group, Yamato Software Laboratory,
1623-14 Shimotsuruma, Yamato-shi, Kanagawa-ken, Japan
ykobayas@jp.ibm.com
[3] Omron Software Co., Ltd., 4th Software Engineering Group,
8 Higashida-chou, Kawasaki-ku, Kawasaki-shi, Kanagawa-ken, Japan
s-miyagi@mx.omronsoft.co.jp

Abstract. Goopas is a location-aware personalized information notification service coupled with automated ticket gates in railway stations. The service was provided to 40,000 users by an earlier system implemented on J2EE, but had performance problems, because location-aware systems must finish user tasks before the users move, and such personalized systems require handling a large number of users. Agent Server was used for Goopas to replace the original system. This paper describes how Agent Server was used for a real service that provides high performance and strong capabilities to 100,000 users.

1 Introduction

Agent Server [5] is middleware that serves large numbers of agents in a server based on the Agent Programming Model [1], which provides a model for program-owner-associated, asynchronous, reactive systems. In the model, agents are represented as independent reactive objects. Each has its own persistent states, and processes tasks asynchronously by reacting to messages from the owner or other agents. By employing the properties of this model, Agent Server enhances concurrency, controllability, cache scalability, and load balancing to provide the capabilities to manage millions of agents.

Our research issues on Agent Server technology are followings: (1) to confirm effectiveness of the technology by applying it to a personalized application which has functionality enough for practical use, (2) and to show software designs and patterns how to apply the technology effectively into the application.

Goopas is a location-aware personalized information notification service. It is linked to the automated ticket gates in railway stations, and when a user of the service passes through the gate, it can send an e-mail message to the user's mobile phone. The user's personal attributes (including such things as age, job, gender, and preferences) are registered to correspond with his or her e-mail address and pass ID.

T. Ishida, L. Gasser, and H. Nakashima (Eds.): MMAS 2004, LNAI 3446, pp. 224–238, 2005.

The resulting e-mail includes information about the neighborhood of that station personalized for the user.

One of the difficulties of location-aware services is a requirement for low latency, because the location-aware systems must complete processing while the user is still at the location. For the Goopas services, the e-mail must be posted to the mail server in 10 seconds. This personalized system requires handling throughput to serve 100,000 users, while still keeping the latency short. To meet these requirements, the delivered information and advertisement content included in the e-mail are prepared for each user using batch processing. However the original system implemented purely with J2EE faced performance limitations blocking expansion of the service area. The preparations for 40,000 users took over 160 minutes for the information content, and another 80 minutes for the advertising. Processing of each gate transit took about 9 seconds when there were 20 gate transit events per second. The refined requirements called for keeping latency within 10 seconds, even if there are 60 events every second, while handling throughput for 100,000 users.

Agent Server was used to implement the improved Goopas system in order to meet these new performance requirements, confirming the effectiveness of Agent Server's approach. As a result, we achieved over 20 times faster performance than in the earlier system (without hardware improvements). Because of the properties of the Agent Programming Model, Agent Server incorporates performance-improving mechanisms into the new Goopas system. In this paper, we describe the new Agent Server-based implementation of the Goopas system, and discuss why Agent Server is so effective for personalized systems such as Goopas.

2 Related Work

There are many different discussions about what is an agent [1]. In this paper, the Agent Programming Model is a model to program owner-representing, asynchronous, reactive systems. In this model each agent has its own persistent states, and each agent processes tasks asynchronously by reacting to messages from the owner or other agents.

Agent Platform [2] is one of the platforms based on the Agent Programming Model. It provides asynchronous, subscription-based messaging using Message-Oriented Middleware. Mobile agent systems such as Telescript [3] and Aglets [4] are also based on the Agent Programming Model. Compared with these platforms, Agent Server provides a capability to manage millions of agents in a server process, and it focuses on a high performance architecture to process the agents.

The architecture of Agent Server does not depends on any lower layer tools except for Java, as was discussed in [5], and Agent Server based on the Java 2 Enterprise Edition (J2EE) [6], which is subject of this paper, was introduced in [7]. It employs the Java Messaging Service (JMS) [8] and Enterprise Java Beans (EJB) [9].

Some experimental platforms for location-aware applications exist. ROVER [10] is a platform for location-aware applications. It provides an action management mechanism. A ROVER controller has a scheduler to execute actions asynchronously according to a specified scheduling policy, but it does not provide any data locality model for processing actions. In the Agent Programming Model, the relationships of a data entity to its actions are important properties of each agent. The properties provide control for concurrency and a clustering mechanism for Agent Server. In this paper, we describe how the Agent Programming Model is effective to process the tasks of the location-aware personalized services.

3 Agent Server

An agent is an entity that reacts to events in the system on behalf of an "owner". An owner usually represents an actual person or an object in the physical world. In order to implement agents using the system, the Agent Programming Model provides a model to program an owner-associated, asynchronous, reactive system. In the Agent Programming Model, agents are represented as independent reactive objects. They have their own persistent states and process tasks asynchronously by reacting to messages from the owner or other agents.

Agent Server is middleware providing the Agent Programming Model. It manages millions of agents in a server process. In the server, agents are represented as persistent objects which have data associated with their respective owners. The messages are delivered to agents, and agents react to them asynchronously. Agent Server provides a function to distribute a message to selected agents.

In this section, Agent Server based on J2EE and database management system is described. In the server, agents are represented as entity beans, and the beans implement a message listener interface to receive JMS messages. The entity beans are stored in the database. JMS messages are delivered to agents by a message distribution mechanism called message resolver, which is provided by Agent Server.

3.1 Architectural Overview

As shown in Fig. 1, a JMS message that comes from a JMS queue is processed by a message resolver of the respective instantiation of Agent Server. A message resolver selects target agents for the message, and fans the message out to them.

Agent Server has in-memory queues associated with respective agents. A scheduler in Agent Server allocates threads to process the messages concurrently. Therefore, even if a message is fanned out to a large number of agents, Agent Server can control the concurrency to utilize the CPU effectively by configuring the number of threads. From the viewpoint of an agent, the messages are processed sequentially.

Agents are selected by matching the properties of the message with attributes of the agents. In a typical application, the agents are stored in a database as entity beans, and the matching logic is written in a query language. Note that for point-to-point, the primary key of the agent is included in the message, and the message resolver selects an agent.

Hash partitioning is used to balance the load of each Agent Server in the cluster. The partitioning method is coupled with a data-dependent request routing that distributes requests to servers based on the allocation of data included in the request.

Each agent is allocated to a server based on the hash value of its primary key. Because the hash values are distributed over the value space of integer, the partition range is decided by dividing the integer space by the number of servers. Each message resolver of a server selects agents within the partition allocated to the server.

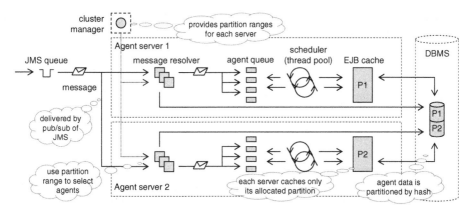

Fig. 1. The architecture of Agent Server

Because of the programming model based on agents, the hash partitioning method can be applied easily. The data and tasks of the agents are independent and well isolated from each other.

Partition ranges are managed by the duplex cluster manager processes. The cluster manager checks the servers in the cluster by using heartbeat queries, and if one of them does not respond, it recalculates the partition ranges for all of the agents to continue working on the live servers.

A well-known hash algorithm provides enough variance and good enough performance to be used for this purpose. According to RFC 1810 [11], MD5 implemented on a Pentium 90 MHz performs at 44 Mbps. Newer chips, such as a 2 GHz system can be considered as performing 20 times faster than this, so we can estimate that a 100-byte primary key is hashed within 1 millisecond.

3.2 High Performance Mechanisms

Agent Server provides mechanisms to provide concurrency control, cache scalability, and properly load-balanced clustering.

Controlling concurrency is needed to deliver high performance when massive number of events are processed, because the CPU utilization ratio depends on the waiting times occurring when any device accesses main memory. By processing tasks concurrently, tasks can be processed during the waiting times of other tasks. Agent Server enhances concurrency by introducing an asynchronous processing model.

A cache mechanism is efficient for processing persistent objects, because the cache reduces database accesses. Agent Server uses entity beans to store the agent's data, and the EJB cache of entity beans is transparent from the viewpoint of the programming model of Agent Server. The details of the effectiveness of the cache and the multi-threaded processing of Agent Server are described in [7].

Hash partitioning is used as the clustering method to achieve load balancing and cache scalability. The partitioning method is coupled with data-dependent request routing which distributes requests to servers based on allocation of the data included in the request. For design simplicity, it is better to use a round-robin request routing, if only the processing power has to scale. However, in using round-robin request routing, both a distributed lock mechanism and a replication mechanism are needed to maintain cache consistency among the servers. In this case, because the cached entities are duplicated, it does not scale even if the number of servers is increased. To serve a large number of agents, Agent Server needs to use a scalable clustering method for cache size. This partitioning method is effective for scaling cache size, because no cache duplication is occurring in the cluster.

4 Goopas

Goopas is an information delivery service coupled with automated ticket gates. As shown in Fig. 2, a user of the Goopas service, such as John, has a pass to go through the ticket gates of train stations, and he has registered an ID number of his pass, the e-mail address of his mobile phone, and some of his personal attributes such as age, gender, and interests. When he goes through a ticket gate with the pass, an e-mail message containing content matching his attributes is delivered to his mobile phone. Not only that, but the delivered content can also include information for the area around that destination station, because the Goopas system is aware of the location of the user (since it knows which ticket gate he passed through).

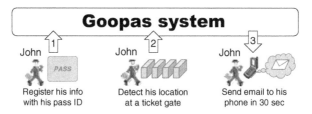

Fig. 2. The service provided by Goopas

4.1 System Overview

An overview of the Goopas system is shown in Fig 3. When a Goopas commuter pass is registered by an automated ticket gate, a passage event is generated and sent to a front end processing (FEP) server. The passage event includes data such as the pass ID, the station, and the passage date and time. The list of the users of Goopas service is registered in the FEP server, so the non-users' passage events can be filtered out, and just the users' events are queued into an MQ server.

The matching application server browses the queue of the MQ server, and processes each queued passage event to match the contents with the attributes of that user. It also sends e-mail to the address of the user's mobile phone if there is matching content. Usually, the e-mail delivered from the Goopas system includes a URL to for the internal site of the Goopas system to count the actual clickthroughs and to navigate to the Web site of the advertiser.

The ticket dispenser provides events for updating the expiration date of the pass. It is processed by the issuance management server in order to synchronize the pass ID information with the database.

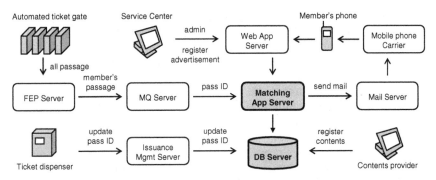

Fig. 3. System overview of Goopas

The most important function of the system is the matching function, because it characterizes how the service matches users with content. This function is provided by the matching application server, and this server is performance critical, because it must keep the latency short to provide location-awareness.

The Agent Server technology is applied to the matching application server that provides the core of the Goopas service. We considered the following when designing it: (1) data and methods can be distributed into isolated objects (agents) which have independent tasks, (2) and they are numerous. The matching application server handles many individual objects that represent users of the Goopas service. In this case, these objects are processed independently. Currently, the number of users of the Goopas service is over 40,000, and it is expected to be over 100,000 users as the service area is expanded. Covering such a large number of users is one of the requirements of the matching application server.

4.2 Service Requirements

To realize a location-aware and personalized service such as Goopas, it is necessary to satisfy the performance requirements. Not only does it often serve a large number of users, but it must also respond quickly to the sensors used to detect the user's location, because the service depends on the user's location, which is a factor that is changing over time. For example, if the e-mail were delivered 10 minutes after a user has passed through a gate, the service is no longer location-aware, because the user has moved over such a long time. It is necessary for the Goopas service to be location-aware and respond within 30 seconds after a user has passed through a gate. That was decided based on the time until a user gets on a train after passing through a ticket gate.

The grace time to deliver the e-mail is divided into three parts by the system. The first 10 seconds is for the queuing from the FEP server to the MQ server. This includes receiving the event of a gate passage from the ticket gate. The next 10 seconds is for the matching application server. This includes browsing the queues, matching the content, creating the e-mail message, and sending it to the mail server. The remaining 10 seconds is the time from the mail server to the user's mobile phone. However this is just an expected value from measured response times, because the time depends on the mobile phone carrier.

The maximum system throughput is expected to be 60 transactions per second. This is estimated based on the following assumptions: There are 300 automated ticket gates that can each process 1 gate passage per second, and 20% of all of the traffic might be users of the Goopas service. This comes to an estimate of 60 events coming to the system in one second.

The functional requirements of the Goopas service are complicated. It was necessary to make the matching function highly customizable, because the matching function is the most important feature that characterizes the service, and it must incorporate the opinions of both the users and the sponsors of the advertisements. Numerous matching parameters are available for the matching application server, in order to be able to adjust the matching rules for the service requirements.

E-mail delivered after a gate passage can include two types of content. "Information content" is content provided by information production companies in a way similar to a sponsored TV program. "Advertisement content" is commercial content provided by sponsors. Both of them have to match the attributes of the user that receives them. In addition, the information should fit into the same genre. The matching function refers to 10 database tables with 54 matching parameters, and 6 of them involve variable length arrays.

4.3 Content Preparation

In this section, we describe the design requirements of the matching application that had to be met in order to satisfy the performance requirements of the service.

The hardware configuration is as follows: two machines which have two processors each are used for the matching application server, and two machines with two processors each are used for the database server. The matching application server uses the cluster configuration described in Section 3.2, so effectively there are four processing units working in parallel. However, one of the database servers is for backup, so there are only two active processing units for the database server.

In the hardware configuration, the processor time which each request can consume is estimated as follows:

According to requirements, 60 requests to the matching application server can arrive each second, and each transaction request must be completed within 10 seconds. Then the 4 processing units of the matching application server have to process 600 transactions in every 10 seconds. Now assuming that all of the processors are utilized 100%, the processor time for each request of the matching application server is 10 seconds / (600 transactions / 4 way) = 66 milliseconds. In the database server, 33 milliseconds can be used.

By prototyping, the processing time was originally estimated as 176 milliseconds for each transaction, so there was a high risk when processing the matching tasks dynamically. To solve this problem, the concept of content preparation was introduced in the design of the matching application server. It was inherited from the design of former system.

Two types of passes used at ticket gates are supported by the service. One is a commuter pass and the other is a kind of credit card. For Goopas, the significance of a commuter pass is the link it establishes between two specified stations. It is reasonable to expect pass users to make a daily round trip between the station near home and the station near the office.

Therefore, the system can anticipate those stations will also be visited tomorrow, and the information content can be prepared by nighttime batch processing. This has roughly four hours for completion, because it starts after the last train (1:00 a.m.), and needs to finish before the first train (5:00 a.m.). However the advertisement content is prepared completely online. Because it executed in the background of the processing of gate passages, it is necessary to prioritize gate passage events over content preparation.

Dynamic matching is still needed because the users with credit cards are not expected to have regular stations, and also because commuter pass users may sometimes use another station. However, the number of database accesses and the processing time can be reduced considerably at gate transit time by early matching of the content when possible.

5 Implementation

In this section, the actual implementation of the matching application server is described. The matching application server is a core performance-critical component of the Goopas system. It receives the messages of the passage events, and generates e-mail that includes the content matching the attributes and preferences of the user. It also prepares the e-mail content for the commuter pass users. In Fig. 4, an overview is shown.

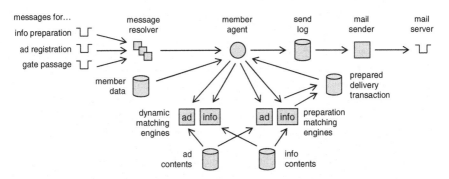

Fig. 4. Architectural overview of the matching application server

Each user agent is associated with a user of the Goopas service, and the agent processes the following tasks: (1) prepare advertisement content for the user when an advertisement is registered, (2) prepare information content for the user at night, (3) if content was not prepared, match both of content types when a user passes the gate, and (4) create the e-mail message to send to the user when the user passes the gate.

As described above, agents are represented as entity beans, and the beans implement the message listener interface to receive JMS messages. Each user agent holds the attributes of a user, and processes the tasks listed above when events are delivered as JMS messages. The advertisement content and the information content are represented as entity beans.

The information content prepared in advance is also part of the data held by the agents. In order to deliver this content, the agent will wait for the proper transit event for the corresponding user.

The matching engine components have the logic to match content attributes with user preferences stored in the agent. The details are described in the following sections.

5.1   Preparation of Advertising Content

The preparation of the advertising content is done during the daytime when the content is registered. An overview of the processing flow is shown in Fig. 5.

When the advertising content is registered with the system, a message that includes the attributes of the content is sent to the matching application server. These attributes are used to select users that have preferences matching the target of the advertisement.

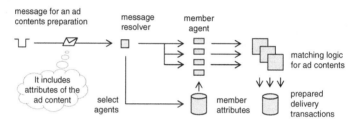

Fig. 5. Preparation of Advertising Content

The executed agents are filtered by the message resolver before the message is distributed. In the case of general publish-and-subscribe messages, subscribers actively register themselves in the messaging system. In contrast, in Agent Server the agents are selected by the message resolver based on their fields. The message resolver can select agents using the query functions of the database server.

Therefore, two steps are used to match the user attributes with contents attributes. First, the message resolver eliminates some of the matched the agents, and then agents that received the message check the remaining matching conditions.

This approach provides some advantages. First, the load of the matching can be distributed between the database server and the application server. Also, the tasks optimized with query functions are handled by the database server. In particular, it is most effective for tasks that can be processed by sorted indexes to be processed by the database server. The ad-hoc matching is best processed concurrently as agent tasks.

The threads for preparation of advertising content have lower priority than the threads for processing gate passages.

The attributes listed in Table 1 are used to select the users matching an ad. These attributes are compared from the left side columns against the two rightmost columns, and thus used to allocate advertising content to users. As described above, there are two kinds of parameters that are to be matched. If the "By query" column contains a

"O", then the matching is done by an EJB-QL query, but for "X" the matching is done in the logic of the agent.

Table 1. Matchable attributes of the advertising content and the users

Attributes of ad	Type, Variation	By query	Attributes of member	Type, Variation
supported carrier	3 booleans	O	used carrier	1~3
target gender	man/woman /any	O	gender	man/woman
target range of age	non-divided range in 0 ~999	O	age	0~999
target jobs	64 booleans	X	job	1~64
being married	yes/no/any	O	being married	yes/no
having children	yes/no/any	O	having children	yes/no
related station	array, 1~200	X	home station	1~200
		X	office station	1~200
related genres	array, 1~50	X	interested genres	array, 1~50

Attributes of ad	Type, Variation		Already allocated ad	Type, Variation
passage timing	1~4	X	passage timing	1~4
available period		X	allocated date	future date

Attributes of ad	Type, Variation		Already allocated info	Type, Variation
passage timing	1~4	X	passage timing	1~4
available period	non-divided range	X	allocated date	future date
related genres	array, 1~50	X	genre	1~50

5.2 Preparation of Information Content

Preparation of the information content for the next day is started after the last train stops. As shown in Fig. 6, when the preparation job starts, the message resolver fans the new content out to all of the agents, and they find matching content and attach it to the table of the prepared delivery transactions. Each delivery transaction is associated with a day and the passage timing of some user, and this represents the delivery of an e-mail message including the selected content.

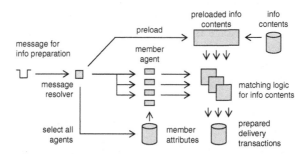

Fig. 6. Preparation of information content

As shown in Fig. 7, the content information has a three-dimensional structure with axes for user types, passage timings, and genres. Users are categorized into several segments based on their attributes such as gender, age, and work. Passage timings are detected as four recorded times for trip events (entering or exiting a gate and going away from or towards their homes) based on the registered home and workplace stations. Each content item is also associated with a genre such as baseball news, movie information, shopping guidance. Different genres are allocated to different slots in the array for each segment and for the timing of the trip. All of the slots are covered by this method, and at least one genre of the content item is selected, as long as a user subscribes to any genre.

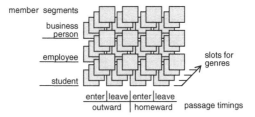

Fig. 7. Structure of information content

This structure is not only used to ensure contents distribution, but is also useful to simplify the matching logic when selecting content. An agent just picks up an array of information content and finds any subscribed genre from the array. However this means that the number of simultaneous database accesses is the same as the number of agents. This is an unrealistic approach, because the number of agents can go up to 100,000. In our implementation, all of the information content for the target day is loaded into an indexed collection with this structure as soon as the message resolver receives a message. This approach is much better, because the number of database accesses is reduced into just one at a time.

5.3 Processing of Gate Passage

The processing flow for a gate passage event is shown in Fig. 8. When the user passes through a gate, the event is sent to the matching application server by a JMS point-to-point message. The message resolver takes a message from the JMS queue, and the pass ID included in the message is used to select the agent for the user who passed through the gate. Then the message is posted to that agent's queue.

When the agent receives the message, it collects the information to create an e-mail message from the prepared content that was stored in the prepared delivery

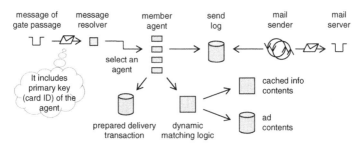

Fig. 8. Processing of gate passage

transaction. If the content has not been prepared, it matches content with the user dynamically. Then the information is stored into a table called a send-log. The mail sender component is given its own threads, and it creates and sends the e-mail by using the information stored in the send-log. The task of the gate passage includes access to the database server and mail server. Because they have different capacities, they should be processed asynchronously in order to tune them separately.

6 Performance Evaluations

As shown in Table 2, compared with the original system, the matching application server based on Agent Server is over 100 to 200 times faster for batch processing, and about 3 times faster for online processing.

Table 2. Performance comparison of the original system with the Agent-Server-based system

	Former system	Agent server system	Gaining ratio
Preparation of advertisement	8.03 trx/sec	934 trx/sec	116 times faster
Preparation of information	4.03 trx/sec	961 trx/sec	238 times faster
Processing of gate passages	20 req/sec, 9 sec/trx	65 req/sec, 6.9 sec/trx	3.25 times faster

In the following subsections, we attribute these performance gains to three layers: hardware enhancement (estimated 6 times better performance), Agent Server (7 times better), and application design (3 to 6 times better).

6.1 Hardware Enhancement

Because almost all of the data is in the cache of the application server, the database server does not cause any bottleneck for the application server. As shown in Table 3, the performance gain of the hardware upgrade is estimated at about 6 times faster than the earlier system, which comes from the gain of doubling the servers for the matching application server. The cluster of the matching application servers scales linear because of the hash partitioning. The utilization ratios of the processing units of the matching servers are nearly 100% in our performance test.

The performance gain of the processing for gate passages depends on the improvements of the database server, because each transaction requires accessing the database. Therefore, the observed number in Table 2 is considered to be the result of bringing out the hardware performance.

Table 3. Hardware comparison of former system and new system

Former system	Agent server system	Enhanced ratio
Matching application server P3 1GHz 2CPU	**Matching application server** IBM x335 P3 Xeon 3.06GHz 2CPUx2	6 times faster
Database server P3 Xeon 700MHz 2CPU	**Database server** IBM p630 Power4 1.2GHz 2CPU	2 times faster

6.2 Agent Server

Table 4 shows the results of an experiment to evaluate the performance improvement of the multi-threading and the database cache of the matching application server. Comparing cached multi-threaded processing with non-cached single-threaded processing, the multi-treaded version is over 7 times faster than the single-threaded approach. Because the original system of the Goopas service accesses the database server directly as a single thread, this suggests that the resulting performance contribution for Agent Server is 7 times the original system.

In our earlier experiment to evaluate the system using an artificial sample [6], the cached multi-threaded processing was found to be 10 times faster than non-cached single-thread processing. This confirms that the estimate is reasonable, because almost the same result was measured in the actual complex application. This also shows that the Goopas service is very suited for Agent Server technology.

Table 4. Performance comparison of the preparation processing of information content

Single thread, no cache	101trx/sec
Multi-threaded, no cache	208trx/sec (2 times faster)
Multi-threaded, cached	714trx/sec (7 times faster)

6.3 Application Design

Many design factors of the application enhance the performance of the new system. By employing messaging, the matching attributes of an advertisement are propagated to the agents without copies. This reduces the database access to 1/100,000 of copying. According to the above attributions, the design for the preparation of advertising content is estimated to contribute the rest of the three-fold performance gain. In the matching task for the information content, the preloading mechanism contributes to reduce the database accesses to 1/5,000. The design for the preparation of the information content is actually estimated it enhance it for a 6-fold gain, in the same manner.

7 Discussion

The reason why Agent Server is effective for the matching application server is that the data handled by the matching application server can be divided into large entities that correspond with their processing tasks. The matching task, the most important function of the matching application server, is executed by using attributes of each user, and the result is written in each record of the user, so the task can be divided for each user.

The matching tasks of the agents need to share the advertising content. Also, the information content is shared by them. Usually this avoids isolated tasks. However this data can be copied and cached because we can assume that it is static during the preparation process. Therefore the preparation tasks for respective users are isolated, even if the tasks are sharing the same content.

It is clear that Agent Server provides more performance for batch processing rather than for request-response according to the experience of this implementation. The request-response processing for gate passages is improved depending on the performance gain of the hardware. On the other hand, the batch processing of the preparations are improved beyond the hardware gain. General server components like EJB container are designed to enhance concurrency against requests, so the former system can exploit the performance of the hardware by employing EJB functionalities. On the other hand, in the case of batch processing, a mechanism to control concurrency in the application layer is needed. We confirmed that Agent Server complements it.

The message resolver provides a good framework for the matching function for the matching application server. In the preparation of advertisement contents, the message resolver narrows down the agents to the set of the potentially matching ones. In this manner, the processing complexity is divided into two parts: database preference tasks and procedural tasks. The tasks to narrow down the number of agents are calculated effectively by using sorted indexes in the database server. Therefore, in the matching task, conditions representing a simple value that can be sorted should be processed by queries of the database server. Other complex conditions or dynamic conditions are processed procedurally in the actions of agents.

8 Conclusion

We confirmed that the personalized location-aware service, Goopas, is effectively implemented by Agent Server. The Agent Programming Model provided by Agent Server introduces a design approach to divide tasks into a large number of isolated actions associated with the users of the service. Associated with the users, the data of the Goopas service can be divided into hundreds of thousands of agents and its tasks can be isolated with respective agents. In Agent Server, data locality and task isolation are the keys to enhance throughput, because they provide capabilities to control concurrency effectively, to balance the server load evenly, and to scale the cache size linearly. In addition, it was also confirmed that Agent Server provides an effective framework to execute batch processes such as the matching tasks of the Goopas case. Agent Server complements the extra functionality of batch processing into the J2EE.

In this paper, our contributions are (1) confirming that Agent Server is effective even in an actual application, (2) and showing a practical design to apply the technology effectively into the application.

References

1. Bradshaw, J.M.: *Software Agents*. The MIT Press (1997)
2. Bellissard, L., De Palma, N., Freyssinet, A., Herrmann, M., Lacourte, S.: An Agent Platform for Reliable Asynchronous Distributed Programming. *Symposium on Reliable Distributed Systems* (SRDS'99), Lausanne, Suisse (1999), p.294-295
3. White, J.E.: *Telescript Technology: An Introduction to the Language*. General Magic, Incorporated, Sunnyvale, CA. (1995)

4. Aridor, Y., Oshima, M.: Infrastructure for Mobile Agents: Requirements and Design. *Proceedings of the Second International Workshop on Mobile Agents* (MA '98), Springer-Verlag (1998), p.38-49
5. Yamamoto, G., Tai, H.: Performance Evaluation of an Agent Server Capable of Hosting Large Numbers of Agents. *AGENTS'01*, Montreal, Quebec, Canada (2001), p.363-369
6. Sun Microsystems: Java™ 2 Platform Enterprise Edition (J2EE) Specification. Version 1.4, Final Release (2003)
7. Yamamoto, G., Neyama, R., Koyanagi, T.: How to Process Many Transactions in Individualized Notification Services based on EJB. IBM Research Report RT0524 (2003)
8. Sun Microsystems: Java Messaging Service Specification. Version 1.1 (2002)
9. Sun Microsystems: Enterprise JavaBeans™ Specification. Version 2.1 (2003)
10. S. Banerjee et al.: Rover: Scalable Location-Aware Computing. *IEEE Computer*, Vol. 35, No. 10 (2002), p.56-63
11. Network Working Group: Report on MD5 Performance. *RFC 1810* (1995)

Needs and Benefits of Massively Multi Book Agent Systems for u-Libraries

Toshiro Minami

Kyushu Institute of Information Sciences, Faculty of Management and
Information Sciences, 6-3-1 Saifu, Dazaifu, Fukuoka 818-0117, Japan
minami@kiis.ac.jp
http://www.kiis.ac.jp/~minami/

Abstract. Libraries are changing. The next stage library is supposed to be
u-library (ubiquitous library) where each material is equipped with an RFID tag
and an agent runs on it. Agents also run on counters, shelves, and other library
equipments. They communicate each other and with book agents. The library
agent systems are unique in the sense: (1) The number is large; thousands in
very small libraries and millions in larger libraries. The total number will rise
up to billion by considering the inter-library loaning system. (2) The supposed
life span is very long, at least twenty years and hopefully more than one hundred years. Due to the rapid progress of information technology agents in a
wide spectrum capability and functionalities form a massively multi-agent system even in one library. In this paper we propose a concept of delegate agent
system in order to uniformly deal with such massively multi-agent systems.

1 Introduction

Libraries are changing. The materials they are dealing with these days are not only
books, magazines and other materials that are printed on paper, but also electronic
and/or digital materials like CD-ROMs, DVDs, e-journals, e-books, etc.. Furthermore,
along with the rapid advancement of information technology, a lot of digital library
projects [5, 11] have been launched and more and more library services are provided
on the Internet. Now the libraries are changing from the traditional "tosho-kan
(book/liber-house)" to "information-kan."

Even though more and more patron services are required and libraries are hoping to
do that, given resources of libraries such as the number of staff, budgets for purchasing materials and constructing digital libraries are generally very limited these days.
In order to put more services into action, libraries are eager to introduce new IT technologies and to reduce the cost and to make the libraries be more informatized.

By attaching RFID (Radio Frequency Identification) tags to materials, libraries and
librarians get great benefits such as reduction of staff's time for inventory and check-
in/check-out of books [4, 6]. Comparing the inventory time of books with RFID tags
and that of with barcode, the former is estimated some twenty to thirty times faster
than the latter. By installing the self check-out machines, the number of staffs at the
circulation counter may reduce to half (e.g. Homer Babbidge Library, University of
Connecticut [10]).

T. Ishida, L. Gasser, and H. Nakashima (Eds.): MMAS 2004, LNAI 3446, pp. 239–253, 2005.
© Springer-Verlag Berlin Heidelberg 2005

More importantly, introducing new technologies will give the libraries new types of data and information that will be useful for improving and extending library services. For example, RFID tags contain IC chips and have memory, from tens of bytes to some kilo bytes in them. Therefore the memory capacity is much more than the size of the barcode, which has the capacity needed for storing the book ID.

So the books can contain other data like, ISBN (International Standard Book Number), the number of times the book is borrowed, the latest dates of borrowing and returning, classification codes, comments and evaluation data of the book, and many others. By these data we are able to know how popular the book is, and it might give patrons some useful tips when they decide whether to borrow the book or not.

The aims of this paper are:

1. to propose an agent model of coming u-libraries, where RFID tags and their agents are put on materials and reader/writers (or R/Ws) with agents are planted on many library equipments, and patrons ID cards are also RFID tags with agents so that the data concerning how the materials are used inside of the library are automatically collected and accumulated by agents, and analyzed for better patron services,
2. to give a preliminary investigation on massively multi-agent systems (MMAS) for u-library where number of book agents may reach as many as several millions and how useful the MMAS is in such environment, and
3. to illustrate the specific features of MMAS for book agents and to inspire that such systems are also important in other application fields.

The rest of this paper is organized as follows. In Section 2, we will take up some component technologies such as RFID and explain what they are like and how they are supposed to be used in library applications.

In Section 3, we will propose a model or an image of u-libraries. In u-library environment, RFID tags, sensors, R/Ws are attached to virtually all objects like book shelves, tables, gates, as well as library materials like books and magazines. They will communicate each other and automatically collect data. These data are supposed to be integrated into information which is useful for librarians to provide better services to their patrons.

In Section 4, we will investigate the multi-agent system where agents run on every book tags, sensors, R/Ws and others. One of the specific features in such an environment is that some agents, e.g. book agents, are "passive" ones. A passive agent is an agent that only runs when available; or when running energy is given. We will consider in what way they can communicate and gain sufficient information. Such an environment inspires a new research topic in multi-agent systems.

In Section 5, we illustrate how RFID equipments and their functionality can be integrated in multi-agent framework. The key idea is to use the concept of delegate, or virtual, agent. A delegate agent is a representative agent running on a server that behaves on behalf of the corresponding RFID tag agent. By taking such model we can uniformly deal with the massively multi library agent system where a wide variety of agents in their capability, performance, accessibility coexist and collaborate.

And finally in Section 6, we will summarize our discussions in the preceding sections and give some further research topics.

2 Components of u-Libraries

RFID technology is considered to be the key technology for ubiquitous computing. One type of its components, called tags, can communicate with another type equipments called reader/writers (R/Ws) which are located in near distance of the tags. In this section we learn what RFID system is all about and we put special focus on how it is currently used in library applications.

Figure 1 shows how (passive) RFID system [3, 9] works. A tag at the right-hand side consists of IC chip and antenna. It has no batteries and thus cannot run standalone. At the left-hand side is a R/W, which gives energy and clock signal for synchronizing the data transmission. A tag gets energy provided from the R/W near it in electro-magnetic induction via the antenna. It waits until sufficient energy is charged. When it is ready, it communicates with R/W and exchange data by making use of the same antenna. At the backend of the R/W are applications such as databases.

The frequencies used in RFID systems range from about 100kHz upto GHz bands, which is in the ISM (Industrial, Scientific and Medical) bands [3]. The most popularly used frequency among them is 13.56MHz. It is mostly appropriate for applications with medium read distance, i.e. from about 1cm to 1m. Currently this frequency is most popularly used also in library applications for book tags and patron cards.

The typical 13.56MHz tag is shown in Figure 2. The black square object in the top-left corner is the IC chip and the coil surrounding it is the antenna of the tag. Such tags in label form are attached to books and similar ones in card form, i.e. in plastic covering, are used for patrons' ID cards. Currently most libraries use the barcode for identifying their patrons. In the future these cards will be replaced with RFID cards with the specification common to book tags.

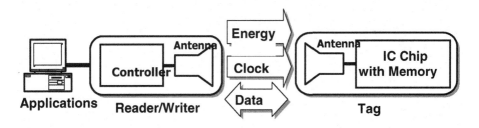

Fig. 1. RFID System

The tags described so far are called "passive" because they have no batteries and need external energy as is shown in Figure 1. There are other types of tags which are called "active" because they are equipped with batteries and thus they can work without external energy supply. The most important advantage of active tags is that the data transmission distance is longer then passive tags and thus the security gate becomes more reliable. On the other hand, active tags have disadvantages such as they are thicker, heavier, much more expensive and shorter lifespan than passive ones. However these problems might be overcome in the future and such tags may be widely used together with passive ones in libraries.

Fig. 2. RFID Tag for Books

As is shown in Figure 3, R/Ws in libraries are typically used in three ways: (a) security gate, (b) circulation processing at the counter, and (c) bookshelf inventory.

A security gate detects materials that are un-processed for check-out when they go through it. If the tags are of RO (Read Only) or WORM (Write Once, Read Many) type, the security gate reads the IDs of the tags that are attached on books, then it enquires to the library server if all the IDs have been properly processed for borrowing. If at least one of the IDs is found not to be properly processed, it will turn on the alarm lamp and make sound so that the librarians can recognize and check which book is/are the non-processed one/ones.

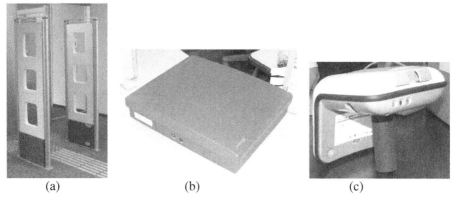

(a)   (b)   (c)

Fig. 3. Reader/Writers for Libraries: (a) Security Gate, (b) Desktop Type for Circulation Counter, and (c) Handy Type for Book Inventory

If the tags are of RW (Read-Write) type, the security gate reads the status data of the tags and determine if all the status are set to be borrowed. This detection is done locally so that it is very fast comparing to the former case. The disadvantage of the RW tags is that they are generally more expensive than RO tags.

The desktop type of R/W is used for processing check-out and returning of books. When a book is borrowed, the librarian scans it over the R/W and the system reads its ID and sends it to the database server of the library so that the book having the corresponding ID is recorded to be borrowed. If the tag is of RW type, the same status data is written on the tag by the R/W at the same time.

The handy type R/W is supposed to be used for inventory. The librarians hold it and scan the data from a bookshelf to another bookshelf. Comparing the speed of inventory with the barcode system and with the RFID system the latter is estimated roughly some twenty to thirty times faster.

3   Services in u-Libraries

In the previous subsection, we have seen how RFID system is typically applied in libraries. By planting R/Ws to other objects, new types of applications can be developed and the libraries can get new types of data that relate to how books and other library materials are used and how patrons move and use equipments inside of the libraries. Most libraries have no such data so far.

Fig. 4. Intelligent Shelf

3.1   Intelligent Shelf

An intelligent shelf is a bookshelf having R/Ws in it so that it can read which books are put in which shelf. It is also called a smart shelf [6]. Figure 4 is an intelligent shelf experimentally developed by a company in collaboration with the author. An antenna can be placed in the backend of each shelf of an ordinary bookshelf so that it is able to recognize in which shelf such and such books locate. A box at the top of the bookshelf is the controller of the antennae. It scans the whole bookshelf by activating the antennae one after another. These two components form a bookshelf type R/W.

Currently the R/W cannot detect in which part the book is located on a shelf. However if we put several antennae for one shelf, we will be able to locate more accurately and eventually to locate exactly where and in what order the books are arranged on a shelf.

By using such bookshelves the library system can detect whenever a book is taken out of the shelf and whenever it is returned on a shelf. For example the library system can make a list of books that were returned on wrong shelves. By using this list librarians are able to relocate such books to their right positions.

Also such data can be used to rank the books according to the frequencies of taking out and returning, which indicate how popularly the books are used in the library. This will give a good tip to librarians when they evaluate their book collection policy.

Currently the intelligent shelf is very expensive though. One example price is one million yen for one bookshelf. It is far too expensive to replace all the bookshelves currently used in libraries. However it is worth considering if we first replace just one or a couple of bookshelves with intelligent shelves.

For such purpose one good candidate is the bookshelves for newly registered books. Such books attract patrons' interest and thus they will be used in high frequencies. By analyzing such data, librarians will be helped by the extracted information with choosing new books to be purchased.

Another candidate is, specifically in university libraries, for the books that are designated as subtexts by teachers. These books usually appear in the syllabuses. It is a great benefit for students to read such textbooks in the library.

If we use the intelligent shelves for such books, the library can collect the detailed data how these books are used; e.g. for each book when it was taken off the shelf and when it was returned, and maybe who did it.

By collecting and analyzing these data, the library might be able to decide how many volumes of a title to buy according to the data. If a book has little or no usage history, the library can let the teacher who recommended this book know this fact. Then he/she may encourage the students of the class so that they use this textbook more on the subject.

3.2 Intelligent Browsing Table

An intelligent browsing table is a table in a library browsing room with R/W(s). Figure 5 is an example browsing table experimented in AIREF Library in Fukuoka City, Japan [1]. On the table a patron is reading a book with some books around him (a) and two RFID readers (b) detect them and send the data to their server.

By analyzing the data from the intelligent browsing table(s), librarians are able to obtain information which books are read, how long, how often and others. Such information is useful for shelf arrangement and book collection. If the table readers can also collect patron IDs, they can get information who reads what books. By analyzing these data we can get which and which books are often read together by such and such patrons. This information is useful for book recommendation service to patrons by use of the collaborative filtering technology [6], which has been well-known in agent researcher's communities.

3.3 Intelligent Reference Desk

Referencing is a key function for libraries. Every library provides the reference service to patrons, and in many libraries have a special reference counters for this purpose. However, at least in Japan, only a limited number of patrons enquire to the reference librarians when they are in trouble searching for appropriate information sources or books.

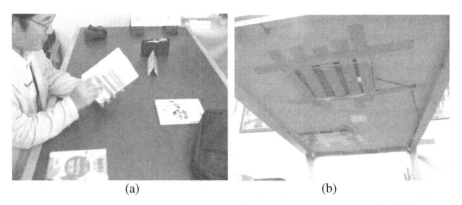

(a)   (b)

Fig. 5. Intelligent Browsing Table: (a) Top Side of the Table and (b) RFID Readers Attached Under the Table

In order to make the libraries more reliable and favorite place for patrons, we have to make more effort to let the patrons know that libraries provide the reference service. At the same time we have to give more helps to librarians for better referencing skills. Education is very important in order to keep their skills up to date. This importance was also indicated in the well-known "The Five laws of library science" by S. R. Ranganathan [7]:

(1) Books are for use,
(2) Every reader his book,
(3) Every book his reader,
(4) Save the time of the reader,
(5) The library is a growing organism.

In addition to these, we have to provide them with some advanced referencing tools. Among them is a reference case database. By fully using such databases it will become much easier for solving the enquiries that were done before.

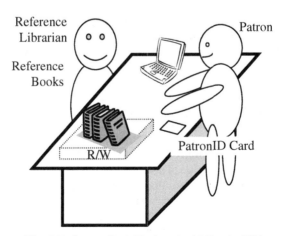

Fig. 6. Reference Desk Equipped with Reader/Writer

However one of the problems in constructing such database is lack of staff's time. If they have to spend too much time to input case records, they will not want to provide sufficient case data. In order to reduce their time for such inputting job, the system is expected to automatically collect as much data that might be useful for constructing the reference database.

Based on the similar idea to the browsing table, and put some R/Ws on a reference desk we can automatically collect data which reference tools are used during referencing. By asking to the enquirer to put her patron card on the desk, the system can automatically detect the patron ID and put it in the patron's name field of the case record.

4   Multi-agent System for u-Libraries

Current RFID tags that are supposed to be used in libraries are not intelligent enough. They have memory inside and they get and put data according to the request from the R/Ws. If we put more intelligent functions into it, the price will be too high for libraries so that most libraries will not be able to purchase them for their books.

However considering the rapid progress of information technology, the cost issue will be solved eventually, maybe in the near future. So now is the good time to start researching on library systems when all the book tags are intelligent enough and work as an agent and communicate with other tag agents and R/W agents.

The most important expected advantage of agentification is that the agents are proactively communicate each other and exchange their data and try to integrate them by themselves. For example a book agent has frequency data how often the book is used by what sort of people, what sort of books are used together with the book, and so on. The book agent can advise the patron agent with in what way it can be used with maximum benefits according to the data or information it has.

By accumulating such data or information owned by the agents, the library agent may know what kinds of books are used in what purpose. Such information is useful for choosing appropriate books for purchasing, determining the arrangement of book shelves, and so on. Current libraries have just a little such objective data that will help them how to decide when they need. So such system must be a great help for libraries. Therefore agentified u-library is a great revolution for libraries.

In this section we consider and investigate what the multi-agent system is like for u-libraries in more detail.

4.1   Agents in a Bookshelf

Now we suppose all the tags and R/Ws are intelligent agents. In a bookshelf each book and the bookshelf itself are agents. The agent systems for libraries are unique in the sense diversity of the capability and performance of the tags, therefore those of corresponding agents, is quite large. This diversity comes that the time span of library equipments are long, hopefully more than one hundred years, thus a wide variety of tags in different specification should exist at the same time and form a system.

Figure 7 is an illustration of book agent and shelf agent systems. At the left-hand side is the shelf agent and in the right-hand side are book agents. The upper book agents are passive and the lower book agents are active. A passive agent is the agent that corresponds to the passive tag and an active agent corresponds to active tag.

A passive agent is able to run only when it gets energy from the R/W agents including shelf agents nearby. The arrows in Figure 7 indicate that passive agents can communicate only with R/W agent. An active agent, on the other hand, can run at any time it needs to, because it has a battery. So an active agent can communicate not only with R/Ws but also with other active agents. It could be realized that even the passive agents can communicate with other agents, both passive and active, in the future.

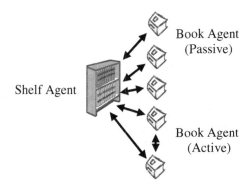

Fig. 7. Agents in a Bookshelf; Shelf Agent and Book Agents

4.2 Possible Exchanged Data Between Agents

First of all we consider what sort of data a book agent has to carry. Note that we choose the items so that they are applicable to both passive and active agents.

- Agent type
- Agent ID
- Meta (or catalog) data about the book. E.g. title, author, publisher, date of publication, classification, etc.
- Frequency data such as:
  - Frequencies to be borrowed according to the patron IDs
  - Frequencies to be used by the same patron according to the book IDs
- Log data such as:
  - Location IDs of shelves, browsing tables, reference desks, etc. with time stamps and patron IDs
  - Names together with time stamp data of other book agents that share the same location of tables and desks
- Home location; i.e. the location agent's ID where the book agent belongs
- Etc.

Suppose two book agents are taken out of shelves and put on a browsing table. Then the table agent will give energy to these agents and they start running. The process goes as follows:

1. First the book agents get the ID of the table agent and recognize where they are.
2. Then they send request to the table agent for asking who are in the neighbor.
3. The table agent will return with other book agent's IDs.
4. Then they recognize that the other one's existence. If the table agent also detects the patron agent, it will also tell the agents who are using them.
5. Then they recognize and record the situation. The communication will be stopped in any seconds so they have to record only those that they can so far have collected.

Their owned data may be sent to the library server when they are requested by a table agent or some other agents. These data are accumulated into such data like how often such and such books are used at the same time. This frequency data is used when the system recommends a book if a patron take one book and does not take the other book that are highly used together.

In another example, a bookshelf agent detects the book agent together with a patron agent. Then the bookshelf agent recognizes that the book is put on the shelf by the patron. If it is the different shelf agent from the home location agent's ID of the book agent, it can report to the librarians that the book is miss-shelved. It can even record who returned the book on a wrong shelf. Librarians may give warning to the patron to be more careful when he/she returns books to shelves.

4.3 Detection of Unprocessed Books at the Security Gate

One of the advantages of RFID tag system for libraries is that it can be used also for detecting the books that are not processed for borrowing when the patron goes through the security gate. Another advantage is not only detecting that the patron has at least one such books but also the system recognizes what the book is. Even though there are no ways to perfectly protect the books from theft, there are many effective ways in order to be closer to the perfect.

Typical security gate system is shown in Figure 8. There are two antennae and the patrons are supposed to go through between them with books. One possible way to have more secure gate system, the detection antennae work in accordance with the door or the bar at the gate so that patrons cannot run through the gate in order to avoid the books to be detected. In addition to it, it is desirable to recognize the patron agent together with the book agents he/she is carrying at the security gate. If the patron moves too fast at the security gate, the gate agent is unable to detect the patron agent and the gate bar will be locked. If the patron moves slowly enough the gate agent will detect both the patron and book agents. When the gate agent gets the book agents' IDs it will check if all the books are in the checked-out mode.

If a theft trial is detected the security gate will make alarm sound and lamp. It might be useful if this data is recorded by the patron agent and book agent. By accumulating these records we are able to have a list of books, hopefully also the types of books that have been stolen in high possibilities, that are frequently tried to be stolen and the list of patrons who might try to steal repeatedly.

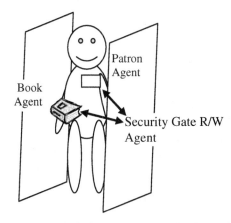

Fig. 8. A Patron with a Book is Going through a couple of Security Gates

5   Virtualized Multi-agent Model for Library Agents

As have been described in the previous subsections, library agents varies a lot in their running environments such as network connection, bandwidth, performance, duration of running time, and so on. The agents on R/Ws have great advantages in these aspects, while the agents on book tags have poorer running environment. On the other hand the book agents vary according to the time it was made.

The equipments used in libraries are supposed to be used for a long time; at least a couple of decades and hopefully more than one century. As the result a wide variety of book agents will run at the same time in library applications.

In order to deal with such a high diversity of agents in their capabilities and characters in a uniform way, we need an integrated and flexible model. In this section, we will first point out how RFID agent environments vary and then we illustrate how RFID equipments and their functionality with such a variety can be interpreted uniformly as agents, which we call delegate, or virtual, agents, and make some preliminary but essential discussions for developing an integrated view for the massively multi book agent systems for u-libraries.

5.1   Variety of Agents' Environment

Thanks to rapid progress of technology, limitations for these environments will be getting to be relieved as time passes. However, this causes another reason of varieties in agents' capabilities. The number of materials of a library is quite large; from tens of thousand to some millions. Thus, the number of tags, and therefore that of the agents on them, is also very large. Libraries can not replace all the tags with new ones even if they are much more advanced and have better performance and functions. What they can do at most is to attach the new tags on the newly purchased books and they may replace just a small percentage of tags already attached on the books. Therefore it is unavoidable that a variety of types of tags is used at the same time in the library.

In this subsection, we will take some aspects on agents and illustrate how much they may be different.

- **Network Environment:**
  Most R/Ws may have broadband connection to the network. Even the handy type R/Ws are able to have the wired or wireless high speed connection. Comparing to these, tags with 13.56MHz have slower communication speed. Future tags may have much faster connection.

- **Power Supply:**
  Basically, the R/Ws are connected to the power line. Exceptionally, the handy readers are equipped with batteries. They have sufficient energy. On the other hand book tags are passive and therefore they have no power in themselves. As the result the agents on R/Ws are able to run in a long time period, normally they can run without stopping. On the other hand the tag agents can run only when the tag is near a R/W and they have enough power supply.

- **Performance:**
  The performance of the agent varies in accordance with the power supplied to the equipment. Generally the tag agents run much slower than that of R/Ws.

- **Memory Size and Type:**
  Roughly the memory of the R/Ws is the same one as that of PCs. Comparing to the number of R/Ws the number of book tags are huge. The cost issue is more important for tags so that the memory size of the tags must be relatively small. Currently, it is about from some tens to mega bits. Three types of memory are used in tags; RO (Read Only), WORM (Write Once, Read Many), and RW (Read and Write). Former is cheaper than latter ones.

- **Sensors:**
  So far just a little number of tags have sensors in them. If a book tag has temperature and humidity sensors we can estimate the aging speed of the book from the data. Such tags equipped with sensors will become popular as the cost of a tag decreases and the application field widens in the future.

- **Frequency:**
  The frequencies that the tags can use are in the ISM (Industry, Scientific, Medicine) bands. Among them the most popularly used frequency is 13.56MHz for book tags. Evaluation of other frequency tags, e.g. some 900MHz or 2.45GHz tags, has just started and such tags may be used widely in the future.

5.2 RFID Equipments as Agents

In order to deal with a variety of equipments of R/Ws and a variety of tags in a uniform way, we will make a multi-agent model so that they share the same fundamental feature. In this model, we interpret both tags and R/Ws as agents and their differences are just the difference of features of basically the same agents.

Currently some libraries use RO or WORM tags, while some other libraries use RW tags. In order to have the integrated model for agent that covers both types, we assume that each tag and each R/W has its corresponding delegate agent. Despite the differences of the actual tags and R/Ws in terms of their properties, the delegate agent has sufficient memory, functionality with it. Connectivity and some other features of them may differ. We realize these delegate agents in the following way in the real system and interpret them as the corresponding delegate agent.

- **R/W Agent:**
  A software agent can run on a R/W. This actual agent has sufficient memory, network connectivity, etc., so we consider this actual agent itself as the delegate agent of the R/W. Some R/Ws in the handy/portable type may need concern similar to the tag agents because they may have intermittent connection to the network.

- **RO/WORM Tag Agent:**
  These two types of tags are almost equivalent so that they can only give their IDs to other agents in most of their operations. We suppose there is a delegate agent server in the network for dealing with this type of delegate agent. The representative agent is located in the server and it contains the related data in their memory that is supposed to be held in the delegate agent of the tag agent. When a R/W detects a RO/WORM tag, the ID of the tag is sent to the delegate agent server and the representative agent moves to the R/W and run on the R/W's running environment. The agent returns to the server when the tag goes away from the R/W.

- **RW Tag Agent:**
  A RW tag has its own memory. If it has sufficiently high performance so that a software agent can run on it, the agent itself is the delegate agent like as of R/W agent. If the tag has poor performance, the delegate agent is constructed in the similar way as of agent for RO tag. Difference lies that the corresponding agent must have some synchronizing process with the memory of the tag.

In the research field for smart objects, the RFID tags are called small SD (Smart Device) and those having more performance, like PDA, are called big SD. They classify the platforms for multi-agents on such SDs in three ways; portal, embedded, and surrogate [2, 8]. The agents discussed in this paper are very similar to their agents. An embedded platform corresponds to the case that real and delegate agents are same. We can realize the actual agent system in such a way so that an agent in the tag and an agent in the R/W work collaboratively and they behave like the delegate agent for the tag. This model corresponds to the surrogate platform. In this way, the portal platform corresponds to the agent for RO tags. The big difference is that they assume that SDs are basically used for interfacing with human users. The agents in this paper do not exist for interfacing but for collecting data and information so that they are accumulated and used for improving the library services for the patrons. Furthermore, we discriminate the delegate and actual agents.

6   Concluding Remarks

As Ranganathan had suggested in his five laws of library science [7], the most important issue for libraries is to do their best in giving (information) services to patrons so that they are considered to be reliable by their patrons. In order to achieve this goal, libraries have been changing. Reflecting the advance of Internet, most libraries provide various network-based services.

Attempts on digital library functions have been pursued from this point of view and much effort has been made not only constructing digital material databases but also useful tools for them [12] in order to adapt to the digital society. Considering that RFID (Radio Frequency Identification) technology is supposed to be the most important ubiquitous society, u-library facilities should be the next issue for libraries. This paper gives a preliminary consideration on this issue and tries to clarify what the u-library is like and what problems should be solved from the massively multi-agent system's point of view.

The key technology for u-library is obviously RFID; tags and their R/Ws. In this paper, we have emphasized that by attaching RFID tags to library materials such as books, magazines, CDs, DVDs, and so on, and put R/Ws (Reader/Writers) on bookshelves, desks, browsing tables, reference counter tables, and so on, we will have an infrastructure for multi-agent system environment. It is a massively multi-agent system in terms of the number of agents. The number of books in a library varies from thousands, in small libraries, to millions, in big libraries. For example, in Kyushu University alone, the number of books is over three million and four hundred thousand. Several hundred billions of books will exist totally in university libraries in Japan. Considering that libraries are virtually collaborating each other by ILL (Interlibrary loaning) system, the book agent system is truly a massively multi agent system in number.

Due to the cost issue is very important currently, most tags are memory-based. Many tags are developed as read-only or write-once-read-only tags. In the near future, tags will be equipped with information processing facilities so that they can make encrypted communication and are intelligent enough so that we can call them agents. Similarly, current book agents are passive for technological reasons including costs. However, by considering the functional advantage, active tags will be the major players as book agents in the future.

Because of the long life-time of library materials and the number of them is very big, it is inevitable that specifications of book tags vary a lot. Suppose technology changes in every ten years and new technology is applied to every new books. Then ten different kinds of agents co-exist one hundred years later. The library system should deal with such a variety of agents in their specifications such as performances and functionalities. Thus the library agent system is massively multi in this respect as well.

In order to deal with such massively multi agent system in such a high diverse environment, it is desirable to make a uniform framework for them. We have proposed the concept of delegate agent system for this requirement in Section 5.

The eventual goal of such systems is to develop a good protocol for accumulating such a small chunk of data into meaningful information so that it gives a good tip to librarians for better patron services. So far the data that can be used for such purpose for libraries are mainly from circulation database; i.e. who borrowed and returned which books and when. Some libraries do not have entrance and exit time data of patrons now.

In the future library, which we would like to make as an agentified u-library, the librarians will give advice to their patrons based on the information extracted by the book and other library agents from the data that are automatically collected and analyzed. It should be a great help for librarians for pursuing their job.

Acknowledgments

I greatly acknowledge my co-researchers Prof Takuya Kida of Hokkaido University, and Profs Kiyotaka Fujisaki and Daisuke Ikeda of Kyushu University for their discussions on digital libraries and RFID technologies. This research was partially supported by the Ministry of Education, Science, Sports and Culture, Grant-in-Aid for Scientific Research (B), 16300078, 2004.

References

1. AIREF Library: http://www.kenkou-fukuoka.or.jp/airef/tosyokan3.htm (in Japanese)
2. Carabelea, C., Boissier, O.: Multi-Agent Platforms on Smart Devices: Dream or Reality?, Proc. Smart Object Conference 2003 (2003)
3. Finkenzeller, K.: RFID Handbook (Second Edition). John Wiley & Sons (2003)
4. Lee, Eung-Bong: Digital Library & Ubiquitous Library. Science and Technology Information Management Association Academic Seminar (V) (2004) (in Korean)
5. Minami, Toshiro: Putting Old Data into New System: Web-based Catalog Card Image Searching. Proc. 2000 Kyoto International Conference on Digital Libraries (ICDL2000) (2000) 296-303
6. Minami, Toshiro: An Approach towards Library Automation with IC-Tags. Bulletin of Kyushu Institute of Information Sciences, Vol.5 No.1 (2003) (in Japanese)
7. Ranganathan, S.R.: The Five Laws of Library Science, Bombay Asia Publishing House (1963)
8. Ramparany, F., Boissier, O.: Smart Devices Embedding Multi-Agent Technologies for a Pro-active World, Proc. Uniquitous Computing Workshop (2002)
9. Resnick, P. and Varian, H. R. (Guest Eds.): Recommender Systems. Communications of ACM, Vol. 40 No. 3 (1997) 56-89
10. University of Connecticut Libraries: http://spirit.lib.uconn.edu/
11. Weis, S.A., Sarma, S.E., Rivest, R.L., Engels, D.W.: Security and Privacy Aspects of Low-Cost Radio Frequency Identification Systems. Proc. First International Conference on Security in Pervasive Computing. Lecture Notes in Computer Science, Vol. 2802. Springer-Verlag (2003) 201-212
12. Witten, I.H.: Digital libraries and society: New perspectives on information dissemination. http://www.cs.waikato.ac.nz/~ihw/DLs.and.society.pdf

Social Network and Spatial Semantics
for Real-World Information Service

Yutaka Matsuo

National Institute of Advanced Industrial Science and Technology (AIST),
Aomi 2-41-6, Tokyo 135-0064, Japan
y.matsuo@aist.go.jp
http://www.carc.aist.go.jp/

Abstract. Several attempts have been made to utilize a large scale multi-agent system for real-world information services in mobile/ubiquitous/pervasive computing environments. In our world, social knowledge, such as human relations and spatial semantics, plays an important role in communication and behavior. Such social knowledge should be incorporated into multi-agent systems to increase the effectiveness of real-world information services. This paper describes an approach for acquisition and utilization of social relationships among people. A web-mining approach is used to obtain a social network, especially that of researchers. We also address semantics of place.

1   Introduction

Recently, various kinds of information support systems are developed in the context of mobile/ubiquitous/pervasive computing. For example, information support at offices and homes [7], tour navigation and shopping navigation [2, 21], and conference support [22] are some major applications. Usually, many sensors are set in an environment and users have information terminals. If thousands or millions of sensors and users are involved in the systems, a large scale multi-agent system is a natural situation [5]. Multi-agent architectures for ubiquitous computing environment play an essential role in that situation [10, 13].

In a ubiquitous information environment, it is important to acquire and utilize lifeworld semantics around us. Development of sensor technology allows us to observe users' behaviors in more detail. Thereby, myriad behavioral data become available. Nevertheless, our world is filled with a variety of semantics: We naturally understand the semantics of place (e.g., we do not speak loudly in a library). We behave consciously according to social relations with others (e.g., we are careful of what we say depending on the listener and their relation to us and others.) In order to make real-world information services more effective, such social knowledge should be incorporated with multi-agent systems.

This paper mainly addresses two issues that are related to the semantics noted previously. First, we focus on social relationships among people. There is a growing interest in obtaining and utilizing social relations online. For example, social networking sites

T. Ishida, L. Gasser, and H. Nakashima (Eds.): MMAS 2004, LNAI 3446, pp. 254–268, 2005.
© Springer-Verlag Berlin Heidelberg 2005

(SNS) such as Friendster[1] and Orkut[2] have grown rapidly: over 200 SNSs exist now. SNS is an online application by which a user can register personal information including personal friends and acquaintances; the systems promote information exchange such as sending messages and reading Weblogs. In the context of the Semantic Web, social networks are used to realize a web of trust that enables estimation of information credibility and trustworthiness [3]. It is also applicable to calculate reputation in multi-agent systems [19] Our approach is to mine a social network from the Web, especially one comprising researchers. We also show a social network constructed from sensory information.

The second half of this paper describes semantics of place for advanced location services. A place has meanings that are shared socially. Our attempt is to describe such semantics of place with respect to spatial function. We show how to record such semantics and explore their potential applications.

Incorporating social relationship among users and semantics of places with multi-agent architecture bring us various applications: For example, in a conference or exhibition site, one may want to find his/her acquaintances. In order to realize it, an agent will seek the user's acquaintances in real world by communicating with other agents. The agent has to consider the context of the user and other agents, where they physically exist and in what social relation they are. Another example is guidance tour at a museum, a university, and a city. A user agent has to consider where to visit and who to meet depending on the social relation and physical location. To provide such appropriate navigation and guidance services in a society scale, massively multi-agent systems are necessary and they should utilize some kind of social knowledge. In this paper, we mainly target on a conference site.

The remainder of this paper is organized as follows. The next section describes social network mining from the Web and sensor information. We then describe semantics of place in Section 3. We present discussion and conclude the paper in Section 4.

2   Social Network Mining

We develop two approaches for automatically obtaining a social network. One is to extract a collaboration network of researchers from the Web. Using a Web search engine and text processing, we can represent a large (up to 3000 nodes) social network. We operated our system at JSAI2003 and JSAI2004 (The 17th and 18th Annual Conferences of the Japanese Society for Artificial Intelligence). Another approach is to obtain a social network from sensor information. Such a network illustrates who meets whom in a ubiquitous computing environment. Such a module to obtain social relationships is incorporated with a multi-agent architecture for advanced information services, such as those for community support at a conference site [16].

2.1   Social Network from Web Information

We assume that nodes of a network are given. In other words, we first identify members of the target network that we want to include. The JSAI has a regular annual conference.

---

[1] http://www.friendster.com/

[2] http://www.or kut.com/

We first choose the contributors to the last four annual conferences (JSAI98, JSAI99, JSAI2000, JSAI2001, and JSAI2002) as active members of the JSAI community. Each active member of JSAI is considered to be a node in a social network. A node is labeled by the name of its corresponding person.

Next, edges between nodes are added using Web information. The fundamental approach is very simple: to measure relevance of two nodes X and Y, we put a query

"X and Y"

to a search engine. We can subsequently measure the relevance of two names based on the number of retrieved results. For example, if we put a query "Yutaka Matsuo and Mitsuru Ishizuka" we get 156^3 hits, whereas we obtain only 7 hits by putting the query "Yutaka Matsuo and Riichiro Mizoguchi." Because both "Mitsuru Ishizuka" and "Riichiro Mizoguchi" have almost the same numbers of hits by themselves (1120 and 1130, respectively), we can conclude that the co-occurrence is biased: "Yutaka Matsuo" tends to appear more often with "Mitsuru Ishizuka" than with "Riichiro Mizoguchi." Actually, Professor Mitsuru Ishizuka (the sixth author of this article) was a supervisor of Yutaka Matsuo (the first author) during his Ph.D. course.

Our approach estimates the strength of relation by the strength of co-occurrence. If X and Y have a strong relation, the retrieved documents might include X's homepage, Y's homepage, their publication pages, a laboratory's member list page, a department student list page, a conference program page, an expert committee's page, and other resources. Succinctly, our hypothesis is: if there are numerous pages including both names, the two subjects have some social relation with high probability.

Many indices are useful to estimate the strength of co-occurrence. Some major indices that estimate overlap or similarity of two sets are [12, 18]:

Frequency $|X \cap Y|$

Mutual information $\log \dfrac{N|X \cap Y|}{|X||Y|}$ (N is the number of Web documents.)

Dice coefficient $\dfrac{2|X \cap Y|}{|X| + |Y|}$

Jaccard coefficient $\dfrac{|X \cap Y|}{|X \cup Y|}$

Overlap coefficient $\dfrac{|X \cap Y|}{\min(|X|, |Y|)}$

Cosine $\dfrac{|X \cap Y|}{\sqrt{|X||Y|}}$

We employ overlapping coefficients with a certain threshold.

$$R(X, Y) = \begin{cases} \dfrac{|X \cap Y|}{min(|X|, |Y|)} & \text{if } |X| > k \text{ and } |Y| > k, \\ 0 & \text{otherwise} \end{cases}$$

---

[3] This figure and the following figures in examples are results by Google (Japan) in Jan. 8th, 2004. Note that the examples are translated from Japanese.

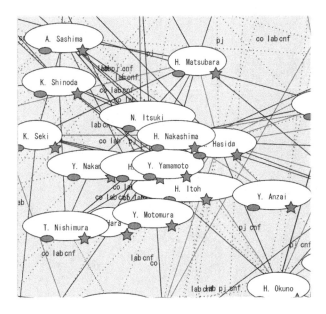

Fig. 1. Social network at JSAI2003 (zoomed)

We set $k = 30$ for JSAI case. If we want to estimate the co-occurrence more precisely to a person garnering few hits, we can pursue other alternatives: we can calculate statistical reliability or use an $m-$estimate.

We then extract edge labels to discriminate the relationship between two persons. Four classes of relationship are defined among researchers as:

– Coauthor: coauthors of a technical paper
– Lab: members of the same laboratory or research institute
– Proj: members of the same project or committee
– Conf: participants of the same conference or workshop

Each edge may have multiple labels. For example, X and Y have the relations of both "Coauthor," and "Lab."

We first fetch the top five pages retrieved by the query "X AND Y." Then we extract features from the content of each page: Attributes NumCo, FreqX, and FreqY are about appearance of name X and Y. Attributes GroTitle and GroFFive are for classifying the content of a page using pre-defined word groups.

We take a machine learning approach to judge classes of relationships automatically. We apply C4.5 [17] to derive classification rules for 275 pages to which we manually assigned the correct labels. Table 1 shows the error rate of five-fold cross validation for 275 training data. Although the error rate for Lab is high, others have about a 10% error rate or less. Precision and recall are measured by manually labeling another 200 Web pages.[4] Coauthor class gives high precision and recall even though its rule is very

---

[4] We do not use these 200 pages for producing discriminant rules.

Fig. 2. Social network of JSAI2003 (for overview)

Table 1. Error rate of edge labels, precision and recall

class	error rate*	precision	recall**
Coauthor	4.1%	91.8% (90/98)	97.8% (90/92)
Lab	25.7%	70.9% (73/103)	86.9% (73/84)
Proj	5.8%	74.4% (67/90)	91.8% (67/73)
Conf	11.2%	89.7% (87/97)	67.4% (87/129)

*: error rate of five-fold cross validation for 225 training data
**: precision and recall for different 200 correct data.

simple. However, the Lab class gives low recall, presumably because laboratory pages have a greater degree of variety. Proj and Conf classes give higher error rates when applied to 200 other data than when they are applied to the 275 training data. Thereby, we infer that Web pages of these classes have a variety of styles, and that the obtained rules are insufficient.

We can employ more advanced algorithms because determination of the relationship class is reduced to a text categorization problem. For example, the support vector machine will improve the performance [6]. Using unlabeled data also improves the categorization [14]. Numerous studies have addressed text categorization, but the present

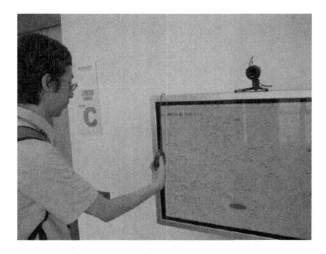

Fig. 3. Social network display at JSAI2003 site

study is intended to use as simple an algorithm as possible. The relationship depends on the target domain; therefore, we must define such classes depending on the domain.

We served a social network display system at JSAI2003 and JSAI2004 in combination with location and schedule information service systems [16, 4]. Figure 1 depicts a part of our obtained social network of the JSAI community. The entire network is shown in Fig. 2. Although the whole network has 1560 nodes, we show only a network with 266 nodes and 690 edges for simplicity. A node is labeled with the corresponding participant name (in Japanese), and edges are labeled as "Coauthor", "Lab", "Proj", or "Conf". The network is represented in SVG format with Java script. We can view the network using an SVG viewer and drag nodes.

2.2   Researcher Retrieval System

We developed a researcher retrieval system based on the extracted social network among researchers. It has the following features:

- We can search for a researcher by name, affiliation, research keyword, and research category, as shown in Fig. 4.
- We can view a list of researchers who show a strong relation to a target researcher, as shown in Fig. 5. If we click one researcher, we can view the detail and related researchers. Thereby, we can surf the social network and understand the community well.
- Centrality analysis is combined. The system can show how central a person is with respect to the degree centrality and eigenvector centrality on top of the hit count of Web pages.
- We can determine a path from one person to another. Several paths are shown. Furthermore, it is possible to discern a path to a person having a certain attributes. For example, we can find a path from me to a researcher who studies robotics who is nearest on the social network.

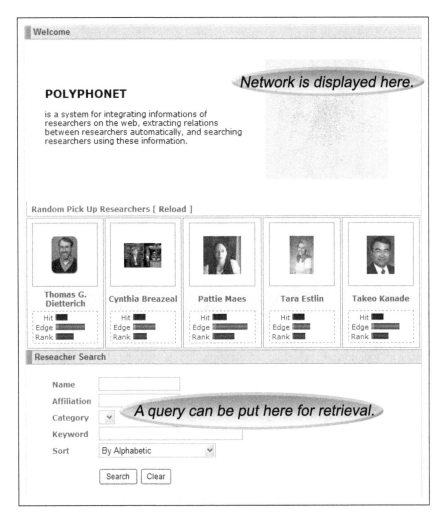

Fig. 4. Researcher retrieval system

- Because we use Web information, we can freely add a researcher if the database does not have information regarding that researcher. All we need input is that person's name and affiliation.

This system is developed so far for AI researchers in Japan (500 persons), robotics researchers in Japan (3600 persons), disaster mitigation researchers in Japan (3000 persons), Hokkaido researchers (1000 persons), and World-wide AI researchers (3000 persons). This knowledge-base can be utilized in a ubiquitous computing environment at academic conferences, possibly using multi-agent architecture.

2.3 Social Network from Sensory Information

In a ubiquitous computing environment wherein many sensors are set, we can obtain users' behavioral data. Especially, if we establish location sensors, we can obtain the

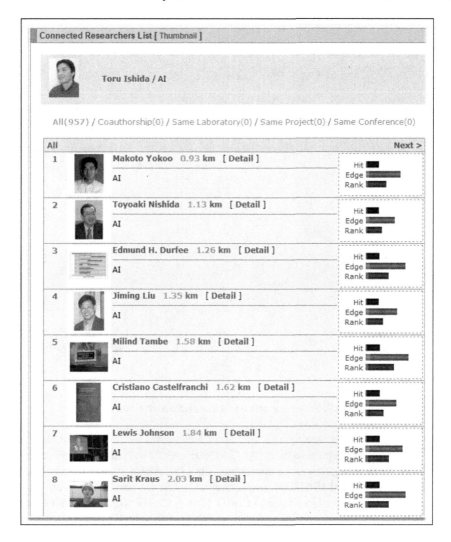

Fig. 5. Researchers showing a strong relation

```
Jun/26 14:43.11, 103, reception
Jun/26 14:48.11, 113, entrance of D room
Jun/26 14:51.26, 114, entrance of E room
Jun/26 14:52.13, 103, reception
Jun/26 14:55.18, 102, front of digital poster
Jun/26 15:11.18, 113, entrance of D room
...
```

Fig. 6. Sample of location history by a user

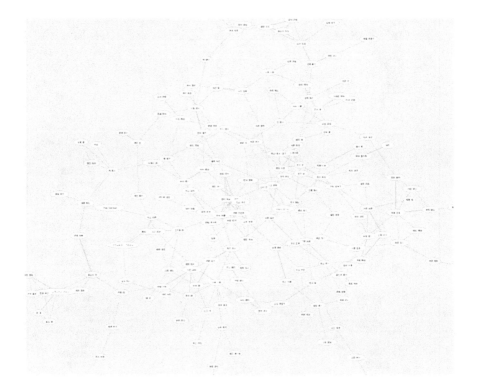

Fig. 7. Encounter network at a conference (for overview)

location history of respective users. At JSAI2003 and 2004, Nishimura and colleagues deployed location sensors at the conference site [15]. About 30 and 100 sensors were used at JSAI2003 and JSAI2004, respectively. Conference participants were provided with an information terminal called a CoBIT [16]. A CoBIT with an ID emitter sends a user's ID by infrared transmission; location sensors detect the ID.

Figure 6 shows a sample of the location history of a user obtained using sensors. We attempt to use that data to extract a social network.[5] We first define "a person meets a person once" as "two persons are detected by the same sensor within 30 s." Subsequently, their strength of co-location is measured by the following function:

$$f(X,Y) = (\#of\ two\ persons\ meet)/(\#\ of\ either\ person\ detected).$$

This is considered as a variant of the Jaccard coefficient.

Figure 7 shows a network using this function. The persons are evenly connected to others compared with Fig. 2. This is true because a person can meet others within the constraint of the conference duration. Especially, we find that persons with high cen-

---

[5] Note that this application entail privacy concerns. Our trial demonstrates the utility of this method in a limited community.

Table 2. Precision and recall of encounter detection

threshold	precision	recall**
0.1	92.3% (12/13)	2.8% (12/416)
0.035	84.8% (28/33)	6.7% (28/416)
0.001	76.4% (68/89)	16.3% (68/416)

trality in a social network by Web information are sometimes located at the periphery of the network obtained by this algorithm. Such persons could remain at the conference only for a short time. Conversely, students and young researchers sometimes comprise highly-connected clusters.

Table 2 shows an evaluation of the network by questionnaire. Precision is high while recall is very low. It is naturally inferred that people meet others at places other than where sensors are set. On the other hand, if two people are detected often at the same point, we can consider, with high probability, that they have talked.

3   Semantics of Place

Spatial information has received much attention recently. A ubiquitous computing environment enables us to monitor user behavior and potentially provide tailored information services depending on the user situations such as location. Navigation and city tours are some major applications that use location information. Nevertheless, most studies emphasize an application aspect: the meaning of space is implicitly incorporated in a system.

We consider that space has a meaning. We attempt to capture the meaning of space according to its functionality. For example, a lounge has functions including "enable one to drink," "provide something to drink," and "enable one to be seated." These functions are realized by the functions of objects that exist in that space. The function of space is sometimes more important than the function of inner objects. According to Sasajima, a function is defined as a result of interpretation of a behavior under an intended goal [20]. We define a spatial function as a result of interpretation of a property that is realized by a spatial structure under an intended goal. The importance of explicit conceptualization for reusability of knowledge has been widely recognized [9].

Developing a spatial representation is an important issue in information support including mass user navigation and disaster mitigation. In combination with multi-agent systems, more tailored information services are possible.

3.1   How to Describe Spatial Functionality

We propose to describe the meaning of a space using a triad:

$$(space\ region)\ (user\ type)\ (function\ type).$$

That is, in a certain region, space has a certain type of function for a certain type of user. The function of space is conditioned mainly on the user type.

```
<space>
 <Rectangle>
  <coordinates 200,120   340,180
 </Rectanble>
 <user>
  <aattr type="position">staff</aattr>
 </user>
 <pprov>coffee</pprov>
</space>
```

Fig. 8. A simple example of a spatial function

A space region can be described using conventional notation. In this study, we use G-XML[6] [1], which is a protocol for encoding spatial data through extensions built upon XML. It supports a variety of spatial models, such as a metrical and topological models, including vector and raster models. We will not address details of G-XML herein.

For example, a space in which a staff member can get a cup of coffee is described as Fig. 8. It is a form of XML. In the rectangle region, the "physically provide" function of coffee exists for a user type whose social attribute of "position" is staff. The following are types of users and types of spatial functions that we propose.

Definition of User Type. Representation of a user is described by the user's physical and social attributes. Physical attributes concern things that the user possesses. Social attributes concern the abstract properties that the user has.

pattr. The `pattr` denotes a physical attribute. It includes `belongings` and `devices`.

aattr. The `aattr` denotes a social (or abstract) attribute. It includes the following types: `position`, `interest`, `knowledge`, `gender`, `age`, `permission`, `appointment`, `ability` and so on.

Definition of Function Type. We categorize spatial functions as four types: that is, physically provide, socially provide, enable, and permit. "Provide" is a spatial function to provide something physically or socially, such as coffee or permission. It may change the user's physical or social attributes. "Enable" is a spatial function to enable some action, and "permit" is a spatial function to permit some action.

pprov. The `pprov` denotes a function of providing physical objects.

aprov. The `aprov` denotes a function to provide an abstract object. An abstract object includes information, permission, an appointment, and so on.

enable. The `enable` is a physical function that allows a user to perform some action.

permit. The `permit` is a social function that permits a user to perform some action that is prohibited in the superspace.

---

[6] Geographic information - XML encoding for geospatial data exchange. XML stands for eXtensible Markup Language.

```
<?xml version="1.0" standalone="yes"?>
<spaces>
 <place type="restaurant" label="Udon">
  <space>
   <user>
    <aattr name="position">guest</aattr>
   </user>
   <permit id="func:permit:eat">eat</permit>
   <enable id="func:enable:eat">eat</enable>
   <service>restaurant
    <achievedby>
     <func ref="func:enable:eat"/>
     <func ref="func:permit:eat"/>
    </achievedby>
   </service>
   <user>
    <aattr name="position">staff</aattr>
   </user>
   <enable>cook</enable>
   </space>
 </place>
</spaces>
```

Fig. 9. An example of spatial function representation

In addition to the above functions, we define a `service` function. Service is a spatial function with human intervention, such as a guide service or a reservation service. Figure 9 is a (simplified version of) spatial function description of a restaurant space.

3.2   Spatial Function Retrieval

The objective of our spatial function representation is to allow a machine to grasp the rough meaning of spaces. Consequently, it enables a machine to make an inference that more closely resembles human reasoning about space than current systems.

For example, assume a user puts an input to a machine – "I am thirsty." If our system can interpret the input, it will search for a place where the user can drink. The current navigation system may have representation with the locations of cafes, so it can recommend the user to go to such places. However, other ways to satisfy the user's need are by showing the location of a vending machine, a convenience store, or a hot-water service room.

The system can also respond to the input "I am hungry": It searches for a place to get something to eat and a place where we can take a seat and eat. Then it can suggest "How about buying sandwiches at the store and going to the park to eat it?" This is a combination of multiple spatial functions.

We call our task *spatial function retrieval* (SFR). An SFR system consists of two parts: (i) interpret a user's demand, and obtain the functions to retrieve, and (ii) search for the functions from a spatial database. The first part (i) is currently solved by con-

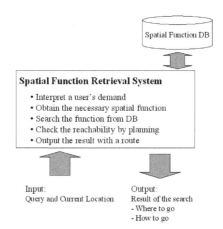

Fig. 10. Spatial function retrieval system

Table 3. Relation between a user's need and spatial functions

Need	required function
I am hungry	service:restaurant, {pprov:food, permit:eat}
I am thirsty	service:cafe, {pprov:drink, permit:eat}
I want to smoke	{permit:smoke}, service:cafe
I want to rest	{enable:sit, permit:sit}
I feel sick	{enable:lie down, permit:lie down}, service:guide
I want to access the Internet	{enable:use LAN, pattr:belongings:PC}
I want to have a meeting	{enable:sit, property:lockable, ex-possession}

sulting a predefined table, a part of which is shown in Table 3[7]. The following is a procedure for the search (ii). As the document retrieval system, it expands the query if our system fails to search.

1. Direct search phase Search for a place to respond to the user's need. If there is no appropriate place, go to Step 2.
2. Decompose into functions and search Decompose the user's need into necessary spatial functions, and retrieve. If there are no functions, go to Step 3.
3. Query expansion and search Expand the necessary functions using default knowledge about a place, or using ontology of target objects.

An overview of the SFR system is shown in Fig. 10. For example, a query "I am thirsty" is input. Then, the system will consult the table in Table 3, and searches for "service: cafe" because there might be a cafe service in a restaurant, a food court, or a lounge. It also searches "pprov: drink & permit: eat." There may be a coffee server that

---

[7] We have already produced more than 40 pairs of needs and spatial functions; they are categorized into six groups.

the user can use and a space where the user can drink. The result is provided to the user by the action sequence using natural language and a path on a map.

Because SFR is one example to use a representation of places, it will potentially enhance several kinds of location-based information services. In contrast to many studies that have explored representation of spatial semantics, we have made an effort to keep ours simple and easy-to-use.

4   Conclusion

This paper specifically addresses two kinds of social knowledge for a ubiquitous environment: social relations among persons and semantics of places. First, Web information and sensor information are used to construct a social network. A researcher retrieval system is introduced to promote collaboration among researchers. Next, a method for representation for semantics of places is proposed. It is used as an advanced navigation system, called a spatial function retrieval system.

For advanced context-dependent information support in a ubiquitous computing environment, it is important to obtain and utilize social knowledge in our world. Our algorithm can contribute large scale multi-agent systems for mass user support in the real-world. It is also a great challenge in artificial intelligence to produce an agent that can behave socially appropriately, known as social intelligence [8] and socially situated intelligence [11], which eventually contribute to large scale simulation for society-centered design [5].

References

1. M Arikawa and K Kubota. A standard XML based protocol for spatial data exchange. In *Int'l workshop on Emerging technologies for geo-based applications*, pages 37–45, 2000.
2. A Butz, J Baus, A Krüger, and M Lohse. A hybrid indoor navigation system. In *Proc. 2001 International Conference on Intelligent User Interfaces*, pages 25–33, 2001.
3. Jennifer Golbeck and James Hendler. Accuracy of metrics for inferring trust and reputation in semantic web-based social networks. In *Proc. EKAW 2004*, 2004.
4. Masahiro Hamasaki, Hideaki Takeda, Ikki Ohmukai, and Ryutaro Ichise. Scheduling support system for academic conferences based on interpersonal networks. In *Proc. ACM Hypertext 2004*, 2004.
5. Toru Ishida. Society-centered design for socially embedded multiagent systems. In *International Workshop on Cooperative Information Agent (CIA-04), LNCS 3191*, pages 16–29, 2004.
6. T. Joachims. Text categorization with support vector machines. In *Proc. ECML'98*, pages 137–142, 1998.
7. C. Kidd, R. Orr, G. Abowd, C. Atkeson, I. Essa, B. MacIntyre, E. Mynatt, and T. Starner. The aware home: A living laboratory for ubiquitous computing research. In *Proc. of the 2nd International Workshop on Cooperative Buildings*, 1999.
8. J. F. Kihlstrom and N. Cantor. *Social Intelligence*, pages 359–379. Cambridge University Press, 2000.
9. Y. Kitamura and R. Mizoguchi. Functional ontology for functional understanding. In *Workshop Notes for QR-98*, pages 88–98, 1998.

10. K. Kurumatani. Social coordination with architecture for ubiquitous agents - CONSORTS. In *Proc. IAWTIC '03*, 2003.
11. Jessica Lindblom and Tom Ziemke. Social situatedness of natural and artificial intelligence: Vygotsky and beyond. *Adaptive Behavior*, pages 79–96, 2003.
12. C. D. Manning and H. Schütze. *Foundations of statistical natural language processing.* The MIT Press, London, 2002.
13. H. Nakashima. Grounding to the real world - architecture for ubiquitous computing -. In *ISMIS2003 invited talk, LNAI 2871, Foundations of Intelligent Systems*, pages 7–11, 2003.
14. K. Nigram, A. McCallum, Sebastian Thrun, and Tom Mitchell. Text classification from labeled and unlabeled documents using em. *Machine Learning*, 39:103–134, 2000.
15. Takuichi Nishimura, Masahiro Hamasaki, Yutaka Matsuo, Ikki Ohmukai, Hironori Tomobe, and Hideaki Takeda. Jsai2003 integrated support system. *Transactions of the Japanese Society for Artificial Intelligence*, 19(1):43–51, 2004.
16. Takuichi Nishimura, Yoshiyuki Nakamura, Hideo Itoh, and Hideyuki Nakamura. System design of event space information support utilizing CoBITs. In *Proc. IEEE ICDCS2004*, pages 384–387, 2004.
17. J. R. Quinlan. *C4.5: Programs for Machine Learning.* Morgan Kaufmann, California, 1993.
18. E. Rasmussen. Clustering algorithms. *Information Retrieval: Data Structures & Algorithms. William B. Frakes and Ricardo Baeza-Yates (Eds.), Prentice Hall*, 1992.
19. Jordi Sabater and Carles Sierra. Reputation and social network analysis in multi-agent systems. In *Proc. International conference on Autonomous Agents (AAMAS2002)*, pages 475–482, 2002.
20. M Sasajima, Y Kitamura, M Ikeda, and R Mizoguchi. FBRL: A function and behavior representation language. In *Proc. IJCAI-95*, pages 1830–1836, 1995.
21. B Schmidt-Belz, P Stefan, A Nick, and A Zipf. Personalized and location-based mobile tourism services. In *Workshop on Mobile Tourism Support Systems*, pages 18–20, 2002.
22. Yasuyuki Sumi and Kenji Mase. Digital assistant for supporting conference participants: An attempt to combine mobile, ubiquitous and web computing. In *Proceedings UBICOMP 2001 (LNCS 2201)*, pages 156–175, 2001.

A Massively Multi-agent Simulation System for Disaster Mitigation

Ikuo Takeuchi

The University of Electro-Communications, 1-5-1,
Chofu, Tokyo, Japan 182-8585

Abstract. We introduce two Japanese national projects on disaster mitigation which seriously involve massively multi-agent simulation system. We describe a simulation integration architecture that combines various natural phenomena and huge number of human activities to estimate and predict a complicated disaster progress and countermeasures effects. We describe the state of the art of our system design and implementation related mainly about multi-agent programming. Finally, we discuss about the rationale of massively multi-agent simulation for the purpose of disaster mitigation.

1 Introduction

One of the most outstanding features of the Integrated Disaster mitigation Simulation System (IDSS) now under the development in the DaiDaiToku project[1] is that this disaster simulation system incorporates massively multi-agent simulation essentially. At a disaster, say, at a big earthquake, human individual and social activities cannot be dismissed in order to estimate and mitigate the disaster damage effectively as well as to predict complex physical phenomena.

In this paper, we will discuss the following issues:

1. How did we design the IDSS architecture so that it can integrate many kinds of simulators and a massively multi-agent system on top of them?
2. How can we exploit a massively multi-agent simulation to mitigate a disaster in reality? It is not an easy problem at all to make the massively multi-agent simulation system useful for decision making just after a big disaster happens.

2 IDSS for the DaiDaiToku and InfoShare Projects

An earthquake is a very complex disaster; it can cause buildings and bridges to collapse, disrupt life lines, and roads and often trigger landslides, liquefaction, fires, and tsunami. Earthquakes are still difficult to predict when and where to happen. Hence we should prepare well for minimizing the damage caused by an unexpected big earthquake in all conceivable ways. The earthquake disaster

T. Ishida, L. Gasser, and H. Nakashima (Eds.): MMAS 2004, LNAI 3446, pp. 269–282, 2005.

simulation is one of the most promising methods to reduce the earthquake damage, if it involves human activities at an earthquake as well as various physical phenomena. It should analyze and/or predict how many buildings collapse, how roads are blockaded obstructing refuge and rescue activities, how fires spread, how humans act, and so on. Such a comprehensive disaster simulation system can be used beforehand to illuminate civilians how to prepare and behave when an earthquake happens, and to provide good suggestions to various emergency responsive professionals how to cooperate with each other. If the disaster simulation system is connected to some sensor systems built in the city or provided with information by humans in the disaster field, it would help the risk management officers to make better decisions in real time, and the officers can give civilians and professionals the forecast of the disaster progress by a variety of communication means.

A comprehensive rescue simulation system for earthquake disaster reduction has been developed in the RoboCupRescue simulation project proposed by Kitano et al[2,3]. Ongoing efforts in the project make the simulation system more realistic for search and rescue at the first chaotic stage of a disaster.

In 2002, the Ministry of Education, Culture, Sports, Science and Technology (MEXT) of Japan started the Special Project for Earthquake Disaster Mitigation in Urban Areas (DaiDaiToku, for short in Japanese) of five year term. This project encompasses themes on disaster mitigation and preparedness, ranging from improvement of building architecture by using world largest 3-D full-scale earthquake testing facility "E-Defence," to exploitation of robotics and information technology (IT). One of the main topics of the IT exploitation sub-project is the development of an integrated earthquake disaster simulation system (IDSS). The final objective of this sub-project is to provide a working prototype simulation system that can be readily used by local government offices.

In 2004, the MEXT started funding on a new 3-year disaster mitigation project for "Risk-Adaptive Information Sharing System for Disaster Mitigation" (InfoShare project). The InfoShare project is deeply related to the DaiDaiToku project in the sense that it will promote information sharing among civilians, local governments, and various disaster responsive organization in the central government by utilizing a number of IT branches which include massively multi-agent simulation and its visualization to help disaster mitigation decision making for a variety of users.

Here we briefly sketch the requirements and issues of the IDSS which are relevant to this paper.

2.1   Simulation Integration

We can estimate primary damages caused by a disaster by running an appropriate simulator. Since sudden, rapid shaking of the Earth will not last long, primary damages of buildings and constructs may happen almost instantly, but fires may quite easily start here and there, and then spread over the city at a certain rate in the dense urban environment. This kind of secondary damages can also be estimated by running appropriate simulators. However, fire fighters and other agents do their best to extinguish fires although they may not have enough fire-plugs or cistern, or they cannot easily access to fires prevented by blockage of roads. Victims do not stay at dangerous area and they move toward would-be-safer area. Mass evacuation may itself cause another kind of secondary damages.

As can be easily seen, a number of different simulators should cooperate with each other in an integrated simulation system in order to be able to provide realistic and truly usable information. The most important requirement to the IDSS is this comprehensive simulation integration. However, there may be so diverse kinds of simulators. For example, time resolution varies from sub-second to minute, space resolution from centimeter to 100 meters, implementation language from Visual Basic, Fortran, C, C++ to Java, implementation platform from Windows, UNIX, to a supercomputer, and so on.

Besides above scale heterogeneity, considered disaster space dimensions are also heterogeneous. Most simulators deal with 2 dimensional city map, but some deal with 3 dimensional map of multi-floor buildings and underground shopping mall. But these are not independent, that is, these maps are connected and there must be bilateral flow of agents and information between them.

The degree of interaction between sub-simulators should also be considered. For example, fire spread simulation has to interact tightly with fire extinguishment simulation, but it does not need to interact much with a seismic intensity simulation.

These requirements and conditions make clear the necessity of developing a set of protocols and APIs between sub-simulators and some system modules.

It is obviously a big challenge to integrate these diverse kinds of simulators somehow without degrading the system performance. As can be easily understood, the IDSS should be implemented on the basis of a large-scale heterogeneous distributed computer systems. But it should also be cost-effective, so that scalable PC clusters would be the best choice of the hardware architecture.

2.2   Information Integration and Its Presentation

These requirements are more related to the InfoShare project, but still some are in the scope of IDSS.

At the first stage of a disaster especially, it is most important to estimate or realize damages as accurately as possible by utilizing every possible information source. However, since information sources (including sub-simulators) vary widely and may even contradict each other, the information gathering and its integration are quite difficult. It is of course expected that the more information is gathered, the more accurately should be the disaster situation grasped. If the simulation system involves prediction such as fire spread and human actions, it will be diverted from the real situation as time passes. It should be amended with information acquired by further observation.

From the viewpoint of the InfoShare project, it is also important to make a common framework or protocol on which different organizations can share information they individually gather. It is now the most urgent topic in the project. And IDSS should be compliant to the protocol.

The information provided by various reports and simulation progress should be displayed to humans lucidly and intelligibly. There are different kinds of users who want different information that is important to themselves. All available information need not, or should not be displayed, of course, since it hinders important information relevant to the user. Instead, some selected information should be presented for emergency responsive officers to make better critical decision in real time. The system should support the user in customizing the information presentation of the simulation. Moreover, officer's commands, for example, "Stop the fire spread around this line!", should be able to be put on the display as easy as possible and immediately announced to fire brigades at the field. These problems turn out to be a good challenge of human computer interface design.

It should be emphasized here that some early disaster alarm systems will also be incorporated into the IDSS, even though few may think of these as simulators. These alarm systems sense the first wave of an earthquake and make alarm as soon as possible to local government offices of the relevant areas to be attacked by the earthquake. This principle shows that the IDSS is not a mere simulation system for virtual phenomena, but it is a real disaster reduction system with the aid of simulation technology.

2.3   Huge Number of Agents

To estimate more accurately how a disaster causes secondary damages and to plan how the damages should be reduced, it is necessary to include relevant human (or agent) activities in the disaster simulation system.

By simulating the activities of emergency responsive professionals such as fire brigades and ambulances, we can estimate in advance the effectiveness of their predetermined criteria for decision and action, and we can also get helpful information for optimal decision making in real time. In the former case, we may be able to explore better criteria by a number of experiments. If some of the agents are rescue robots, their AI programs can be tested and improved by experimental simulations without deploying them at costly semi-real or infrequently occurring real disaster fields.

By simulating the actions taken by civilian victims, we may be able to find a bottleneck for safe evacuation, and we can make a good evacuation code, which will be taught to every civilian in disaster preparedness education. Showing the virtual simulation progress visually serves as a good education of civilians as well as local government officials responsible to disaster prevention.

By simulating the functions of various IT devices that can be available to disaster countermeasure, for examples, PDAs for fire fighters and police forces, and some sensor infrastructure built in the city, we can estimate their effectiveness and find functions to be improved or added. This estimation is important to estimate the cost effectiveness of such IT investment.

These sort of simulations will be best performed by agent-oriented programming, because every human or agent can be modeled in a more realistic and detailed manner than other ways of mathematical modeling. However, such a huge number of agents itself, say, at least 10,000, raises a challenge from the viewpoint of massively multi-agent system.

3   Outline of the System Structure

The requirements to the IDSS are so complicated that a simple-minded extension of the current RoboCupRescue simulation system does not seem to work well. We also departed from the HLA[4,5,6] after long discussions.

Figure 1 shows the state-of-the-art IDSS structure in 2004. We will describe some details of the architecture.

First of all, we classified sub-simulators to be connected to the IDSS into two categories; those for (1) disaster analysis and estimation, and those for (2) disaster prediction and response which include massively multi-agent simulation.

Sub-simulators for disaster analysis and estimation calculate, say, probability distributions of various damages and detect dangerous areas from given (maybe imprecise) information. Hence, they do not, in general, involve much computation about long time-series and mutual dependency with other sub-simulators. These can be considered to give initial values of the complex disaster environment. Some may be connected by causality; for example, a seismic intensity sub-simulator will surely affect a building collapse simulator. But the causality does not involve longer time series, so that only a little time-evolving computation is needed, or at least very short time-evolving computation with much finer time resolution. Traditional simulators, or analyzing programs about earthquake, tsunami, road blockage and so on are classified into this category. Note that real time information acquired by sensors and humans are also classified as that given by a sub-simulator of this type. Simulators of this type only may be quite useful to most local government offices, since these help preventing information blackout at the very fast stage of a big earthquake provided that the system is connected to a real-time sensor infrastructure.

Sub-simulators for disaster prediction and response deal with those secondary damages evolving as time passes such as fire propagation, and human activities responding to the disaster such as fire extinguishing, both of which have to interact with each other, and therefore need a sort of concurrent and distributed computation under rigorous timing control. A protocol called Sub-simulator API (S-API) was designed to implement this rigorous timing control[7].

Multi-agent programming approach is also expected to model individual human activities, by regarding individual human as independent agent which is simulated by its own modeling program of this type. There will be a huge number of agents in the IDSS, each of which interacts with others and with its environments, so that enormous amount of information exchange will be needed. These interactions will be handled by a ways better than the current RoboCupRescue simulation system. As we describe later, we use agent proxy modules (APX) with an Agent API (AG-API) for bundling agents in a cluster.

Conceptually, this dichotomy would not be necessarily introduced. However, most implementers of the first type do not want to step into rigorous timing

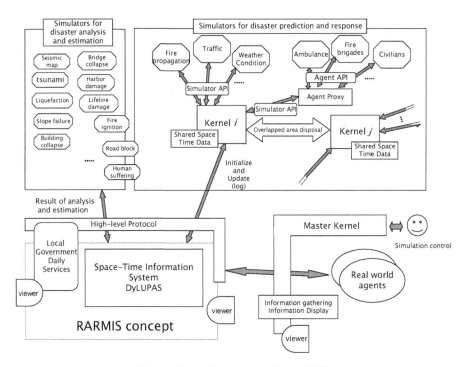

Fig. 1. Overall structure of the IDSS

control protocol between different sub-simulators. We decided that it is enough that sub-simulators of this type run at most only in cascaded manner, passing data only via the underlying geographic information database. That is, for example, after a seismic sub-simulator writes the distribution of seismic intensity and the shaking velocity on the city map, then a building collapse sub-simulator exploits the written information to estimate the collapse probabilities of individual buildings. No information feedback is needed in this case.

As shown in Figure 1, sub-simulators for disaster analysis and estimation are connected directly to a common space-time geographic information system called DyLUPAS via an appropriate network protocol based on XML. Information accuracy would be better as time passes and more amount of information is piled up on the DyLUPAS.

Sub-simulators for disaster prediction and response are distributed according to a number of divided regions for the sake of space scalability. That is, the city is divided into small enough regions on which RoboCupRescue-like simulation can run with a performance at least, say, ten times faster than real time. According to this division, the simulation kernel is also distributed to control individual regions. This regional division allows a little overlap between neighbor regions so that simulation progress in a region can be properly propagated to its neighbors through distributed simulation kernels[8]. Agent programs are connected to the distributed kernels via agent proxy module (APX), and the agent migration is properly dealt with by the APXs and kernels.

Each distributed kernel maintains its own space-time database (called SSTD, coming from Shared Space Time Data)[9]. This is because it incurs too heavy network load if every transaction is done through the DyLUPAS. Hence, each kernel makes a logically equivalent copy of the DyLUPAS of the relevant region, probably after converting it into its own format. The kernel does only inform of logs to the DyLUPAS periodically.

This simulation structure has an obvious flaw. That is, while the DyLU-PAS will be more accurate reflecting gradually gathered information, simulation progress controlled by the distributed kernel will be more inaccurate because it is based on the old initial copy of the DyLUPAS and the simulation is never as exact as real world progress.

Provided that the simulation progress is much faster than the real clock, the officers can simply restart the simulation with more accurate DyLUPAS from the console at the control kernel written in the right bottom in Figure 1. We decided not to embed a complicated roll-back mechanism into the IDSS, though sub-simulators for prediction and response should be aware of the simulation restart (or update) at arbitrary but predefined simulation clock, if they have internal states for their computation.

The DyLUPAS data format is capable of dealing with time-varying objects such as moving cars and shape-changing flood of water, and to maintain some kinds of parallel world models. Since the DyLUPAS maintains all the information acquired by real world observation and the IDSS simulation, a viewer can select appropriate information to display, and it can accept officer's command and then feed it back to simulation via the DyLUPAS.

4   Agent Programming

On the basic IDSS design principle, each agent itself would be an independent sub-simulator that directly communicates with the distributed kernel. However, such implementation is not feasible because more than tens thousands of sub-simulators will not be efficiently controlled in the system. We have to devise a simpler and more efficient mechanism for huge numbers of agents[10].

We have to consider the following conditions at the design of the IDSS agent programming interface (AG-API):

1. Programming Ease: Agent program (or simply agent, hereafter) can be so easily constructed as to encourage wide variety of experiments that will enhance disaster prevention study. Don't bother agent programmers with details of this complicated distributed simulation system.
2. Performance: We have to make the CPU and network load as little as possible.
3. Modeling: We need to choose an appropriate modeling capability level for agent programming. It is a trade-off problem between degree of reality and computational/programming load.

We decided the minimum time resolution of an agent action is 5 seconds; that is, each agent can perceive, think, and take an action in a cycle of 5 seconds. This

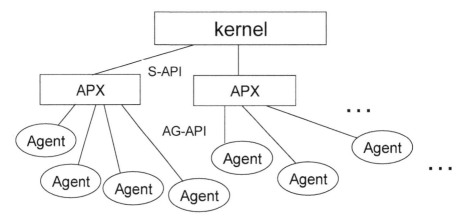

Fig. 2. APX and agents

time resolution affects other kinds of resolutions such as space resolution, unit of actions, objects dealt within the simulation. For example, driving a car does not involve any detailed actions such steering, braking etc.; it only designates a planned path to the target with every 5 second sensing of its environment.

4.1 Agent Proxy (APX)

We introduced a special kind of sub-simulator called agent proxy (APX) in order to bundle a number of agents, and make it easy to control nearby agents and decrease the network packets exchanged between agents and the (distributed) kernel. APX bundles the decisions of agents together and sends them in unity to the kernel as the simulation result of the APX sub-simulator. There may be more than one APX under a kernel (Figure 2).

An APX and agents under it usually run under a single process, sharing memory space, to avoid process switch overhead. This means agent program execution under an APX are serialized. However, under transitive occasion such as in the course of agent migration to other region, some agent programs are invoked by remote method (procedure) call.

4.2 Agent Perception

Figure 3 shows the communication between APX and its agent. APX calls an agent every 5 seconds in simulation clock with a method `cycle` with notable events as its argument if any. This method call is a trigger of agent computation. Other than notable events taught by APX, the agent has to perceive the situation around it as needed by issuing some probing queries to the shared space time data (SSTD) in the kernel; naturally, some data of interest are cached into APX.

To make the interface simple and efficient, APX does not send would-be-relevant information particular to an agent because some special sensory robot wants only special kind of gas, and it may discard all other information. Moreover, APX does not do any check about agent sensing commands so that any

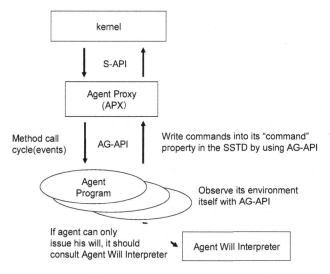

Fig. 3. Agent perception-action cycle

agent can know more than he could know. Unlike RoboCupRescue simulation league, the IDSS is not for competition. It is completely under the agent programmer's control how to restrict the information accessible to each agent. Hence, each agent program may have a sort of front-end module that controls the accessible information of the agent independently of the agent core program. Agent programmers can easily develop a new kind of robot with special sensing capabilities. By this loose interface, the performance degradation would be lessened.

4.3   Agent Action

At the last of a 5 second cycle, the agent may issue a set of action commands such as *walk*, *drive*, *extinguish* and *say*. The commands represent the agent action to be executed in the next 5 seconds. Commands in the set should be able to be executed simultaneously, for example, *walk* and *say*. This clarifies the meaning of 5 second time resolution – within 5 seconds, no two consecutive actions can be performed . The commands are written into the corresponding variables in the SSTD, and the relevant sub-simulators will process the commands.

Action commands allowed to issue to agents are rather of low level; that is, there is no command that represents agent's desire such as "I want to go my home". Such desire should be broken down into a concrete plan to achieve the desire, such "I walk to a house at the position (x, y) through the $road_1$ and $road_4$". This is of course for the performance reason of traffic simulator and other simulators.

However, admitting the burden of agent program side, there will be an Agent Will Interpreter (AWI) nearby APX which interprets agent's desire and breaks down it into a sequence of action commands or concrete moving plan which can readily understood by the traffic simulator.

There remains a subtle problem related to the causality of agent actions. For an agent, the result of his/her/its actions should be observed within the next cycle. Since the clock tick of the simulation is much finer than the agent perception-action cycle, we devise some clock shifting technique of synchronization to resolve the problem.

If all agents are very busy to iterate this shortest cycles, the simulation performance would be not much improved. But we expect that most of agents are not so busy. In that case, an agent can enlarge its cycle unless some important event happens; this is very plausible for victims buried under collapsed houses.

4.4   Agent Movement and Communications

We found that, in the distributed simulation system, agent movement, or traffic simulation is the most difficult problem. In our distributed simulation framework, every agent has to belong to a certain APX for its perception-action cycle execution. However, if agents moves by walk or car, they had better change its APX, or migrate to another APX to lighten their computation load.

It seems indispensable to divide the wide urban area into some number of regions to assure the scalability of the distributed simulation, but frequent agent migration needs much communication packets between processors. Moreover, high speed movement could easily violate the integrity of the regionally distributed simulation, because such high speed movement need wider interaction with the environment that cannot be coped within our distributed simulation framework based on information exchange over a small overlapped region segments between adjacent regions. If the interaction causality range is wider than the overlapped region segment, we cannot be sure of the correct simulation.

Another problem is the telecommunication between agents. Our distributed simulation system is designed as an asynchronous one, but if agents that belong to different distributed kernels, or different regions, want to communicate by their telecommunication devices, two distributed simulation subsystems over the two regions have to synchronize each other. Hence, though our simulation integration is planned to be asynchronous, it is virtually quite synchronous at last.

4.5   Geographic Model for Agents

In the RoboCupRescue simulation, the geographic model for agents is simply a network model as shown in Figure 4(c). However, civilian victims at an earthquake often take actions in more spatial geography; that is, they often refuge in a big railroad station which has no clear network geographic model; it is a space spread in two dimensions.

In the current IDSS implementation, we only adopt the network model, but soon incorporate the mixture of network model and spatial model as shown in Figure 4(b). Agents have to select which geographic model they rely on at every move command, because different kinds of traffic simulators will process their commands.

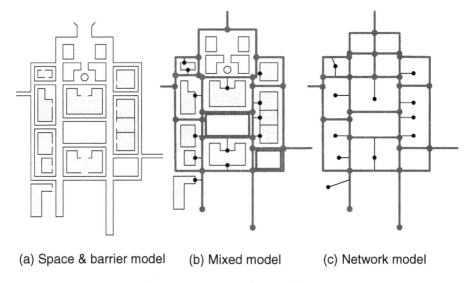

(a) Space & barrier model   (b) Mixed model   (c) Network model

Fig. 4. Geographic models

5 Rationale of Massively Multi-agent Simulation

Both in the DaiDaiToku and InfoShare projects, agent simulation is highlighted in the master plans. However, we have to assess the rationale of massively multi-agent simulation in the disaster mitigation context. That is, we have to rationalize the usability and usefulness of massively multi-agent simulation for various aspects of disaster mitigation. For example, how can we exploit massively multi-agent simulation results for local government officers to make better decision?

Unlike large scale military simulations, most agents, say civilians (some are victims and some are volunteers rescuing victims, etc.), in the disaster field are not grasped precisely by the simulation system; only the activities of emergency responsive professionals such as fire brigades can be correctly reflected into the simulation. Civilians cannot be controlled by the simulation results. Nevertheless, individual civilian's safety is the most important mission of the simulation, in spite of being based on massively multi-agent system technology.

The IDSS has two kinds of usages: one for beforehand simulation, the other for real-time simulation just after an actual disaster. The meanings of massively multi-agent simulation would be different in these usages.

5.1 Beforehand Simulation

We found that a simple simulation like RoboCupRescue gave a deep impression to many civilians residing in the simulated area, because the very their houses were threatened by spreading fire but fire fighters seemed to ignore and concentrate on other fires. Such experience gives civilians strong motivation for their self aid and mutual aid activities. They realize public aid may easily fail. In this case, reality about their houses gave strong impact to the civilians.

If each of the huge number of agents corresponds quite naturally to each inhabitant in the town, and looks like an "agent" that reflects individually his/her own reality, there will be much more impact on the civilians, at least, in beforehand disaster simulations.

Therefore a good multi-agent simulation is very useful to enlighten civilians on how to prepare and act at a big disaster. For this purpose, we will conduct a variety of experiments by mixing people characteristics, say, civilians in panic, civilians who tend to take leadership in a disaster, civilians who simply follow people around them, civilians who know the location of refuges or not, etc. according to social surveys after earthquakes. This sort of simulation will reveal out how civilians' preparedness affects the disaster reduction.

This benefit will be readily able to be extended to the training of professionals, and even the design of their behavior standard manual, because their behaviors directed by the manual can be more accurately simulated; that is, the quality of the manual may be more directly reflected to their disaster response effectiveness. The remaining biggest problem, however, is whether the bureaucracy admits the results demonstrated by the IDSS as an advice of its manual design improvement.

In the InfoShare project, we are planning to show the usefulness of good information sharing framework by experiments that controls the parameters of the "degree" of information sharing. Firstly, the participatory experiments will involve humans who play a role of chief commanders in disaster responsive organizations, and control the degree of information sharing among them; for example, restriction of the communication channels usable by the human players, addition of delay and errors, etc. We measure the affection to player's decision. Then, we replace the human players by the agents in the simulation system, and evaluate the adequacy and accuracy of the agent modeling.

5.2   Real-Time Simulation

But it is by no means an easy problem to make the simulation system useful just after a big disaster happens. That is, it is a big challenge to associate the simulation of a huge number of virtual agents with real behaviors taken by a huge number of real humans in the disaster field in order to make the real-time simulation fully exploitable to mitigate the ongoing disaster.

Multi-agent simulation can provide a microscopic view of happenings in a disaster field. But most of the happenings predicted by the simulation would not be real. How can we rely on the microscopic simulation results to make a decision? However, if we see the simulation results in a macroscopic view, say, if we can know where most civilians need help, an officer can deploy his units to that area, without knowing the individual details.

It is important to assess the difference between a macroscopic view of microscopic multi-agent simulation results and macroscopic simulation results. For example, a macroscopic traffic simulator can be made based upon a flow graph theory, which can estimate the maximum traffic flow of the road network part of which has been blockaded, and give advice which roads should be cleared in higher priority. But it may not be able to deal with time varying traffic. A finer traffic simulator can simulate every car and human moving on the partly block-aded road network based on some fluid dynamics model or cellular automaton model, and help finding plausible traffic jams that prevent emergency response. A truly multi-agent traffic simulator can simulate every car and human based on individual perception-action model, and may give more qualitative evalua-tion of evacuation and logistics. However, it is still a remaining problem how can we be confident of the advantage of the multi-agent simulation in the real-time simulation just at an ongoing disaster.

One plausible answer to this problem is that after iterating a number of be-forehand experimental simulations with continual improvement of agent behavior modeling, we would acquire far better simulation model than other analytical, rather macroscopic simulation models, and thereby we will be able to get more accurate macroscopic view of the disaster by doing massively multi-agent simu-lation.

Another idea for the solution is a huge number of on-the-spot simulations and their loose summation with a central simulation system. For example, a rescue professional at the spot where he has to dig out a buried person has a PDA and runs a local simulation how to dig out the person with some small amount of information from the center such as how quick the fire spreads toward the spot. This local simulation can be more accurate and timely because its initial values and observation inputs are quicker and easily corrected. The result of the simulation helps the professional immediately, and is reported in some abstract form to the center. In this case, large part of the massively multi-agent simulation is left to massively distributed local simulations. The central simulation system does some global simulation, compensates local simulations that are not done locally in the disaster field, and integrates all the simulation results for global decision making.

6   Conclusion

In this paper, firstly we introduced the integrated disaster simulation system (IDSS) whose development is still on the way. We can summarize the character-istics of the IDSS with respect to MMAS as follows:

1. It will integrate a number of diverse kinds of simulators to cooperate with each other with as little effort as possible. It is open in the sense that any new simulator can join only with a small effort and also the system itself would be gradually improved.
2. A huge number of humans, cars, robots, and organizations in the disaster field are represented by agents. Each agent is deemed as an individual simu-lator, but bunch of agents are serialized under a simulator called agent proxy (APX) for the sake of performance.
3. The simulation framework is not limited to earthquake so that other kinds of disasters can be well simulated by this structure.

4. It would accelerate the development of intelligent rescue robots and sensor infrastructure of a city, because it gives a good testing environment for their development.

Then we described consideration on the assessment of the massively multi-agent system in the IDSS. We have to prove the advantage of the massively multi-agent simulation framework in the IDSS project.

The authors would like to thank all members of the IDSS project to make up the architecture of the IDSS through discussions; especially, Itsuki Noda, Yoshitaka Kuwata, Tetsuhiko Koto, Hiroki Shimora, Takuya Morishita, Michinori Hatayama, Tomoichi Takahashi, and Nobuhiro Ito. This research is conducted as part of the Special Project for Earthquake Disaster Mitigation in Urban Areas under a grant of the Ministry of Education, Culture, Sports, Science and Technology of Japan, and also supported by the Project for Risk-Adaptive Information Sharing for Disaster Mitigation under a grant of Japan Science and Technology Agency.

References

1. I. Takeuchi, Rescue Simulation and Its Road Map, *Proceedings of SICE Annual Conference 2002 in Osaka*, MA15-6, pp.1056-1061, 2002.
2. S. Tadokoro et al. The RoboCup-Rescue Project: A Robotic Approach to the Disaster Mitigation Problem, *Proc. IEEE International Conference on Robotics and Automation*, pp. 87-96, 2000.
3. T. Takahashi et al. Rescue Simulation Project and Comprehensive Disaster Simulator Architecture, *Proc. IEEE/RSJ International Conference on Intelligent Robots and Systems*, pp. 1894-1899, 2000.
4. F. Kuhl, R. Weatherly and J. Dahmann, *Creating Computer Simulation Systems: An Introduction to the High Level Architecture*, Prentice Hall, 1999.
5. R.M. Fujimoto, *Parallel and Distributed Simulation Systems*, John Wiley & Sons, Inc., 2000.
6. B. Logan and G. Theodoropoulos, The Distributed Simulation of Multi-Agent Systems, *IEEE Proceeding Journal*, Vol 89, No 2, pp 174–185, 2001.
7. I. Takeuchi, T. Koto, I. Noda, Y. Kuwata, H. Shimora and T. Takahashi: Topics on the Control Mechanisms for a Large-scale Earthquake Disaster Mitigation Simulation System, *2nd International Workshop on Synthetic Simulation and Robotics to Mitigate Earthquake Disaster*, Lisbon, 2004.
   http://www.rescuesystem.org/robocuprescue/SRMED2004/proceeding.html
8. T. Koto and I. Takeuchi, Distributed Disaster Simulation that Integrates Sub-simulators, *1st International Workshop on Synthetic Simulation and Robotics to Mitigate Earthquake Disaster*, Padova, 2003.
9. H. Shimora, I. Noda, Y. Kuwata, T. Koto, and I. Takeuchi, Design of Application Programming Interface for Distributed Simulation Systems, *1st International Workshop on Synthetic Simulation and Robotics to Mitigate Earthquake Disaster*, Padova, 2003.
10. T. Koto, I. Takeuchi, I. Noda, N. Ito, H. Shimora, T. Morisita, K. Honji, T. Takahashi, and Y. Kuwata: Agent management architecture for a large-scale earthquake disaster mitigation simulation system, *2nd International Workshop on Synthetic Simulation and Robotics to Mitigate Earthquake Disaster*, Lisbon, 2004.

Designing Emergency Guidance
in a Social Interaction Platform

Hideyuki Nakanishi and Toru Ishida

Department of Social Informatics, Kyoto University,
Yoshida-Honmachi, Sakyo-ku, Kyoto 606-8501, Japan
{nakanishi, ishida}@i.kyoto-u.ac.jp
http://www.lab7.kuis.kyoto-u.ac.jp/

Abstract. Future computing systems interact with a large number of users moving around buildings and streets. In this paper, we propose an example of such systems and how to evaluate ubicomp systems equipped with a large-scale physical environment that includes a large number of people inside. In our emergency guidance system, off-site guiding staff monitors a crowded large-scale public space to understand its situation, and instruct on-site guiding staff how to guide crowds effectively. Our system tracks and synthesizes the public space to enable the off-site staff to grasp it, and support communication between the on-site and the off-site staffs. Because it is not affordable to use the physical public space and a lot of human subjects to evaluate the system, we used our social interaction platform to simulate our guidance system. We could successfully construct simulations, in which the crowds are replaced with social agents in the virtual public space.

1   Introduction

Development of ubiquitous computing (ubicomp) systems compels us to explore their design space in physical environments. Physical part of ubicomp systems is usually much larger than that of desktop computing systems. In terms of ubicomp systems, 1) offices, home, and classrooms have been a major development field [1]; 2) navigation in shopping malls is one of promising applications [4]; and 3) streets can be a playfield of mixed reality games [7]. In this regard, designing ubicomp systems is very different from designing desktop computing systems, most of which can be accomplished in digital environments.

This nature of ubicomp systems interferes seriously with their design process since it is expensive to test them in an actual physical environment. We need many people and an experimental field to evaluate a system. Consequently, development of ubicomp systems tends to give birth to a compromise in order to make it feasible. For instance, 1) context information was simulated to compensate for lack of sensor devices [16]; 2) a university building was used to evaluate a navigation system for shopping malls [4]; and 3) entertainment was selected as an application domain to take advantage of errors produced by unreliable communication and positioning systems [7].

T. Ishida, L. Gasser, and H. Nakashima (Eds.): MMAS 2004, LNAI 3446, pp. 283–294, 2005.
© Springer-Verlag Berlin Heidelberg 2005

Designing an ubicomp system becomes extremely difficult if it is supposed to be used in indoor large-scale environments such as tall buildings, central railway stations, and airports. GPS is unavailable in indoor situations and wide-area positioning sensors are not very affordable. Because indoor large-scale environments may contain a large amount of people inside, a lot of human subjects are needed to analyze the effectiveness of the system especially when interaction between the system and each person generates significant side effects on others' behavior. An example of such massively multiagent ubicomp systems is our emergency guidance system explained in next section.

To support the design process of massively multiagent ubicomp systems, we have created methods to simulate a situation where those systems interact with many people. In these methods, human observers are substituted for sensing functionality of a system, physical environments are changed into virtual environments, and most subjects are replaced with social agents, which are software agents equipped with social interaction capability [17]. Our social interaction platform introduced in the third section enables these replacements. We discuss the replacing methods in the fourth section.

2   Emergency Guidance System

In large-scale public spaces like central railway stations, appropriate guidance for crowd control is critical because a vast amount of people visits. There are two ways to guide visitors. Staff in a control room provides overall guidance for all visitors through announcement speakers while on-site staff working in a public space gives location-based guidance for each visitor. At the present time these two guidance do not seem to be tied together very much, and collaboration between the off-site and the on-site staffs has not been extensively considered.

We propose an efficient means of crowd control, in which the off-site and the on-site staffs cooperate with each other. In this guidance illustrated in Figure 1, the off-site staff monitors an overall public space to find an unsafe group of crowd, and then instruct the nearby on-site staff how to guide the crowd effectively. According to this instruction the on-site staff tries to modify the crowd's behavior. Since current facilities, which are surveillance cameras and announcement speakers, cannot support such operations very well, technologically advanced systems are necessary. Our emergency guidance system is an asymmetric communication environment which connects people who can remotely perceive an entire situation of a large-scale physical space and people who exist in the space [18]. This system is an example of massively multiagent ubicomp systems.

Figure 2 depicts the first prototype of the guidance system installed in Kyoto Station, which is a central railway station where more than 300,000 passengers visit per day. The movements of the people on a station's platform are tracked by using a vision sensor network. We attached 12 sensors to the concourse area and 16 sensors to the platform as shown in Figure 3's floor plan, on which the black dots show the sensors' positions. The movement data are transmitted to the control room where the off-site staff is viewing the synthesized platform to find a location where their remote help is needed. They can see a bird's-eye view of the platform, which cannot be taken directly through cameras attached to the ceiling of the platform. When they notice a dangerous spot, they point at human figures which correspond to the on-site staff around the spot so as to establish vocal communication channels between their headsets and the on-site staff's mobile phones. This trick is possible because their phone numbers are registered at the system beforehand.

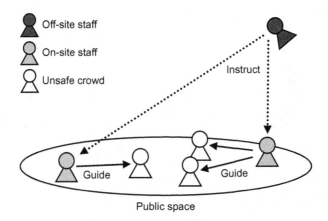

Fig. 1. Collaboration in Emergency Guidance

It is hard to guess what happens when the guidance system is used in actual emergency situation, because many people behave autonomously and complex interaction occurs. We need to carry out a lot of experiments in the station, but that is faced with several problems. Even though the installation of the sensor network is a result of our considerable efforts, its covered area is merely a very small part of the station, and its accuracy is not sufficient for earnest evaluation of the system's performance. Furthermore, it is enormously difficult to conduct an experiment with many subjects to evaluate the systems' effectiveness in such a public space. Simulating techniques which can solve these problems are very helpful in designing this kind of systems.

In the case of massively multiagent ubicomp systems, human-computer interaction is only a part of all interactions. Human-computer interaction between a system and users can cause face-to-face interaction between users and other people who are not using the system. And moreover, this interaction can affect everyone's behavior in the same physical space. The emergency guidance system deals with the following three interactions: 1) interaction between the system (namely the off-site staff) and on-site staff, 2) interaction between the on-site staff and the crowd, and 3) interaction among the crowd. The social interaction platform described in the next section makes it possible to construct and execute a simulation of these interactions.

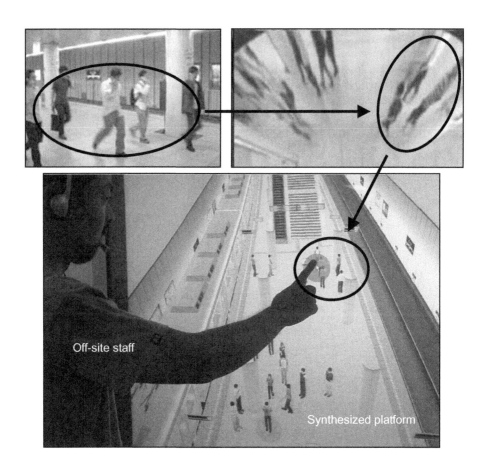

Fig. 2. Emergency Guidance System

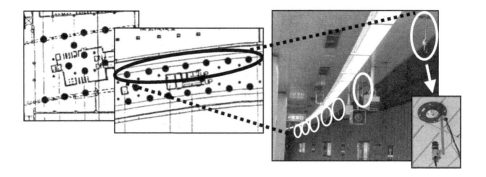

Fig. 3. Vision Sensors in Kyoto Station

3   Social Interaction Platform

There are various technologies which can be utilized for simulating social interaction in a physical space, e.g. embodied conversational agents [5], collaborative
virtual environments [3], virtual cities [14], and multiagent-based simulations [8].
Our social interaction platform called "FreeWalk/Q" is an integration of these
technologies [19]. As the result of that integration, people's avatars and social
agents can socially interact with one another in a shared virtual space. The
platform is a combination of the two components: "FreeWalk" and "Q." Q is a
scenario description language, in which we can describe interaction scenarios as
explained below [11]. FreeWalk is an interaction platform which mingles agents
and avatars based on the interaction model detailed later.

An interaction scenario is a definition of a social role. It is a collection of
scenes, each of which includes a set of interaction rules that define the agent's
social behavior in the situation. Each rule is a couple made up of a conditional
cue and the consequent series of *actions*. A short example is presented below.
Cues start with a question mark and actions start with an exclamation point. In
scene1, the agent says "Hello" and its state switches to scene2 when it hears
someone say "Hello." But if the agent observes someone wave his/her hand in the
same scene, its state switches to scene3. The same cue yields different actions in
different scenes. In scene2, the agent approaches the person and responds with
"Yes, may I help you?" when it hears "Hello" again.

```
(defscenario reception
  (scene1
   ((?hear "Hello" :from $x)
    (!speak "Hello" :to $x)
    (go scene2))
   ((?observe :gesture "wave")
    (go scene3)))
  (scene2
   ((?hear "Hello" :from $x)
    (!walk :to $x)
    (!speak "Yes, may I help you?" :to $x)))
  (scene3 ...
```

In the interaction model of FreeWalk, each action is mapped to a modification
of the walking, gestural, and speech parameters of the agent. Other agents' cues
can inspect these action parameters if such perception parameters as visual and
hearing powers of those agents allow them to perceive the action parameters.
In this manner, the virtual space of FreeWalk transmits verbal cues and such
nonverbal cues as interpersonal distance [9], gaze direction [13], and pauses in a
conversation [6]. These cues influence each agent's next action and finally invoke
group behaviors. For example, an agent's walking direction may change and this
change may form a flow of other following agents [23] when the agent observes
a pointing gesture produced by the gestural parameters of another agent.

In the platform FreeWalk/Q, people's avatars and social agents can share
the same virtual space, the same interaction model, and the same interaction

scenario. Agents are controlled through the application program interface (API). API functions are called to evaluate cues and actions described in the current scene of the assigned scenario. On the other hand, avatars are controlled through the user interface (UI). The action parameters are modified based on how the input devices are controlled. The perception parameters determine the distance of the far clipping plane in the view displayed on the screen, and the sound volume.

Based on the framework of "Society-centered Design" [12], we have created methods to simulate the emergency guidance system on the platform. The platform is useful for constructing a simulated collaborative guidance as well as executing it. When we construct the simulation, the platform becomes an environment for experiments from which we can retrieve interaction models and scenarios of social agents that act as the crowd. In the society-centered design framework, this construction phase corresponds to the "participatory simulations," which are multiagent-based simulations that include avatars. When we execute the simulation, the platform not only produces the simulated crowd but also functions as a tool to track subjects playing a role of the on-site staff. In the framework, this execution stage corresponds to the "augmented experiments," which are real-world experiments augmented by simulated users.

4   Simulating Methods

4.1   Describing Interaction Among Agents

To replace human subjects who play the role of an escaping crowd with extra agents, we need to simulate humanlike decision-making capability to form a group behavior. First, we describe an interaction scenario of the group behavior to construct its simulation as realistic as possible. Next, we conduct an experiment in which subjects take part in the simulation to experience the group behavior. Our social interaction platform can support this participatory simulation. After that experiment, we ask the subjects what decisions they have made throughout the virtual group behavior. In this interview, we show the subject a replay of his/her recorded first-person view which was displayed on the screen so that he/she can easily recall and answer what he/she was doing every moment. For example, we ask what they were paying attention to, what they were thinking about, and what they were trying to do per second. Finally, we can improve the scenario based on the interview result.

To simulate the emergency guidance system, we need a simulation of following behavior of the crowd. Previous studies gave us a basis for describing an interaction scenario of the following crowd [25, 15]. In the experiment, subjects experienced the described behavior and we interviewed them as shown in Figure 4. We successfully obtained deeper decision-making rules of the following crowd. For example, one of the prepared rules was "if you find a leading person, you follow his/her instruction." But, we found this was imperfect. The obtained rule is "if you find a leading person and observe others are following him/her, you follow his/her instruction."

Participatory simulation

Interview

Fig. 4. Interviews after Participatory Simulations

When we model a group behavior based on recorded materials of past real-world events [10], we can observe what happened actually in the event but have to make enormous efforts to interview people there. In a physical-space simulation [25], we can interview the subjects but it is difficult to record their first-person views without distracting them who are being engaged in the group behavior. In virtual-space simulations, it is very easy to record exactly the same views and replay it in the interviews.

4.2   Modeling Interaction with Humans

In terms of agent-human interaction, we have focused on designing humanlike response in non-conversational interaction because we suppose that conversational interaction would be a territory of human subjects. In the emergency guidance system, interaction between the off-site and the on-site staffs is conversational, but in the other interactions in which the crowd participates, non-conversational interaction is very influential as described below. Hence, subjects are in charge of the staff and social agents constitute the crowd in the simulations.

A kind of nonverbal communication is much related to non-conversational interaction. It has been reported that nonverbal communication has several different functions [21]. Some functions are related to conversational interaction. A typical one of them is to provide information. For instance, nods and frowns transmit the meanings of yes and no. Another conversational function is to co-ordinate interaction, e.g. beginning a conversation and taking a turn. There are also non-conversational functions, which strongly influence human communication and relationships. For example, people use nonverbal cues to bolster inter-

Fig. 5. Role-reversal Experiments

personal connections, such as building intimacy by increasing gaze and moving closer to the other person [26].

When the staff tries to guide the crowd in an emergency guidance, they usually shout something like, "the exit is over there!" The influencing power of this verbal cue shifts according to the nonverbal cues which accompany the words [28]. If the nonverbal cues do not indicate enough implicit influence that is trustworthiness, the crowd will not follow the staff's verbal instructions.

We created a method to develop social agents that can perceive implicit influences as humans do [20]. In this method, human perception mechanism is analyzed in psychological experiments, and then the mechanism becomes embedded in agents. At first, qualitative model to interpret nonverbal cues that provide implicit influences is fabricated based on social scientific knowledge of human responses to other humans. Next, the model is quantified by using the results of the experiments in which subjects respond to agents that emit the varied nonverbal cues as stimuli. Finally, we construct agents that can respond to multi-modal input data which compose the nonverbal cues. In the experiments, subjects play the role of the agents that perceive implicit influences in a simulation and the agents play the role of humans who try to make the influences. Thus, the method is called role-reversal experiments, which is presented in Figure 5. Findings from past media studies [22] enable the transition from the first step to the second step. Statistical analysis enables the transition from the second step to the third step. The social interaction platform is useful for making agents in both the second and the third steps.

A self-confident person speaks loud and fast [24]. A self-confident person tends to use gesture more [27]. Extended gaze into another's eyes is the strongest cue to provide the impression of self-confidence [21]. If the staff speaks loudly and quickly, points to the destination clearly, and makes steady eye contact, you will probably follow their instructions. We can develop this qualitative model into a quantitative model according to the result of an experiment to observe how four cues–gaze ratios, gesture sizes, voice volumes, and speech speeds–contribute to trustworthiness. Using the questionnaire data, we are able to find the threshold of each cue's positive effect and the relative influence of that cue. We can use ANOVA analysis to determine which level's effect is significantly stronger or weaker than another level's effect and how independent the cues are. If each cue is independent and their influences are linear, we can also use multiple linear regression analysis to make a formula that calculates the degree of trustworthiness based on each cue's input data. In Figure 5, you can see an example of the input interface that is a combination of motion tracking sensors (detecting gesture sizes), an eye tracking sensor (detecting gaze ratios), and a microphone (detecting voice volumes and speech speeds).

4.3   Tracking Without Sensors

The installation of sensors in an experimental physical environment is always problematic. Our idea is that someone (may be an experimenter) becomes the wizard who provides the system context information instead of the sensors that would be attached to the environment. Please suppose that the system is connected to a virtual space that is a copy of the physical environment. In the same or a remote place, the wizard observes what the subject is doing. By this observation, the wizard controls the avatar which corresponds to the subject in order to make it do the same thing in the virtual space. Lastly, the ubicomp system obtains the subject's context information from the virtual space.

In the simulation of the guidance system, the movements of the subjects who play a role of on-site staff are converted into the avatars' movements so that the guidance system can track the subjects without using a positioning sensor network. As a result of this tracking, human figures in the synthesized public space can walk along the same route as that of the subjects. The tracking also enables the subjects to see the simulated crowd on their see-through face-mounted displays or other display devices since positional relationships between the subjects and the crowd can be calculated.

In the experiment to simulate interaction between the off-site and the on-site staffs at Kyoto Station, the subject who played a role of off-site staff was viewing the virtual station synthesized by the guidance system running on the PC in our laboratory. This laboratory is about three kilometers distant from the station where the subject who was playing a role of on-site staff was being tracked by the wizard person. As you can see in the left picture of the Figure 6, the wizard was carrying a laptop PC which sends the avatar's position to the PC in the laboratory through wireless networks. The subject in the laboratory could understand the location of the on-site subject and could talk with him/her by phone.

There are two ways for the wizard to observe a subject walking around in a large-scale physical space. If the wizard can have a bird's-eye view of the

Fig. 6. Tracking by Observation

whole space and look down the subject from some higher location, pointing at his/her position on a 2D map would be better than controlling the avatar in a 3D space. However, there was not any good location to keep watch over the subject continuously because Kyoto Station has a complex structure, which fosters many blind spots. In such an environment, the other way in which the wizard keeps following the subject is an acceptable option. In this case, a 3D navigating interface is a good solution. In the experiment, the wizard could make use of the third-person viewpoint located behind the avatar very well since it was possible to move the avatar precisely just by keeping coincidence between the displayed view and his sight as given in Figure 6. This way of observation is more effective also in acquisition of such detailed context as gestural movements.

5   Conclusion

We could successfully simulate interactions necessary to evaluate the emergency guidance system, which is the example of massively multiagent ubicomp systems. We have tackled scalability issues about smart environments and people inside them [2]. We showed that virtual space can be a participatory simulation platform of smart environments.

We have focused on the case that many people are moving around and interacting with each other in a large-scale crowded smart environment. In that situation, the three different interactions occur. We proposed the three methods, each of which simulates each kind of interaction. Our future work includes unification of the methods.

Acknowledgement. We express our thanks to the Municipal Transportation Bureau and General Planning Bureau of Kyoto city for their cooperation. This work would have been impossible without the invaluable participation of Hideaki Ito, Shinya Shimizu, Tomoyuki Kawasoe, and Toyokazu Itakura. We thank Shigeyuki Okazaki, Toshio Sugiman, Ken Tsutsuguchi, Satoshi Koizumi, CRC Solutions, Mathematical Systems, and CAD Center for their support in the development of the guidance system and the social interaction platform. The platform is available at `http://www.lab7.kuis.kyoto-u.ac.jp/freewalk/` and `http://www.digitalcity.jst.go.jp/Q/`.

References

1. Abowd, G. D., Atkeson, C. G., Bobick, A. F., Essa, I. A., MacIntyre, B., Mynatt, E. D. and Starner, T. E. Living Laboratories: The Future Computing Environments Group at the Georgia Institute of Technology. ACM CHI2000 extended abstracts, 215-216, 2000.
2. Abowd, G. D. and Mynatt, E. D. Charting Past, Present, and Future Research in Ubiquitous Computing. ACM TOCHI, 7(1), 29-58, 2000.
3. Benford, S., Greenhalgh, C., Rodden, T. and Pycock, J. Collaborative Virtual Environments. CACM, 44(7), 79-85, 2001.
4. Bohnenberger, T., Jameson, A., Kruger, A. and Butz, A. Location-Aware Shopping Assistance: Evaluation of a Decision-Theoretic Approach. Mobile HCI 2002, LNCS 2411, 155-169, 2002.
5. Cassell, J., Sullivan, J., Prevost, S. and Churchill, E. Embodied Conversational Agents. MIT Press, 2000.
6. Clark, H. H. Using Language, Cambridge University Press, 1996.
7. Crabtree, A., Benford, S., Rodden, T., Greenhalgh, C., Flintham, M., Anastasi, R., Drozd, A., Adams, M., Row-Farr, J., Tandavanitj, N. and Steed, A. Orchestrating a Mixed Reality Game 'On the Ground'. ACM CHI2004, 391-398, 2004.
8. Drogoul, A., Vanbergue, D. and Meurisse, T. Multi-Agent Based Simulation: Where are the Agents? MABS2002, LNCS 2581, 1-15, 2002.
9. Hall, E. T. The Hidden Dimension. Doubleday, 1966.
10. Helbing, D., Farkas, I. J. and Vicsek, T. Simulating Dynamical Features of Escape Panic. Nature, 407(6803), 487-490, 2000.
11. Ishida, T. Q: A Scenario Description Language for Interactive Agents. IEEE Computer, 35(11), 54-59, 2002.
12. Ishida. T. Society-Centered Design for Socially Embedded Multiagent Systems. CIA2004, LNCS 3191, 16-29, 2004.
13. Kendon, A. Spatial Organization in Social Encounters: the F-formation System. A. Kendon, Ed., Conducting Interaction: Patterns of Behavior in Focused Encounters, Cambridge University Press, 209-237, 1990.
14. Linturi, R., Koivunen, M. and Sulkanen, J. Helsinki Arena 2000 - Augmenting a Real City to a Virtual One. Digital Cities, LNCS 1765, 83-96. 2000.

15. Murakami, Y., Ishida, T., Kawasoe, T. and Hishiyama, R. Scenario Description for Multi-agent Simulation. AAMAS2003, 369-376, 2003.
16. Nagel, K., Kidd, C. D., O'Connell, T., Dey, A. K. and Abowd, G. D. The Family Intercom: Developing a Context-Aware Audio Communication System. Ubicomp2001, LNCS 2201, 176-183, 2001.
17. Nakanishi, H., Nakazawa, S., Ishida, T., Takanashi, K. and Isbister, K. Can Software Agents Influence Human Relations? - Balance Theory in Agent-mediated Communities -. AAMAS2003, 717-724. 2003.
18. Nakanishi, H., Koizumi, S., Ishida, T. and Ito, H. Transcendent Communication: Location-Based Guidance for Large-Scale Public Spaces. ACM CHI2004, 655-662, 2004.
19. Nakanishi, H. and Ishida, T. FreeWalk/Q: Social Interaction Platform in Virtual Space. ACM VRST2004, 97-104, 2004.
20. Nakanishi, H., Shimizu, S. and Isbister, K. Sensitizing Social Agents for Virtual Training. Applied Artificial Intelligence, 19, 2005. (to appear)
21. Patterson, M. L. Nonverbal Behavior: a Functional Perspective, Springer-Verlag, 1983.
22. Reeves, B. and Nass, C. The Media Equation: How People Treat Computers, Television, and New Media Like Real People and Places. Cambridge University Press, 1996.
23. Reynolds, C. W. Flocks, Herds, and Schools: A Distributed Behavioral Model. ACM SIGGRAPH87, 25-34, 1987.
24. Scherer, K., London, H. and Wolf, J. The Voice of Confidence: Paralinguistic Cues and Audience Evaluation. Journal of Research in Personality. 7, 31-44, 1973.
25. Sugiman T. and Misumi J. Development of a New Evacuation Method for Emergencies: Control of Collective Behavior by Emergent Small Groups. Journal of Applied Psychology, 73(1), 3-10, 1988.
26. Tepper, D. T. and Haase, R. F. Verbal and Nonverbal Communication of Facilitative Conditions. C. E. Hill Ed., Helping Skills: The Empirical Foundation, 211-223, 1978/2001.
27. Timney, B. and London, H. Body Language Concomitants of Persuasiveness and Persuasibility in Dyadic Interaction. International Journal of Group Tensions, 3, 48-67, 1973.
28. Zimbardo, P. G. and Leippe, M. R. The Psychology of Attitude Change and Social Influence. McGraw-Hill, 1991.

SmartRescue: Multi Agent System Based on Location and Context Aware Information

Jung-Jin Yang and Dong-Hoon Lee

School of Computer Science and Information Engineering,
The Catholic University of Korea,
Yeouido Post Office, P.O.Box 960,
35-1 Yeouido-dong, Yeongdeungpo-gu, Seoul, Korea (150-010)
Tel: +82-2-2164-4377, Fax: +82-2-2164-4777,
{jungjin, rephaser}@catholic.ac.kr

Abstract. Computing environments are now evolving into ubiquitous environments upon this new infrastructure. The mobile device in a ubiquitous environment provides services that do not restrict the user from accessing the data wherever the person may be. Various mobile services have been modeled upon this environment, and due to the increasingly refined tastes and desires of the customers, intelligent agents with high performance levels along with user view interface are in demand.

Diverse tools and information resources undergo interactions and mutual communication in a ubiquitous environment. To improve such interoperability, this article suggests a multi-agent system through web ontology links. In particular, the work presents an effective model for an Emergency Search and Rescue System based on the mobile service and multi-agents which aid in improving the existing system, and also discusses the base technology and limitations that may occur in the process of establishing this system.

Keywords: Ubiquitous Computing, Semantic Web Service, Negotiation, Context-Aware System.

1 Introduction

Our nation's drastic increase of the cell phone user population of more than 30 million people and the growth of mobile technology have contributed in building an infrastructure that enables individuals to connect to network terminals. Moreover, services beyond the basic phone call, such as mobile banking or game and data services are now on the rise owing to the portability of the cell phone. Recent computing environments are now advancing into ubiquitous environments on the basis of such new infrastructures. The purpose of the ubiquitous environment is to fulfill the "5A Rule" in which readily "Accessible" and "Affordable" data is available to "Anybody," "Anytime," "Anywhere." The mobile device in a ubiquitous environment provides services that do not restrict the user from accessing the data wherever the person may be. Various mobile services have been modeled upon this environment, and due to the increasingly refined tastes and desires of the customers, agents with high performance levels along with user view interface are in demand.

T. Ishida, L. Gasser, and H. Nakashima (Eds.): MMAS 2004, LNAI 3446, pp. 295 – 308, 2005.

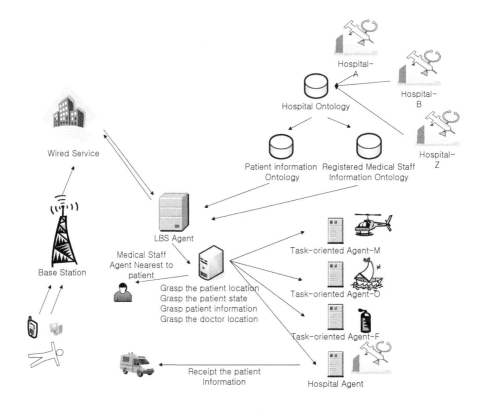

Fig. 1. System Framework

Diverse tools and information resources undergo interactions and mutual communication in a ubiquitous environment. To improve such interoperability, this article suggests a multi-agent system through web ontology links.

A constituent of community computing in a ubiquitous computing environment is a basic unit enabled with autonomous ability to achieve a goal given through interaction with others. Including micro agents suitable for constituents of community computing with limited resources, massively multi agent system is also required to support both massive parallelism and mutual assistant relationships among numerous constituents in this environment.

This article 1) presents a system model employing mobile services 2) lists required technologies 3) proposes the processes that must precede this model 4) suggests the linkage between the service model and ontology in order to understand the user's request and 5) suggests a negotiation model that would be created by the exchange in messages by the brokers and service providers. In chapter 2, an emergency rescue scenario employing the suggested system model is introduced. In chapter 3, the system framework is discussed in relation to the scenario. In chapter 4, the methodology of establishing the system is introduced. In chapter 5, the structural limitations of the current system and new directions for improvement and future work are discussed.

2 Motivating Scenario

This is an example of a hypothetical scenario in which the suggested system model is employed.

A person hurt himself by stumbling over a rock in the mountains. He is able to send an emergency rescue request and information about his state of breathing difficulties possibly related his genetic disorder via his mobile device, which is then delivered to the broker. The broker identifies the location of the injured person, and according to the information given by the user decides which emergency service to provide. The broker recognizes that the injured person is unable to move and therefore requests the mountain rescue squad for help. At the same time, the broker contacts the closest hospital to quickly supply medical treatment, and informs a person in the vicinity who is registered and capable of first aid treatment (usually a doctor) about the emergency. The doctor receives information (such as previous medical records, physical state, particular details etc.) and the location of the injured person through his/her mobile device, which ensures the injured person of a speedy and accurate emergency treatment.

Figure 1 shows the flow of the emergency rescue service based on the scenario. The scenario above functions on the following assumptions.

- Services are provided within Location Based Services limits
- The user's requests are sent to a mediator (broker)
- The broker uses Context Aware System to select the task to be executed
- A registered agent exists for every service that is executed upon the request of a broker
- Service providers maintain and update scattered databases.

3 System Framework

This chapter discusses the system organization required to properly execute the scenario presented in the previous chapter. The user in Figure 1 possesses a mobile device of Wipi platform, and the telecommunication company has a LBS agent that is capable of locating the user with a device ID. There is also a broker between the user and the provider, which is responsible for identifying the situation and negotiating. Moreover, in case of emergency, the ontology of the user profile functions to provide information about the user. The order of services provided upon receiving an emergency help request is as follows.

3.1 Information Transmission

Upon receiving an emergency help request, the LBS agent locates the user by identifying the user's device and transmits the user's information to the broker. To establish the LBS technology and system, the following issues must be considered. The LBS system can be divided into Position Determination Technology using communications network or GPS to locate mobile devices, and applied technology such as the LBS platform technology. [Figure 2] shows a general LBS system configuration diagram [1].

3.1.1 Position Determination Technology

Position Determination Technology is employed to identify the location of a mobile device. PDT methods may be categorized as Network-based if it employs the communications network reception signals, Handset-based if it uses the GPS receptor mounted on the mobile device, or Hybrid if these two methods are mixed.

The Network-based method does not require a special installation, but the accuracy in locating a user differs greatly depending on the size of a base station or the gauging methods. Normally, the error span ranges from 100 meters to several kilometers. The Handset-based method requires additional GPS reception apparatus and is comparatively more accurate than the Network-based method. However, in cities with many skyscrapers or in forests with a dense tree population, signal reception may be obstructed therefore hindering the decision of determining the location of the user. The Hybrid method or the Assisted-GPS technology is undergoing research to overcome the limitations the two former methods carry by combining the two. Since the Position Determination Technology is the fundamental base of LBS, various

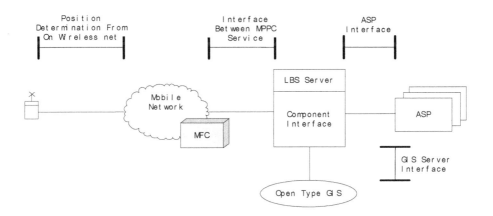

Fig. 2. LBS System Framework

Table 1. Major Features of LBS Technology

	Cell-ID	AOA	TOA	TDOA	E-OTD	A-GPS
accuracy (m)	in radius of cell	According to LOS	150	100~500	50~150	5~100
terminal modification	×	×	×	SW	SW	SW/HW
net modification	×	Array	○	SW	SW/HW	SW/HW
response time	20 seconds	10 seconds	some seconds	some seconds	5 seconds	5 seconds
environment	besides of shadow area	LOS service area	city	city	city	satellite signal good area

studies are conducted to reinforce the two major axes of this research, which are time and location, in other words, to reduce the response time and increase the accuracy of locating a user. Cell-ID, AOA, TOA, TDOA, E-OTD are technologies that employ the Network-based method. A-GPS uses the Handset-based technology that depends on the GPS receptor installed in the mobile device.

Table 1 explains the major features of each technology. The rescue system suggested in this article requires maximum accuracy in minimum response time. Also, the user should not be restricted by the surrounding environment in requesting emergency rescue. The Hybrid method, in which the GPS and the Network-based methods are combined, seems to be the most plausible method that suffices the requirements above and therefore will be assumed as the suitable method in this rescue system.

3.1.2 Position Determination Technology

LBS Platform Technology is responsible for network access and network management between mobile communication network and the LBS applied technology. It also manages location information and provides supplementary functions required to properly execute services. LBS platform provides the most fundamental and essential functions for the LBS, which is composed of various parts which are as follows: the LBS Server provides location services such as communication network access and management, location and information services, taxation and roaming services; the Location Data Server is responsible for the real time processing of the mass of mobile device location information; the Location Application Server provides the common facilities of various methods needed to support LBS through a Standard Interface.

3.2 Context Awareness System

The suggested scenario mentions a hospital ontology which includes an adequate plan and procedure in handling an emergency. This ontology and the user cooperate under a Query model to acquire appropriate information that corresponds to a certain situation. This chapter introduces the ontology and Query model methods used for situation-recognition. Situation-recognition procedures will be discussed in part 4.

3.2.1 Ontology

The term "ontology" carries a slightly different meaning from the generic database. The general database is a mere data storage tank, but an ontology redefines the existing data according to consistent formats (XML, RDF, OWL). The Query model mentioned in this article is also a type of an ontology [2]. Once it receives a rescue request query from a user, the ontology perceives information that the user needs via the broker's Query model, and the ontology searches for a solution to provide the appropriate service to the user. The ontology is created and shared by the experts of each field and is, therefore, the most dependable source of information.

3.2.2 Query Model

The Query model in Figure 3 is used to sort the accurate understanding of the user's rescue request and the corresponding rescue methods [3].

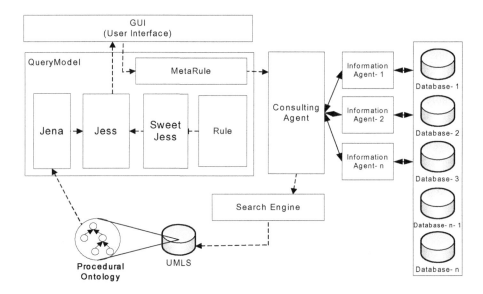

Fig. 3. Query Model

- Meta Rule - The Meta Rule is employed when selecting the most appropriate ontology from various fields of study. Since the scenario suggested concerns emergencies and patients requesting immediate attention, the Meta Rule would fix the hospital ontology as the default so that the time spent in finding the information would be reduced [4].

- Consulting Agent - The Consulting Agent searches for an Information Agent based on the queries from users or queries resulting from the Query model. UMLS and other components of the Query model are utilized to rephrase a query given by a user.

- UMLS Search Engine - This is the engine used to locate the UMLS.

- UMLS - The UMLS carries all of the ontologies, and it searches the adequate ontology that possesses the pertinent information of the UMLS based on the information submitted by the Consulting Agent. The suggested scenario framework is structures upon an emergency, therefore, several ontologies concerning emergency procedures are set as the default which will reduce the time needed to search certain data.

- JENA - The JENA switches the ontology information (in RDF format) into RuleML format of the JESS, which handles the inferential function.

- SweeJess - The SweeJess switches previously stipulated rules (about emergencies) into RuleML format of the JESS, which handles the inferential function.

- JESS - The JESS combines the information and rules deriving from the ontologies to create re-queries. [5]

This system employs ontologies and the Query model to accurately determine and quickly understand the user's situation. The broker in this framework uses both the ontology and the Query model.

3.3 Negotiation

The broker searches for the most appropriate service provider by negotiating with the closest emergency agent, according to the information about the emergency situation acquired by the Query model mentioned above, and upon recognizing the situation, provides information of the situation and the user to the service provider. Negotiation results will differ for each case. For example, if a person who is lost requests rescue, the person's user information would not be transmitted since the location information given to the LBS Agent would suffice in the rescue process. Detailed framework of the negotiation process is discussed in chapter 4.

3.4 Resolving the Situation

Numerous agents participate in effectively resolving the situation. Agents associate with the service provider and utilize the ontologies to provide the optimal information. In our model, the details regarding the issue of user privacy is excluded and it presumes user information exposed under prior user permission.

3.4.1 Emergency Agent
The emergency agent closest to the scene of emergency occurrence provides the user information to the appropriate service provider (the hospital in the case of the suggested scenario). The emergency agent employs the ontology related to the service provider to analyze past records and infer the user's current status, which enables the agent to properly manage the situation. Such analyses and inferences are transmitted to the service providers who discuss the matter with other experts based on the information retrieved by the agent.

Though the inferences drawn by the ontology are appropriate, unexpected situations may occur in case of emergencies; therefore, experts undergo another round of thorough analyzing process. For example, if natural disasters (such as a snow storm or heavy rainfall) were to occur after receiving the information, weather factors could not have been reported by the user at the time of a rescue request, hence the Query model modeled upon this request cannot properly execute the rescue process without considering these exceptional factors.

3.4.2 Provider
The providers are the service experts who are the actual people providing the service in the rescue process. The providers depend on the information given about the emergency situation and the appropriate process of resolving this situation in order to execute the rescue process quickly and accurately.

- Medical institutions - The medical institutions receive information beforehand to analyze and prepare for the situation and readily deal with the problem as soon as their services are requested.

- Rescue institutions - When an emergency situation occurs, the rescue institutions receive the user's information and dispatch rescue teams that are most compatible with the situation or the place of emergency. Detailed information on the user's status is constantly updated and transmitted to the rescue team by the rescue institution.

Emergency Personnel Service
The broker receives information about the service providers from the emergency agent and transmits this information to the LBS agent, which in turn requests rescue to the emergency personnel (usually doctors) who are closest to the user or in the same communication network as the user.

4 Methodology

Chapter 4 discusses the technology and methodology of executing the suggested system model.

4.1 Three-Tier Based M-Service

In the suggested system model, the broker receives a request from the user and searches an agent that would provide sufficient services to the user. This is based on a Three-Tier M-Service Negotiation model.[6] The Three-Tier M-Service system is composed of the following: the Data View which stores mass data and retrieves the pertinent data according to the user's needs, the Process View which connects the user and the Data View, and the User Interface View which provides different interfaces according to the different mobile devices of the users. Each component of the Three-Tier M-Service model is explained in detail below.

4.1.1 User Interface View
The User Interface serves to provide the appropriate interface to the user according to the compatibility of different mobile devices. The capacity and limitations differ for each mobile device. The same information is displayed in a different fashion depending on the type of the user's mobile device (such as the PDA or WAP). The implementation of such User Interface is easy with the current XML technology. The XML document object can be transformed into a XML Scheme by the XML processor and a presentation object by the XSL style sheet. Information with User Interfaces can be diverse with multi-modality.

4.1.2 Process View
The Process View in a negotiation model is the link between the Interface View and the Data View. Numerous Base Processes, or the basic execution routine exists in this model. The Process View is the structural subset of the process defined by and deriving from the Base Process. It acts as the main functioning mechanism in the negotiation model.

4.1.3 Data View

The Data View is the set of tables carrying the information needed in executing a process. The Data View is the database possessing the information requested by the user. The user's request is transmitted to the Data View via the Process View, and the data is appropriately displayed since it has been customized according to the User Interface. The following shows the methods of implementing the components in a Three-Tier M-Service model.

4.2 User Interface View

The User Interface View functions on the premise that a Wipi platform is employed. The simplest method should be used when making a speedy rescue request in an emergency. For example, on pressing the special function button of the mobile device registered by the user, the rescue request application operates and the broker registers the report. The broker possesses a Plan Structure within the database which defines the Query model to execute the situation-recognition process. The broker transmits the first query (the root node in the query tree, see Figure 4) to the rescue request application. The user sends a response (chooses from the closes node) to the broker and the broker sends the next query. This process is repeated (until the external node of the query tree is reached by depth expansion) to collect the information needed to perceive the situation.

The user application, like the User Interface View, also functions on the premise that the application is performed on the Wipi platform. The advantage of using a Wipi platform is that the User Interface application does not have to be implemented for each communication network that the user has subscribed since the platform has been standardized [7].

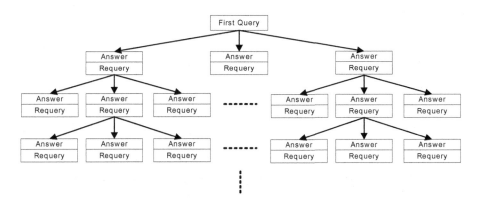

Fig. 4. Query Tree Example

4.3 Process View

4.3.1 Sequence Diagram

The system process can be divided into two sequential parts. Figure 5 shows the process among the user, LBS agent, and the broker through a sequence diagram. The process is initiated with the transmission of the user's information in an emergency, and is continued by the LBS agent which sends location information of the user and the emergency personnel based on the basic information of the subscribers. The broker, upon receiving the information, communicates with the situation-recognition and service agents and reports the progress and the result to the user. However, only after brokers execute their main task of recognizing the situation and negotiating are such processes able to operate properly.

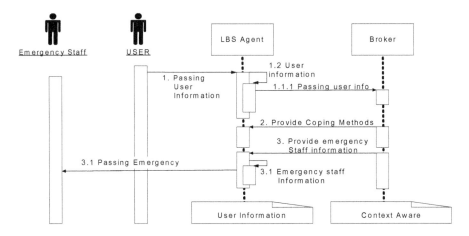

Fig. 5. Sequence Diagram for System Process

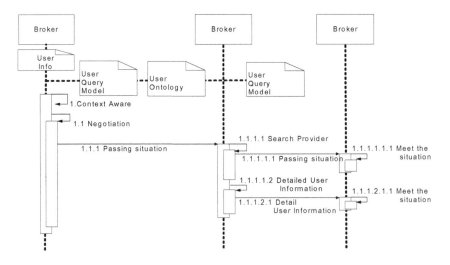

Fig. 6. Sequence Diagram for Emergency Situation

Figure 6 shows the process among the broker, emergency agents, and the provider through a sequence diagram. Based on the information provided by the user, the broker connects to the shared ontologies and employs the Query model for situation-recognition. The results acquired through situation-recognition become the object of negotiation between the broker and the providers to select the adequate service and provider for the user. The information, resulting from the negotiation that is transmitted to emergency agents, searches for adequate providers by presenting inferred material about the user. Figure 6 is the handling process of an emergency situation deriving from negotiation, but not all cases experience the handling process mentioned above. The role of the broker is the most important part in this model. Depending on the broker's situation-recognition and negotiation, the sequence diagram above would change drastically.

4.3.2 Context Aware System
There are two approaches in implementing the Context Aware System. The first approach is when a designer implements the application by combining structural services or traits. The second approach employs abstraction by the designer so that the designer may consider the application of the object on a more sophisticated level. Required instrumental techniques that avail in improving the situation-recognition application and development are as follows: acquiring and approaching a situation, independently storing, distributing and executing situation-recognition information deriving from situation-recognition application. Upon this framework, the method of combining the structural services is used.

If the state of a situation is considered when providing sufficient information or services to the user, this process is identified as the situation-recognition system and the general information of the state is classified as follows: 1) user status 2) physical environment status 3) computing system status 4) user-computer interaction history 5) other unclassified status. User status and physical environment status are required in the framework of a general situation-recognition classification. In analyzing the user status, the user's identification and medical records are transmitted from the user ontology, and by cooperating with the medical ontology and the Query model, the user's emergency situation is recognized. The information that has undergone this process is then transmitted to the hospital agent. Technical support is necessary for situation-recognition that depends on physical status information such as the pulse, blood pressure, body temperature, amount of blood flow, and dormant characteristics.

In the case of the physical environment status, corresponding agents or communication networks rather than brokers function to filter status information that is sent to rescue agents. The user is located via LBS and the location information is sent to communication networks or other agents in order to notify the location of the emergency and its physical environment status. In other words, the physical status does not recognize the user status nor the situation but only receives the situation information [8]. Medical ontology (or certain database are also eligible) must be established by experts in order to accurately diagnose the patient's status in an emergency. This process must precede the service suggested in this article for the service to be implemented properly.

The broker possesses a type of medical diagnosis to analyze the patient's status. The medical diagnosis is the collection of all the information gathered from medical ontologies and the user's query process. The broker executes re-queries until the medical diagnosis is sufficiently completed. After completing the medical diagnosis, the broker transmits the set of information to the medical center agents where the patient's status may be analyzed beforehand to make appropriate preparatory measures in advance. The broker functions to provide pertinent services effectively upon a user's request. Therefore, the broker must accurately recognize the situation based on the provided user information. The broker determines service providers and the level of service provided according to the user request information.[9]

The worst situation that may occur in the suggested scenario is when a user requests rescue with a mere location information. The user may not even respond to re-queries. In this case, the broker must deduce the service providers and the degree of service that is necessary. Even in cases where there is a lack of situation-recognition information, the broker must be ready to make the best decision for the user.

Therefore, the broker uses the location information with the provided data and cooperates with emergency information ontologies to infer the services the user may need. The JADE (Java Agent Development Environment) is used as the middleware in this framework to support Agent Management, Agent Communication, and Agent Interaction protocols as in Figure 7.

4.3.3 Negotiation

Negotiation is the communication between more than two agents endeavoring to fulfill their individual tasks. Each agent draws up a "deal" to make a common plan that would satisfy every party participating in the negotiation.

The Contract Net Protocol functions to resolve cooperative efforts among agents, provides solutions to connection problems, and searches for agents that would execute the given tasks. The scenario is based on a FIPA Contract Net Interaction Protocol (IP), which has been modified with added functions of "communication acts," such as

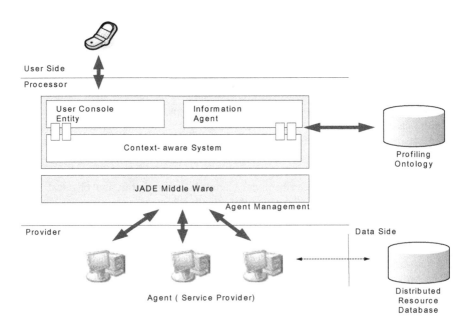

Fig. 7. JADE-based Agent Platform

rejection and confirmation, from the previous Contract Net Interaction Protocols. The initiator assures that more than one participant executes a task, functions as a Manager to maximize the usage of certain ability, and either approves or rejects agents in a given process. Emergency Rescue scenario depends heavily on the urgency of service request, and therefore, it is assumed that the maximum level of service is offered by the service provider. The broker begins negotiating with the provider after selecting the service provider and the level of service to be provided.

The broker tries to obtain the maximum service options from the provider and compares this with the minimum options obtained through the deduction process that must be provided to the user. If no information overlaps, the standard service level is applied, according to the degree of urgency. If information overlaps, the service level and congestion levels of the Service Provider Profiling Ontology are considered in determining the final service level.

5 Discussion and Future Work

This article suggests a web service model that introduces multi-agents and brokers based on the growing population of mobile device users and new infrastructures resulting from the drastic increase of such users.

Brokers were defined as the mediator that classified agents according to their roles, and the message transmission process between the broker and the agents were introduced. In this framework, the brokers are responsible for the collection and dispersion of multi-agents. The broker transmits individual tasks from the central unit to each agent and by distributing the functions, traffic and actual costs of status information transmission are reduced. Moreover, brokers interact with other agents which enable the brokers to function as multi-brokers that are able to carry out the tasks of brokers from different fields.

Also, as a methodology of implementing the system, usable current technology and issues concerning current technology have been discussed. Before implementing the system, several issues must precede the system. First, information must be secured. User and location information are constantly exchanged among brokers and agents to provide the adequate services for the user. The protection of personal information must be guaranteed for every process of the system.

Second, the assumptions of the system framework must be implemented. The medical information database and the medical personnel information database are some of the presupposed functions that need to be established.

Third, the standardization of the Wipi platform must be completed. The Wipi platform is undergoing standardization processes for various fields, but especially, the standardization process for LBS and XML support is imperative for the system.

The model exhibits its limitation when unintended situations occur (when the emergency is unable to be transmitted to the broker). To overcome this limitation, the connection may be substituted by a constantly open mode as opposed to the existing temporary connectors that would always wait on the agent, which would exclude the user's actions from the interaction process. Hardware technology that can recognize the situation is necessary to implement a waiting mode for the no-hand status. This framework depends mainly on the possibility of providing the LBS service and its negotiation process with other agents. A system that would provide location information must also be implemented in order to transmit location information to rescue agents.

Acknowledgement

This work has been supported by both the KISTEP under grant number M10430010004-04L3001-00400 and the grant of the Korea Health 21 R&D Project, Ministry of Health & Welfare, Republic of Korea under grant number 0412-MI02-0404-0002.

References

1. Institution of Korea Patent Information, "LBS: Location Based Service."
2. World Wide Web Consortium (W3C), http://www.w3.org/2001/sw.
3. Grosof, B.N., Gandhe, M.D., and Finin, T.W.(2003). "SweetJess: Inferencing in Situated Courteous RuleML via Translation to and from Jess Rules," Working paper, version of May, 2003.
4. Rule Markup Language Initiative. http://www.ruleml.org   and http://www.ebusiness.mit. edu/bgrosof/#RuleML.
5. Jess, http://herzberg.ca.sandia.gov/jess/.
6. Dickson K. W. Chiu, S. S. Sheung, Eleanna Kafeza, Ho-Fung Leung "A Three-Tier View-Based Methodology for M-Services Adaption"
7. The Korea Standards Forum of Wireless Internet. http://www.kwisforum.org
8. Mostefaoui, G.K.; Pasquier-Rocha, J.; Brezillon, P., "Context-aware computing: a guide for the pervasive computing community" In. Proceedings of the IEEE/ACS International Conference on Pervasive Services , July 2004 Pages:39 - 48
9. Chen, H.; Finin, T.; Joshi, A., "Semantic Web in the context broker architecture", In Proceedings of the Second IEEE Annual Conference on Pervasive Computing and Communications, March 2004.

Multiagent-Based Demand Bus
Simulation for Shanghai

Zhiqiang Liu[1], Toru Ishida[2], and Huanye Sheng[1]

[1] Department of Computer Science and Engineering, Shanghai Jiao Tong University,
200030, Shanghai, China
zqliu@sjtu.edu.cn, hysheng@mail.sjtu.edu.cn
[2] Department of Social Informatics, Kyoto University, Kyoto, Japan
ishida@i.kyoto-u.ac.jp

Abstract. Demand Bus System, a new public transportation system, is expected to be a convenient service for special transportation demands to solve more and more serious traffic problems concerning metropolises as Shanghai. Under this background, this paper focuses on evaluating the usability of the demand bus system rather than on the algorithms as the previous researches did. As a useful evaluation tool for achieving this objective, Multi-Agent Based Simulation is used to obtain a better understanding of such system in particular when lacking real applications for a large scale. By using the participatory solution, we propose a multiagent simulation framework to include domain experts, stakeholders, system users, as well as computer scientists to build and modify the computational model directly. The implementation of the prototype system shows that it is easy to build such system from scratch to mega by this mechanism. Initial analysis shows the demand bus system is a convenient service supplement to the fast transportation for community in Shanghai.

1 Introduction

Shanghai, which is one of the biggest cities in China with a population of about 18 million, is faced with more and more serious traffic problems along with the city's development in size and economy. The latest statistic of traffic flow at rush hours shows 20,000 per hour in the main entrances of Central Business District. The average velocity of bus is less than 9 km. per hour. People have to spend lots of time back and forth for work because of the long distance and the terrible traffic jams. More and more people turn to use the bicycles as main mode for their daily trips. However, there are no fixed bicycle lanes in most areas, the bicycles have to occupy the automobile lanes, which has aggravated the deterioration of the traffic jams. It is estimated that the average daily passengers of Shanghai is about 35 million. But public transit is far away from meeting the people's needs. Table 1 shows the traffic situation of Shanghai in 2003. Public transportation only accounted for 21 % of total passenger traffic. Bus, as the most important mode of public transportation, is complained for its slowness, inconvenience, and inflexibility. Most buses are

T. Ishida, L. Gasser, and H. Nakashima (Eds.): MMAS 2004, LNAI 3446, pp. 309–322, 2005.

centralized in the main areas. Those people who live a bit far away from these areas should schedule their outgoing plan carefully to catch the buses. Furthermore, no matter crowded or not, buses move along fixed route and stop at every station even no passenger gets on/off the bus.

Many policies had been proposed to improve the traffic situation, which include how to induce the vehicles and how to control the automobiles in rush hours. But they could not overcome the shortcomings of bus service and could not change the situation of those people who live in the area with few buses. We seek a more flexible service to improve the convenience of people's trip and decrease the number of bicycles used.

Table 1. The public transportation statistic in Shanghai (2003)

Transportation	Route Length	Vehicle Amount	Passengers	Percentage
Bus	22,110 km	18,625	7,460,000	21
Taxi	-	48,672	1,360,000	0.4
Subway	108.65 km	445	1,110,000	0.3

Demand Bus System (DBS), also called Demand Response System, is thought to be a new way to provide convenient transportation services for special demands. The user calls a bus center and states his location, destination and the preferred time. After the bus center arranges a suitable bus to execute the task, user waits for the bus coming. It's faster and more convenient than public bus service, and cheaper than taxi service. With the development of Shanghai, the city is divided into many small parts with different functions. Some are living centers, some are working centers, and others are shopping or entertainment centers. It's convenient for several people to take one car for work or shopping. Such Car-sharing activities are burgeoning fast in Shanghai, but they are spontaneous actions and it is difficult to say what role they act in improving the situation in large areas because they are still limited by many facts. We hope DBS can be a community transportation service to meet people's needs and to improve the fleet utilization in Shanghai, which in turn, would decrease the number of automobiles and bicycles. Before applying such service, we need look deeply, and make suitable strategies to operate a system suitable for Shanghai.

Different demand bus services had been provided for people all over the world. But people found it's difficult to build perfect DBSs in different situations and there is no successful application used for large city as one of main service modes. A rich variety of demand bus problems emerge from the characteristics of the servers, the rides, the metric space, and the objective function. The problems have been studied extensively in the literature, for example, by Hunsaker and Savelsbergh[1], Diana and Dessouky[2], and Healy and Moll[3].These researches mainly concentrated on the algorithms to optimize the solutions, and few done on the framework to investigate the effectiveness and the strategy. This has induced the need for suitable methodologies and tools to help in investigating the effectiveness and the strategy of DBS. A useful evaluation tool for achieving this objective, in particular when lacking real applications for large scale is Multi-Agent Based Simulation (MABS). In this context, it is used as the process of designing and creating a model of a likely or expected public transportation system for conducting numerical experiments. The purpose is to obtain a better understanding of the behaviors of such a system in a given set of conditions, even with uncertain treatment of events. In order to describe the interaction between human and agents, we use the interaction design language Q, which has been proved to be a good language, to build such simulation.

In section 2, we propose a multiagent simulation framework. A prototype system using this framework is implemented, and some simulations and experimental results for using demand bus in Shanghai are made in section 3. Conclusion and future work are discussed in the last section.

2   DBS Simulation Framework

2.1   Problem Description

The problem under consideration is related to a number of other well-studied routing problems, among which more closely relevant is a variation known as the dial-a-ride problem, which can be specified informally as follows. Servers are traveling in some metric space to serve requests for rides. Each request is characterized by two points in the metric space as $R(s,d,tw)$: a source (s), the starting point of the ride, and a destination (d), the end point of the ride. The tw means the time window of the ride. It can be defined as the start time or the arrival time. This is a combined routing and scheduling problem. Generally, routing and scheduling problems involve both task precedence relations and time window constraints. Task precedence relations force the pickup activity for a task to precede the delivery activity for the task. The time window constraints require that a task should be finished even it would possibly violate optimality criterion.

In the demand bus system, the customer origins are unknown in advance and are served at a time, thus the problem is to design routes dynamically for the servers through the metric space, so that all requested rides are made and some optimality criterion is met. Metrics to be minimized could be number of buses, distance traveled, lateness at customer sites, etc. Many variations of the problem exist, such as time windows within which customers must be served, multiple depots, etc.

Considering the complex situation mentioned above, we look forward a simulation system to be designed and implemented flexibly. In the design process, not only computer professionals, but those domain experts, stakeholders in the field of bus system operation should be involved. Further more, as users of demand bus system, people's experiences and requirements to the service should also be considered carefully. People should easily be involved to try the new service, not only by giving advices before the system is designed, but also by participating in the experiment through analyzing the simulation reports. That is to say, we need a platform to design the simulation for different roles and an easy way to realize the system. Thus, one of the most necessary requirements placed on agents is the capability to interact with users. To unify agent-to-agent and human-to-agent interaction, we introduce Q language - a scenario description language for describing interaction among agents and users.

2.2 Interaction Design Language: Q

Some inter-agent protocol description languages, such as KQML and AgenTalk, often regulate an agent's various actions on the basis of computational model of agent's internal mechanisms. Obviously, these agents based on strict computational models have to be designed and developed by computer experts. In order to build a model more close to reality, participatory method is involved during the design process. Participatory method is a kind of way by which participants work together to share the understanding and to build a computational model to simulate research phenomena. It is necessary to design a new agent interaction description language, which makes it possible that those non-computer-professional application designers, such as sales managers and consumers, might write scenarios that describe and model the behaviors of agents, so that a practical multiagent system can be easily established and modified. Under the background, we start working on Q language [4] - a scenario description language for designing interaction among agents and humans. This kind of scenario-based language is used to design interaction from the viewpoint of scenario description, but not for describing agent's internal mechanisms.

Q extends scheme by introducing sensing /acting function and guard command to realize scenario description. The basic facilities of Q language for scenario description include Cue, Action, Scenario and Agent.

Cue is defined as a sensing function, which represents agent's perception to its outside environment. A cue doesn't produce any side effect on the environment. For example, we define cue a sensing function as following:

```
(defcue ?getDemandRequest (from out) (request in))
```

It is used to sense any request form user. When Demand Bus Service Center gets request form user, it will start to deal with the request. The action Demand Bus Service Center will take in Q language is defined as Action function. Action may change and impose effects on the environment of agent system. We defined an action function:

```
(defaction !broadcastRequest (to out) (request out))
```

It is used for Demand Bus Service Center to announce a new request for all buses to bid for the task. Lots of such Cues and Actions compose a Scenario that represents the situation agents would act. A simple scenario as following shows what an agent would do when it senses the environment.

```
(defscenario scenario-buscenter(&pattern ($request ""))
  (WaitingforServiceRequest
   ((?getUserRequest :request $request)
    (!broadcastRequest :to bus :request $request)
    (go WaitingforServiceRequest))))
```

The Executable structure of Q scenario, shown in Fig1, consists of Control Layer and Execution Layer [8]. In the Control Layer, when Q scenario is assigned to one agent, the message processor would be created and be bound to this agent. At the same time, Q interpreter would send the cues and actions to agent to execute according to the scenario. Q language focuses on the logic representation of

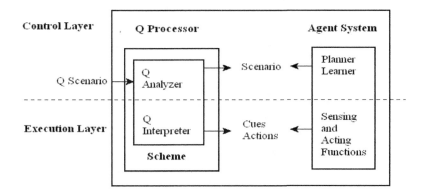

Fig. 1. Executable Structure of *Q* Scenario

interaction of human and agent. It does not care the implement method. So it is easy to create system with different algorithms and different situations. A complex behavior of agent can be realized by the combination of scenarios. We can extend agent system flexibly by creating lots of scenarios and implemental module warehouse.

Conclusively, the most prominent property of *Q* language is its simplicity on both design and application of agent systems. *Q* language can support many totally different agent systems, such as FreeWalk [5] and Crisis Management [6] for its powerful ability of describing human requests to agents. As mentioned in the previous part, DBS is such a complex system that we need lots of interactions between agents and humans. *Q* language provides a very simple but   highly practical and realistic way to design such system.

2.3 Simulation Framework

Generally speaking, as to large scale events simulation, computer scientists used to build computational model based on researchers' experiences and implement the platform for domain experts to do some experiments. They would improve the model according to the simulation result until researchers are satisfied with the simulation performance. That is to say domain experts are only involved before the model is designed and after the simulation system is implemented. This method could not overcome the fundamental limitations and pitfalls of computer modeling – the gap between the computational model and reality. In most occasions, computer scientists would not completely comprehend the research problem simply by requirement analysis process. Furthermore in a complicated system, it's impossible for people to have a whole view to such system, especially to a new kind of service. So the model might be far away from what we really need to examine in experiment. In order to walk more close to the reality, we hire participatory solution- let domain experts and system users design the system by themselves. This kind of participatory solution is used not only during the design period, but also in the experiments. As we discussed before, no mater in which period, people can modify or add the scenario which

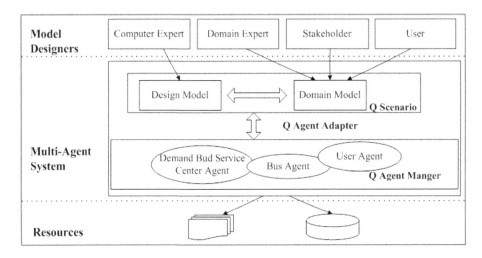

Fig. 2. Multiagent Framework for Demand Bus Simulation

describes the agent action. Computer scientists only need to implement the actions designed in the scenarios. It's very convenient to improve the performance and extend the system form scratch to mega by this mechanism.

According to this, we divide the system framework into three parts (Fig 2): Model designers, multiagent system and resources.

In the design process, we divide the whole computational model into two parts: design model and domain model. Design model shows us the structure of system, the relationship of system components, protocols, and other elements. It's mainly created by the computer scientists. At the same time domain experts, stakeholders, and users would exchange their knowledge to build the domain model, which focuses on the mechanism of research domain such as logic of behavior. Another work the computer scientists should do is to integrate the two parts. As shown in Fig 3, the simulation design is a circulative process to improve the performance step by step. During the process, computer scientists, domain experts and stakeholders would set up an ideal system and group the agents. In order to understand the behaviors of agents, the state transition of each group is built. In the state transition, I means input, that is information agent gets in the environment and O means output, that is action agent would take. In each state, agent may be faced with much different information and it will take many different actions. This kind of state machine mechanism provides domain experts a simple but powerful tool to describe the logic of agent behavior. After the computational model is created, scenario writers interpreter it into Q scenario and programmers implement actions and cues in the scenario. Researchers observe the simulation performance and modify the domain model. By setting up code warehouses and scenario depositary, we can improve domain model in a flexible way and reduce the dependence on computer scientists. After repeating such process for lots of time, we can get the best simulation system and experiment result.

Multiagent system includes three parts: Q scenario, Q agent manager, Q agent adapter. Q scenario describes agents' states, cues and actions, which are designed according to the simulation model. *Q* agent manager, who is in charge of the management of agents, includes the implementation of cues and actions described in scenario. It also serves as a message layer for the communication between agents. We had discussed the execution of *Q* agent manager in Section 2.2. *Q* agent adapter creates a link between above two parts.

The resources part includes all digital maps, traffic statistics, and route history et al. Agents could not own all information they need during the simulation. All of these outer resources help us apply more complicated scenarios and to examine more facts that would have influence on the behaviors of agents.

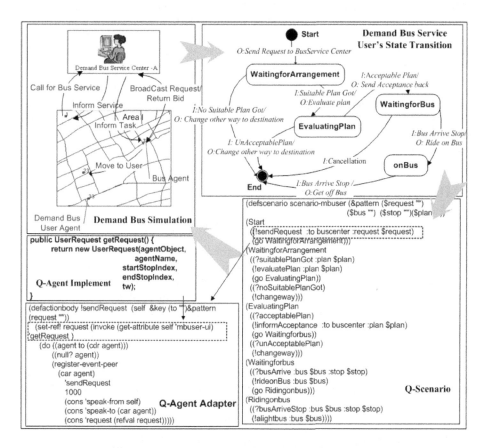

Fig. 3. Illustration of Multiagent System Design Process

2.4 Simplified Sequential Insertion Heuristic Algorithm

There are lots of algorithms proposed for Dial-a-Ride problem. Among them, some are used in the static system, and some are used in dynamic system. The best methods that can be directly used into a dynamic environment are the insertion methods.

Sequential insertion heuristic was proposed by Wilson and has been improved by different researchers. When a request was received, the algorithm inserted the passenger on an existing vehicle route without changing the order of the stops previously scheduled. The feasible route minimizing the additional time required to pickup and drop off the new customer that was chosen. Routes that satisfied the guaranteed service bounds were preferred over all others. However, the algorithm would specify routes that violated the service guarantees if no others were found. The aim was to maintain a minimum level of service while having enough flexibility to allow the vehicles to service unknown future requests. This algorithm was a greedy local-search procedure. To prevent the search from being too myopic, the algorithm maintained a collection of "good" feasible routes for each vehicle. The size of this collection as well as the coefficients of the objective function was user specified parameters, customized for the demand probability distribution.

We speed up the algorithm simply by considering the geographic information, that is to say, we will consider geographically close user to route for insertion. The method to schedule a new request is as following:

Step 1: Search for all feasible insertions of new customer for each vehicle and find the insertion that results in minimum increase of objective function value.

Step 2: If it is infeasible to insert customer in one of the routes, the customer will be rejected. Otherwise, the customer will be served by the vehicle whose additional cost is minimal.

3   Demand Bus Shanghai

3.1   Simulation Design

The aim of this research is to find a solution to evaluate the usability of demand bus system in Shanghai. What we need to do is to find out what kinds of areas are suitable to operate this service, which kind of people is the potential users, and what kind of operation policy should be taken. They are mainly influenced by two objectives: maximization of the profitability and best service quality. These two goals interact as improvements in the quality raise costs and thus reduce profitability. These variables can be manipulated in order to identify the optimal combination with respect to the performance measures.

We suppose that there is only one Demand Bus Service Center dealing with the user's request for demand bus service. When it receives a request, it will immediately try to find a suitable bus and inform the task. If there is no bus available, the user's request would be rejected. All buses are treated as independent individuals and can compete for the task to take users. When user gets a service plan, which includes the waiting time and service time, he would compare it with the public bus service , if he does think the demand bus service is better than public bus service, he would accept the demand bus service. On the other hand he would reject to use demand bus service and takes public bus.

Simulation System is implemented in java based on the framework proposed above. In all experiments, all roles are controlled by agents. Contract Net Protocol [7] is a well-known protocol for assigning subtasks to agents involved in distribution problem solving, which supports economic model of negotiation. We design our system by using this protocol. The system architecture is shown in Fig 3. The algorithms used to calculate shortest path and to choose best bus to insert new request respectively are A star and simplified sequential insertion heuristic method. We store all traffic information in the digital map which can be handled by GIS component in our simulator and select four districts in Shanghai as experimental zone, in which the travel time between any pair of points by taxi would not be longer than twenty-five minutes. Other parameters in the system such as bus velocity, frequency of public bus, and waiting time for public bus in these four areas are estimated according to the situation in Shanghai. In order to create a dynamic environment, all demand bus service requests occur random and the source and destination of users are also decided randomly. Considering the dynamic character of demand bus service, we add variables to the waiting time and service time in the service plan. One more important thing is to decide the objective function to deal with a new request form user. Our aim is reduce the distance all buses travel on the premise of guaranteeing service level.

System behavior is investigated by performing a series of experiments. We do our experiments on a laptop with a Centrino 1.6G process and 512 Mb memories. In order to simplify the situation, we assume that all users in our simulation would select one from Demand Bus service and public bus service. Furthermore, we supposed:

1. There are no traffic jams;
2. All buses stay at the last drop-off location and no expense happen when bus stops.
3. Once a user's request is assigned to a bus, the pick-up and delivery activity should be done by the same bus.
4. If one user rejects to use demand bus service, he can find a suitable public bus to meet his request. We can get the travel time only by using distance and speed of public bus.

$$wt = \sum_{i=1}^{j} (pt_i - rt_i) \Big/ j \ . \tag{1}$$

$$st = \sum_{i=1}^{j} (dt_i - pt_i) \Big/ j \ . \tag{2}$$

$$r_{loaded} = \sum_{i=1}^{k} S(u_i) / \sum_{j=1}^{l} S(b_j) \ . \tag{3}$$

$$r_{rej} = n_{rej} / n_r \ . \tag{4}$$

For one hand, waiting time and service time are two important facts when we evaluate the service quality. Waiting time is the time period from the time when the user got response from Bus Center to the time when he is picked up by one bus. Service Time is the time when user stays on the bus. The less waiting time and service time are the better service quality user can get. We used Equation 1 to represent the average waiting time (wt), rt_i is the response time when the DBS center replies to the ith user's request, and pt_i is the pick-up time of this user. Equation 2 is the representation of service time, and dt is the drop-off time.

For the other hand, better service needs more buses used for people, which increases the cost. The maximization of the profitability can be measured by Loaded

Rate (r_{loaded}) and Rejection Rate (r_{rej}). Loaded rate (Equation 3) is used to measure the profit based on the fact that people buy ticket to use demand bus service which is similar to that of public bus. It is evaluated by total distance of all buses traveled and total distance of all users need traveled. We omit the time when empty buses stop according to our assumption that no expenses happen when bus stops. $S(u_i)$ is the distance of the ith user traveled and $S(b_j)$ is the distance of the jth bus run. For instance, one bus drives from A to B. If it serves for one user in the middle way, the loaded rate would be 50 %. If it serves for three people, the loaded rate would be 300 %. The higher the loaded rate is, the larger the profit is. Furthermore we can use loaded rate to estimate the ticket price in the operation. Rejection rate (Equation 4) shows whether or not people want to use demand bus service compared with public bus service. People mainly consider the time used to complete a task and the price of ticket when they evaluate these two services. Because public bus has fixed route, and scheduled timetable, waiting time is almost fixed and service time only concerns with distance. In order to simplify the evaluation between these two services, we set that the speed of demand bus is two times of that of public bus and if the time user takes public bus is less than two times of that of demand bus, user would reject to use demand bus service. The parameter is set according to the situation of some shuttle buses in Shanghai. n_{rej} is the amount of people who reject to use demand bus service and the n_r is the total number of requests for demand bus service excluding the number of refused by bus center. The smaller the rejection rate is, the more people want to use demand bus service, and the larger the profit is.

The policy is the number of buses placed in service under various request patterns and the extension of service areas. The number of requests and buses directly impact the performance measures. While lots of system strategies could be tested, investigation in this research is limited to two representative dispatching strategies. The first experiment involves using all buses for new request, common area with randomly requests. In this experiment, the sources of buses would be set randomly, and the source and destination of user would also be set randomly. We call this as Ordinary Type, which is distinguished from the Community Type in the second experiment. It is mainly used to compare the usability of demand bus service and the public bus service. We also want to find out the relationship between the number of buses and the number of requests. One would expect that when request rate increases, the waiting time decreases and the rejection rate decreases. As to the loaded rate, it would also increase. The second experiment involves using community type area and other conditions that are same to first one. Community area means lots of people with similar situation. The sources or destinations would be centralized in some communities. What we expect to see is the difference between the two kinds of demand bus service.

3.2 Result and Discussion

The experiment results for the first experiment are shown in the Fig 4-Fig 7. As shown in Fig 4, we choose one bus from each simulation result to observe the change of passengers in each bus in the experiments when we use 10 buses in the simulation. In these experiments the demand rates vary from 50 requests per hour (r/h) to 300 r/h. In order to distinguish the time, we count one when user gets on/off the bus each time.

The average number of passengers is no more than three and the max number is five when the demand rate is 300 r/h. The same phenomenons are found when we use 20 or 30 buses. The average number of passengers is slightly changed and the max number is about nine. It is meaningless to use a big bus for this kind of service.

In other figures, each line in the graph represents a performance for a given situation. Average waiting time, average service time, rejection rate, and loaded rate are plotted against a variable demand rate.

In Fig 5, waiting time is greater than service time while there are only 10 buses. And with the growth of the demand, waiting time increases rapidly while service time does not change lot. This indicates the quantity of bus is far away from the need of system's demands. Fewer users can share a bus because of limitation of the time windows (in Fig 4, the passengers is two or three when the demand rate is not high) and they have to reject the demand bus service (in Fig 7 – the rejection rate of 10 buses is the highest).or wait for a long time (in Fig 5, the waiting time of 10 buses is the longest but service time almost equals to the one of 20 or 30 buses). Obviously, by adding more buses in the system, waiting time could decrease as shown in Fig 5.

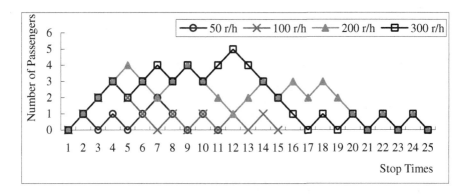

Fig. 4. Passengers on Each Bus under Four Kinds of Demand Rate

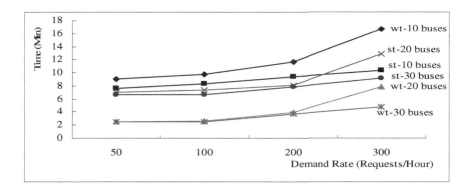

Fig. 5. Waiting Time/ Service Time in Experiment I

The Service time is slightly greater than waiting time while there are 20 buses. In the earlier stage when the requests increase, waiting time and service time have not grown simultaneously, but they continue increasing after requests reaching certain stage (300 r/h). The change is exactly a result influenced by the characteristic of demand bus service and our objective function. According to our objective function, when we need choose a bus to handle a new request, we will find the one who will drive less to finish the task. That is to say we will calculate the distance exclusive of overlapped route. At this time, bus with passenger would easily be selected. Then waiting time and service time of all passengers would increase and the loaded rate would be high. These changes are exactly as what we find in the Fig 5 and Fig 6 when the demand rate increases from 200 r/h to 300 r/h. But more and more buses have to detour, and then if there are free buses, free buses would easily be selected firstly. That is why the situation with 30 buses is similar with that with 20 buses uses in the system except waiting time and service time did not change much when the demand rate reached 300 r/h. So the loaded rate of 30 buses would less then that of 20 buses as shown in Fig 6 and the rejection rate would be low as shown in Fig 7.

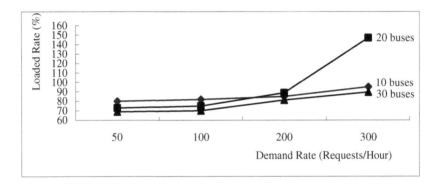

Fig. 6. Loaded Rate in Experiment I

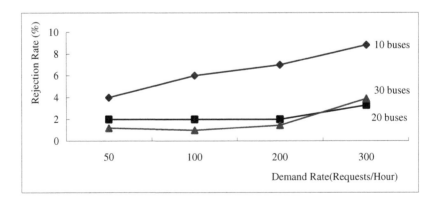

Fig. 7. Rejection Rate in Experiment I

According to our definition of rejection rate, from Fig 7 we can also know that demand bus service is more attractive than public bus service because the reject rate is less than 10 % in all kinds of situations. That is to say it's a convenient point-to-point and time-saved service for people.

The result of second experiment is shown in Table 2. As we mentioned before, the aim of this experiment is to compare performances of two different situations of demand bus service: ordinary type and community type. In the ordinary type situation, all uses are distributed randomly in the experimental areas. And in the community type situation, people can have similar origin locations or destinations inside one kind of communities, such as living center, shopping center, et al. The average waiting time and service time of community type is a little bit longer then ordinary type, but the loaded rate is six times of that of ordinary one. From the view of profitability, for a given number of users we can use less buses to achieve the same service quality .From the rejection rate, we can know DBS has its significant advantage in the aspect of convenience for community service.

Table 2. Performances for Experiment II

	wt(min)	st(min)	r_{loaded}	r_{rej}
Ordinary Type	6.87	10.42	0.88	4
Community Type	9.35	14.5	5.1	2

4   Conclusion and Future Work

In this paper, we proposed a multiagent simulation framework to evaluate the usability of demand bus system. Massively Multi-Agent Based Simulation has been widely used to evaluate system by creating a model to conduct numerical experiments. In our work, we divided the computational model into design model and domain model. Design model created by computer scientists shows us the structure of system, the relationship of system components, protocols, and other elements. Domain model created by domain experts, stakeholders, and users focuses on the mechanism of research domain such as logic of behavior. The implementation of prototype system shows that it is easy to build such system from scratch to mega by this mechanism. Initial results show that for our experimental areas with low request frequency, Demand Bus service has low rejection rate about 10 % compared with public bus service. It also has significant advantage in the aspect of convenience and profitability for community in Shanghai. It could be a service supplement to the fast transportation, such as subway. We also found that for a given number of requests, we could reach a balance point to improve service quality and profitability by providing enough buses. It is useful to estimate the quality of bus we need to operate demand bus service.

The difficult point of evaluating the service is how to model people's attitude to the system. Utility function is too simple to get a better result. In the future, we want to do some simulation with many people involved.

Acknowledgement. This work was supported by Association of International Education, Japan (AIEJ). The authors would thank Daisuke Torii and Yohei Murakami in Kyoto University for their help during the conceiving of this paper. Cheng Zhu and Donghui Lin in Shanghai Jiao Tong University also gave many suggestions to this paper. This work was partly supported by the Research on the modern logistics key technology and its application project (No.03dz15008).

References

1. Hunsaker B., Savelsbergh M.: Efficient feasibility testing for dial-a-ride problems. Operations research letters. 30 (2002) 169-173
2. Diana M., Dessouky M. M.: A new regret insertion heuristic for solving large-scale dial-a-ride problems with time windows. Transportation Research Part B. 38 (2004) 539–557
3. Healy P., Moll R.: A new extension of local search applied to the Dial-A-Ride Problem. European Journal of Operational Research. 83 (1995) 83-104
4. Ishida T.: Q: A Scenario Description Language for Interactive Agents. IEEE Computer, Vol.35.No. 11 (2002)54-59
5. Ishida T.: Digital City Kyoto: Social Information Infrastructure for Everyday Life. Communications of the ACM (CACM), Vol. 45, No. 7. (2002) 76-81
6. Ishida T.: Society-Centered Design for Socially Embedded Multiagent Systems. International Workshop on Cooperative Information Agents (CIA-04), Lecture Notes in Computer Science, 3191, (2004)16-29
7. Smith R. G.: The Contract Net Protocol: High Level Communication and Control in a Distributed Problem Solver. IEEE Transactions on Computers, C-29(12). (1980) 1104-1113
8. Gao Z.Q., Kawasoe T., Yamamoto A., Ishida T.: Meta-Level Architecture for Executing Multi-agent Scenarios, Pacific Rim International Workshop on Multi-Agents(PRIMA 2002),Lecture Notes in Artificial Intelligence, 2413, (2002) 163-177

Scalability of Dial-a-Ride Systems—A Case Study to Assess Utilities of Ubiquitous Mass User Support

Noda Itsuki

Information Technology Research Institute, AIST,
2-41-6 Aomi, Koto-ku, Tokyo 135-0064, Japan
i.noda@aist.go.jp

Abstract. Evaluation of scalability and usability of dial-a-ride systems is reported as a case study to assess utilities of ubiquitous mass user support. One of applications of ubiquitous and multi-agent systems is transportation system in urban area. While multi-agent and ubiquitous systems are considered to support next-generation social systems, it is not clear how it provides advantage in usability and benefit. We will show a result of comparison between dial-a-ride bus systems, one of possible multi-agent application of transportation systems, and traditional fixed-route bus systems.

We conduct experiments of various situation and show how the advantage of dial-a-ride is robust to the variation of social conditions. For example, when many demands occur from/to a certain point like railway stations or shopping centers, improvement of usability of dial-a-ride systems is better than one of fixed-route systems so that a break-even point between the two systems is reduced. This means that dial-a-ride systems are useful even in 'rush-hour'. Through these experiments, we will figure out the conditions where multi-agent like systems have advantage against traditional systems.

1 Introduction

While ubiquitous computing and multi-agent systems get many attention for the next generation of information infrastructures for mass user support, it is not clear what are the benefits and what killer applications of these technologies. It is difficult to figure out such benefits because utilities of these technologies are not tangible until they are deeply incorporated in social systems.

Transportation systems in urban area are one of possible application area of ubiquitous and multi-agent technologies, because these technologies enable flexible control of mass-transportation according to various demands and situations: Sensor networks and ubiquitous network will collect and summarize detailed information about demand and traffic situation in real-time, while multi-agent systems will help the management of a large number of vehicles. For example, in the case of dial-a-ride systems, ubiquitous networks enable to take passenger's

T. Ishida, L. Gasser, and H. Nakashima (Eds.): MMAS 2004, LNAI 3446, pp. 323–334, 2005.

requests on demand, then negotiation protocols among multi-agents will solve the bus-assignment problem effectively.

However, it is not obvious that such systems works as well as we image. For example, if passenger's requests occur quite systematically, traditional fixed-route bus systems may work more effectively than dial-a-ride systems.

In order to show the benefit of dial-a-ride system, we introduced a way to compare efficiency of a traditional fixed-route system and a dial-a-ride system in a virtual city in our previous work [NOS+03]. In this work, usabilities of the two systems are compared under the same condition of system costs. As the result, we showed that the dial-a-ride system can be more efficient under a certain condition.

In this article, I will investigate that the efficiency of the dial-a-ride system is kept under several conditions, and figure out changes of advantage of the dial-a-ride system according to varied social situations.

2   Problem Domain and Formalization

2.1   Dial-a-Ride System

Dial-a-ride is a system in which a passenger calls a control center of buses and states a destination; the center assigns an appropriate bus and re-plans its route for the request. The dial-a-ride system is attracting attention as a new public transportation system that provides convenient transportation for disabled persons while solving traffic-jams in urban areas.

There are several variations of frameworks of dial-a-ride systems according to combinations of styles to receive *demands* [1] and policies of bus routing. Two major styles to receive demands are:

- **reservation style:** A passenger makes a demand to the bus control center a certain period ahead of the expected departure time. For example, a passenger must make a reservation one day before riding.
- **real-time style:** A passenger can make a demand when she wants to ride: that is, she simply calls the control center when she wants to move.

This study presumes the **real-time** style because it can be applied more generally to various conditions under which the fixed-route systems can be operated.

The bus routing policies also have some variations. The followings are two typical policies:

- **basic-route with optional detour routes:** A bus mainly follows a basic route; it turns into predefined optional detour routes according to demands. A passenger can embark or disembark at any place along these routes.
- **free-routing:** A bus can run on any road in a certain area. A passenger can embark or disembark any place in the area.

---

[1] We refer to a passenger's request to move from one place to another as a *demand*.

We focus the **free-routing** in these policies because it provides a typical merit of the dial-a-ride system.

2.2   Usability and Profitability

We take *usabilities* for passengers and *profitabilities* for bus companies as measures of efficiency of two bus systems, dial-a-ride and fixed-route bus systems. Generally, the evaluation of such criteria is difficult because usabilities depend on subjective factors and profitabilities may be affected by various social conditions. In order to avoid these difficulties and to enable such evaluation by simulation, we simplify usabilities and profitabilities as follows.

For *usability*, we specifically address the primary purpose of a bus system: to provide a way for a passenger to reach her destination as quickly as possible. From this point of view, *usability* can be defined as follows:

> **usability:** average elapsed time since a demand is told to the bus center until the demand is satisfied.

Note that we use the time when the demand is stated instead of the time when the passenger departs because we need to compare dial-a-ride and fixed-route systems in the same condition. In the case of a fixed-route system, a passenger goes to a bus-stop when he/she has the demand. This means that the elapsed time is measured from then. So, we need to use the same measure in the case of a dial-a-ride system.

In addition to it, we suppose that a passenger never changes buses. The first reason is that it is difficult to measure physical and mental costs of the transfer. People may use a slower bus route instead of a faster one when the latter one requires many transfers. This implies that we need to interpret such costs into *usability*, which is measured by time by definition. To avoid complexity, we do not consider cases in which a passenger changes buses.

Profitability is formalized as follows. Profit (or deficit) of a bus company depends on maintenance, fuel and labor costs, and fare incomes, which are affected by social and economic conditions. In addition, fare-pricing causes secondary social effects like changes of the number of passengers. Therefore, it is difficult to quantify profits directly. Instead, we simplify it as a balance between fare revenue and cost, where revenue and cost change in proportion to the number of passengers and buses, respectively. In other words, *profitability* is defined as follows:

> **profitability:** the number of demands occurring in a unit period per bus.

2.3   Virtual Town

We compose the following virtual town as a field for this simulation:

- Streets in the town are arranged in a grid pattern as in Kyoto and New York.
- The town shape is a square.

- All stops are at crossings.
- There are no traffic jams.
- A bus goes through, turns left or right at a crossing with the same time-cost.
- There are no limitations in the passenger capacity of individual buses.
- Getting on and off buses require no time.

In this virtual town, demands occur under the following conditions:

- Demands occur with constant frequency.
- If a passenger reaches a the destination on foot faster than riding a bus, the passenger refuses to use a bus. In this case, the time to walk is treated as the elapsed time to complete the demand.

3   Simulation Setup

3.1   Fixed-Route Systems

Usability of a fixed-route system varies according to bus-routes. It is difficult to find the optimal set of routes to cover a town theoretically because it is affected by many factors like the number of buses, average bus speed, the number of routes, the shape of the town, and so on. Therefore, we apply a genetic algorithm (GA) to find a semi-optimal set of routes.

In this simulation, an individual of GA consists of a set of bus-routes. We suppose that the number of routes is fixed, and that just one bus runs on one route. Therefore, the number of buses is equal to the number of routes. There are two route types: *normal* routes and *loop* routes. On a *normal* route, a bus runs back and forth between two terminals. On a *loop* route, a bus circulates in the loop.

As mentioned in Section 2.2, usability is measured by *average time to complete a demand* (ATCD). When a passenger decides which route to use, the ATCD (T_{demand}) can be calculated as

$$T_{\mathrm{demand}} = (L_{\mathrm{src}} + L_{\mathrm{dst}})/V_{\mathrm{walk}}$$
$$+ L_{\mathrm{route}}/(M_{\mathrm{bus}} \times V_{\mathrm{bus}})$$
$$+ L_{\mathrm{bus}}/V_{\mathrm{bus}}, \qquad (1)$$

where L_{src}, L_{dst} and L_{bus} are distances between a departure-point and a embarkation stop, between a disembarkation stop and a destination-point, and between the two stops, respectively. L_{route} is the length of the whole route. V_{walk} and V_{bus} are walking speed and bus speed; M_{bus} is the number of buses per route [2]. In the equation, the first, second, and third terms of the right-hand side indicate "time of walking", "average time of waiting at bus stop", and "time of riding a bus", respectively.

---

[2] As mentioned above, M_{bus} is fixed to be 1 in this simulation.

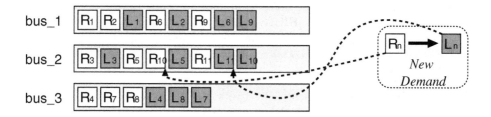

Fig. 1. Successive best insertion: When a new demand occurs, the system seeks the best pair of insertion positions for two new via-points (departure-point (R) and destination-point (L)) without changing existing orders in queues

In order to evaluate the best performance of an individual (a set of bus-routes), the system seeks the best route from the set of routes and determines the best combination of stops to embark and disembark for a given demand. Note that evaluation includes ATCD of the case where a passenger chooses to walk the whole journey to the destination because walking is faster than using a bus. In this case, L_{route} and L_{bus} are assumed to be zero; $L_{src} + L_{dst}$ is equal to the distance between the departure-point and the destination-point.

A generation consists of 100 individuals. Each individual is evaluated by calculating average ATCD based on Eq. 1 using 50 randomly generated demands. Then, the top 10 individuals are selected and survive to the next generation. The next generation consists of 10 survivors, 70 descendants generated from the survivors (7 descendants per surviver), and 20 new randomly-generated individuals. Detailed operation of GA is described in [NOS+03].

3.2   Dial-a-Ride System

For simulation of a dial-a-ride system, we must decide a way to assign a new demand to buses and to re-plan a path for each bus. This is a kind of dynamic traveling salesman problem. Moreover, the problem includes a more complex constraint that each demand is refused when the expected arrival time is overdue for its deadline. [3] Therefore, it is hard to find the optimal assignment in a reasonable time.

Many researchers have already attacked the first issue. Assignment of passengers' request and planning of bus routes is considered as a variation of the *traveling-salesman problem* [KdPPS01, BMRS94] and the *vehicle routing problem* [BC87, SS95, BGAB83, RR97, LL01]. Various optimization techniques are used to solve the problem. [HM95] makes use of local search and tab search respectively.

---

[3] Deadline of a demand is defined as the latest time the demand should be completed. In our simulation, the deadline is the time when the demand will be completed if the passenger walks the entire distance to the destination.

Simulated annealing and GA are also applied in [Sil01, Sil00]. Complexity of calculation is investigated in [HKRW01].

In this work, we take a relatively simple and light-weight way to find a semi-optimal assignment called *successive best insertion* (Fig. 1) described as follows.

1. Each bus stores assigned demands in a via-point queue in which an assigned demand is represented by two via-points: the departure-point and destination-point. The bus always runs toward a via-point at the top of the queue, and removes it from the queue upon arrival. We suppose that the order of via-points in the queue is not changed after the assignment.
2. Each bus also keeps the expected time to complete each assigned demand. The expected time is calculated by supposing that the bus will run according to the *current* queue of via-points.
3. When a new demand occurs, each bus seeks the best pair of positions to insert two via-points of demand according to the minimum of the total delay of existing demands and expected time to complete the new demand. If a deadline of existing or new demand expires by insertion, the bus reports that it has *no solution*.
4. The control center assigns the demand to a bus whose cost is minimum in all buses. When all buses report *no solution*, then the demand is refused.

4   Results and Discussion

In the previous work [NOS+03], we supposed that demands occur uniformly over the town. This means that each passenger chooses its departure- and destination-point completely random. Such a situation may occur when people goes around in a huge shopping center randomly. On the other hand, a more typical situation in town is that most of people want to depart from and/or reach to a certain center of a town like a central station, city hall, or shopping-complex. In order to compare efficiency of the bus systems under such various situations, I conduct various simulation where occurrence of demands are concentrated to one or two certain points.

4.1   Changes of Usability Against Concentrated Demands

In [NOS+03], we showed that the usability of the dial-a-ride system is improved faster than one of the fixed-route system when the frequency of demands increases. Fig. 2-(a) shows the changes of average times to complete a demand in both systems. In the figure, thin lines indicate changes of the average time of dial-a-ride systems where the ratio between the frequency of demands and the number of busses is fixed as a certain value (frequency of demands/number of buses = $1, 2, 3, 4, 5, 8$ or 16). For example, the ratio = 1 means that a bus is operated for only one passenger in average, so that the system looks like a taxi system. Generally, the ratio should be high for the profit of bus companies because the fare of buses is paid per person.

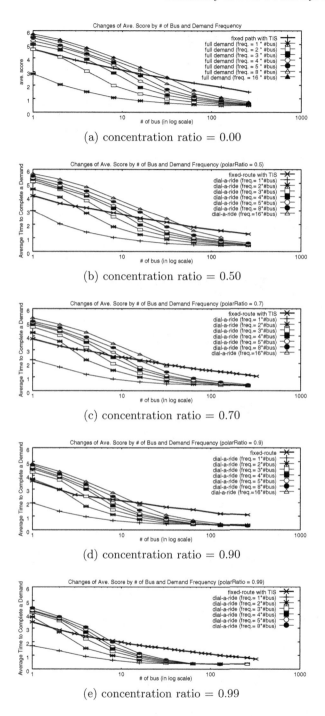

(a) concentration ratio = 0.00

(b) concentration ratio = 0.50

(c) concentration ratio = 0.70

(d) concentration ratio = 0.90

(e) concentration ratio = 0.99

Fig. 2. Changes of average time to complete a demand when the profitability is fixed with concentrated demands

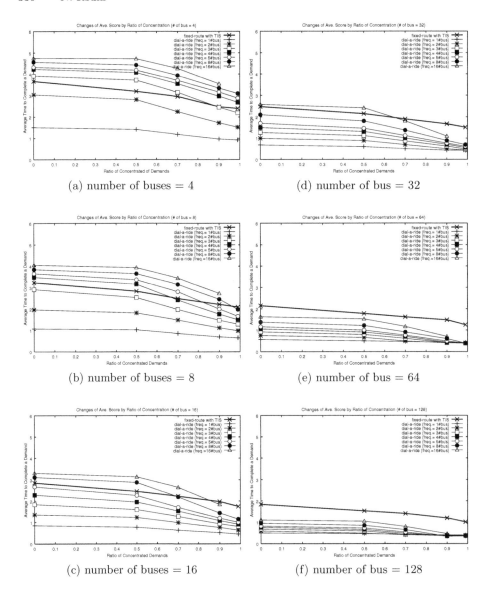

Fig. 3. Changes of average time to complete a demand when the ratio of concentrated demands is changed

A thick line in the figure indicates changes of the average time of the fixed-route system when the number of buses increases. There are only one line for the fixed-route system because its usability (the average time) depends only on the number of buses but does not on the frequency of demands.

From Fig. 2-(a), we can see that the dial-a-ride system can be more reasonable when the frequency of demands are enough because improvement of the dial-a-ride system is faster than one of the fixed-route system even if the ratio of frequency of demands and the number of buses is large.

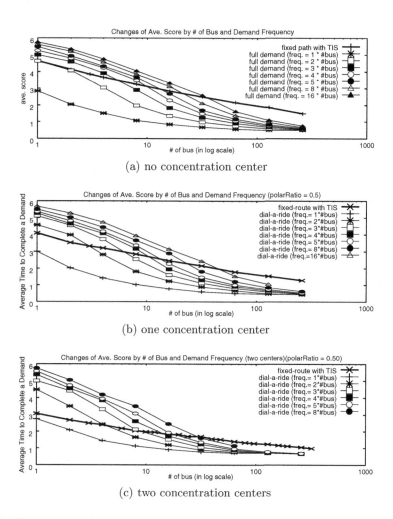

(a) no concentration center

(b) one concentration center

(c) two concentration centers

Fig. 4. Comparison of average time when the number of concentration centers is changed

This feature is kept even when the demands are concentrated. Fig. 2-(b), -(c), -(d), and -(e) show the changes of average time under the condition where a certain ratio of demands are concentrated in the center of town, that is, departure- or destination point of a demand is set at the center of town in a certain probability. Fig. 2-(b), -(c), -(d), and -(e) are the case the probabilities that the departure- or destination-point of a demand is concentrated to the center are 0.5, 0.7, 0.9 and 0.99, respectively, while Fig. 2-(a) corresponds to the case there are no concentrated demands (departure- and destination-points are selected randomly).

From these figures, we can see that the average time is improved in both case when the ratio of concentrated demands increase. The degrees of improvements are similar in both case, so that the dial-a-ride system keeps the feature that its average time decreases more rapidly than one of the fixed-route system.

4.2   Effect of Ratio of Concentrated Demands

It is meaningful to investigate how the usability changes in both systems with the fixed number of buses when ratio of concentrated demands changes. For example, we like to know which of dial-a-ride and fixed-route systems is better when there is a special event where many people gather into a center.

Fig. 3 shows the result of the simulation of such cases. Each graph shows changes of the average time to complete demands when the ratio of concentrated demands changes under the condition where the number of buses is fixed. As same as Fig. 2, each thin line indicates a case of dial-a-ride systems with various ratio of the frequency of demands per a bus, and a thick line indicates the case of fixed-route system. In each case of (a)-(f), usabilities of the dial-a-ride systems are improved relatively quickly than that of the fixed-route system. This means that the dial-a-ride system is more reasonable when the ratio of concentrated demands is very high, especially in the case the number of buses is relatively large. For example, in the case of the number of buses = 16, the bus company should switch the system from fixed-route to dial-a-ride when the concentration ratio becomes greater than 0.7.

4.3   Effects the Number of Concentrated Centers of Demands

How do the usabilities of both bus systems when the town has more than one concentration centers ? Such a condition happens, for example, when the town has central station and a business center at different locations. Fig. 4 shows the result of experiments under such conditions. In these graphs, Fig. 4-(a) and -(b) are the same as Fig. 2-(a) and -(b) respectively. Therefore, (a) is the case that the town has no center, and (b) is the case that the town has one center where half of demands depart from or arrive to the center. Fig. 4-(c) is the case the town has two centers. In the last case, half of demands depart from and/or arrive to two centers.

Fig. 4-(c) tells that the efficiency of the fixed-route system is, by its nature, relatively high in the case of two centers, while the dial-a-ride systems show similar results as the case of one center. Therefore, the balancing point moves right so that more demands are required for the dial-a-ride system to get better usability than the fixed-route system. It is easy to understand this phenomena because the fixed-route system can improve its usability by putting one or more routes between two centers.

5   Concluding Remarks

Results showed in Section 4 tells that, although overall features of dial-a-ride and fixed-route systems are kept under concentrated demands condition, advantages of each system may changed according to the number of attracting centers in town. The benefit of dial-a-ride systems is enhanced when the town has a single center to attract people, while fixed-route systems get large advantage when many people move between two centers in town.

These features of both systems tells us that we should focus on the case of non- or single-centered towns as an application domain when we consider to utilize ubiquitous mass user support technologies to bus systems. This kind of analysis is important for ubiquitous computing to justify its huge cost to use in real world.

References

[BC87]   William A. Bailey Jr. and Thomas D. Clark Jr. A simulation analysis of demand and fleet size effects on taxicab service rates. In *Proceedings of the 19th conference on Winter simulation*, pages 838–844. ACM Press, 1987.

[BGAB83] L. D. Bodin, B. L. Golden, A. Assad, and M. O. Ball. Routing and scheduling of vehicles and crews: the state of the art. *Computers and Operation Research*, 10:63–211, 1983.

[BMRS94] L. Bianco, A. Mingozzi, S. Riccaiardelli, and M. Spadoni. Exact and heuristic procedures for the traveling salesman problem with procedence constraints, based on dynamic programming. In *INFOR*, volume 32, pages 19–31, 1994.

[HKRW01] Dietrich Hauptmeier, Sven Oliver Krumke, Jorg Rambau, and Hans-Christoph Wirth. Euler is standing in line dial-a-ride problems with precedence-constraints. *Discrete Applied Mathematics*, 113(1):87–107, 2001.

[HM95]   P. Healy and R. Moll. A new extension of local search applied to the dial-a-ride problem. *European Journal of Operations Research*, 83:83–104, 1995.

[KdPPS01] Sven O. Krumke, Willem E. de Paepe, Diana Poensgen, and Leen Stougie. News from the online traveling repairman. *Lecture Notes in Computer Science*, 2136:487, 2001.

[LL01]   Haibing Li and Andrew Lim. A metaheuristic for the pickup and delivery problem with time windows. In *IEEE International Conference on Tools with Artificial Intelligence*, volume 13, pages 160–167, 2001.

[NOS+03] Itsuki NODA, Masayuki OHTA, Kosuke SHINODA, Yoichiro KUMADA, and Hideyuki NAKASHIMA. Evaluation of usability of dial-a-ride systems by social simulation. In *Proc. of Fourth International Workshop on Multi-Agent-Based Simulation*, pages 139–152, Jul. 2003.

[RR97]   K. S. Ruland and E. Y. Rodin. The pickup and delivery problem: faces and branch-and-cut algorithm. *Computers Math. Applic*, 33(12):1–13, 1997.

[Sil00]   Zbigniew Czech Silesia. Parallel simulated annealing for the set-partitioning problem. In *The 8th Euromicro Workshop on Parallel and Distributed Processing*, pages 343–350, 2000.

[Sil01]   Zbigniew Czech Silesia. Parallel simulated annealing for the delivery problem. In *The 9th Euromicro Workshop on Parallel and Distributed Processing*, pages 219–226, 2001.

[SS95]   M. W. P. Savelsbergh and M. Sol. The general pickup and delivery program. *Transportation Science*, 29(1):17–29, 1995.

Distributed Visitors Coordination System in Theme Park Problem

Takashi Kataoka[1], Hidenori Kawamura[1],
Koichi Kurumatani[2], and Azuma Ohuchi[1]

[1] Graduate School of Information Science and Technology, Hokkaido University,
North 14, West 9, Kita-ku, Sapporo 060-8628, Japan
{kataoka, kawamura, ohuchi}@complex.eng.hokudai.ac.jp
http://ses3.complex.eng.hokudai.ac.jp/index_e.html
[2] Information Technology Research Institute,
National Institute of Advanced Industrial Science and Technology,
Aomi 2-41-6, Koto-ku, Tokyo 135-0064, Japan
k.kurumatani@aist.go.jp

Abstract. A distributed visitors coordination system is proposed as an application of a massively multi-agent system. In the system, some agents register their next destination using an information device such as a cellular phone, and this information is used to reduce the effect of the time delay between decision-making and effect-emergence. This delay causes queue lengths to oscillate. However, it is troublesome for agents to continuously register their next destination. To compensate them, exclusive queues are made available to agents registering their next destination. Computer simulation of the theme park problem, showed that when all agents avoid the congestion by registering their next destination, the total waiting time is minimized and queue length oscillation is reduced.

1   Introduction

The ubiquitous environment is now being realized with the growing use of such devices as personal digital assistants (PDAs) and cellular phones and advances in the network environment using proximity communication represented by wireless LAN[1]. A ubiquitous environment enables users to share and transmit information easily, anytime and anywhere. For example, it enables realization of a navigation system, which provides information in real time. Moreover, it enables a user to make a reservation at a hotel or to operate household appliances while away form home[2, 3]. Thus, people's lives can be made more convenient by developing various types of user supports. A new type of support for the ubiquitous environment is called "mass user support"[1]. This support aims at not only optimizing individual utility but also supporting a social system consisting of many users. One important research area in mass user support is flow control in which there are many people and each person has individual utilities based on his or her preference and restrictions. An example application area is a congestion information service. Such services are gradually being realized though the

T. Ishida, L. Gasser, and H. Nakashima (Eds.): MMAS 2004, LNAI 3446, pp. 335–348, 2005.
© Springer-Verlag Berlin Heidelberg 2005

use of information providing systems such as a vehicle information and communication system (VICS)[4]. Particularly important in such systems is a control for reducing congestion based on global information. Research on this has been done using simplified models of theme parks[7], event halls[5], traffic[2, 6], and so on. In these models, visitor agents select the next destination "congestion disregarding behavior" or "congestion avoiding behavior" by using congestion information. Simulations have shown that, the waiting time for all agents is not necessarily minimum if too many agents avoid congestion.

In a network, one way to solve the problem caused by time delay is to use a congestion avoidance algorithms, such as RED[10]. A packet routing algorithm may thus be applicable to theme parks, for example. In RED, some packets are discarded if crowding occurs, and they are transmitted again after a while. However, although it may be easy to discard packets, it is hard to make visitors leave a theme park. Therefore, applying congestion avoidance algorithms to a theme park is challenging.

We previously clarified the relationship between the waiting time for all agents and congestion avoiding behavior[7]. We showed by experiment that congestion avoiding agents continually went to the emptiest place if they received congestion information within a certain time frame, and they concentrated there. Since that place remains the emptiest until agents begin arriving there, other congestion avoiding agents continue to receive the same congestion information, despite the fact that some agents are already moving toward that place. Therefore, that place becomes overcrowded due to excessive agent concentration. Another place then becomes the emptiest place, and the cycle repeats. The queue length in each place thus oscillates. This is because it takes time from when agents select their next destination based on the latest congestion information to when they join the queue at the destination. Briefly, there is a delay existed between decision-making and effect-emergence. We can reduce total waiting time by reducing this delay.

A congestion information system that provides global information based on the current state of each service facility is thus not very effective. It is necessary to provide information that is calculated discretely as an application of a massively multi-agent system. To solve time delay problem, a method is needed that will enable the system server to estimate the future congestion situation at each service facility, discretely. The situation in which many agents share limited resources has been modeled as El Farol Bar problem[8] and the minority game[9]. In these models, many agents select one of two resources based on the past winners' selections. If the number of past selections is suitable, the resources are shared well. As the result of individual agent's selection based on the same information, optimal resource sharing is achieved. However, when the ratio of sharing the resources changes, these models are not effective.

Rump and Stidham tested a model in which each agent avoided congestion by estimating the future congestion situation and then visiting a service facility[11]. As a result, the queue lengths oscillated chaotically. Ikeda and Tokinaga achieved higher dimensional accuracy with genetic programming[12] and managed to control the chaotic oscillation . However, in these studies, there was only one service facility, and agents only selected whether to visit the facility or not. It may be more difficult to control the oscillation with genetic programming if there are multiple facilities. When an agent performs an action determined by genetic programming and the action is fed back to the environment, a more complicated phenomenon may appear that is impossible to control by genetic programming.

It is difficult to estimate future states based only on for the current congestion situation. To solve this problem, we developed the distributed visitors coordination system (DVCS). Visitor agents select a destination based on either congestion disregarding behavior or congestion avoiding behavior. The congestion avoiding agents register their next destination into a system server using some kind of information device, such as a cellular phone. This enables the server to estimate future queue lengths with more accuracy and provide congestion information that moderates the oscillation in queue lengths. However, it is troublesome for an agent to continually register its next destination. To compensate them for their efforts, we added exclusive queues for them. We evaluated the effectiveness of this system for the theme park problem with two types of agents, ones not using the congestion information provided and ones using it.

In Section 2 we introduce the general definition of the theme park problem. Section 3 describes the distributed visitors coordination system, and Section 4 describes the simulation. Section 5 presents some experimental results, and the results are discussed in game-theoretic terms in Section 6. We conclude in Section 7 with a summary and a look at future work.

2 Theme Park Problem

The objective in the theme park problem is to maximize the satisfaction of all agents by controlling their visiting schedule. Many agents visit a theme park consisting of several attraction, roads, and so on, as shown in Fig. 1. We model the theme park using a directed graph in which each segment is a node.

Segment i has three static attributes and three dynamic ones. The static ones are capacity (c_i), service time (st_i) and visited probability, p_i. Capacity is the maximum number of visitor agents who can be served at one time by a segment. Service time in the number of steps a visitor agent wait at each segment. Visited probability is a parameter of the attractions. The higher the probability, the more agents who visit. The dynamic ones are $Ls_i(t)$, the list of agents being served by a the segment at time t, $Lq_i(t)$, the list of agents waiting for service by a segment at time t, and the remaining service time, $st_{rest,i}(t)$, which is a parameter of the attractions. Initially, this value is equal to st_i, is decremented in steps while Ls_i has at least one agent. When it reaches 0, it is set to st_i again.

Agent j has p_{ji}, v_{ji}, des_j, wt_j, mt_j, and pt_j as parameters, v_{ji} represents the state whether agent j has visited segment i or not. This value is initially 0, it is set to 1 if the agent visits segment i. Preference value p_{ji} represents the agent's preference degree for attraction i, and the value is 0 or 1. If it is 1, the agent wants to visit attraction i, if it is 0, the agent does not want to visit there.

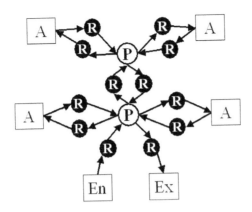

Fig. 1. Example theme park modeled by directed graph. Notations, A, R, P, En, and Ex represent attraction, road, plaza, entrance, and exit, respectively

The preference values are decided randomly for all attractions based on p_i when an agent enters the park. The current destination segment is des_j, wt_j and mt_j represents total waiting time and total moving time, respectively. Past time pt_j is the time that agent j was on the list of agents being served by the present segment.

An agent coming to segment i at time t is added to the end of queuing list $Lq_i(t)$. If the transition condition is satisfied, the agent at the head of $Lq_i(t)$ can transit to $Ls_i(t)$, the list of agents being served. An agent who transits to $Ls_i(t)$ is deleted from Lq_i. Thus, an agent's priority is FIFO (first-in first-out) queuing. The transition condition is as follows.

if segment i is an attraction, $st_{rest,i} = 0$ in time t
otherwise, $|Ls_i(t)| + 1 \leq c_i$

The $|Ls_i(t)|$ represents the number of agents on the list of agents being served. We set that an attraction cannot service visiting agents until it finishes serving the previous visiting agents. For the other segments, an agent can transit to list $Ls_i(t)$ from list $Lq_i(t)$ even if the segment is serving another agents in time t.

At time t, the agents act in turn based on their numbers. All agents necessarily belong to one of two lists, $Lq_i(t)$ and $Ls_i(t)$, in one of the segments. If agent j is on queuing list $Lq_i(t)$ and the transition condition described above is satisfied, it transits to $Ls_i(t)$, otherwise,

$$wt_j \leftarrow wt_j + 1, \tag{1}$$

and the agent remains on the list Lq_i. If agent j is on the list $Ls_i(t)$, segment i is an attraction, and $st_{rest,i} = 0$, agent j selects an attraction as his next destination based on a strategy described later. Then, des_j is changed to that attraction, and agent j transits to the queuing list of the next segment. If segment

i is an attraction and $st_{rest,i} \neq 0$, agent j does nothing special. If segment i is not an attraction,

$$pt_j \leftarrow pt_j + 1, \qquad (2)$$

and if it is a road,

$$mt_j \leftarrow mt_j + 1. \qquad (3)$$

Then, if $pt_j \geq st_i$, $pt_j = 0$ and agent j transits to the queuing list of the next segment.

3   Distributed Visitors Coordination System

As mentioned above, the waiting time for all agents is not necessarily minimum if too many agents try to avoid congestion by using current congestion information. This is because there is a delay between decision-making and effect-emergence. Therefore, the attractions in turn become overcrowded due to excessive agent concentration, and their queue lengths oscillate.

To prevent this, the system server must provide congestion information that reduces the effect of the delay. One approach is to have the system server estimate the future state of each attraction's queue and provide information to the agents that stimulates them to visit attraction that will become empty in the future . To achieve high accuracy, the system server needs to know agent's next action. Therefore, we considered making agents register their next destination into the server. If the server knows the number of agents moving toward each attraction at a certain time beforehand, it can prevent agent concentrate on at those attractions. In our proposed distributed visitors coordination system, agents register their next destination into the system server using some kind of information devices, such as a cellular phone, immediately after they select next destination. In particular, the system server provides agents the estimated wait time at each attraction as congestion information. At time t, the estimated wait time at attraction i is

$$EstimatedTime_i(t) = \alpha(|Lq_i(t)| + |Lq_{ex,i}(t)|) + \beta num_{i,reg}(t), \qquad (4)$$

where $Lq_{ex,i}$ denotes the exclusive queue, described later, and $num_{i,reg}(t)$ denotes the number of agents who have registered attraction i as their next destination. It is decremented by 1 when an agent who has registered it as their next destination arrives there and is added to either of the two queuing lists, $Lq_i(t)$ or $Lq_{ex,i}(t)$.

Provision of the estimated wait time calculated using (4) makes the attraction with the minimum value the emptiest one when a congestion avoiding agent using this information arrives there. The result is no overcrowding. However, it is troublesome for agents to always register their next destination. To compensate them for their trouble, we added another queue, $Lq_{ex,i}(t)$, at each attraction. It is an exclusive queue for agents who registered attraction i as their next destination. The other agents stand in either $Lq_i(t)$ and $Lq_{ex,i}(t)$, depending on

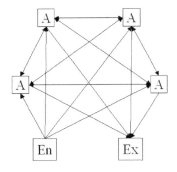

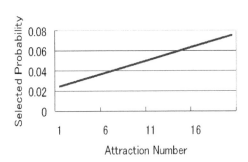

Fig. 2. Example situation for simulation. Each arrow represents a road segment

Fig. 3. Selected probability of each attraction

which one. When agents transit from $Lq_i(t)$ or $Lq_{ex,i}(t)$ to $Ls_i(t)$, they transit alternately from the two lists. Therefore,

$$\forall t, |Lq_i(t)| \geq |Lq_{ex,i}(t)|. \tag{5}$$

The agents who registered the attraction as their next destination have a shorter wait, which promotes agent registering.

While this system may seem like a "time-specific reservations" system, which is being used in some theme parks, the waiting time for all agents may not be reduced as much with a "time-specific reservations" system. This is because the waiting time of an agent who has been able to make a reservation decreases while that of an agent who has not been able to make a reservation increases inversely. The advantage of that system is that the agent who has been able to make a reservation can receive service with a shorter waiting time at certain attractions. On the other hand, in our proposed system, the objective is to reduce the effect of time delay by increase the accuracy of estimating future queue lengths by learning agents' actions beforehand.

4   Simulation

We simulated our system using the theme park model shown in Fig. 2. Each attraction is connected to every other attraction by a road segment. Service time st_i for each road segment was 30, meaning it takes 30 steps to traverse each road segment. These 30 steps are the time delay because it takes 30 steps for agents to arrive at their destination from the time they select their next destination immediately after visiting the current attraction. There were 20 attractions in the park.

Each agent used one of two strategies for destination selection. With the congestion disregarding (CD) strategy, the agent does not consider congestion and

Table 1. Parameter settings

Capacity of attractions	10
Service time of attractions	15
Capacity of roads	∞
Service time of roads	30
Average arrival rate	0.8

selects attraction i randomly as his next destination from among the attractions for which p_{ij} is maximum, from the non-visited attractions. With the congestion avoiding (CA) strategy, the agent selects the attraction with the shortest expected wait time, which was received as congestion information, from the non-visited attractions.

An agent enters the theme park at the average arrival rate, λ, of 0.8. When an agent enters, he is defined as either a CD agent or a CA agent with probability P_{CA}, which is the ratio of CA agents in the park. Once an agent is defined as one or the other, he cannot change. Each agent selects 15 attractions to visit based on each selected probability at the entrance. The selected probability of each attraction is shown in Fig. 3. Agent j is set to $p_{ji} = 1$ with a higher probability for an attraction that has a large i. That is, more agents visit attractions with a large i. The selected probability of each attraction means the degree of its popularity. We set the attraction visited by many agents and not one purposely. Therefore, it is necessary to evenly distribute the agents by providing them congestion information. Since the average arrival rate was 0.8, there were empty attractions and overcrowded ones at a just suitable rate.

We simulated three cases to determine the effect of using our system.

1. onlyCA

In the first case, CA agents avoid congestion based on the estimated wait time, which is calculated simply from the queue length at each attraction at that time. That is, CA agents are provided the estimated wait time at each attraction as congestion information, which is the value given by Eq. (4) when $\alpha = 1$ and $\beta = 0$. CA agents do not register their next destination, and there is no exclusive queue at each attraction.

2. CA_noDelay

In the second case, the service time of the road segments between attractions is set to 0, i.e., no time delay. This means that agents can join the queue of the emptiest attraction instantly. Although this situation is unachievable, we used it for comparison. The other settings were the same as in case 1.

3. CA_DVCS

In third case, we applied our proposed distributed visitors coordination system (DVCS). CA agents register their next destination and can stand in an exclusive queue. They are provided the estimated wait time at each attraction as congestion information, which is the value given by Eq. (4) when $\alpha = 1$ and $\beta = 1$. These parameters were selected to equally treat the queue length and number of agents registering as factors of congestion information. However, they must be investigated further to determine which value is optimal. On the other hand, CD agents select their next destination randomly and cannot stand in the exclusive queues.

The parameter values for the simulations are shown in Table. 1. Each simulation ended once 5000 agents had left the park. We used the waiting time as the measure of satisfaction, averaged over 100 simulations.

5   Results

The average waiting time for all agents is shown in Fig. (4). A ratio of CA (congestion avoiding) agents equals 0.0 means there are only CD (congestion disregarding) agents, and $P_{CA} = 1$ means there are only CA agents. In the onlyCA case, the average waiting time for all agents was not minimum at $P_{CA} = 1$, as in previous studies[5, 6, 7], which is the situation in which all agents simply avoid congestion. In the range of $P_{CA} \leq 0.3$, the average waiting time increased as P_{CA} decreased because of the time delay. In the CA_noDelay case, which is the ideal situation, the average waiting time decreased as P_{CA} increased and was minimum at $P_{CA} = 1$. Without a time delay, CA agents do not crowd excessively, and they fill the attraction queues uniformly. In the CA_DVCS case the tendency was the same as in the CA_noDelay case. This means that CA agents are directed toward the attractions uniformly if the system server knows the number of agents moving, even if an agent cannot immediately actually stand in a queue. As shown in Fig. 4, the average waiting time for all agents in the CA_DVCS case was almost equal to that in the CA_noDelay case. However, in

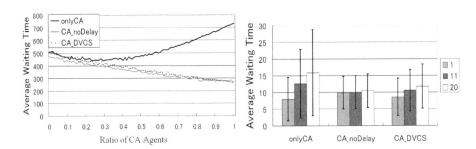

Fig. 4. Average waiting time for all agents in each case. X-axis indicates P_{CA}, ratio of CA agents, and Y-axis indicates average waiting time of whole agents

Fig. 5. Average waiting time and standard deviation for agents who visited attractions 1, 11, and 20. X-axis indicates each case, and Y-axis indicates average waiting time. Vertical lines show standard deviations. Each number indicator corresponds to attraction number

Table 2. Average waiting time for attractions 1, 11, 20

onlyCA	CA_noDelay	CA_DVCS
36.54120751	30.3851502	30.93780554

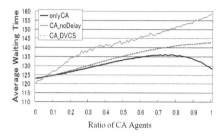

Fig. 6. Average waiting time for all agents in each case with average arrival rate of 0.3. X-axis indicates P_{CA}, ratio of CA agents, and Y-axis indicates average waiting time for all agents

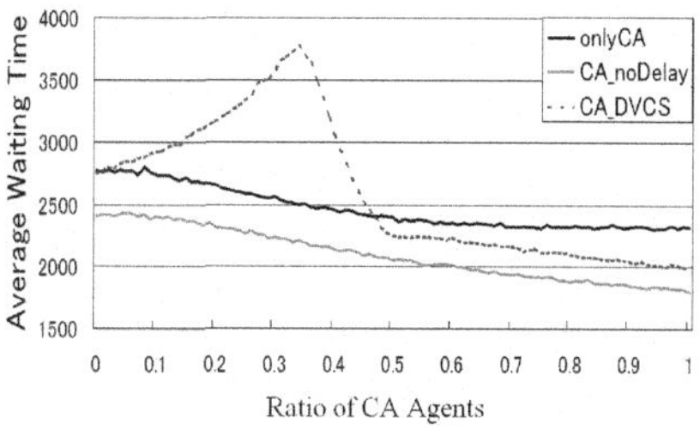

Fig. 7. Average waiting time for all agents in each case with average arrival rate of 1.1. X-axis indicates P_{CA}, ratio of CA agents, and Y-axis indicates average waiting time for all agents

the real world, the distances between attractions are not equal, so users do not take the same number of steps to get to the next attraction. These factors are not serious although they do have somewhat of an effect. Therefore, the average waiting time for all agents in the CA_DVCS case is no longer than that in the onlyCA case. However, it may be longer than that in the CA_noDelay case.

Figure 5 shows the average waiting times and standard deviations for agents who visited attractions 1, 11, 20, for $P_{CA} = 1$. Table 2 shows the average waiting times. Since more agents visited the attractions with a higher number, i, the average waiting time of agents who visited attraction 20 was maximum in all cases. However, the average waiting times in the CA_noDelay case did not differ much between attractions. This is because providing congestion information that did not include the time delay prevented the CA agents from crowding certain attractions, so they stood in the attraction queues uniformly, as mentioned above. In the CA_DVCS case, CA agents went to empty attractions although not as effectively as in the CA_noDelay case. In the onlyCA case, the queue lengths oscillated greatly, as shown by the large standard deviations. On the other hand, in the CA_noDelay and CA_DVCS cases, the oscillations were moderated. That is the distributed visitors coordination system reduced the effect of the time delay and moderated the oscillations in the queue lengths.

Figure 6 shows the average waiting time for all agents with average arrival rate of 0.3, meaning there were few agents in the park. The average waiting times in each case increased with P_{CA}, so providing congestion information was not effective. The magnitude relation of the average waiting times in two cases was inverse to that in Fig. 4. Service at the attractions begins when agents enter the queue, even if there is only one agent. In the CA_noDelay case, agents still had to wait until a few agents, which was much less than capacity c_i, finished being served even if they arrived there immediately. Since this was repeated, their waiting time increased. On the other hand, in the onlyCA case, some CA agents visited the same attraction at the same time. Since the attraction could service many agents at once, their waiting times were shorter than in the CA_noDelay case. The average waiting time in the CA_DVCS case was between those in the onlyCA and CA_noDelay cases.

Figure 7 shows the average waiting time for all agents with average arrival rate of 1.1, meaning there were too many agents in the park. In the range of $P_{CA} \leq 0.5$, the average waiting time in the CA_DVCS case was much longer. Since attractions had an exclusive queue, many CD agents waited for a longer time while CA agents waited for a shorter time by standing in the exclusive queue. The advantage of this queue decreased gradually as P_{CA} increased, and it was mostly gone at about $P_{CA} = 0.5$. However, as the number of CA agents increased, the effect of registering their next destination grew, and the average waiting time for all agents decreased. Finally, the average waiting time in the CA_DVCS case is between those in the onlyCA and CA_noDelay cases.

Thus, the distributed visitors coordination system is not necessarily effective. When there are few agents or too many agents, it is less effective. Otherwise, it is effective, such as when the average arrival rate is 0.8. We can thus say that the distributed visitors coordination system is effective in most situations.

6   Discussion

Our testing showed that having agents register their next destination reduces the time delay effect and moderates the oscillations in queue lengths. Then, what was the effect of the excusive queues for agents registering their next destination? To investigate this, we defined another case, CA_noEQ, in which there are no exclusive queues although CA (congestion avoiding) agents register their next destination. They stand in the same queues as the CD (congestion disregarding) agents. The other settings are the same.

Figure 8 shows the average waiting times of CD and CA agents in the CA_noEQ case. Figure 9 shows them in the CA_DVCS case. Figure 10 shows the average waiting time for all agents in the CA_noEQ and CA_DVCS cases. In the CA_noEQ and CA_DVCS cases, the average waiting times of CD and CA agents differed greatly although it did not differ for all agents. In the CA_noEQ case, the average waiting times of CD and CA agents were almost the same. However, the average waiting time of CA agents was slightly longer than that of CD agents, consistently. This is because the CA agents postponed visiting the crowded attractions until they became less crowded. On the other hand, in the CA_DVCS case, the average waiting times of CD and CA agents differed greatly. In the range of $P_{CA} \leq 0.8$, the average waiting time of CA agents was shorter

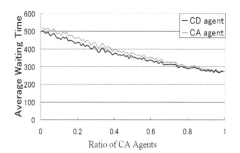

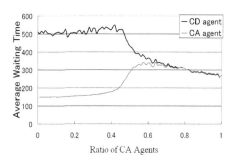

Fig. 8. Average waiting times of two kinds of agents in the CA_noEQ case. X-axis indicates P_{CA}, ratio of CA agents, and Y-axis indicates average waiting time of each agent

Fig. 9. Average waiting times of two kinds of agents in the CA_DVCS case. X-axis indicates P_{CA}, ratio of CA agents, and Y-axis indicates average waiting time of each agent

than that of CD agents, although it was longer in other range. The average waiting time changed at around $P_{CA} = 0.5$ because the advantage of standing in the exclusive queues drops when the number of agents eligible to stand in them exceeds 50%.

In the CA_noEQ and CA_DVCS cases, when each agent rationally selects one of the two strategies, what ratio of strategies does it become? In the CA_noEQ case, although the average waiting time for all agents was minimum at $P_{CA} = 1$, the average waiting time of CA agents was consistently longer than that of CD agents. When there are n CA agents out of $(N - 1)$ agents, and Nth agent's profit, which is less waiting time, is $CA(n+1)$ or $CD(n)$ according to his selection of strategy,

$$CA(n + 1) \leq CD(n), \qquad n = 0, 1, 2, \cdots, N - 1 \qquad (6)$$
$$CD(0) \leq CA(N). \qquad (7)$$

That is, a CD agent's profit is always larger than a CA agent's one, but the profit when all agents select the CD strategy is smaller than when all agents select the CA strategy. In game theory, this is called the dilemma game of N agents. Figure 11 shows the profit function of the dilemma game with N agents, and the situation in Fig. 8 shows the same tendency because an agent's profit is less waiting time in a theme park. In Fig. 11, the Pareto optimal point is at $n/N = 1$, and the equilibrium point is at $n/N = 0$. Similarly, in Fig. 8, the Pareto optimal point is at $P_{CA} = 1$, and the equilibrium point is at $P_{CA} = 0$. That is, in the noEQ case, if each agent selects a strategy rationally, his profit will be the waiting time for $P_{CA} = 0$ because all agents select the CD strategy. This is an undesirable state.

In contrast, the two waiting times in the CA_DVCS case seem like the profit function of the minority game, which is a game in which selecting different

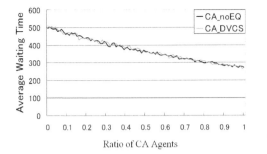

Fig. 10. Average waiting times of whole agents in the CA_noEQ and CA_DVCS cases. The X-axis indicates P_{CA}, ratio of CA agents, and Y-axis indicates average waiting time for all agents

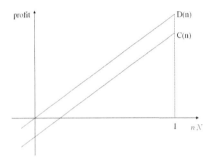

Fig. 11. Profit function of dilemma game with N agents. X-axis indicates ratio of agents who select strategy C, and Y-axis indicates profit of each strategy

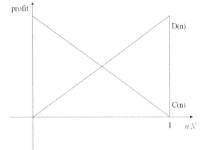

Fig. 12. Profit function of minority game with N agents. X-axis indicates ratio of agents who select strategy C, and Y-axis indicates profit of each strategy

strategies results in the optimal state. (Fig. 12 shows the profit function of the minority game.) However, in the range of $P_{CA} \geq 0.8$, both waiting times are downward-sloping although the magnitude relation of the average waiting times in two cases was inverse to that in other range. This is different them in the minority game. In the CA_DVCS case, the Pareto optimal state is also the state in which all agents select the CA strategy. This means that the situation in the CA_DVCS case is also dilemma game in the range of $P_{CA} \geq 0.8$. Therefore, the equilibrium point is at $P_{CA} = 0.8$.

If each agent learns repeatedly and selects a strategy rationally in such situation, the ratio of CA agents will converge at $P_{CA} = 0.8$, which is the equilibrium point, although this depends on the learning method. The average waiting time for all agents at $P_{CA} = 0.8$ is less than at $P_{CA} = 0$. This means that the average waiting time for all agents balances out at a more desired state than in the CA_noEQ case.

In addition, the onlyCA and CA_noDelay cases did not have exclusive, as in the CA_noEQ case, and they resulted in the dilemma game, which has a Pareto optimal point at $P_{CA} = 1$ and an equilibrium point at $P_{CA} = 0$.

Thus, adding exclusive queues shifts the equilibrium point in the increasing P_{CA} direction, although there was no change in these situations being dilemma game. In short, adding exclusive queues for agents who have the same strategy as many other agents is effective way to make agents select the same strategy.

7   Conclusion

We have described own distributed visitors coordination system that reduces the effect of the time delay between decision-making and effect-emergence. In this system, CA (congestion avoiding) agents register their next destination and can stand in exclusive queues. Simulation showed that an increase in the number of CA agents registering their next destination reduced the waiting time for all agents. Providing congestion information, the estimated future state of each attraction's queue based on knowing agents' next actions, effectively reduced the effect of the delay.

Whether the exclusive queues are added or not, the profit function for whole agents did not differ. However, doing so shifted the equilibrium point in the state where more CA agents avoided congestion, although there was no change in these situations being dilemma game. Therefore, the distributed visitors coordination system encouraged the rational agents to register their next destination, which reduced the waiting time for all agents.

Thus, our system effectively stimulates agent coordination and reduces global congestion, even if the number of agents is massive.

Some settings were simplified for the simulation. For example, the number of steps between attractions was uniform. In the real world, the number differs, so the effect of using our system may differ from the experimental one. Investigation of this is future works.

References

1. Koichi Kurumatani: User Intention Market for Multi-Agent Navigation - An Artificial Intelligent Problem in Engineering and Economic Context. In Working Note of the AAAI-02 Workshop on Multi-Agent Modeling and Simulation of Economic Systems, MAMSES-02, Technical Report WS-02-10, AAAI Press (2002) 1–4
2. Tomohisa Yamashita, Kiyoshi Izumi, Koichi Kurumatani: Effect of Using Route Information Sharing to Reduce Traffic Congestion. Multi-Agent for Mass User Support, International Workshop, MAMUS Acapulco, Mexico, August 10, 2003 Revised and Invited Papers (2003) 86–104

3. Hidenori Kawamura, Koichi Kurumatani, Azuma Ohuchi: Modeling of Theme Park Problem with Multiagent for Mass User Support. Working Note of The IJCAI-03 Workshop on Multiagent for Mass User Support, Acapulco, Mexico (2003) 1–7

4. VICS (Vehicle Information and Communication System) is the information service in ITS (Intelligent Transport Systems): http://www.its.go.jp/ITS/

5. R. Suzuki, T. Arita: Effects of Information Sharing on Collective Behaviors in Competitive Populations. Proceedings of the Eight International Symposium on Artificial Life and Robotics (2003) 36–39

6. T. Shiose, T. Onitsuka, T. Taura: Effective Information Provision for Relieving Traffic Congestion. the Proceedings of ICCIMA'01, 4th International Conference on Intelligence and Multimedia Applications (2001) 138–142

7. Hidenori Kawamura, Takashi Kataoka, Koichi Kurumatani, Azuma Ohuchi: Investigation of Global Performance Effected by Congestion Avoiding Behavior in Theme Park Problem. IEEJ Transaction EIS, Vol. 124, No. 10 (2004) 1922–1929

8. W.B. Arthour: Inductive Reasoning and Bounded Rationality. American Economic Association Papers Proceedings, Vol. 84, No. 2 (1994) 406–411

9. D. Challet, Y.C.Zhang: Emergence of Cooperation and Organization in an Evolutionary Game. Physica A, Vol. 246 (1997) 407–418

10. S. Floyd, V. Jacobson: Random Early Detection Gateways for Congestion Avoidance. IEEE/ACM Transactions on Networking, Vol. 1 (1993) 397–413

11. C.M. Rump, S. Stidham,Jr.: Stability and Chaos in Input Pricing for a Service Facility with Adaptive Customer Response to Congestion. Management Science, Vol. 44 No. 2 (1998) 246–261

12. Y. Ikeda, S. Tokinaga: Controlling the Chaotic Dynamics by Using Approximated System Equations Obtained by the Genetic Programming. Trans. IEICE, Vol. E84-A, No. 9 (2001) 2118–2127

Author Index

Lecture Notes in Computer Science

For information about Vols. 1–3464

please contact your bookseller or Springer

Vol. 3515: V.S. Sunderam, G.D.v. Albada, P.M.A. Sloot, J.J. Dongarra (Eds.), Computational Science – ICCS 2005, Part II. LXIII, 1101 pages. 2005.

Vol. 3514: V.S. Sunderam, G.D.v. Albada, P.M.A. Sloot, J.J. Dongarra (Eds.), Computational Science – ICCS 2005, Part I. LXIII, 1089 pages. 2005.

Vol. 3513: A. Montoyo, R. Muñoz, E. Métais (Eds.), Natural Language Processing and Information Systems. XII, 408 pages. 2005.

Vol. 3512: J. Cabestany, A. Prieto, F. Sandoval (Eds.), Computational Intelligence and Bioinspired Systems. XXV, 1260 pages. 2005.

Vol. 3510: T. Braun, G. Carle, Y. Koucheryavy, V. Tsaousidis (Eds.), Wired/Wireless Internet Communications. XIV, 366 pages. 2005.

Vol. 3509: M. Jünger, V. Kaibel (Eds.), Integer Programming and Combinatorial Optimization. XI, 484 pages. 2005.

Vol. 3508: P. Bresciani, P. Giorgini, B. Henderson-Sellers, G. Low, M. Winikoff (Eds.), Agent-Oriented Information Systems II. X, 227 pages. 2005. (Subseries LNAI).

Vol. 3507: F. Crestani, I. Ruthven (Eds.), Information Context: Nature, Impact, and Role. XIII, 253 pages. 2005.

Vol. 3506: C. Park, S. Chee (Eds.), Information Security and Cryptology – ICISC 2004. XIV, 490 pages. 2005.

Vol. 3505: V. Gorodetsky, J. Liu, V. A. Skormin (Eds.), Autonomous Intelligent Systems: Agents and Data Mining. XIII, 303 pages. 2005. (Subseries LNAI).

Vol. 3504: A.F. Frangi, P.I. Radeva, A. Santos, M. Hernandez (Eds.), Functional Imaging and Modeling of the Heart. XV, 489 pages. 2005.

Vol. 3503: S.E. Nikoletseas (Ed.), Experimental and Efficient Algorithms. XV, 624 pages. 2005.

Vol. 3502: F. Khendek, R. Dssouli (Eds.), Testing of Communicating Systems. X, 381 pages. 2005.

Vol. 3501: B. Kégl, G. Lapalme (Eds.), Advances in Artificial Intelligence. XV, 458 pages. 2005. (Subseries LNAI).

Vol. 3500: S. Miyano, J. Mesirov, S. Kasif, S. Istrail, P. Pevzner, M. Waterman (Eds.), Research in Computational Molecular Biology. XVII, 632 pages. 2005. (Subseries LNBI).

Vol. 3499: A. Pelc, M. Raynal (Eds.), Structural Information and Communication Complexity. X, 323 pages. 2005.

Vol. 3498: J. Wang, X. Liao, Z. Yi (Eds.), Advances in Neural Networks – ISNN 2005, Part III. XLIX, 1077 pages. 2005.

Vol. 3497: J. Wang, X. Liao, Z. Yi (Eds.), Advances in Neural Networks – ISNN 2005, Part II. XLIX, 947 pages. 2005.

Vol. 3496: J. Wang, X. Liao, Z. Yi (Eds.), Advances in Neural Networks – ISNN 2005, Part II. L, 1055 pages. 2005.

Vol. 3495: P. Kantor, G. Muresan, F. Roberts, D.D. Zeng, F.-Y. Wang, H. Chen, R.C. Merkle (Eds.), Intelligence and Security Informatics. XVIII, 674 pages. 2005.

Vol. 3494: R. Cramer (Ed.), Advances in Cryptology – EUROCRYPT 2005. XIV, 576 pages. 2005.

Vol. 3493: N. Fuhr, M. Lalmas, S. Malik, Z. Szlávik (Eds.), Advances in XML Information Retrieval. XI, 438 pages. 2005.

Vol. 3492: P. Blache, E. Stabler, J. Busquets, R. Moot (Eds.), Logical Aspects of Computational Linguistics. X, 363 pages. 2005. (Subseries LNAI).

Vol. 3489: G.T. Heineman, I. Crnkovic, H.W. Schmidt, J.A. Stafford, C. Szyperski, K. Wallnau (Eds.), Component-Based Software Engineering. XI, 358 pages. 2005.

Vol. 3488: M.-S. Hacid, N.V. Murray, Z.W. Raś, S. Tsumoto (Eds.), Foundations of Intelligent Systems. XIII, 700 pages. 2005. (Subseries LNAI).

Vol. 3486: T. Helleseth, D. Sarwate, H.-Y. Song, K. Yang (Eds.), Sequences and Their Applications - SETA 2004. XII, 451 pages. 2005.

Vol. 3483: O. Gervasi, M.L. Gavrilova, V. Kumar, A. Laganà, H.P. Lee, Y. Mun, D. Taniar, C.J.K. Tan (Eds.), Computational Science and Its Applications – ICCSA 2005, Part IV. LXV, 1362 pages. 2005.

Vol. 3482: O. Gervasi, M.L. Gavrilova, V. Kumar, A. Laganà, H.P. Lee, Y. Mun, D. Taniar, C.J.K. Tan (Eds.), Computational Science and Its Applications – ICCSA 2005, Part III. LXV, 1340 pages. 2005.

Vol. 3481: O. Gervasi, M.L. Gavrilova, V. Kumar, A. Laganà, H.P. Lee, Y. Mun, D. Taniar, C.J.K. Tan (Eds.), Computational Science and Its Applications – ICCSA 2005, Part II. LXV, 1316 pages. 2005.

Vol. 3480: O. Gervasi, M.L. Gavrilova, V. Kumar, A. Laganà, H.P. Lee, Y. Mun, D. Taniar, C.J.K. Tan (Eds.), Computational Science and Its Applications – ICCSA 2005, Part I. LXV, 1234 pages. 2005.

Vol. 3479: T. Strang, C. Linnhoff-Popien (Eds.), Location- and Context-Awareness. XII, 378 pages. 2005.

Vol. 3478: C. Jermann, A. Neumaier, D. Sam (Eds.), Global Optimization and Constraint Satisfaction. XIII, 193 pages. 2005.

Vol. 3477: P. Herrmann, V. Issarny, S. Shiu (Eds.), Trust Management. XII, 426 pages. 2005.

Vol. 3476: J. Leite, A. Omicini, P. Torroni, P. Yolum (Eds.), Declarative Agent Languages and Technologies II. XII, 289 pages. 2005. (Subseries LNAI).

Vol. 3475: N. Guelfi (Ed.), Rapid Integration of Software Engineering Techniques. X, 145 pages. 2005.

Vol. 3474: C. Grelck, F. Huch, G.J. Michaelson, P. Trinder (Eds.), Implementation and Application of Functional Languages. X, 227 pages. 2005.

Vol. 3472: M. Broy, B. Jonsson, J.-P. Katoen, M. Leucker, A. Pretschner (Eds.), Model-Based Testing of Reactive Systems. VIII, 659 pages. 2005.

Vol. 3468: H.W. Gellersen, R. Want, A. Schmidt (Eds.), Pervasive Computing. XIII, 347 pages. 2005.

Vol. 3467: J. Giesl (Ed.), Term Rewriting and Applications. XIII, 517 pages. 2005.

Vol. 3466: S. Leue, T.J. Systä (Eds.), Scenarios: Models, Transformations and Tools. XII, 279 pages. 2005.

Vol. 3465: M. Bernardo, A. Bogliolo (Eds.), Formal Methods for Mobile Computing. VII, 271 pages. 2005.